Woodrow Wilson

John A. Thompson

An imprint of **Pearson Education**

London • New York • Toronto • Sydney • Tokyo • Singapore • Hong Kong • Cape Town
New Delhi • Madrid • Paris • Amsterdam • Munich • Milan • Stockholm

PEARSON EDUCATION LIMITED

Head Office:
Edinburgh Gate
Harlow CM20 2JE
Tel: +44 (0)1279 623623
Fax: +44 (0)1279 431059

London Office:
128 Long Acre
London WC2E 9AN
Tel: +44 (0)20 7447 2000
Fax: +44 (0)20 7240 5771
Website: www.history-minds.com

_____

First published in Great Britain in 2002

© Pearson Education Limited 2002

The right of John A. Thompson to be identified as Author
of this Work has been asserted by him in accordance
with the Copyright, Designs and Patents Act 1988.

ISBN 0 582 24737 3

British Library Cataloguing in Publication Data
A CIP catalogue record for this book can be obtained from the British Library

Library of Congress Cataloging in Publication Data
A CIP catalog record for this book can be obtained from the
Library of Congress

10 9 8 7 6 5 4 3 2
07 06   05 04 03

Typeset by 35 in 10/12 pt Janson Text
Produced by Pearson Education Asia Pte Ltd.
Printed in Malaysia, LSP

The Publishers' policy is to use paper manufactured from sustainable forests.

For Dorothy

CONTENTS

Preface

Like the other volumes in this series, this is not a biography but a study of a political leader. As the 28th president of the United States, Wilson left a much larger mark on history than most of his predecessors. During his eight years in the White House, he secured enactment of some of the most significant legislation of the 'progressive era.' He shaped America's response to revolutions in Mexico and in Russia. Above all, he directed American foreign policy during the First World War, leading the United States into the conflict in 1917 and playing a major role in the Paris peace conference. His name became, and has remained, associated with both a particular set of objectives for US foreign policy, and a distinctive approach to the understanding of international relations. This book seeks to describe and interpret the part played by Wilson in these momentous developments.

In taking this new look at Wilson, I have been enormously reliant upon the magnificent edition of *The Papers of Woodrow Wilson*, published by Princeton University Press in 69 volumes (1966–94). This edition, for which Arthur S. Link was primarily responsible, is generally acknowledged to have set new standards for such documentary series. Much material, particularly in the early volumes, was previously unknown, and for the period of Wilson's political career the edition includes not only the great majority of Wilson's own letters, speeches and papers but also the most significant of the letters he received, together with extracts from the diaries and other records of those who had meetings with him. I am also greatly indebted to the extensive and excellent scholarship that exists on the various aspects of Wilson's career, and I have in addition drawn on my own research on the World War I period.

The very scale of the *Papers* highlights the need in a book of this size to make choices of emphasis and omission. Some of these have flowed from the focus upon Wilson as a political leader. Thus, I have paid greater attention to his public utterances, from which he derived so much of his power and influence, than to his private relationships, which in my view had much less importance in determining his behavior than some biographies and attempts to analyze his psychological development have suggested. I have also devoted the greatest amount of space to Wilson's conduct of American foreign policy during World War I and its aftermath, on the grounds that this was the aspect of his presidency with the widest and most enduring significance, but I believe that relating it to his whole career and way of thinking illuminates both.

The book takes the form of a narrative. This is not an alternative to analysis, but the indispensable framework for an attempt to probe the reasons for Wilson's words and actions. His various statements have often been taken to be unmediated expressions of durable personal convictions, but they were addressed to particular audiences on specific occasions and can only really be understood within their context. Likewise, reconstructing the sequence of events helps to answer such crucial questions as why Wilson responded to German submarine warfare in a manner that eventually brought the United States into the war, and why he later refused to compromise with the Senate over the League of Nations, even though this resulted in America's not joining an organization that he had done more than anyone else to establish. All political leaders need to work within the constraints of their political systems, and to take account of the domestic and international balance of forces at the time. The analytical narrative design of this book is an attempt to show the extent to which this was true of Wilson, and hence to supplement, and in places contest, interpretations that focus on his own thought and personality.

Acknowledgments

I wish to thank the friends and colleagues whose advice has done much to improve this book. Richard M. Abrams, Christopher M. Clark, Peter Clarke, Stefan Collini, John M. Cooper, James T. Patterson, Keith Robbins and Robert W. Tucker all read the manuscript, in whole or in part, and made valuable comments. So did my wife, Dorothy J. Thompson, and my father-in-law, Frank W. Walbank. Between them, they saved me from several errors and infelicities, but, of course, bear no responsibility for those that remain.

I also wish to acknowledge the very generous gift of a complete set of *The Papers of Woodrow Wilson*, made to me by Professor William A. Link after the death of his father, Arthur S. Link, in 1998. This was not only extremely helpful to me in this project but also a much valued memorial to a great scholar whose friendship, together with that of his wife, Margaret, enriched our lives.

Chronology

28/29 December 1856	Thomas Woodrow Wilson born, Staunton, Virginia
1858	Wilson family moves to Augusta, Georgia
1870	Wilson family moves to Columbia, South Carolina
1873–74	Attends Davidson College, North Carolina
1874	Wilson family moves to Wilmington, North Carolina
1874–75	Studies at home
1875–79	Attends the College of New Jersey at Princeton (later Princeton University); BA, 1879
1879–December 1880	Attends the University of Virginia Law School
1881–82	Completes study of law at home
1882–83	Practices law in Atlanta, Georgia
September 1883	Engagement to Ellen Louise Axson
1883–85	Graduate student at Johns Hopkins University (PhD, 1886)
January 1885	Publication of *Congressional Government*
June 1885	Marriage to Ellen Axson
1885–88	Teaches at Bryn Mawr College, Pennsylvania
1888–96	Guest lecturer on administration at Johns Hopkins
1888–90	Teaches at Wesleyan University, Middletown, Connecticut
1889	Publication of *The State*
1890–1902	Professor of Jurisprudence and Political Economy, Princeton
1893	Publication of *Division and Reunion, 1829–1889*

1896	Publication of *George Washington*
May 1896	Wilson's right hand partially incapacitated (possibly a small stroke)
Summer 1896	First trip to Great Britain
October 1896	Sesquicentennial address, 'Princeton in the Nation's Service'
Summer 1899	Trip to Great Britain
1902	Publication of *History of the American People* (five vols)
June 1902	Elected President of Princeton
January 1903	Death of Wilson's father, Joseph Ruggles Wilson
1904	Curricular reform approved
1905–06	Inauguration of preceptorial system
February 1906	George Harvey introduces Wilson to the Lotus Club as a possible presidential candidate
May 1906	Temporary blindness in one eye, possibly caused by a stroke
July–August 1906	Trip to Great Britain with family
December 1906	Broached 'quad' plan
January–February 1907	First trip to Bermuda, meets Mary Hulbert Peck
Ocober 1907	'Quad' plan rejected by Board of Trustees
January–February 1908	Second trip to Bermuda
1908	Publication of *Constitutional Government in the United States.*
October 1909	Princeton trustees accept offer of $500,000 from W.C. Procter to build a graduate college off campus
January 1910	Procter offer withdrawn
May 1910	Wyman bequest to Princeton with Dean Andrew West as executor
September 1910	Nominated as Democratic candidate for Governorship of New Jersey
November 1910	Elected as Governor of New Jersey with 54 per cent of the popular vote

July 1911	Wilson presidential campaign headquarters opens in New York
Autumn 1911	Meets Edward M. House
November 1911	In New Jersey elections, Republicans regain control of state legislature
2 July 1912	Nominated as Democratic candidate for President on 44th ballot at Baltimore convention
5 November 1912	Elected as US President after carrying 40 (of 48) states, though with only 42 per cent of the popular vote
4 March 1913	Inaugurated as US President
3 October 1913	Signs Underwood Tariff
23 December 1913	Signs Federal Reserve Act
21 April 1914	Military intervention at Vera Cruz
2–4 August 1914	World War I begins in Europe
6 August 1914	Ellen Wilson dies
26 September 1914	Signs Federal Trade Commission Act
15 October 1914	Signs Clayton Antitrust Act
4 February 1915	German declaration of 'war-zone' around British Isles in which submarine warfare will be conducted
March 1915	Meets Edith Bolling Galt
28 March 1915	Sinking of *Falaba* – one American (Leon C. Thrasher) killed
7 May 1915	Sinking of *Lusitania* – 1,200 deaths, including 128 Americans
13 May 1915	First *Lusitania* note
7 June 1915	W. J. Bryan resigns as Secretary of State rather than sign second *Lusitania* note – succeeded by Robert Lansing
21 July 1915	Third *Lusitania* note
28 July 1915	Military intervention in Haiti
19 August 1915	Sinking of *Arabic* –48 deaths, including two Americans
8 September 1915	*Arabic* pledge – Germany promises no more liners will be sunk

6 October 1915	Engagement to Edith Bolling Galt announced
19 October 1915	*De facto* recognition of Carranza government in Mexico
4 November 1915	Wilson publicly calls for preparedness
18 December 1915	Marriage to Edith Bolling Galt
22 February 1916	House–Grey memorandum signed
24 February 1916	Wilson letter to Senator Stone calling for defeat of Gore and McLemore resolutions
9 March 1916	Pancho Villa raid on Columbus, New Mexico
15 March 1916	Punitive military expedition under Pershing enters Mexico
24 March 1916	Sinking of *Sussex* – about 80 killed or injured; four Americans injured
4 May 1916	*Sussex* pledge – conditional German undertaking to follow rules of cruiser warfare against merchant ships
15 May 1916	Military intervention in Dominican republic
27 May 1916	Addressing the League to Enforce Peace, Wilson declares US willingness to join a post-war league of nations
1 September 1916	Signs Keating–Owen Child Labor Act
3 September 1916	Signs Adamson Act establishing eight-hour day on the railroads
7 November 1916	Reelected as President, carrying 30 states with over 49 percent of the popular vote
27 November 1916	Strengthens Federal Reserve Board warning against purchase of foreign Treasury bills
18 December 1916	Sends note asking belligerents to state peace terms
22 January 1917	In address to Senate, calls for 'a peace without victory'
31 January 1917	German announcement of unrestricted submarine warfare
3 February 1917	Breaking of diplomatic relations with Germany

26 February 1917	Wilson requests congressional authority to arm merchant ships
28 February 1917	Zimmermann telegram published
5 March 1917	Second inauguration as president
15 March 1917	Abdication of Tsar in first Russian revolution
18 March 1917	News reaches Washington of sinking of three American ships by German submarines
2 April 1917	Wilson's War Address to Congress
6 April 1917	US declaration of war on Germany
18 May 1917	Signed Selective Service Act
27 August 1917	Reply to Pope Benedict XV's call for peace
September 1917	Establishment of 'Inquiry' to prepare for peace conference
5 November 1917	Bolshevik revolution in Russia
26 December 1917	Government takeover of railroads
8 January 1918	Fourteen Points Address
3 March 1918	Treaty of Brest-Litovsk taking Russia out of the war
20 March 1918	War Council created
6 April 1918	Speech in Baltimore calling for 'Force without stint or limit'
July 1918	Approves US participation in military expedition to Siberia
27 September 1918	Speech in New York insisting that League of Nations must be incorporated in peace treaty
6 October 1918	German note to Wilson asking for peace on basis of Fourteen Points and Wilson's other speeches
5 November 1918	In congressional elections, Republicans win control of both houses
11 November 1918	Armistice ending World War I
4 December 1918	Sails from New York for Europe
January 1919	Paris peace conference begins
14 February 1919	Presents draft of League of Nations Covenant to conference

Chapter 1

Images of Wilson

Woodrow Wilson was at one time the most famous political figure in the world. When in December 1918 he became the first serving US president to leave North America, his arrival in Europe to take part in the peace conference following the First World War was treated by multitudes like the Second Coming. One young American on his staff described his reception in Paris:

> The parade from the station to the Murat house in Rue de Monceau, which is to be his official residence, was accompanied by the most remarkable demonstration of enthusiasm and affection on the part of the Parisians that I have ever heard of, let alone seen . . . Troops, cavalry and infantry, lined the entire route and tens of thousands of persons fought for a glimpse. The streets were decorated with flags and banners, Wilson's name was everywhere, and huge 'Welcome Wilson' and 'Honor to Wilson, the Just' signs stretched across the streets from house to house.[1]

Wilson's receptions in England and Italy matched those given to him in France. What were the reasons for this popular acclaim? Many, including the President himself, took it to be a response to the ideals and principles he had proclaimed. In a series of speeches in Washington, both before and after American entry into the war, Wilson had called for 'a new international order based upon broad and universal principles of right and justice', including a league of nations that would afford 'mutual guarantees of political independence and territorial integrity to great and small nations alike', and thus 'make it virtually impossible that any such catastrophe should ever overwhelm us again'.[2] These speeches, even the Fourteen Points address of January 1918 that referred to specific territorial questions, had consisted more of the elegant proclamation of general principles than of the formulation of precise proposals. But this had done nothing to diminish their moral force and popular appeal. 'To Europeans generally', Victor Mamatey has written, 'his speeches, circulated in hasty and execrable newspaper translations, in enemy countries moreover censored, were impressive but largely incomprehensible – a fact which stimulated rather than weakened the growth of the Wilsonian myth. The exalted and inscrutable are natural ingredients of myths.'[3] British liberals took a less cynical view. 'For a brief interval Wilson stood alone for mankind', H.G. Wells recalled.

> And in that brief interval there was a very extraordinary and significant wave of response to him throughout the earth. So eager was the situation that all humanity leapt to accept and glorify Wilson – for a phrase, for a gesture. It seized upon him as its symbol. He was transfigured in the eyes of men. He ceased to be a common statesman; he became a Messiah. Millions believed him as the bringer of untold blessings; thousands would gladly have died for him.[4]

To the authority of a pope, Wilson seemed to add the might of an emperor. Indeed, many of those cheering him were probably expressing gratitude for the American contribution to the Allies' victory or hailing the man that they thought would dominate the peace conference. In 1918, even more clearly than in 1945, American power had determined the outcome of the European conflict. Although the United States had not entered the war until April 1917 and the 115,000 members of the American Expeditionary Force (AEF) who lost their lives represented only a fraction of the combat deaths suffered by the other major belligerents, it is quite possible that Ludendorff's great offensive in the spring and early summer of 1918 would have succeeded had it not been for the Americans who came into the line in substantial numbers at this point and were blooded at Belleau Wood and Château-Thierry. Certainly, the psychological collapse of the German army in the autumn owed much to the seemingly endless supply of fresh American troops, then arriving at the rate of nearly 10,000 per day. By the time of the armistice, the two million American soldiers in France already outnumbered the British; had the war lasted a few months more, they would have outnumbered the French, too.

Even more important than its military and naval contribution to the defeat of the Central Powers had been America's economic and financial strength. The enormous productive capacity of the American economy was heavily drawn on by the Allies before the United States itself became a belligerent, to the extent that by the autumn of 1916 almost 40 percent of the British Treasury's war spending was in North America.[5] The consequent trade imbalance was hard to finance and the British had almost run out of means to do so when the American declaration of war on Germany solved the problem by opening the way for intergovernmental loans. By

1919, the United States was owed over $10 billion by its co-belligerents and had in addition become a net creditor on its international private investment account to the tune of more than $3.5 billion.[6] 'Mr Wilson had not invented any new political philosophy', the British diplomat and writer, Harold Nicolson, later observed. 'The one thing which rendered Wilsonism so passionately interesting at the moment was the fact that this centennial dream was suddenly backed by the overwhelming resources of the strongest Power in the world.'[7]

In whatever proportion it was the warrior or the priest that the European crowds were hailing, their acclaim itself enhanced the perception of Wilson's power. For this was a moment, in the wake of the collapse of the Tsarist, Habsburg, Hohenzollern and Ottoman empires, when democratic values were enjoying a new and much wider legitimacy. In a famous tract, John Maynard Keynes observed that

> When President Wilson left Washington he enjoyed a prestige and a moral influence throughout the world unequalled in history. His bold and measured words carried to the peoples of Europe above and beyond the voices of their own politicians. The enemy peoples trusted him to carry out the compact he had made with them; and the Allied peoples acknowledged him not as a victor only but almost as a prophet. In addition to this moral influence the realities of power were in his hands. The American armies were at the height of their numbers, discipline, and equipment. Europe was in complete dependence on the food supplies of the United States; and financially she was even more absolutely at their mercy. Europe not only already owed the United States more than she could pay; but only a large measure of further assistance could save her from starvation and bankruptcy. Never had a philosopher held such weapons wherewith to bind the princes of this world.[8]

Keynes penned these words in a spirit of disillusionment, having been shocked and depressed by the extent to which the Treaty of Versailles departed from the terms of the Fourteen Points and the 'spirit of unselfish and unbiased justice' in which Wilson had said the settlement should be made.[9] The vision of a new world order was shattered even more emphatically when the failure of the Senate to approve the peace treaty prevented the United States itself from participating in the League of Nations. In his attempt to rally public support for ratification, Wilson embarked in September 1919 on a speaking tour across the country in which he traveled 8,000 miles in 22 days and delivered 32 major addresses – all but one of them without benefit of amplification. This tremendous physical effort by a man already in poor health had to be cut short when he collapsed shortly after speaking in Pueblo, Colorado; a few days after his return to Washington, he suffered a severe stroke from which he never really recovered. The contrast between the pathetic invalid in the White House and the triumphant figure who had arrived in Europe a year earlier vividly symbolized Wilson's failure to achieve his high goals.

It has also shaped the images of Wilson that have persisted down the years. These have always diverged sharply. To those brought up in the Christian tradition, the rejection of his message by the forces of selfish nationalism and hatred on both sides of the ocean, and his own 'martyrdom' in the cause of world peace, could easily be assimilated to the story of an earlier Messiah. 'Not Wilson, but humanity, failed at Paris', declared the South African leader, Jan Christiaan Smuts.[10] Certainly, many have shared Patrick Devlin's view that 'Wilson in the twentieth century represents idealism in action.' Devlin, an eminent British jurist and Catholic, was inspired to make a detailed study of Wilson's policy during the period of neutrality by the belief that the President was 'under the control of an ideal' that 'sought to introduce into international affairs the Christian ideal of peace upon earth for men of goodwill to be brought about through the Christian ethic of service to others'.[11] The leading modern authority on Wilson, Arthur S. Link, has described him as '*primarily* a Christian idealist ... a man who almost always tended to judge policies on a basis of whether they were right by Christian standards, not whether they brought immediate material or strategic advantage'.[12]

This picture of Wilson has been broadly accepted by some who have seen it in a less favorable light. As Link himself has observed, there has always been a tendency in Europe to see him as

> a well-intentioned idealist, a man good by ordinary Christian standards, but essentially a destructive force in modern history because he was visionary, unrealistic, provincial, and ignorant of European problems, and zealous and messianic in conceit but devoid of either practical knowledge or the humility to follow others better informed than he.[13]

This image owed something to the portraits painted by Keynes and Harold Nicolson, both of whom had served as junior members of the British delegation in Paris and had been bitterly disappointed by the extent to which the treaty violated the principles Wilson had laid down. Neither man was impressed by Wilson's skill as a negotiator and Keynes concluded that 'the President was like a nonconformist minister, perhaps a Presbyterian. His thought and his temperament were essentially theological not intellectual, with all the strength and the weakness of that manner of thought, feeling, and expression.'[14]

If Keynes's condescending tone was very much his own, it also seemed to reflect the somewhat snobbish disdain that marked the attitude of many upper-class Europeans to the representatives of this new world power.

> The first glance at the President [he remarked] suggested not only that, whatever else he might be, his temperament was not primarily that of the student or the scholar, but that he had not much even of that culture of the world which marks M. Clemenceau or Mr Balfour as exquisitely cultivated gentlemen of their class and generation.[15]

As well as arousing hopes and receiving plaudits in Europe, Wilson was the target of much hostility. No one expressed this more unreservedly than Sigmund Freud, viewing events from Vienna, that special victim of the First World War. 'The figure of the American President, as it rose above the horizon of Europeans, was from the beginning unsympathetic to me', Freud confessed in the introduction to 'a psychological study' of Wilson that he composed in collaboration with the American diplomat William C. Bullitt who, as a young man, had resigned from the US delegation to the Paris peace conference in protest against the harsh terms of the German treaty. Freud stressed what he believed to be Wilson's ignorance of European languages, culture, and geography, and his immersion in 'the ideas and ideals of the middle-class Bible-reading British'. On the basis of biographical data supplied by Bullitt, Freud diagnosed Wilson as suffering from an unresolved Oedipus complex that caused him subconsciously to identify his father (who was a clergyman) with God and himself with Jesus Christ.[16] None of this, in Freud's view, enhanced Wilson's grip on reality and, like others, Freud compared Wilson to Don Quixote, remarking that 'many bits of his public activity almost produce the impression of the method of Christian Science applied to politics'.[17] The same analogy appealed to the British Foreign Office, where for a time the code word for a league of nations was 'Christian Science'.[18]

Skepticism about the Wilsonian ideal of collective security persisted among professional diplomats in Britain as elsewhere through the interwar years.[19] It found academic expression in an influential work by a former Foreign Office official holding (somewhat ironically) the Wilson Professorship of International Relations in the University of Wales at Aberystwyth. In *The Twenty Years' Crisis*, originally published in 1939, E.H. Carr contrasted the approach to politics of 'the "intellectual" and the "bureaucrat", the former trained to think mainly on *a priori* lines, the latter empirically'. In Carr's view, 'utopianism with its insistence on general principles may be said to represent the characteristic intellectual approach to politics', with 'some supposedly general principle, such as "national self-determination", "free trade" or "collective security"' being 'taken as an absolute standard'. Not surprisingly, Carr saw 'the most perfect modern example of the intellectual in politics' as Wilson, whose 'whole conception of the League of Nations was from the first closely bound up with the twin belief that public opinion was bound to prevail and that public opinion was the voice of reason'.[20]

Carr's book is often regarded as one of the precursors of 'the Realist school' that emerged in the United States in the 1940s and 1950s. Writing during World War II, the celebrated journalist and commentator Walter Lippmann argued that Wilson's condemnations of traditional diplomacy, national armaments and the idea of a balance of power were 'prejudices formed in the Age of Innocence, in the century of American isolation' when 'the United States had no need to arm, no need to find alliances, no need to take strategic precautions'.[21] The emigré political philosopher Hans J. Morgenthau, lambasting the 'utopianism', 'legalism', and 'sentimentalism' that he saw as the abiding faults of American foreign policy, described Wilson's experience as 'a tragedy not of one man, but of a political doctrine and, as far as the United States is concerned, of a political tradition'.[22] The distinguished former diplomat and policymaker, George F. Kennan, likewise saw Wilson as epitomizing persistent and deplorable American attitudes to foreign affairs, notably a 'legalistic–moralistic approach to international problems' and 'the colossal conceit of thinking that you could suddenly make international life over into what you believed to be your own image'.[23]

The burden of the criticism of Wilson's approach by these American writers was that he should have based his policies directly upon a clear conception of the national interest rather than attempting to reform the nature of international politics in accordance with universal ideals. However, it had been an important aspect of Carr's 'Realist critique' that these supposedly universal ideals, such as the supreme importance of maintaining peace, in fact served the interests of 'satisfied' powers like the United States and Great Britain at the expense of others less favorably placed in the existing order.[24] This interpretation of Wilson's policy as a sophisticated program to reshape the world in accordance with America's national interest, particularly the interests of its capitalist economic system, was developed by 'New Left' historians in the 1960s. The 'ultimate Wilsonian goal', according to N. Gordon Levin, 'may be defined as the attainment of a peaceful liberal capitalist world order under international law, safe both from traditional imperialism and revolutionary socialism, within whose stable liberal confines a missionary America could find moral and economic pre-eminence'.[25] 'Shaping the peace', Samuel F. Wells writes,

> became for Wilson the means of global reform which would bring an automatic expansion of America's political and economic influence ... The man behind the rhetoric on self-determination, the open door, and international cooperation was at heart the secular evangelist of American political economy.[26]

The realism of Wilson's program has been defended in a less equivocal way by the many who have seen the Second World War as a vindication of his approach rather than, like Lippmann, as a consequence of it. According to this view, it was the failure of the United States to join the League of Nations that undermined that organization and doomed the hope that 'collective security' would make another major war impossible. 'Solely from the standpoint of the interest of the American people themselves, who saw straight and who thought straight twenty years ago?', Undersecretary of State Sumner Welles asked rhetorically on Armistice Day, 1941. The answer, of course, was 'that great statesman, patriot, and lover of his fellow men – Woodrow Wilson'. As the campaign to develop support for a new international organization gathered momentum in the later years of the Second World War, Wilson was apotheosized again. 'The Unforgettable Figure Who Has Returned to Haunt Us', as he was called in a pictorial biography in *Look* magazine, became the hero of a lavish Technicolor film produced by Darryl Zanuck in 1944.[27] More recently, Arthur Link has vigorously disputed the notion that Wilson was 'an impractical idealist and visionary', pointing out that he was prepared to use armed force to achieve diplomatic objectives, recognized the relevance of material interests, and understood the concept of a balance of power. Link argues that what he sees as Wilson's consistent stand for a settlement to the First World War that would command the durable support of all the major powers represented a 'higher realism' than that of 'the European leaders who thought that they could win decisive victories on the battlefields and on or under the seas, and who thought that they could impose their nations' wills upon other great peoples'.[28]

These various images of Wilson differ not only in whether they present him in a favorable or unfavorable light, but also in the extent to which they portray his policies and programs as expressive of his personal temperament and idealism rather than simply as representative – whether of general American attitudes and ideas or of the values and interests of a ruling capitalist class in particular. However, they share the assumption that Wilson's actions and utterances arose directly from his beliefs, with the implicit corollary that attempts to explain them should focus on his own intellectual formation. The fact that Wilson was an academic until he entered politics at the age of fifty-three seems to have strengthened this assumption. 'He was by no means a business man or an ordinary party politician', Keynes noted. 'After all, he had spent much of his life at a university.'[29] For many, this led naturally to the conclusion that Wilson was, in the phrase Margaret Thatcher used as a proud self-description, a 'conviction politician'. Yet there has always been an alternative view – one deeply held by some of Wilson's contemporary political opponents. This was that, as a practicing politician, he traveled with very little ideological baggage, adopting and abandoning positions as they suited his political interests at the time, and deftly using his exceptional rhetorical ability to cover his tracks. 'I think he would sacrifice any opinion at any moment for his own benefit and go back on it the next moment if he thought returning to it would be profitable', Henry Cabot Lodge wrote in 1912, long before his bitter disagreements with Wilson over the First World War and the League of Nations.[30] Nor was it only those who opposed his policies who doubted whether Wilson was moved by simple conviction. Lord Robert Cecil, the most devoted supporter of the idea of a league of nations in the British government, noted in his diary after some meetings with the President: 'He supports idealistic causes without being in the least an idealist himself, at least so I guess, though perhaps I misjudge him.'[31]

One thing that is evident from these very diverse perceptions of Wilson is that he has aroused particularly strong feelings both of admiration and of hostility. In this, as in other ways, he resembles the hero of his youth: the British statesman William Gladstone. The emphasis both men laid on the place of moral principles in politics has generated very different responses. Many have been inspired by what they have seen as an attempt to elevate the standard of political behavior by appealing to altruistic impulses and a broad conception of humanity's interest. Others, however, have been repelled by what has seemed to them an expression of moral conceit, at once naïve and hypocritical, and a refusal to recognize that the apparently dirty compromises of political dealing represent the only practicable way to adjust real differences of interests and values without conflict and bloodshed.

In Wilson's case there has been an additional element, also evident in many of the reactions described above. He led the first major intervention into world politics of the United States, a country that had hitherto played little part in international diplomacy. In doing so, he articulated distinctively American values and prejudices in a manner that led the statesmen and peoples of other countries to associate these with him personally, and also did much to set the agenda for the power that has done more than any other to shape the history of the twentieth century. Moreover, undertaking this intervention required Wilson to persuade his own countrymen to make real sacrifices of money and lives, and to abandon a policy of non-involvement that had become a cherished and hallowed tradition. In making this persuasive effort, Wilson developed a rationale for the deployment of American power overseas that has remained central to subsequent debates in the United States over the role that the country should play in the world. Both abroad and at home, therefore, Wilson has been indissolubly associated with a particular, very American, version of internationalism that has continued to be the subject of lively debate.

This association was strengthened by the very personal way in which Wilson directed American policy. In part, this was a consequence of the fact that the United States had not yet established any elaborate machinery for the handling of foreign relations. In 1913 the State Department employed only 213 people in Washington (including clerks, messengers, and manual workers), and fewer than 450 in all the overseas diplomatic and consular offices combined.[32] In those days before the CIA there was no apparatus for gathering and analyzing intelligence and, unlike the other great powers, the United States did not operate an espionage system. Nor was there a unified Defense Department or Joint Chiefs of Staff; the army and navy departments were autonomous organizations related at least as closely to the congressional committees that closely controlled their budgets as to the administration. Whereas nowadays the White House staff numbers thousands, it then consisted only of Wilson's political secretary, Joseph P. Tumulty, his personal stenographer, and a few clerks.

As well as this lack of institutional depth, however, Wilson's domination of what in modern parlance would be called 'the decision-making process' reflected both the unique position of the president in the American system of government and his own personality and method of working. Under the US Constitution, the nation's executive authority is vested in the president, who is the only official to be elected – all the others are appointed by him (though some appointments also need congressional approval). It is rare for other members of the administration to have the kind of independent political standing commonly enjoyed by senior cabinet ministers in parliamentary systems; in the Wilson administration the only one who did so, Secretary of State William Jennings Bryan, resigned in 1915. Unlike some other presidents, Wilson did not informally share the power and responsibility with which he was formally endowed by his office. The adviser with whom he had the most prolonged discussions on the widest variety of matters, Colonel E.M. House, held no official position at all until 1917, but enjoyed his status simply as 'the President's friend'. House played an important role during World War I, but even he did not share in the shaping of policy in the way that, say, Dr Henry Kissinger did under President Nixon.

Wilson's concentration of authority in his own hands was facilitated by the habits that he carried over from his academic life. He was the last American president to compose all his own speeches, even on the rare and important occasions on which he read from a fully prepared text. He also personally wrote not only instructions to administration officials and press releases but also major diplomatic notes (though for protocol reasons these were signed by the Secretary of State). Many of these papers were drafted on an old portable typewriter which Wilson took with him into the White House, and which became his trademark and even, perhaps, his talisman. One British official at Paris recorded his astonishment when, after a session of the conference, the President

> gave someone instructions to telephone for his typewriter. We conjured up visions of a beautiful American stenographer, but in a short time a messenger appeared, bringing with him a battered typewriter on a tray . . . The typewriter was placed in a corner of the Conference Room and the President proceeded to tap out a long memorandum. It is a strange sight to see one of the greatest rulers in the world working away in this fashion.[33]

These working practices, together with the very small White House staff, have led Patrick Devlin to comment, with only mild hyperbole, on the way that Wilson conducted American policy during the momentous period of neutrality:

> Mrs Wilson coded and decoded and blotted signatures. Tumulty was invaluable in party matters but not equipped to serve in any other sphere. The President might almost have been running a parish with the help of his wife and a curate and a portable typewriter.[34]

The personal and apparently untrammeled way in which Wilson directed American policy, combined with a recognition of the enormous and potentially decisive strength of the United States, led many to see him as an individual in the rare position of being able to determine the course of history. In his large-scale history of *The World Crisis*, Winston Churchill declared that

> It seems no exaggeration to pronounce that the action of the United States with its repercussions on the history of the world depended, during the awful period of Armageddon, upon the workings of this man's

mind and spirit to the exclusion of almost every other factor; and that he played a part in the fate of nations incomparably more direct and personal than that of any other man.[35]

Churchill wrote this in the context of American intervention in the war but, as we have seen, a similar view was taken by many observers of the peace conference, particularly by those who had pinned their hopes on Wilson and been disappointed. 'Rarely in human history has the future course of world events depended so greatly on one human being as it depended on Wilson in the month which followed his return to Paris', Bullitt asserted. 'The whole stream of human life may be deflected by the character of a single individual.'[36]

Such perceptions have naturally led to a great interest in Wilson's biography and the factors that may have shaped his personality or caused it to change over time. Freud and Bullitt have been by no means the only authors to attempt to bring the insights of modern psychology to bear on these questions; indeed, the wealth of such studies has led the historian Dorothy Ross to conclude that 'if a case can be made for psychohistory ... Woodrow Wilson would seem to provide the ideal forum'.[37] Much attention has also been focused on Wilson's medical history, and the argument has been made that ill health affected his behavior and impaired his performance at certain crucial times before his disabling stroke in the autumn of 1919.[38]

All this would seem to make Wilson a highly appropriate subject for a 'profile in power'. However, in drawing such a profile, we first have to recognize that the observations of Churchill, Keynes, Bullitt and others are somewhat misleading. In the United States, the sovereign power rests not with the president but with the American people. No one was more aware of this than Wilson, who constantly insisted both that it was his duty to represent their views and that it was the fact that he did so which gave weight to his words and actions. Throughout his life, he was absorbed by the nature and potentialities of leadership in a democracy. So it is this particular variant of the old question about the extent to which an individual can shape history that a study of his career may illuminate. Focusing on the challenges and constraints presented by the task of exercising leadership in a democratic system also, incidentally, provides an approach to understanding Wilson's actions that has been relatively little explored in the extensive literature on him.[39]

Wilson's record as a democratic leader is especially interesting because of the scale of both his achievements and his failures. Wilson entered the White House as only the second Democratic president since the Civil War, and at a time when the Republicans were the normal majority party. His victory in 1912 owed much to a split in the Republican ranks, but his reelection in 1916 in the face of a reunited opposition was a striking tribute to his political skill. In his first term, he had provided leadership that succeeded in enacting a more substantial program of domestic legislation than any of his predecessors; among his successors only Franklin D. Roosevelt and Lyndon Johnson could boast of a comparably impressive record. He had also sustained broad public support for a foreign policy that had succeeded in preserving peace with honour in very difficult circumstances. In his second term, Wilson mobilized American resources (and American opinion) for an overseas military expedition of a scale quite unprecedented in the nation's history. As we have seen, this achievement and the reception of his public pronouncements gave him enormous international prestige. Yet in Paris he was generally judged to have failed to gain the kind of peace he had sought, and the Senate's rejection of the treaty and the League of Nations was a humiliating personal defeat for him. The Democratic party suffered a crushing defeat in the 1920 election and observers agreed that this was largely due to its association with the by now very unpopular President.

In reviewing this record of remarkable achievements and spectacular failures, I shall focus on Wilson's style of leadership, its strengths and weaknesses, and the extent to which it varied in different situations. It is noteworthy that critics at the time and since have attacked his conduct in contradictory ways. He has been accused in some contexts of abandoning principles, and in others of stubbornly refusing to compromise. This raises general questions about the place of both firmness and flexibility in successful leadership. However, we shall also need to explore the issue of how far Wilson's successes and failures were due to his own actions and how far to other factors beyond his control. In this connection, we might reflect whether any American president has really succeeded in solving the problem of finding a foreign policy that would be both effective abroad and popular at home. For it may be that Wilson's career illustrates the limits, as much as the extent, of a democratic leader's power to shape the course of history.

Notes

1 Diary of Raymond B. Fosdick, 14 December 1918, Arthur S. Link et al. (eds), *The Paper of Woodrow Wilson* (henceforth *PWW*), 69 vols, Princeton, NJ, 1966–94, vol. 53, pp. 384–5.

2 Addresses to Congress, 11 February 1918, 8 January 1918, address to the Senate, 22 January 1917, *PWW*, vol. 46, p. 320, vol. 45, p. 538, vol. 40, p. 534.

3 Victor S. Mamatey, *The United States and East Central Europe 1914–1918: A Study in Wilsonian Diplomacy and Propaganda*, Princeton, NJ, 1957, p. 107.

4 H.G. Wells, *The Shape of Things to Come: The Ultimate Revolution*, London, 1933, p. 96.

5 Arthur S. Link, *Wilson: Campaigns for Progressivism and Peace 1916–1917*, Princeton, NJ, 1965, p. 184.

6 Melvyn P. Leffler, '1921–1932', in William H. Becker and Samuel F. Wells, Jr (eds), *Economics and World Power*, New York, 1984, p. 227.

7 Harold Nicolson, *Peacemaking 1919*, London, 1933, p. 191.

8 *The Collected Writings of John Maynard Keynes*, vol. 2, *The Economic Consequences of the Peace*, London, 1971, p. 24.

9 Address to Congress, 11 February 1918, *PWW*, vol. 46, p. 320.

10 Quoted in Walter Lippmann, *US War Aims*, Boston, MA, 1944, p. 170.

11 Patrick Devlin, *Too Proud to Fight: Woodrow Wilson's Neutrality*, London, 1974, pp. 464, 678.

12 Arthur S. Link, *The Higher Realism of Woodow Wilson*, Nashville, TN, 1971, p. 129.

13 Ibid., p. 128.

14 *The Economic Consequences of the Peace*, p. 26; Nicolson, *Peacemaking 1919*, especially pp. 52–3, 163–71, 183–4, 196–205, 209–10.

15 Keynes, *The Economic Consequences of the Peace*, p. 25.

16 Sigmund Freud and William C. Bullitt, *Thomas Woodrow Wilson: A Psychological Study*, London, 1967, pp. 93–4, 133, 44–55, 245, 252. The limited and dubious factual basis of this book is stressed by Link in *The Higher Realism of Woodrow Wilson*, pp. 143–53.

17 Freud and Bullitt, *Thomas Woodrow Wilson*, pp. xii–xiii. For other comparisons of Wilson with Don Quixote, see Keynes, *The Economic Consequences of the Peace*, p. 26 and Hans J. Morgenthau, *Scientific Man vs. Power Politics*, Chicago, IL, 1946, p. 36.

18 Arthur Walworth, *America's Moment: 1918: American Diplomacy at the End of World War I*, New York, 1977, p. 65n.

19 See, for example, Michael Howard, *War and the Liberal Conscience*, London, 1978, pp. 91–4.

20 Edward Hallett Carr, *The Twenty Years' Crisis: An Introduction to the Study of International Relations*, New York, 1964, pp. 14, 17–19, 32–4.

21 *U.S. War Aims*, pp. 171–5.

22 Hans J. Morgenthau, *American Foreign Policy: A Critical Examination*, London, 1952, p. 28.

23 George F. Kennan, *American Diplomacy 1900–1950*, Chicago, IL, 1951, pp. 82, 61–2.

24 Carr, *The Twenty Years' Crisis*, pp. 75–88, 105.

25 N. Gordon Levin, Jr, *Woodrow Wilson and World Politics: America's Response to War and Revolution*, New York, 1968, p. vii.

26 Samuel F. Wells, Jr, 'New Perspectives on Wilsonian Diplomacy: The Secular Evangelism of American Political Economy', *Perspectives in American History*, 6 (1972); 419.

27 Robert A. Divine, *Second Chance: The Triumph of Internationalism in America During World War II*, New York, 1967, pp. 45, 167–74. The $3 million budget for *Wilson*, starring Alexander Knox, was larger than that for any previous film except *Gone with the Wind*.

28 *The Higher Realism of Woodrow Wilson*, especially pp. 134–9.

29 *The Economic Consequences of the Peace*, p. 26.

30 Quoted in William C. Widenor, *Henry Cabot Lodge and the Search for an American Foreign Policy*, Berkeley, CA, 1980, p. 173.

31 Cecil diary, 6 February 1919, *PWW*, vol. 54, p. 514.

32 Rachel West, *The Department of State on the Eve of the First World War*, Athens, GA, 1978, p. 4.

33 Lord Riddell's diary, 22 January 1919, quoted in G.R. Conyne, *Woodrow Wilson: British Perspectives, 1912–21*, London, 1992, p. 158.

34 Devlin, *Too Proud to Fight*, p. 468.

35 Winston S. Churchill, *The World Crisis, 1916–1918*, London, 1927, Part I, p. 229.

36 Freud and Bullitt, *Thomas Woodrow Wilson*, pp. 205, 224. See also Keynes, *The Economic Consequences of the Peace*, p. 23.

37 Dorothy Ross, 'Woodrow Wilson and the Case for Psychohistory', *Journal of American History*, 69: 3 (December 1982): 659–68.

38 See, in particular, Edwin A. Weinstein, *Woodrow Wilson: A Medical and Psychological Biography*, Princeton, NJ, 1981; Bert Edward Park, MD, T*he Impact of Illness on World Leaders*, Philadelphia, PA, 1986, Chapter 1.

39 Wilson has, however, come to occupy a central place in the political science literature on the evolution, and proper nature, of the American presidency. Both his own writings and his conduct as president have been widely seen as marking the emergence of a 'modern' conception of the office that some have celebrated and others have deplored. For a review of these divergent views, see Terri Bimes and Stephen Skowronek, 'Woodrow Wilson's Critique of Popular Leadership: Reassessing the Modern–Traditional Divide', *Polity*, 29 (fall 1996): 27–39.

Chapter 2

The Making of a Political Leader

When Keynes observed that Wilson was 'like a nonconformist minister, perhaps a Presbyterian', he was certainly right about the President's background.[1] Not only was he born in a manse but his mother was the daughter and sister, as well as the wife, of a Presbyterian minister. Jessie Woodrow, though herself born across the English border in Carlisle, was descended from a Scottish family that had produced churchmen, scholars and lawyers over several generations. Her husband, Joseph Ruggles Wilson, could not trace his ancestry back so far but his parents too had been immigrants to the United States, in their case as part of the large wave of Scottish–Irish from Ulster who arrived in the early nineteenth century and spread across the South and Midwest. The Wilsons, like the Woodrows, settled in Ohio and it was there that the recently ordained minister and the young student married in 1849.

After a few years combining supply preaching with professorships at small colleges, the Revd Dr Wilson obtained the pastorate of the First Presbyterian Church of Staunton, Virginia, and moved his growing family into the handsome new manse provided. Here the third child and eldest son, Thomas Woodrow Wilson, was born shortly after midnight on 28 December 1856.[2] Before Tommy (as he was called) was two, the family moved to Augusta, Georgia, where they remained until 1870 when Dr Wilson accepted a professorship in a seminary at Columbia, South Carolina. This was the zenith of his career and it proved to be a brief one. After a row which split the seminary and reached the General Assembly of the Church, Dr Wilson in 1874 accepted a call from the First Presbyterian Church of Wilmington, North Carolina.

The Wilson family thus lived in the South during the period when the sectional conflict was at its height, before, during and after the Civil War. Though not a Southerner by origin, Joseph Wilson identified with the regional cause. In a sermon in 1861 he declared that slavery was 'imbedded in the very heart of the moral law itself' and that, 'by saving a lower race from the destruction of heathenism', it might help 'to refine, exalt, and enrich its superior race'.[3] In the same year, he issued the invitation that led to a separate General Assembly for the Southern Presbyterian Church. During the war, he served for a season as an army chaplain and after one battle his church in Augusta became a hospital and the church-yard a detention camp for Union prisoners.

These incidents must have made an impression on his son, who later recalled that his earliest memory was hearing a passerby say that Lincoln had been elected and there would be war.[4] Woodrow Wilson was to live in the South, apart from his time as an undergraduate in Princeton, until he was almost twenty-seven years old. He shared the general white Southern detestation of the 'carpetbagger' regimes established under the Republican Congress's Reconstruction legislation that imposed negro suffrage on the ex-Confederate states; he also acquired an unquestion-ing, lifelong allegiance to the Democratic party.[5] After moving to the North Wilson took some pains to lose such regional accent as he had, but he retained a taste for Southern food, such as fried chicken.[6] His years in the South also left Wilson with a stock of 'darky stories' and the conven-tional racial attitudes of a middle-class Southerner – a paternalistic benevolence premised on an assumption of white superiority. Addressing a Southern audience in 1909, he said that 'the only place in the world where nothing has to be explained to me is the South'.[7] But he later made the same remark about America as a whole, and there can be no question that in his mature years the broader identification was by far the more important to him.[8] Even at the age of twenty-three, as a law stu-dent at the University of Virginia, he declared, rather boldly in that con-text, that 'because I love the South I rejoice in the failure of the Confederacy'.[9] Both as a scholar and a politician, he came to adopt a view of the sectional conflict that combined doing honor to the conception of the Union for which the South had fought with the view that the North stood for the future of the nation and that it was a good thing that it had won.[10]

Nevertheless, the environment in which he grew up naturally helped to shape Wilson's personality, and in this respect what mattered was not simply region but class. In the small and medium-sized towns in which they lived, his family was always one of those at the apex of the social pyramid. Although they occupied large houses in reasonably comfortable circumstances, neither their status nor their self-esteem derived primarily from wealth. Even in the nineteenth century, being a minister or college teacher was rarely the road to riches, and Dr Wilson was always concerned about his income. (When one of his Wilmington parishioners observed that his horse looked better groomed than he did, he retorted that he took care of his horse but it was his congregation that took care of him.) But Woodrow Wilson was brought up as a gentleman in a society in which there was no higher status. As he rose in the world and came to move in the highest circles in America and Europe, he never seems to have experienced any sense of social dislocation or lack of assurance. He had the manners of his class – a touch reserved, very courteous to ladies and servants – and also a lively sense of honor (which may well be seen as particularly Southern). So much does he seem to have taken for granted the genteely cultured values in which he had been bred that he rarely articulated them, but he did occasionally register distaste when confronted with others. As a young lawyer in Atlanta, he complained that 'here the chief end of man is certainly to make money, and money cannot be made except by the most vulgar methods'.[11]

This did not mean that Wilson lacked ambition. On the contrary, he had a fierce desire to make a name for himself. This was a trait that he inherited (or perhaps absorbed) from his father. It was one of the unspoken bonds in a relationship that was special to both. Some psychologically-minded historians have suggested that Joseph Wilson was a dominating figure who generated in his son a repressed anger as well as a lasting sense of inadequacy and need to prove himself.[12] They attribute the remarkable fact that the boy did not learn his letters until he was nine and could not read easily until he was eleven or twelve to an unconscious resentment of his father's pressure. Also easily seen as a form of escape is the rich fantasy life that Tommy Wilson developed in his teens, in which he played the part of a hero in a romantic world of derring-do, often involving ships and islands – those more manageably contained environments that appeal to many children. Even as an undergraduate, he made out cards in the name of 'Thomas Woodrow Wilson, Senator from Virginia'.[13] In a letter, his father urged him not 'to feed on dreams – daydreams though they be. The roast beef of hard industry gives blood for climbing the hills of life.'[14]

Such a preacherly admonition might seem to confirm the view of Dr Wilson as a stern and rather forbidding figure. This, contrasted with the evidently very protective attitude of Jessie Wilson, has been seen as explaining both the animus that Wilson later directed at those he identified as enemies and his need for reassurance from people close to him, particularly women.[15] Such analyses, however, rest on an interpretation of Wilson's relationship with his father that is very questionable. Although Dr Wilson could be an exacting mentor, insisting particularly on precision in verbal expression, he also provided unstinted love and support to his favored son. The letters he wrote to the college student contain much praise as well as guidance, and one of the few replies of Woodrow's that has survived has a relaxed, self-mocking tone that suggests an underlying assurance.[16] Nor, as we shall see, did the mature Wilson manifest any lack of self-confidence. Edwin A. Weinstein has suggested that Wilson's difficulty in learning his letters may have been due to a form of dyslexia, which would also explain why he remained a very slow reader as an adult.[17] Moreover, although Dr Wilson, extroverted and intellectually assured, was clearly quite a formidable figure in his prime, as his own career declined and his ambitions came to be increasingly focused on his son, the balance of power in the relationship shifted. Arthur Link has observed that 'Woodrow was the dominant partner at least from the mid-1880s onward.'[18] He effusively dedicated his first book, *Congressional Government*, to 'the patient guide of his youth, the gracious companion of his manhood, his best instructor and most lenient critic', and for the rest of his life continued to pay tribute to his 'very wonderful father', but it is difficult to imagine that he remained in awe of him.[19]

Nevertheless, his relationship with his immediate family was clearly fundamental in Wilson's early life and did much to shape his personality. Although he had three siblings, his only brother was ten years younger (and much less able) and Tommy was clearly the chief focus of his parents' attention (augmented if anything by that of his two elder sisters). Jessie Wilson fussed about his practical and psychological welfare while Dr Wilson devoted many hours to teaching his eldest son about all manner of things; a relative recalled how, on walks around Augusta, the frock-coated minister would explain to the bespectacled boy the arcane workings of the city's mills and industrial plants.[20] Such formal education as Wilson had before going to college was from tutors in small private schools. It is not surprising that he acquired some of the characteristics of an only child, including a drive to high achievement and the need to report all his doings to someone close to him (a role later fulfilled by his wife).[21] Although he developed an independence of judgment and decision, Woodrow Wilson never rebelled against his parents or repudiated their values.

It is probably in this context that his religious commitment is best understood. As we have seen, both sympathetic biographers such as Link and Devlin and hostile ones like Bullitt and Freud have suggested that Wilson's Christian convictions did much to shape his actions on the political stage. There is no question about the reality of his faith or of its importance to him. Not only was he a regular churchgoer throughout his life but he maintained in his own home the Presbyterian tradition of family prayers and bible reading with which he had been brought up. He frequently testified to how much strength he drew from his faith. As president, he told his doctor and confidant Admiral Cary Grayson that 'so far as religion is concerned, argument is adjourned'.[22]

Yet this much-quoted comment had a slightly double-edged character. Wilson came to maturity at a time when biblical criticism and Darwinism were raising serious questions about traditional theological axioms, and when many Anglo-American intellectuals were experiencing an agonizing loss of faith. His response to this situation, as he made clear in an entry in his confidential journal on his 33rd birthday, was to fence his religion off from the ordinary working of his intelligence:

> I used to wonder vaguely that I did not have the same deep-reaching spiritual difficulties that I read of other men having. I *saw* the intellectual difficulties, but I was not *troubled* by them: they seemed to have no connection with my faith in the essentials of the religion I had been taught ... I am capable, it would seem, of being satisfied spiritually without being satisfied intellectually.[23]

Much later, Wilson rationalized this position by saying that 'there are people who *believe* only so far as they *understand* – that seems to me presumptuous and sets their understanding as the standard of the universe'.[24]

But the barrier that Wilson erected between his faith and his intellect worked in both directions. On the one hand, his religion seems to have been very much an emotional matter. He particularly valued Communion and hymn-singing (which he greatly enjoyed), and as a young man once fled a service because he found the preacher too academic and lacking the proper feeling.[25] A longtime friend recalled that he 'always took his religion very simply. His father and the Presbyterian Church must be unquestionably right; having accepted these premises he dismissed theology from his mind and enjoyed his Bible, his God and his prayers without the least struggle with his intellect.'[26] On the other hand, his religious commitment did not constrain his thinking in other areas. In this, too, he was upholding family tradition. His maternal uncle, James Woodrow, a scholar and scientist who had a doctorate from Heidelberg, lost his post at the Columbia Theological Seminary after he had been accused of heresy because he taught Darwin's theory of evolution. As a graduate student, Wilson wrote scornfully of the way a previous generation of economists had treated the subject as a branch of religion, criticizing Francis Wayland for his 'constant tendency to call all seemingly established principles of the science laws of Divine Providence'.[27] His own writings in the field of politics were entirely secular in character, so much so that there was opposition in the strongly Presbyterian board of trustees to Wilson's appointment to the Princeton faculty.[28] In the 1890s the line Wilson drew between the religious sphere and the ordinary affairs of the world enabled him to endorse what he took to be the Burkean view that political morality 'has no other standard than that of Expediency'.[29] Unlike some of his contemporaries, such as William Jennings Bryan, Wilson did not see politics primarily as an arena for the realization of Christian values.[30]

Insofar as his religious background affected Wilson's political style and conduct, it was in less direct ways. The tone and language of his speeches unquestionably carried echoes of the Bible and of inspirational preaching. Though particularly marked in this minister's son, this was a characteristic of much political rhetoric, and indeed of public discourse generally, in the America of his era. Somewhat more personal was Wilson's frequent evocation of 'Providence' in accounting both for the course of his own life and of the nation's history. Finally, Wilson seems to have derived from the Calvinist–Presbyterian mindset, and particularly from his father, certain psychological characteristics, including both a disposition to divide the world into the elect and the damned, or friends and enemies, and a tendency towards self-righteous obstinacy when under stress in conflict situations.

Although the young Wilson appears to have had no inclination to enter the ministry himself, he fully shared his father's interest in the technique of preaching. From an early age, he was fascinated by oratory. At Davidson College in North Carolina, to which he went when he was sixteen, his chief interest was the campus debating society. Having left Davidson for somewhat obscure reasons after his freshman year to live once more with his family in their new home in Wilmington, he started college again when he went to Princeton in 1875. Here he immediately joined the American Whig Society and threw himself into its program of oratorical contests and debates on a wide variety of subjects. As a sophomore, Wilson organized another debating club, for which he wrote the constitution. When he became editor of the student newspaper, *The Princetonian*, he used its columns not only to offer extensive guidance on how to raise the standard of the football team but also to urge that opportunities for debate be introduced into the formal curriculum. As a law student at the University of Virginia, he became the president of the literary and debating club there and also rewrote its constitution, a pattern repeated yet again when he became a graduate student at Johns Hopkins. While completing his law studies at home, Wilson, as he wrote to a friend, spent about an hour a day practicing elocution and making 'frequent extemporaneous addresses to the empty benches of my father's church in order to get a mastery of easy and correct and elegant expression for the future'.[31] In a letter to his fiancée, Wilson explained why public speaking appealed to him so much:

> I have a sense of power in dealing with men collectively which I do not feel always in dealing with them singly. In the former case the pride of reserve does not stand in my way as it does in the latter. One feels no sacrifice of pride necessary in courting the favor of an assembly of men such as he would have to make in seeking to please one man.[32]

This candid confession is, of course, grist to the mill of those who read Wilson's career as compensation for some form of psychological disability. It is true that he tended to be rather reserved in his personal relations with those not close to him. This did not, however, prevent him making good friends in college, in whom he seems to have confided quite completely. Such friendships clearly meant a lot to him, particularly before he was married. In some of the writings on Wilson's personality there is also the suggestion that he was lacking in virility. This probably originated with the contemporary comments of Theodore Roosevelt, who so prided himself on his own masculinity. Bullitt and Freud make much of the alleged fact that Wilson 'never fought a fist fight in his life'.[33] If this was the case, it probably owed more to a sense of gentility than to a deficiency of testosterone. When Wilson reported home on the high emotions aroused at Princeton by the disputed presidential election of 1876, his mother responded anxiously: 'Tommy dear don't talk about knocking anybody down – no matter what they do or say ... Such people are beneath your notice.'[34] As a politician, Wilson was to display no lack of either courage or combativeness. Nor, *pace* Freud and Bullitt, is there any reason to doubt that he was endowed with at least the normal quotient of sexual libido. Circumscribed as he was by the conventions of his circle, this first found expression in the notice he took of the number of 'pretty girls' in church. At the age of twenty-three, he fell in love with a cousin and subsequently suffered the pains of rejection. Three years later, during his brief, unhappy period as a lawyer, Wilson met Ellen Axson and soon afterwards (following a romantically chance meeting in Asheville, North Carolina) they became engaged. Also descended from two generations of Presbyterian ministers, Ellen shared Wilson's background and values but she had broader literary interests as well as some talent as an artist. The marriage was to be a great source of strength and happiness to Wilson. The letters that the two wrote during their long engagement, and in later periods of separation, have survived and not only provide touching testimony to their mutual devotion but also indicate the passionate nature of the relationship.

Wilson's engagement coincided with a change of course in his career. In 1883 he decided to give up practicing law in Atlanta and applied for a fellowship at Johns Hopkins University to pursue graduate studies in history and political science. As he explained to Ellen, however, his basic interest remained the same. 'I left college on the wrong tack … The profession I chose was politics; the profession I entered was the law. I entered the one because I thought it would lead to the other.' But although this had once been true, now, if anyone was to make a living at the bar, 'he must be a lawyer *and nothing else*'. So he had concluded that

> a man without independent fortune must in any event content himself with becoming an *outside* force in politics, and I was well enough satisfied with the prospect of having whatever influence I might be able to exercise make itself felt through literary and non-partisan agencies … [and that] a professorship was the only feasible place for me, the only place that would afford leisure for reading and for original work, the only strictly literary berth with an income attached.

In this letter, Wilson referred to 'a solemn covenant' he had made with his college friend, Charles Talcott,

> that we would school all our powers and passions for the work of establishing the principles we held in common; that we would acquire knowledge that we might have power; and that we would drill ourselves in all the arts of persuasion, but especially in oratory (for he was a born orator if any man ever was), that we might have facility in leading others into our ways of thinking and enlisting them in our purposes.[35]

There is no doubt that Wilson had long dreamed of being a political leader. As well as the senatorial cards he wrote as an undergraduate, we have his cousin's recollection of the sixteen-year-old boy, sitting at his desk and explaining that the portrait above it was of 'Gladstone, the greatest statesman that ever lived' and announcing that 'I intend to be a statesman, too.'[36] But to Ellen, Wilson insisted that his 'regret at being shut out from the life towards which my first and strongest desires drew me' was not 'accompanied with anything like *pain* or with a sense of failure'. He drew on his faith in providence to conclude that he had been 'directed to the path which is the only one that leads to the successes I was meant to attain' and that 'the latent powers of oratory and statesmanship which I possess – if indeed, I possess them at all – were intended to complete my equipment as a *writer*'.[37]

The change of direction was greatly eased for Wilson by the fact that for many years he had devoted much thought and energy to literary production. Possibly because of the lingering effects of dyslexia, this extended to the physical techniques involved. From the age of sixteen, he had taught himself a complicated system of shorthand and began what became a lifetime practice of using it for first drafts of speeches and articles. In like fashion, he acquired his first typewriter (a Calligraph) in 1883, when the machines had been in use only nine years and before keyboards had been standardized. Apart from his editorials in *The Princetonian* and a few early pieces on religious subjects for a magazine edited by his father, Wilson's writing had concentrated on political subjects. One of the essays he had composed while an undergraduate at Princeton had achieved the distinction of being published in a national journal (where, ironically, the editor who accepted it was the young Henry Cabot Lodge, later to be Wilson's foe and nemesis). While reading for the bar and practicing law, Wilson had produced a book-length manuscript entitled 'Government by Debate' which another college friend, Robert Bridges (who had acquired a position on the staff of the *New York Evening Post*), unsuccessfully hawked around publishers in New York.

In his writing as in his speaking, Wilson was particularly concerned to develop a good style. This was the quality he looked for in the authors he read, mostly English historians such as Macaulay, J.R. Green and Gibbon, and on which he valued his father's advice. As an undergraduate, he had copied out a lengthy passage from one of Dr Wilson's letters, entitling it 'Guide in Writing'.[38] Explaining to Bridges his decision to abandon the law, he wrote that 'I feel as if, after a thorough and undiscourageable discipline of my faculties, and an ample storing of my mind, I could write something that men might delight to read, and which they would not readily let die.'[39]

The desire to play a part directly on the political stage had not been killed. In 1892 he referred to 'the latent politician within me' in explaining why he was tempted by an offer to become president of the University of Illinois, and a few years later, after watching Congress in session in Washington, he confessed to Ellen that 'the old longing for public life comes upon me in a flood'.[40] But whether or not Wilson had quite given up the dream of being another Gladstone when he started to see himself as a budding author, there can be no doubt that it was an intensely ambitious and unusually focused young man of twenty-six who left the South again (for good as it turned out) to begin his graduate studies in Baltimore.

Studying politics

When Wilson arrived there in September 1883, the Johns Hopkins University was barely eight years old but had already made its mark through its pioneering graduate school that was selfconsciously introducing the academic methods and standards of German universities to the English-speaking world. The department of history, politics and economics, which attracted more students than any other, was headed by Herbert Baxter Adams who had gained a PhD *summa cum laude* from Heidelberg. The faculty also included J. Franklin Jameson, who was to become a leading American historian, and Richard T. Ely, another Heidelberg PhD, who was busy evangelizing the challenge of German historical economists to the purportedly timeless axioms and *laissez-faire* orthodoxies of those they described as 'the Manchester school'. Although there were classes in which the instructors lectured, the key teaching forum was the 'seminary' at which the students presented their own work.

Wilson did not fit easily into this setting. In his application for admission, he had stated that his purpose in engaging in graduate work was 'to fit myself for those special studies of constitutional history upon which I have already bestowed some attention', and he seems to have felt that the wide-ranging courses took him too far afield from this central interest.[41] Complaining that the students were expected to cover too much too quickly, he cited his father's comment that 'the mind is not a prolix gut to be stuffed', and insisted that he needed time to digest what he read if he was to think about it properly.[42] Nor did he relish the kind of research that Adams' interest in the origins of American political institutions led him to demand of his students, which Wilson described as 'digging into the dusty records of old settlements and colonial cities ... and other rummaging work of a like dry kind'. Within a month of his arrival in Baltimore, Wilson went to see Adams and 'made a clean breast' of his unhappiness and his desire to pursue what he described as 'a hobby which I had been riding for some years with great entertainment and from which I was loath to dismount'. As Wilson happily reported to Ellen, Adams 'readily freed me from his "institutional" work', saying that 'the work I proposed was just such as he wanted to see done!'[43]

The 'hobby' horse that Wilson referred to was a critique of the American political system based on a comparison with that of Britain. In the article he had published as an undergraduate, he had argued that the cabinet should sit in Congress and, like a British ministry, resign their positions if they lost its confidence. This would remedy what Wilson saw as a despotism, at once irresponsible and fragmented, exercised in secret by Congressional committees.[44] In essays he had written since leaving Princeton and in the ill-fated book manuscript, 'Government by Debate', Wilson had further developed this argument. It can be seen as reflecting various aspects of the mental world he inhabited.

One was his awareness of, and respect for, things English. In the nineteenth century the culture in which young Americans (at least middle-class ones) grew up was centered on Britain, and this may have been accentuated in the Wilson household by the comparatively recent migration from the British Isles of both parents' families. When Dr Wilson read aloud to his family, as he liked to do, it was nearly always from British authors. He subscribed to the *Edinburgh Review* as well as to the New York *Nation*, which itself contained much news from London. Not only did his son acquire a lifelong love of some English poetry (particularly Wordsworth's) but in his youthful fantasies he usually imagined himself to be a British hero, such as 'Thomas W. Wilson, Duke of Eagleton, vice-admiral of the red' or 'Lord Wilson', commanding the 'Royal Lance Guards'. The speeches and essays he composed as a student were mostly on British writers and politicians; even when he wrote about France, the perspective was very much an English one. Strikingly, these writings made casual allusion not only to figures in British history but to contemporary parliamentarians of the second rank such as Robert Lowe and Sir William Harcourt. The senior thesis he read at his Princeton commencement was on 'Our Kinship with England', and his later published works refer unselfconsciously to 'our English cousins' and the characteristics of 'English-speaking peoples'.[45]

In addition to this general British orientation, Wilson was influenced by one English writer in particular, the political journalist and essayist Walter Bagehot. Referring to Bagehot as 'my master', Wilson imitated his style, at once conversational and epigrammatic.[46] His article on 'Cabinet Government in the United States' had freely adopted sentiments and phrases from Bagehot's book, *The English Constitution*.[47] Indeed, it was from Bagehot that Wilson derived the whole notion of 'cabinet government' as a system that fused the legislative and executive powers and in which ministries rose or fell through their ability to command parliamentary majorities after free and open debate of the great issues of the day.

Yet in comparing this favorably with what he called 'its great competitor', the American system, Bagehot had consistently called the latter, 'Presidential Government'.[48] In seeking to understand why Wilson described it instead as 'Congressional Government' (which he did first in an unpublished essay written in 1880), we may point to two factors. One is the passage of time between the two works. Bagehot composed his book originally during the American Civil War, when Lincoln both symbolized and largely exercised federal authority, while Wilson wrote after the period of Reconstruction, during which Congress had been dominant and

President Andrew Johnson had been impeached by the House of Representatives. The other factor is Wilson's Southernness, which seems to have been more important to him as a young man than it later became. It was Northern Republican 'Radicals' that his mother had been afraid he would get into a fight with in the excitement over the disputed election of 1876. The view that Congress had so overturned the balance of powers in the original Constitution as to become despotic was more likely to be held by a white Southerner than by other observers. In making the case that Congress had usurped authority both from the president and from the states, Wilson cited such features of Radical Reconstruction as the Tenure of Office Act prohibiting a president from dismissing cabinet members without the consent of the Senate, and the 'rather hateful privileges' enjoyed by federal supervisors of state elections. He noted that 'the tide of federal aggression probably reached its highest shore in the legislation which put it into the power of the federal courts to punish a state judge for refusing, in the exercise of his official discretion, to impanel Negroes in the juries of his court'.[49]

However, it is important not to exaggerate the extent to which Wilson's viewpoint represented a Southern perspective. In the first place, it was not really the case that he deplored the concentration of power in Congress. Not only did he see legislative supremacy as 'the natural, the inevitable tendency of every system of self-government', but it would have been further enhanced by his proposal that Congress, rather than the president, should appoint cabinet officers.[50] Nor should we attribute his dissatisfaction with the current state of American government simply to regional grievances. For the 1870s and 1880s was one of those periods in which educated Americans generally were inclined to take a dim view of their nation's politics. With the parties apparently fighting largely over the 'spoils' of office, it was widely regarded as a petty and sordid business, as the writings of Henry Adams and Mark Twain (among others) indicate. Some laid the blame on universal manhood suffrage, still of course little known outside the United States and now including the recently freed slaves as well as newly arrived immigrants. In 1876 Wilson himself had noted privately in his diary that 'universal suffrage is at the foundation of every evil in this country', prophesying that 'the American Republic will in my opinion never celebrate another Centennial. At least under its present Constitution and laws.'[51] However, in his published article three years later, Wilson referred to 'the right of every man to a voice in the government under which he lives' as 'that principle the establishment of which has been regarded as America's greatest claim to political honor', and argued that 'while it is indisputably true that universal suffrage is a constant element of weakness, and exposes us to many dangers which we might otherwise escape, its operation does not suffice alone to explain existing evils'. As to what those evils were, Wilson shared the common view among those who read such journals as the New York *Nation* that the level of American public life had declined because 'the best men' no longer entered politics.

Wilson argued that this was because the American political system did not provide any positions of 'commanding authority' to attract 'men of real ability'. 'It is opportunity for transcendent influence,' he wrote, 'which calls into active public life a nation's greater minds, – minds which might otherwise remain absorbed in the smaller affairs of private life.' A cabinet system would provide such opportunities and, by making the possession of office dependent upon 'might in debate' rather than 'supremacy in subterfuge', it would also force parties to choose as their leaders 'men of the strongest mental and moral fiber' since 'none but the ablest can become leaders and masters in this keen tournament in which arguments are the weapons, and the people the judges'. In this way, the nation might hope to find 'worthy successors' of Alexander Hamilton and Daniel Webster.[52]

This argument reflected an aspect of Wilson's thinking that went deeper than Anglophilia, his Southern perspective or even the influence of Bagehot – his preoccupation with political leadership and its relationship to public speaking. A high proportion of his early essays were studies of such individuals as Bismarck, the elder Pitt, John Bright and Gladstone. From these it is clear that what most fascinated him about such men was their oratorical and debating skills. Thus, he wrote that 'the British Parliament, the English nation, harkened with glad eagerness to the organ tones of Pitt's eloquence, and dared not disobey' and that 'it is as an orator that Mr Gladstone most forcibly appeals to our imaginations'.[53] The 'general hints' he wrote himself for 'Government by Debate' emphasized the questions, 'Why have we no great *statesmen*? ... Why have we no great political *orators*?'[54]

Licensed by Professor Adams, Wilson in the winter of 1883–84 returned to the subject about which he had now been thinking and writing for the best part of a decade. Inspired by a rereading of *The English Constitution* in the summer of 1883 (and possibly influenced by his academic environment), he decided to write a book that was less directly a piece of advocacy and more, like Bagehot's work, a realistic analysis of how a political system actually worked in practice, rather than in theory. As he declared in a letter to Bridges, 'I have abandoned the evangelical for the exegetical – so to speak.'[55] He did, indeed, produce quite lengthy descriptive accounts of how the House of Representatives went about its business, stressing the power and autonomy of its committees, and of the process by which revenue was raised and appropriations made. Throughout these, however, there were frequent comparisons with British practice and the moral, always implicit, was quite often explicitly pointed – that American government suffered in many ways from the lack of a clear and responsible center of authority like the British cabinet:

> *Power and strict accountability for its use* are the essential constituents of good government. A sense of highest responsibility, a dignifying and elevating sense of being trusted, together with a consciousness of being in an official station so conspicuous that no faithful discharge of duty can go unacknowledged and unrewarded, and no breach of trust undiscovered and unpunished, – these are the influences, the only influences, which foster practical, energetic, and trustworthy statesmanship.[56]

Congressional Government made Wilson's name and launched him on his new career. Even before it was published, his submission of three chapters had won him the fellowship at Johns Hopkins he had failed to gain the previous year. So energetically had he set about his task that by September 1884 he had a complete manuscript. This time he had no difficulty finding a publisher, and in January 1885 Wilson proudly sent the first two copies to his father and his fiancée. Before the year was out the book had been twice reprinted, after having been widely and favorably reviewed. In the *Nation*, Gamaliel Bradford (who had himself advocated cabinet government for the United States as early as 1873) hailed it as 'one of the most important books, dealing with political subjects, which have ever issued from the American press'.[57]

Recent assessments of *Congressional Government* have tended to attribute its impact principally to its stylistic qualities. One biographer has suggested that it 'was in essence a work of the imagination', while another has criticized 'the substitution of rhetoric for facts'.[58] Such verdicts are apparently the result of judging the book by the criteria applied to modern works of academic political science. Thus, we are told that it 'is not a work of original scholarship' since there were a limited number of citations and these were mostly to a narrow range of secondary sources.[59] Much has been made of the fact that while writing the book Wilson never made the short journey to Washington to observe Congress in action. In addition, the young Arthur Link's criticism that *Congressional Government* showed 'an amazing neglect or ignorance of economic factors in political life' has become standard.[60] All this, however, seems to rest on the assumption that Wilson was seeking to provide a comprehensive description of the American political system, and even of its relationship to the wider society. Yet his real aim was surely to offer a diagnosis of what seemed to him to be the system's weaknesses, and of the reasons for them. The criticisms directed at the book do not engage with its central thesis – that American government suffered from the lack of a single center of authority that both had the power to act effectively and could be held publicly responsible for the things that were done. In presenting this case, Wilson sought to make connections and draw comparisons, not to produce new information about the way the system worked. The argument he made was a powerful one, which can still be seen as a valid critique of the American political system of his day – and, indeed, in its essentials of ours, too.

The ten or fifteen years following the publication of *Congressional Government* may well have been the happiest period of Wilson's life. Keen to acquire an income with which he could set up home properly with Ellen, he took a teaching post in 1885 at the new women's college of Bryn Mawr in Pennsylvania, leaving Johns Hopkins without having completed his doctorate. (A year later he was awarded the degree on the strength of *Congressional Government* and a gentlemanly oral examination.) Although his well-prepared lectures on ancient and modern history were appreciated by the students at Bryn Mawr, Wilson did not get on with the feminist Dean, Carey Thomas, who was the effective power in the college. His views on female higher education were fairly unreconstructed and, after two years' experience, he complained in his journal that 'lecturing to young women of the present generation on the history and principles of politics is about as appropriate and profitable as would be lecturing to stonemasons on the evolution of fashion in dress'.[61] 'I have for a long time been hungry for a class of *men*', he wrote to Bridges in 1888, explaining why he was leaving Bryn Mawr to take up an appointment at Wesleyan University in Middletown, Connecticut.[62] In 1890, to his great satisfaction, he returned to Princeton as Professor of Political Economy and Jurisprudence.

During these years, then, Wilson's life was that of a professor in a liberal arts college in a small community. His brother-in-law, Stockton Axson, himself a college teacher of English, later sought to convey the quiet tenor of such an existence, where

> social pursuits were very simple: little dinners of a few friends attended by the professors and their wives; an occasional meeting of a literary or scientific or philosophic club, at which 'papers' were read and discussed … In these simple surroundings, Mr Wilson really formed his life habits. They were not the habits of a recluse, neither were they the habits of a gregarious animal.

Axson recalled it as 'a rather beautiful atmosphere', and for Wilson its attractions were obviously enhanced by his happy home life with Ellen.[63]

Their three daughters, Margaret, Jessie, and Eleanor, were born in 1886, 1887, and 1889, respectively.

Unlike many professors at this time, however, Wilson was by no means content just to do his teaching and enjoy family and college life. It was not for that that he had abandoned the law and his ambition to enter politics. Indeed, when writing to Ellen about the opening at Bryn Mawr, he had explained that 'it is not my purpose, you know, my darling, to spend my life in teaching. It is my purpose to get a start in the literary work which cannot at first bring one in a living.'[64] As an academic, Wilson was remarkably productive. An article on 'The Study of Administration' in the July 1887 issue of the *Political Science Quarterly* led to an invitation from Adams to give a course of lectures on the subject at Johns Hopkins, something which Wilson then did annually until 1897. The article, which pointed out that the modern age was going to impose 'enormous burdens of administration' even on democratic states, urged Americans to be prepared to learn from foreign experience how these might be best handled.[65] It drew upon the work Wilson was doing for a large-scale comparative and historical study of government. Describing this to Ellen with some distaste as a 'fact book', Wilson wrote it quickly and with heavy reliance on secondary authorities, particularly a recently published series of German scholarly volumes.[66] But *The State*, published in 1889, was conceived as a textbook, and as such it was certainly successful, going through many reprintings and eventually being translated into six foreign languages.[67] As he was finishing *The State*, Wilson received an invitation from the Harvard historian, Albert Bushnell Hart, to write a volume in a series on American history to be published by Longmans, Green. *Division and Reunion, 1829–1889*, which appeared in 1893, was marked not only by careful research in printed original sources but by an interpretation, stressing economic factors and the role of the West, that anticipated later historiography. Wilson had discussed his ideas with Frederick Jackson Turner, whom he had met at Johns Hopkins when he lectured there in 1889 and with whom he had developed a friendship and intellectual companionship.

Wilson's subsequent historical works, a short biography of *George Washington* (1897) and a five-volume *History of the American People* (1902), were more popular in character and seem to have been inspired by literary rather than intellectual ambition. They were also written to make money. Both works originated as a series of articles for *Harper's* magazine for which Wilson was well paid. Wilson had been accustomed to living in large houses, and in Princeton he first rented one (in what is now Library Place) and then had one built on the neighboring lot. These provided spacious accommodation not only for the nuclear family and the governess but also for visiting relatives, many of whom stayed for long periods. But the new house cost almost twice the original estimate. As well as making *Harper's* offers irresistible, Wilson's domestic expenses were one reason why he was so eager to accept the many invitations that came in to give lectures around the country.[68]

Increasingly, then, Wilson had become tempted to exercise his facility as a writer and speaker to enhance both his income and his public visibility by undertaking a variety of assignments. Yet he retained the ambition to make a serious contribution to the theoretical understanding of politics. He had conceived this project while at Bryn Mawr and its first manifestation was a typescript of over a hundred pages on 'the modern democratic state' that he sent to his father in December 1885. In the following year, he wrote to a publisher outlining his plan: 'I would apply the now common inductive method to the study of democratic government – to the study of the genesis and development of *our* democratic government in particular.' In the 1890s Wilson continued to conceive of this as his *magnum opus*, though he now put off writing it since he did not feel he had read and thought enough to be able to do the subject justice. 'In the family circle, this prospective work was always referred to as "POP" which, being interpreted, meant "The Philosophy of Politics"', Stockton Axson recalled. 'He whimsically added that Montesquieu had stolen his title when the great Frenchman of the eighteenth century gave to his book the title *The Spirit of the Laws*.' Soon after his 44th birthday, Wilson asked the Princeton trustees for a year's leave of absence so that he could concentrate on preparing the work that had been forming in his mind 'these twenty years and more', but his father's illness and his own election to the presidency of the university scuppered this plan. Even after Wilson had retired from the White House, broken in health, Ray Stannard Baker recorded that 'the old vision flared up again. He will yet write the great book! The *Novum Organon* of politics!' But 'when he closed his tired eyes, for the last time, the *magnum opus* was still unpenned'.[69]

No doubt, Wilson's failure ever really to undertake, let alone complete, this project was due to more than simple contingencies. The leading authority on his academic writings has observed that Wilson 'betrayed little awareness of the methodological problems involved when the inductive method is applied to social and political phenomena'.[70] As Wilson himself seems to have recognized, his *forte* was imaginative insight conveyed with vivid images and epigrams rather than the mastery of complex detail or sustained and systematic theoretical analysis.[71] In his journal, he noted that he 'chose for my chief ambition the historical explanation of the modern democratic state' because he conceived it to be

> a task, not of origination, but of interpretation. Interpret the age: i.e. inter-
> pret myself … Institutions have their rootage in the common thought
> and only those who share the common thought can rightly interpret
> them … Why may not the present age write, through me, its political
> *autobiography*?[72]

The realization that generating a work that engaged with the likes of Herbert Spencer and Henry Maine would require more than intelligent introspection may explain Wilson's procrastination about embarking on 'The Philosophy of Politics'.

Yet the drafts and synopses that Wilson did produce, together with his published writings and the lectures he gave, are sufficient to indicate the nature of his serious thinking about politics. In the course of the hundreds of thousands of words he wrote and delivered (now brought together in the magnificent edition of his *Papers*), he expressed opinions (not always consistent ones) about many issues. But two central and enduring features were a general approach to understanding the subject and a particular preoccupation.

The general approach was that commonly characterized as the organic analogy – in other words, that society should be conceived of as a living organism. The significance of this approach was that it ran counter to many of the assumptions and principles of the Anglo-American liberal tradition. In the first place, it implied that it was wrong to conceptualize political phenomena in mechanical terms – as in the image of a balance of power. Wilson rejected what he called 'the Whig theory of political dynamics', which he saw as based on a Newtonian model: 'government is not a machine, but a living thing. It falls, not under the theory of the universe, but under the theory of organic life. It is accountable to Darwin, not to Newton.'[73] If societies, like all living things, were in a constant process of development, they could only be understood historically. This necessitated the empirical study of particularities, a process that could not be short-circuited through logical deduction from some abstract, theoretical model. Furthermore, adherents of this approach generally insisted that the proper unit of study was not the individual but the collectivity – many, including Wilson himself, compared the social organism with the human body, with the different 'organs' all performing their specialized functions for the good of the whole. A corollary of this was the rejection of the whole tradition of seeking the origins and justification of government, and indeed of society itself, in a 'contract' in which individuals had foregone certain 'natural rights' in exchange for specific goods. As an academic, Wilson was no admirer of Thomas Jefferson and 'his speculative philosophy'.[74]

It was no doubt at Johns Hopkins that Wilson was impressed with the intellectual authority in the later nineteenth century of an evolutionary approach to social phenomena and the appropriateness of the organic analogy; he would have imbibed it from the German-inspired teaching of Adams and Ely, and in particular perhaps from a course given by George Sylvester Morris, a professor of philosophy.[75] But the seed fell on fertile ground. Wilson's early model, Bagehot, had made much of the difference between 'the literary theory' of the English Constitution and 'the living reality'.[76] Initially, the phrase 'living reality' may have meant little more to Wilson than what he called 'a just understanding of the conditions of practical politics', something he felt was missing in most works of political philosophy and constitutional law; by contrast, he saw Bagehot and de Tocqueville as '*men of the world*, for whom the only acceptable philosophy of politics was a generalization from actual daily observation of men and things'.[77] But already, as an undergraduate at Princeton, Wilson had encountered a writer for whom the organic analogy had much wider implications, and who was to have a more profound influence on him even than Bagehot. At first, characteristically, it had been Edmund Burke's style that had captivated him, but the emphasis he placed on 'political habits' in his essay on 'Self-Government in France' in September 1876 showed that the Burkean perspective had entered into Wilson's own thinking.[78]

There were several references to *Reflections on the Revolution in France* in *Congressional Government* and Wilson's other writings of the 1880s, but both his knowledge of and his allegiance to Burke deepened in the early 1890s, at which time he wrote to a friend that 'if I should claim any man as my master, that man would be Burke'.[79] In 1894 Wilson delivered a paper on 'the Man and his Times' that was an encomium on Burke's character as well as his political philosophy. The picture he painted was of a very Wilsonian hero. Not only was Burke's genius essentially literary but, 'indubitable Irishman though he was', his was 'the authentic voice of the best political thought of the English race'. Wilson argued that Burke's call for conciliation of the American colonists in the 1770s and his passionate opposition to the French revolution in the 1790s were consistent since they were both founded on a hostility to 'abstract reasoning' in politics. In the first case, that reasoning was represented by the North ministry's insistence on parliament's legal sovereignty in the face of the colonists' practical self-government and belief in their rights as Englishmen; in the latter, it was 'the French revolutionary philosophy' that held that 'government is a matter of contract and deliberate arrangement, whereas in fact it is an institute of habit, bound together by innumerable threads of

association, scarcely one of which has been deliberately placed'. By contrast, Wilson saw Burke as 'the apostle of the great English gospel of
Expediency'. While this was 'profoundly practical and utilitarian' in its
treatment of 'men and situations ... as they are found at the moment of
actual contact', it was not unprincipled; on the contrary, Burke 'perceived
that questions of government are moral questions, and that questions of
morals cannot be squared with the rules of logic, but run through as many
ranges of variety as the circumstances of life itself'.[80]

Burke is generally seen as a conservative and, indeed, his writings of
the 1790s had a decidedly reactionary flavor. Wilson endorsed the view
that 'no result of value can ever be reached in politics except through slow
and gradual development, the careful adaptations and nice modifications
of growth'.[81] But even in 1894, when his own political outlook was more
conservative than it later became, he observed that Burke 'erred when he
supposed that progress can in all its stages be made without changes
which seem to go even to the substance'.[82] It was not only that he felt that
in the late nineteenth century a Burkean respect for 'circumstances'
involved the need to adapt political institutions to the enormous and rapid
changes taking place in other areas of life. In common with almost all his
contemporaries, Wilson also believed, much less equivocally than Burke,
that such changes and adaptations did, indeed, constitute progress.

Wilson's belief in progress is reflected in his attitudes to modern
democracy, the subject of his projected major work. He made it clear that
he regarded it as an advanced condition, observing that 'government by
discussion comes as late in political, as scientific thought in intellectual
development'. But he described the nature of the advance in different, not
altogether consistent, ways. On the one hand, he linked democracy with
the general process of modernization – the growth of commerce, the
development of printing and newspapers, rising levels of literacy and
popular education. On the other, he associated it with the 'maturity' of a
people, the product of a long and particular history in which the requisite
habits of 'freedom and self-control' had been built up. This explained why
democracy had 'been a cordial and a tonic to little Switzerland and big
America, while it has been as yet only an quick intoxicant or a slow poison
to France and Spain, a mere maddening draught to the South American
states'.[83]

Wilson's failure to explain how these ideas fitted together may have
reflected the fact that he was less interested in defining the preconditions
of democracy than with analyzing its true nature. He insisted that popular sovereignty in the modern age was 'unlike the sovereignty of a king or
of a small, easily concerting group of men' because 'the people ... do not,

in any adequate sense, govern': 'questions of government are infinitely complex questions, and no multitude can of themselves form clear-cut, comprehensive, consistent conclusions concerning them'. 'The freedom of the democratic nation' really consisted of 'making undictated choice of the things it will accept and of the men it will follow'. In addition to granting or withholding consent, the people 'produce the stuff out of which governors and kings are made', for, in a democracy, 'not a few men of privileged blood only, but all men of original force are quickened to make the most of themselves'.[84]

Wilson thus highlighted the role in modern democracies of leaders, and it is this that runs as a persistent preoccupation through his thinking about politics in his years as an academic. Pointing to 'the virtual absence of any sustained reflection upon the notion of leadership within the liberal tradition', the historian Niels Thorsen has claimed it as Wilson's distinctive contribution to political theory.[85] Be that as it may, it is hard to avoid seeing it, as Wilson himself seems to have done at some level, as preparation for his future career. As we have seen, Wilson had been fascinated since his youth by the personalities and qualities of famous political figures, and the animating argument of his earliest published writings, including *Congressional Government*, had been that both administrative efficiency and proper democratic accountability required that there be in a political system some clearly identifiable and adequately empowered leader. He reiterated this case over the years, adding the argument that the greater demands on government produced by the industrial revolution and the rapid pace of economic and social change made such leadership the more necessary.[86] But he also explored further the relationship between a democratic leader and public opinion, and the qualities and techniques that made for successful leadership.

In his writings on democracy Wilson stressed the limitations of public opinion. Contrary to the common, pious pretence, it was not qualified to govern:

> We know that the making and the modification of laws is fit matter for study; that questions of policy, whether domestic or foreign, are full of intricacy: we know that there is almost no subject upon which there can be said to be in any community a *single* prevalent opinion, at once diffused and intelligent: and yet we assume that the people are constantly getting definite convictions ready for the measurement of each question of government![87]

Nor did 'the mass of citizens' wish to give much thought to such matters: 'they are too tired and too teased by daily toil and care to have more than a few breaths of their life to give to public affairs'. It followed that 'neither legislation nor administration can be done at the ballot box'; they should be left to 'the few who act for the whole'.[88] The true role of public opinion was 'to play the part of authoritative critic': 'Self-government does not consist in having a hand in everything, any more than housekeeping consists necessarily in cooking dinner with one's own hands. The cook must be trusted with a large discretion in the management of the fires and the ovens'.[89]

Yet, pursuing Wilson's analogy, what the cook produced would depend upon the taste of the housekeeper. The organic view itself stressed the limitations of a leader's freedom of action: even

> the despot's power, like the potter's, is limited by the characteristics of the materials in which he works, of the society which he manipulates; and change which roughly breaks with the common thought will lack the sympathy of that thought, will provoke its opposition, and will inevitably be crushed by that opposition.'[90]

In a democracy, those who sought to lead had first to study the 'great dominating currents of the public thought', which Wilson likened to a force of nature: 'In the great nations of the earth their season is as regular and their direction as steady as the trade winds which sweep their sure course across the oceans. Bold sailors may cross them athwart, but none may venture to go in their teeth.'[91]

Again, though, Wilson's image conveyed a complex thought. The sailor set his own course, he did not just go where the wind blew. Wilson remained attached to a more heroic conception of leadership than that of a mere follower of public opinion. It was why he objected to the 'Rousseauite' view of popular sovereignty, which he thought would lead one to 'endeavor to catch the common thought, the cant phrases, and repeat them continually'. On the other hand,

> if we live in a nation that waits to be led, and which has sovereign liberty to follow even us, if we can convince or move it, what an incentive we have to be ourselves in all sincerity, press our claims, fit our thought to effect its purpose betimes, mend our lives to suit the station we would achieve!

He suggested 'the democratic nation' should be thought of as 'a great, sensitive registering machine': 'we may study to play upon it, – we *must*, – *study to play upon it*, and make it register our best suggestions.'[92]

One can construct a fairly coherent, if multifaceted, model of the proper relationship between a democratic leader and public opinion from these various observations of Wilson's. In this model, it is the responsibility of the leader and his colleagues to make policy since the electorate as a whole does not have the information, the inclination or the trained intelligence to do this. However, in taking a position, the leader must always be conscious of the need to develop support for it. So the course he adopts must be in accordance with the fundamental dispositions and values of the people he is leading. This done, the leader exercises his talents, studied skills and force of character to bring public opinion behind him and his policy. As Wilson summed it up on one occasion, 'policy – where there is no absolute and arbitrary ruler to do the choosing for a whole people – means massed opinion, and the forming of the mass is the whole art and mastery of politics'.[93]

Such a synthesis, however, does not do justice to the tension between conflicting feelings which Wilson's writing on this theme seems to display. This tension is perhaps most clearly apparent in the lecture entitled 'Leaders of Men', composed in his last year at Wesleyan. Here Wilson went further than usual in stressing the need for leaders in a modern democracy to be in tune with the thoughts and feelings of the majority. From the Burkean proposition that 'leadership, for the statesman, is *interpretation*', he concluded that 'the ear of the leader must ring with the voices of the people'. Appealing to a minority was no use. Nor should one be ahead of one's time: 'If you would be a leader of men, you must lead your own generation, not the next.' It was wrong to imagine that people could be persuaded by new information or new ideas: 'Men are not led by being told what they do not know ... Their confidence is not gained by preaching new thoughts to them. It is gained by qualities which they can recognize at first sight, by arguments which find easy and immediate entrance into their minds.' Such arguments should be simple and have moral appeal. Wilson cited the example of the leaders of the Anti-Corn Law League in England, Richard Cobden and John Bright: 'Mark the simplicity and directness of the arguments and ideas of such men. The motives which they urge are elemental; the morality which they seek to enforce is large and obvious; the policy they emphasize purged of all subtlety.' 'The arguments which induce popular action must always be broad and obvious', Wilson concluded. 'Only a very gross substance of concrete conception can make any impression on the minds of the masses.'

All this meant that 'some of the gifts and qualities which most commend the literary man to success would inevitably doom the would-be leader to failure'. Since those qualities included subtlety of thought, imaginative insight and originality, one could infer that politics was an arena for the second-rate. Perhaps for this reason, Wilson pointed out that sometimes leaders appeared of a very different stamp: 'Men of strenuous minds and high ideals come forward, with a sort of gentle majesty, as champions of a political or moral principle' and 'only speak their thought, in season and out of season'. Such figures were now and again successful, but generally 'for the advancement of but a single cause'. This was because 'a wide sympathy and tolerance is needed in dealing with men, and uncompromising men cannot lead'.

In this lecture, which the editors of the *Papers* describe as 'a highly personal statement', Wilson explicitly emphasizes the contrasting qualities needed for success in the two fields on which his ambition had focused – the political and the literary. Implicitly, he also seems to be torn about the style of political leadership that he most admires and identifies with. On the whole, it is that which he sees as the most conducive to success in practice – responsive, pragmatic, consensual, prepared to compromise and giving eloquent expression to the common thought. But he also seems almost romantically attracted to a more lonely and prophetic mode, inspiring the people with a new vision. It is not difficult to see his later career as reflecting this tension.[94]

As Wilson developed his conception of the nature of leadership in a democracy, he still faced the problem that had troubled him since his undergraduate days of where within the American system such a leader could operate. 'We are', he lamented in 1897, 'without leaders who can be held immediately responsible for the action and policy of the government, alike upon its legislative and upon its administrative side.' Largely repeating the analysis of *Congressional Government*, he observed that the only form of leadership in the legislature was that exercised 'by management and not by debate', preeminently by the Speaker of the House of Representatives. On the other hand, the President could not be looked to for leadership because he had no real power over Congress and 'in the last resort, it lies with Congress, and not the executive, to choose what the government shall be and do'. Moreover, the White House was no longer occupied by men of the stature of the early presidents, which Wilson saw as a consequence of the way parties now chose their nominees, through conventions dominated by 'an incalculable number of local influences' unconnected with questions of national policy. Anticipating later progressive critiques, Wilson again pointed out that this system of 'leaderless government' obstructed democratic accountability: 'I, for my part, when I vote at a critical election, should like to be able to vote for a definite line of policy with regard to the great questions of the day.'[95]

By the early twentieth century, however, Wilson had come to a much more optimistic view about the opportunities the American system provided for a potential leader. An invitation to inaugurate a recently endowed lecture series at Columbia University led Wilson to write his last academic work, *Constitutional Government in the United States,* which was published in 1908. This restated many of his old themes but it also included a new focus on the office of president. Indeed, he cited it as 'proof that our government is a living, organic thing' that 'we have grown more and more inclined from generation to generation to look to the president as the unifying force in our complex system'. As the business of government had become more extensive, the President had had to delegate the detailed execution of the laws to 'the now innumerable body of federal officials throughout the country'. But, as the only official who represented 'the people as a whole, exercising a national choice', he was uniquely positioned to be 'the leader both of his party and of the nation'. A decade earlier Wilson had suggested that the President was little better placed to affect legislation than 'any other influential person who might choose to send to Congress a letter of information and advice'. Now, in the era of Theodore Roosevelt, Wilson observed that the President not only had the right under the Constitution to make legislative proposals to Congress but could back them up with his 'personal force and influence' and rally public opinion behind them: 'Let him once win the admiration and confidence of the country, and no other single force can withstand him, no combination of forces will easily overpower him.' The recent growth of America's international power and interests had further enhanced the President's position since he had a 'very absolute' control of foreign affairs: 'Our President must always, henceforth, be one of the great powers of the world, whether he act greatly and wisely or not.' Altogether, 'the office will be as big and as influential as the man who occupies it'.[96]

Notes

1 J.M. Keynes *The Collected Writings of John Maynard Keynes*, vol. 2, *The Economic Consequences of the Peace*, p. 26.

2 Technically, therefore, Wilson's birthday was 29 December, but it was always celebrated on the 28th.

3 John M. Mulder, *Woodrow Wilson: The Years of Preparation*, Princeton, NJ, 1978, pp. 9–10.

4 Address in Chicago on Lincoln, 12 February 1909, *PWW*, vol. 19, p. 33.

5 'Stray Thoughts from the South', February 1881, *PWW*, vol. 2, p. 27.

6 Wilson to Ellen Axson, 17 February 1885, *PWW*, vol. 4, pp. 263–4. On first meeting him in Paris, Harold Nicolson noted in his diary that the President had 'a Southern drawl', but this was not the usual perception. Harold Nicolson, *Peacemaking 1919*, London, 1933, p. 236.

7 Address on Robert E. Lee at the University of North Carolina, 19 January, 1909, *PWW*, vol. 18, p. 631.

8 Address in New York, 4 March 1919, *PWW*, vol. 55, p. 419.

9 August Heckscher, *Woodrow Wilson: A Biography*, New York, 1991, pp. 50–51.

10 Arthur S. Link, 'Woodrow Wilson: The American as Southerner', in *The Higher Realism of Woodrow Wilson*, Nashville, TN, 1971 pp. 21–37.

11 Wilson to Robert Bridges, 13 May 1883, *PWW*, vol. 2, p. 355.

12 Alexander L. George and Juliette L. George, *Woodrow Wilson and Colonel House: A Personality Study*, New York, 1956, pp. 6–13.

13 Ray Stannard Baker, *Woodrow Wilson: Life and Letters*, vol. 1, London, 1928, p. 104.

14 Joseph Wilson to Wilson, 25 January 1878. *PWW*, vol. 1, p. 345.

15 George and George, *Wilson and House*, pp. 5–6, 30–33, 43–6, 121–3, 272–3. When his mother died, Wilson wrote to his wife that 'I remember how I clung to her (a laughed-at "mamma's boy") till I was a great big fellow: but love of the best womanhood came to me and entered my heart through these apron-strings'. The context of these much-quoted remarks is rarely taken into account. Wilson to Ellen A. Wilson, 19 April 1888, *PWW*, vol. 5, pp. 719–20.

16 Wilson to Joseph Wilson, 23 May 1877. *PWW*, vol. 1, pp. 265–6. (This letter may not have been sent.)

17 Edwin A. Weinstein, *Woodrow Wilson: A Medical and Psychological Biography*, Princeton, NJ, 1981, pp. 15–19.

18 Link, *The Higher Realism of Woodrow Wilson*, p. 147.

19 E.g. Wilson to Hamilton Holt, 27 February 1918, *PWW*, vol. 46, p. 469.

20 Baker, *Woodrow Wilson*, vol. 1, p. 37; Heckscher, *Woodrow Wilson*, p. 17.

21 Stockton Axson, *'Brother Woodrow': A Memoir of Woodrow Wilson*, Princeton, NJ, 1993, pp.171–2.

22 Baker, *Woodrow Wilson*, vol. 1, p. 68; Axson, *'Brother Woodrow'*, p. 229.

23 Wilson's Confidential Journal, 28 December 1889, *PWW*, vol. 6, p. 462.

24 Diary of Nancy Saunders Toy, 3 January 1915, *PWW*, vol. 32, p. 9.

25 Wilson to Ellen Axson, 9 October 1887, *PWW*, vol. 5, p. 614.

26 Edith Gittings Reid, *Woodrow Wilson: The Caricature, the Myth and the Man*, New York, 1934, p. 16. His brother-in-law likewise observed that 'Wilson's critical mind was never so uncritical as when he attended a church where the preacher spoke simply and expounded the Presbyterian doctrines. Wilson sat like a docile child.' Axson, *'Brother Woodrow'*, p. 275.

27 Mulder, *Woodrow Wilson*, p. 84.

28 Heckscher, *Woodrow Wilson*, p. 104; Francis Landey Patton to Wilson, 18 February 1890, *PWW*, vol. 6, pp. 526–7.

29 Mulder, *Woodrow Wilson*, pp. 127–9.

30 On this point, see John Milton Cooper Jr, *The Warrior and the Priest: Woodrow Wilson and Theodore Roosevelt*, Cambridge, MA, 1983, p. 19.

31 Wilson to Robert Bridges, 24 May 1881, *PWW*, vol. 2, p. 70.

32 Wilson to Ellen Axson, 18 December 1884, *PWW*, vol. 3, p. 553.

33 Sigmund Freud and William C. Bullitt, *Thomas Woodrow Wilson: A Psychological Study*, London, 1967, p. 225. Also pp. 9, 61, 181, 213–14.

34 Jessie Wilson to Wilson, 15 November 1876, *PWW*, vol. 1, p. 228.

35 Wilson to Ellen Louise Axson, 30 October 1883, *PWW*, vol. 2, pp. 499–501.

36 Baker, *Woodrow Wilson*, vol. 1, p. 57.

37 Wilson to Ellen Louise Axson, 27 February 1885, *PWW*, vol. 4, p. 305.

38 J.R. Wilson's Advice to his Son, 14 January 1878, *PWW*, vol. 1, p. 340.

39 Wilson to Robert Bridges, 29 April 1883, *PWW*, vol. 2, p. 343.

40 Wilson to Ellen Wilson, 9 May 1892, 4 February 1898, *PWW*, vol. 7, p. 628; vol. 10, pp. 374–5.

41 Baker, *Woodrow Wilson*, vol. 1, p. 172.

42 Wilson to Ellen Axson, 22 December 1883, *PWW*, vol. 2, p. 596.

43 Wilson to Ellen Axson, 16 October 1883, ibid., 479–80.

44 'Cabinet Government in the United States', August 1879, *PWW*, vol. 1, pp. 495–510.

45 *PWW*, vol. 1, pp. 637, 492; *Congressional Government: A Study in American Politics*, Baltimore, MD, 1981, p. 154; 'Edmund Burke: The Man and his Times', *PWW*, vol. 8, p. 342. In 1897 (when addressing a Virginia audience), Wilson spoke of 'the English race itself, to which we belong', *PWW*, 10, p. 288.

46 Wilson to Ellen Axson, 22 November 1884, *PWW*, vol. 3, p. 471.

47 The debt is clearly brought out by Henry Wilkinson Bragdon in *Woodrow Wilson: The Academic Years*, Cambridge, MA, 1967, pp. 59–61.

48 Walter Bagehot, *The English Constitution*, Oxford, 2001, Chapters 1–2.

49 *Congressional Government*, pp. 51–2, 39–40, 42–3.

50 Ibid., pp. 203, 177–8.

51 Wilson's shorthand diary, 19 June 1876. Also 4 July 1876, *PWW*, vol. 1, pp. 143, 148–9.

52 'Cabinet Government in the United States', *PWW*, vol. 1, pp. 494, 504–7.

53 Ibid., pp. 307–13, 407–12, 608–21, 624–42 (quotations on pp. 411, 637).

54 *PWW*, vol. 2, p. 155.

55 Wilson to Robert Bridges, 19 November 1884, *PWW*, vol. 3, p. 465.

56 *Congressional Government*, p. 187.

57 Arthur S. Link, *Wilson: The Road to the White House*, Princeton, NJ, 1947, pp. 14–15, 17–18.

58 Heckscher, *Woodrow Wilson*, p. 76; Mulder, *Woodrow Wilson*, p. 79.

59 Bragdon, *Woodrow Wilson*, p. 127.

60 Link, *The Road to the White House*, p. 15. See also Mulder, *Woodrow Wilson*, p. 81; Kendrick A. Clements, *Woodrow Wilson: World Statesman*, Boston, MA, 1987, p. 15.

61 Confidential Journal, 20 October 1887, *PWW*, vol. 5, p. 619.

62 Wilson to Robert Bridges, 26 August 1888, ibid., p. 764.

63 Axson, *'Brother Woodrow'*, pp. 78–9.

64 Wilson to Ellen Axson, 30 November 1884, *PWW*, vol. 3, p. 499.

65 *PWW*, vol. 5, pp. 357–80.

66 Wilson to Ellen Wilson, 9 March 1889, *PWW*, vol. 6, p. 139.

67 Japanese, French, Russian, Italian, Spanish and German. Mulder, *Woodrow Wilson*, p. 103; 'Wilson's *The State*', *PWW*, vol. 6, pp. 244–52.

68 Heckscher, *Woodrow Wilson*, pp. 113–14, 119, 131–2.

69 'Wilson's First Treatise on Democratic Government'; Wilson to Horace E. Scudder, 10 July 1886, *PWW*, vol. 5, pp. 54–8, 301–4; Axson, *'Brother Woodrow'*, p. 77; Heckscher, *Woodrow Wilson*, pp. 133–5; Baker, *Woodrow Wilson*, vol. 1, p. 274.

70 Niels Aage Thorsen, *The Political Thought of Woodrow Wilson, 1875–1910*, Princeton, NJ, 1988, p. 223.

71 Wilson to Ellen Axson, 13 February 1885, *PWW*, vol. 5, pp. 56–7.

72 Confidential Journal, 28 December 1889 (Wilson's 33rd birthday), *PWW*, vol. 6, p. 463.

73 *Constitutional Government in the United States*, 1908, *PWW*, vol. 18, pp. 105–6.

74 Thorsen, *Political Thought*, p. 221.

75 Ibid., *Political Thought*, pp. 75–6.

76 *The English Constitution*, p. 1.

77 'Of the Study of Politics'. c. November 1886, *PWW*, vol. 5, pp. 395–406 (emphasis in original).

78 Thorsen, *Political Thought*, pp. 36–8.

79 Wilson to Caleb T. Winchester, 13 May 1893, *PWW*, vol. 8, p. 211.

80 'Wilson's First Lecture on Burke', *PWW*, vol. 8, pp. 313–43.

81 *The State*, *PWW*, vol. 6, p. 310.

82 'Edmund Burke: The Man and His Times', *PWW*, vol. 8, p. 340.

83 'The Modern Democratic State', December 1885, *PWW*, vol. 5, pp. 61–92 (quotations on pp. 71, 63); 'Democracy', December 1891, *PWW*, vol. 7, pp. 345–68 (especially p. 358).

84 'The Modern Democratic State', *PWW*, vol. 5, p. 75; 'Democracy', *PWW*, vol. 7, pp. 359, 357.

85 Thorsen, *Political Thought*, p. 63.

86 See, especially, 'Leaderless Government', an address to the Virginia Bar Association, 5 August 1897, *PWW*, vol. 10, pp. 288–304.

87 'Democracy', *PWW*, vol. 7, p. 354.

88 'The Modern Democratic State', *PWW*, vol. 5, pp. 91, 75, 85–6.

89 'The Study of Administration', ibid., p. 374.

90 *The State*, *PWW*, vol. 6, p. 257.

91 'The Modern Democratic State', *PWW*, vol. 5, p. 91.

92 'Democracy', *PWW*, vol. 7, p. 359.

93 'Leaderless Government', 5 August 1897, *PWW*, vol. 10, p. 290.

94 'Leaders of Men', June 1890, *PWW*, vol. 6, pp. 644–71.

95 'Leaderless Government', 5 August 1897, *PWW*, vol. 10, pp. 288–304.

96 *Constitutional Government in the United States*, Chapter 3, 'The President of the United States', *PWW*, vol. 18, pp. 104–23; 'Leaderless Government', *PWW*, vol. 10, p. 292.

Chapter 3

Practicing Politics, 1902–12

President of Princeton

If Wilson had remained simply a professor, teaching and writing, he would almost certainly never have entered politics. In June 1902, however, at the age of forty-five, he became President of Princeton University. The position gave Wilson a public standing and visibility that he took advantage of to make occasional addresses on national politics, and in some of these he spoke as an avowed member of the Democratic party. Such addresses, along with the dynamic and high-profile manner in which he led the university, gave rise as early as 1906 to mention of him as a possible candidate for the US presidency. But between then and 1910, when he entered the arena by accepting nomination for the Governorship of New Jersey, the tone of his public utterances changed markedly and with it his perceived position in the political alignments of the period.

Although he expressed regret at the further postponement of work on his projected *magnum opus*, his elevation to the presidency of Princeton was a source of great satisfaction to Wilson. 'It has settled the future for me and given me a sense of *position* and of definite, tangible tasks which takes the *flutter* and restlessness from my spirits', he explained to Ellen. He clearly saw it as an opportunity to put into practice his ideas about political leadership. 'I feel like a new prime minister getting ready to address his constituents', he wrote as he worked on his inaugural address.[1] Wilson's eight years as President of Princeton were to follow a trajectory that has often been seen as foreshadowing that of his later eight years in the White House – a period of remarkable accomplishment and acclaim followed by failure to achieve overambitious goals and final defeat in an atmosphere of bitter personal conflicts and animosity.[2] The apparent recurrence of this pattern has been the basis of those interpretations of his career that see Wilson as in the grip of unconscious psychological drives. More recently, his behavior in his later years at Princeton, like that in 1919–20, has been attributed to the effects of ill-health, specifically cerebral vascular disease.[3]

43

Both these approaches seek to explain what they see as a stark contrast between Wilson's conduct in the losing battles and the manner in which he had achieved his earlier successes, thereby discounting the continuities in his style of leadership and in his own priorities. Moreover, drawing a parallel between the course of Wilson's two presidencies involves over-looking the notable difference in the way they ended – whereas he left the White House discredited as well as defeated, when he departed from Princeton for the world of politics his public reputation was high.

Wilson's election as the first lay president of Princeton followed the forced resignation of his predecessor, the Reverend Dr Francis Patton, who had been resisting the changes that a majority both of the faculty and of the Board of Trustees felt were necessary. In 1896, on the occasion of its sesqui-centennial, the College of New Jersey had been officially renamed Princeton University. However, the transformation of a denominational country col-lege into a modern university that could be ranked with Harvard, Yale and such new institutions as Johns Hopkins and Chicago required much more than a change of name. In 1901 the majority of the 117 graduate students were attached to the Presbyterian Theological Seminary and the only other professional schools were in engineering and electrical engineering. Nor were the undergraduates who constituted over 90 percent of the student body characterized by a strong academic commitment. On the contrary, the main preoccupation of many was election to one of the lavishly endowed and socially prestigious eating clubs for upperclassmen. Although the fac-ulty contained some impressive figures, it consisted largely of Princeton graduates, many of whom were more notable for their Presbyterian ortho-doxy than their scholarship; the science side was particularly weak.

This situation did much to set Wilson's goals. He sought to raise the academic standing of the university, with respect both to undergraduate education and to scholarship and research. In this ambition he was repre-sentative of the faculty, particularly its abler members. But although, as he said, he had never thought of himself 'as a professional "educator"' or 'worked out the argument on liberal studies', Wilson did have some per-sonal views that helped to shape his program. One was that the university had a responsibility to the nation to produce young men with the quali-ties of intellect and character that would fit them for leadership – this was the central theme both of his speech at the sesquicentennial celebrations that had done much to promote him to the presidency ('Princeton in the Nation's Service') and of his inaugural address ('Princeton for the Nation's Service'), though in the latter he had placed equal weight on 'the produc-tion of a small body of trained scholars and investigators'. A second was that the right model for the kind of undergraduate education that would do this was the colleges of Oxford and Cambridge, by which he had been entranced on the two visits he made to Britain in the 1890s. A central feature of this model was the 'tutorial' in which undergraduates met with academic staff individually or in small groups to have their work supervised and to discuss their reading. Contrasting this with 'the old system of lectures and quizzes', Wilson declared that the recruitment of 'a body of such tutors' would 'transform' Princeton 'from a place where there are youngsters doing tasks to a place where there are men doing thinking, men who are conversing about the things of thought, men who are eager and interested in the things of thought'. He also had firm ideas about the content of undergraduate education, believing that this should be reasonably general and have a coherent structure; although he favored the introduction of new subjects into the curriculum, he disapproved of the system at Harvard by which students could freely 'elect' which courses they took.[4]

It was, however, less the distinctive nature of Wilson's vision of Princeton's future than the qualities he brought to the effort to realize this vision that made his presidency a landmark in the university's history. He was bold in setting targets and energetic in pursuing them. In his very first report to the Board of Trustees, he calculated that, whereas the existing productive endowment was about four million dollars, six million more were required to meet 'present needs' (including 50 tutorships) and a further six and a half million for the developments, such as a Graduate School and 'School of Jurisprudence' (Wilson's preferred term for a Law School), that would 'create a real university in Princeton'. He then embarked on a tour to sell this program to the alumni and to ask for contributions. 'I hope you will get your whistling over, because you will have to get used to this', he told a New York audience startled by the scale of his demands. A faculty committee, chaired by Wilson himself, was established to review the undergraduate course of study, and the completely new structure it proposed won the unanimous approval of the faculty. Although widespread discontent with the status quo no doubt helped to overcome the vested interests and variety of views that usually obstruct curricular reform in academic institutions, this achievement was a striking tribute to Wilson's leadership skills, which in this instance consisted mostly in reconciling and coordinating the ideas of others. 'We began a group of individuals and ended a *body* agreed in common counsel', Wilson reported to Ellen of the committee's deliberations. 'It is not, as it stands now, exactly the scheme I at the outset proposed, but it is much better.' In other areas, Wilson displayed a tougher form of leadership. Undergraduate discipline was tightened up, admission standards raised, and students whose grades were unsatisfactory found themselves being 'dropped'. Nor did Wilson shrink from securing the resignation of profes- sors whose performance in the classroom he deemed to be unsatisfactory. But he devoted more attention to the positive side of strengthening the faculty, and some notable scientists and scholars were among those he succeeded in bringing to the campus. Several had been attracted by Wilson's own qualities and enthusiasm, and this was even more true of the 50 tutors (now called 'preceptors') that he recruited in 1905. 'Had Woodrow Wilson asked me to go with him and work under him while he inaugurated a new university in Kamchatka or Senegambia I would have said "yes" without further question', one of these young men recalled. The markedly stimulating effect of Wilson's reforms on the intellectual life of the university won recognition within the Princeton community and beyond it. Early in 1907 Ellen proudly retailed the sardonic comment of the *New York Evening Post* that 'he has ruined what was universally admit- ted to be the most agreeable and aristocratic country club in America by transforming it into an institution of learning'.[5]

By this time Wilson had begun advocating another major innovation. In a confidential report to the Trustees, he had condemned the effects of the eating clubs in fostering a social ambition and competitiveness that distracted undergraduates from academic pursuits and impaired 'the democracy of the place'. Acknowledging the loyalties attached to the clubs, Wilson proposed that they be transformed into colleges, with dormitories and resident faculty members. This idea, too, clearly drew on the model of Oxford and Cambridge, although when Wilson submitted a definite pro- posal in June 1907 he made it clear that the envisaged 'residential quad- rangles' would not have the autonomy of 'the English colleges'. He now said that the object was further 'to quicken and mature the intellectual life of the University', and that 'the clubs simply happen to stand in the way'. It is a measure of the standing Wilson had achieved as well as of his powers of persuasion that the Board quickly approved this far-reaching and expensive project. However, publication of the plan evoked a strongly negative reaction from alumni and from some senior members of the faculty. Even John G. Hibben, the philosophy professor who was Wilson's closest friend, opposed it. Some of his supporters advised Wilson to con- tent himself with securing a reform of the clubs, but, confident of the backing of the trustees and of his own power, he showed no interest in such suggestions. After the summer break, he rallied the support of a large majority of the faculty (including the preceptors) with speeches that audi- tors described as 'wonderful' and 'inspiring'. But the Board, alarmed by alumni reaction and the university's financial position, now reversed itself and called for the withdrawal of the plan. The chairman, M. Taylor Pyne, was to follow this up by indicating that his own substantial donations would cease if the president continued to pursue further what he now called this 'absolutely Utopian' scheme. In the face of this 'complete defeat and mortification', Wilson came close to resigning. However, supportive trustees assured him that the Board had expressly left him free to continue to campaign for his plan.[6]

Wilson had launched the initiative that culminated in this débâcle within weeks after returning to Princeton from an extended leave that had been granted to him for health reasons. In May 1906 he woke one morning to find himself blind in one eye, due to a burst blood vessel. In retrospect, this seems likely to have been a small stroke, like a previous incident in 1896 that had for some months incapacitated his right hand. At the time, it was recognized to be a symptom of arterial tension, and doctors advised a period of total rest. Wilson spent the whole summer with his family in England, at Rydal in his beloved Lake District, and seemed to have recovered fully by the autumn. But, as had been the case ten years earlier, those close to Wilson felt that he reacted to the physical setback by becoming more focused and hard-driving, and some have seen this as the explanation for his putting his scheme to the Trustees without first consulting the faculty.[7] On the other hand, Wilson had indicated before his illness that he wanted to convert the clubs into institutions that would foster rather than detract from the educational process and, as we have seen, he had from the beginning of his presidency moved swiftly and boldly to achieve his purposes – as in instituting the preceptorial system before the necessary endowment had been raised.[8] (Cleveland H. Dodge, a wealthy classmate and friend, had agreed to meet any deficit.)

A more revealing aspect of the episode from the perspective of Wilson's later career may have been the nature of the opposition he encountered, and his own reaction to that opposition. A strong thread in the objections to the 'quad' plan among both alumni and contemporary undergraduates was that power would be transferred from the self-governing clubs to the university authorities. Likewise, the opposition of some senior members of the faculty, notably Andrew West, a classics professor who had for long been a major player in the university's affairs, was inspired as much by what they saw as Wilson's autocratic manner of handling the issue as by dislike of the plan itself.[9] On his part, the 'mortification' Wilson felt clearly reflected wounded pride, and he was to display a similar sensitivity to what he perceived as attempts to curb his prerogatives, and combativeness in responding to them, when he was in the White House.[10]

The hard feelings engendered on both sides over the quad plan embittered, and to some degree provoked, the other controversy that darkened the last years of Wilson's tenure – that over the location of the graduate college. In this case, the issue of control became openly central. The Graduate School had been established in 1900 and its development was agreed by all to be an essential element in the making of Princeton into a first-rank university. In his first speech laying out to alumni his 'dream' of a future campus, Wilson had pictured a beautiful quadrangle for graduate students 'in the midst of it', so that undergraduates might be inspired by the example of young men committed to the pursuit of 'truth itself'.[11] Priority having been given to the preceptorial system, funds had not been available for such a building and, in the meantime, graduates had been accommodated in a large house off the campus where West, who was Dean of the Graduate School, had introduced all the formalities and rituals of an Oxbridge college and become desirous of maintaining such an arrangement. A bequest for the construction of a graduate college specified that it must be on university grounds, but West trumped this by inducing the soap millionaire, William C. Procter, to give half a million dollars on condition that the college be built on a site that was about a mile from the campus proper. After the Board by a narrow majority had voted to accept Procter's gift on these terms in the face of Wilson's strong opposition, he wrote to Pyne that this 'had taken the guidance of the University out of my hands entirely' and that he would have to resign. When Procter (at Pyne's instigation) then accepted a compromise proposal Wilson had made for two buildings. Wilson, with some embarrassment, explained that the real issue was not the site but Procter's endorsement of West's ideals for a graduate school, which 'were not the ideals of Princeton University'. Though Wilson's desire that the graduate college should not be controlled by West was shared by several of the professors most involved with the Graduate School, his actions completely alienated Pyne who now intrigued to force him out of office. Henceforth, the Board, along with the whole Princeton community, was bitterly divided between Wilson's opponents and his supporters. Wilson appeared victorious in the conflict when Procter withdrew his offer in February, but three months later West secured a further, apparently much larger, sum for the building of a graduate college from a bequest that named West as an executor. Wilson recognized that this was decisive, and accepted defeat with good grace but expressed private misgivings about how long he would be able to go on working with either West or the Board.[12]

These controversies attracted attention outside Princeton and gave Wilson both a heightened public profile and a new political identity. After the quad plan had been rejected by the Board, Wilson had sought to develop support for it among the alumni through speeches in various cities across the East and Middle West. This tactic of appealing to a wider constituency was one that he was to employ several times in his later political career, and it has often been seen as a very personal one, reflecting Wilson's conception of how a British prime minister could win authority by 'going to the country' and a confidence in his own skills on the platform. However, as E.E. Schattschneider points out, it is a natural and very common move for the loser in any political contest to seek to alter the outcome through widening the circle of those involved.[13] In his campaign for the quad plan, Wilson at first made the case in strictly educational terms, stressing the need to promote intellectual over social concerns among the undergraduates.[14] Nonetheless, in common with those trustees who were his supporters, he did from the start associate the opposition to the quad plan with the wealthy and socially prominent segment of the alumni upon whom the university was largely dependent financially, and his stand over the Graduate College could also easily be interpreted as a fight against the power of money and the values of social privilege. This was how he presented it in confidential guidance to a sympathetic journalist on the *New York Times* in January 1910, and the paper duly ran an editorial (to the great anger of the Pyne camp), in which the ideals of democracy and intellectual endeavor were seen as pitted against the 'dilettante' values of 'exclusive social cliques'. When Procter's withdrawal of his gift was announced, Wilson received many letters of support and much favorable press comment. Shortly after a Board meeting in which his proposal to refer the administration of the Graduate School to the faculty had been rejected, Wilson presented the social issue in extreme terms in a speech to alumni in Pittsburgh. 'The colleges are in the same dangerous position as the churches', he warned. 'They serve the classes not the masses.' Claiming that 'you can't spend four years at one of our universities without becoming imbued with the spirit most dangerous, that if you are to succeed you must train with certain influences which now dominate the country', he declared that he had 'dedicated every power that there is within me to bring the colleges that I have anything to do with to an absolutely democratic regeneration in spirit'.[15]

This sort of rhetoric outraged many Princeton alumni but it accorded with the temper of the times. The power of big business 'interests' in the nation's economic and political life had been the subject of a growing agitation over the previous decade, stimulated by the formation of giant corporations in the 'merger boom' at the turn of the century, 'muckraking' articles in the new, more popular, national magazines, and a number of spectacular scandals. In 1910 the resultant 'progressive movement' was at its height, and the most prominent figures in national politics, such as ex-President Theodore Roosevelt and Senator Robert M. La Follette of Wisconsin on the Republican side, and the Democratic presidential contender, William Jennings Bryan, were associated with it. However, Wilson's previous comments on the political scene had reflected a quite different perspective, that of the conservative wing of the Democratic party, followers of former president Grover Cleveland whom the party had repudiated when it first nominated Bryan for president in 1896. At that time, Wilson had written admiringly of Cleveland (who was to retire to Princeton and become a rather conservative trustee of the university), and in a speech in 1904 Wilson called for the Democratic party to throw off the 'populists and radical theorists, contemptuous alike of principle and of experience' who had 'got the use of its name' since 1896, and to become again 'a party of conservative reform, acting in the spirit of law and of ancient institutions'. In a private letter to a Princeton alumnus a little later, Wilson pointed these Burkean sentiments more sharply by expressing the wish that 'we could do something, at once dignified and effective, to knock Mr Bryan once for all into a cocked hat'. Such views were very much to the taste of Colonel George Harvey, editor of the prestigious *Harper's Weekly*, who had been greatly impressed by Wilson since hearing him speak at Princeton. In early 1906 Harvey began promoting the idea that the Democrats should nominate Wilson for the presidency of the United States.[16]

Wilson was obviously intrigued by this suggestion, which struck so directly at his earliest and deepest aspirations for fame and fulfillment. In 1908 his name was mentioned in connection with both the presidential and vice-presidential nomination, and Wilson, again spending the summer in Britain, deliberately remained in Edinburgh for news of the convention, feeling, as he wrote Ellen, 'a bit silly waiting on the possibility of the impossible happening'. After Bryan had gone down to another heavy defeat that November, Wilson wrote to Mrs Mary Peck, with whom he had become very close during two winter vacations he had taken alone in Bermuda, of the need for a movement to rehabilitate the Democratic party 'along lines of principle and statesmanship'. Discussing the possibility that he might take the lead in such an enterprise, he declared that 'the fray would be delightful, and would be free of all the polite restraints of academic controversy!' 'This is what I was meant for', he wrote, after completing a hard-hitting article condemning the Republicans' handling of the tariff, 'this rough and tumble of the political arena. My instinct all turns that way'.

The route into the arena was obviously through the Democratic party of New Jersey, with whose leading figure, former Senator James Smith, Harvey had good relations. Having paved the way, Harvey early in 1910 urged Wilson to allow himself to be nominated as candidate for governor. Wilson was noncommittal but he was clearly attracted by the idea. 'It would be rather jolly, after all, to start out on life anew together, to make a new career', he wrote to Ellen from Bermuda; she replied that the fact that he had not had his way over the Graduate College would make it easier for him to leave Princeton for politics, and also that the controversy had 'strengthened you *immensely* throughout the whole country'. When the moment for decision came in June, Wilson sought the advice of his friends among the trustees, but made a point of explaining that running for the governorship was 'the mere preliminary of a plan to nominate me in 1912 for the presidency'. When these men assured him of their support in whatever he wished to do, Wilson publicly announced his willingness to accept the gubernatorial nomination.[17]

Wilson thus owed his entry into politics to the efforts of conservative Democrats. Yet he was to campaign for the governorship, and later the presidency, as a progressive, and, once in office, he was to promote and enact extensive reform measures both in Trenton and in Washington. In some ways the change in his views was less dramatic than it has often been presented as being.[18] There was not a world of difference between his endorsement in 1906 of Jefferson's principle 'that there must be as little government as possible' and his 1912 declaration that 'the history of liberty is the history of the limitation of governmental power, not the increase of it'. Throughout this period, he articulated the traditional Democratic opposition to a high tariff, and also called for the modernization of the banking and currency system. It is true that neither of these reforms directly addressed the matters of central concern to most progressive campaigners – the power of 'the trusts' and of political 'bosses'. But on these issues, too, there were elements of continuity in Wilson's positions. Thus, he recognized that large corporations were an inescapable feature of modern civilization in 1912 as he had in 1906; in 1906, as in 1912, he insisted that their activities should be subject to the law in a manner that kept open the doors of opportunity for competitors.[19] With regard to constitutional and political change, he had already by the 1890s become less radical than he had been in his youth, but in accepting the presidency of the Short Ballot Organization in 1909, Wilson was acting in accordance with a lifelong commitment to enhancing both the powers and the accountability of elected officials.[20] Yet, adopting these approaches was quite consistent with opposing other measures advocated by reformers for, as historians have come to recognize, progressivism was a protean phenomenon, incorporating ideologically diverse elements. Thus, Wilson strongly opposed attempts to regulate economic activity through government commissions, arguing that this substituted the discretionary power of public officers for the rule of law. Similarly, the short ballot, which meant reducing the number of officials who were directly elected rather than appointed by a chief executive, differed greatly from reforms that would increase the role of voters, such as the direct election of senators, primary elections, and the initiative, referendum and recall. In the 1900s Wilson opposed such measures, and also the enfranchisement of women, though he later came to endorse them all.[21]

Less easily definable but more significant than such changes in Wilson's position on specific issues was the alteration in the whole tenor of his speeches. Whereas in the mid 1900s his targets had been 'populists and radical theorists' and 'the nostrums of the Socialists', by 1912 he was warning of 'the pervasive power of the great interests which now dominate our development'.[22] A comparable shift can be discerned in the stance of many American politicians in these years as they adjusted to what one called 'the present popular unrest', and the inclination to see Wilson as similarly responsive is strengthened by his own longstanding views about what politics required.[23] 'If you want to win, you have got to fish for the majority', he reiterated in 1907. 'A politician, a man engaged in party contests, must be an opportunist.' Yet, on other occasions, Wilson indicated that he believed that political leaders should act in accordance with their own convictions. Thus, he lauded Cleveland, a 'man of integrity', for his 'singular independence and force of purpose', and said that the Democratic party needed leaders 'as unlike Mr Bryan as principle is unlike expediency'. Similarly, though he continued to extol 'the doctrine of expediency', he described it as referring to the 'pace' of change; the 'direction' was 'a matter of principle', with respect to which an individual should be 'indomitable'.[24]

The timing of the change in the tone of Wilson's public utterances suggests that it owed at least as much to his personal experiences as to political calculation. In private letters, he made clear his conviction that he had been defeated in the Board of Trustees over both the quad plan and the Graduate College 'because money talked louder than I did'. It was following another such defeat that, in his Pittsburgh speech, he first expressed the kind of populist, anti-elitist sentiments that he had earlier deplored:

All the fruitage of the earth comes from the black soil, where are the elements that make for strength, for beauty. Is strength in the fruit? Not at all; it is in the black soil. Every great force comes from below, not from above ... And we should cry out against the few who have raised themselves to dangerous power, who have thrust their cruel hands into the very heartstrings of the many, on whose blood and energy they are subsisting ... The great voice of America does not come from the seats of learning, but in a murmur from the hills and the woods and the farms and the factories and the mills, rolling on and gaining volume until it comes to us the voice from the homes of the common men.

'All my life I have been an insurgent against the class in which I was born', Wilson declared in 1912 as he was running for the Democratic presidential nomination.[25] This was hardly true, but for the rest of his career he did harbor a real dislike and distrust of the East Coast upper class that gathered in city clubs and other exclusive establishments. However, for a time the Pittsburgh speech remained an isolated outburst and Wilson said little else to disturb Harvey and his friends before securing the New Jersey nomination.

Indeed, as some historians have pointed out, the conservative views that Wilson expressed in the 1900s are at least as easily attributable to circumstance and opportunism as his later progressivism.[26] Such views would be commonplace among the wealthy alumni from whom Wilson was seeking large donations to fund his ambitious programs. Moreover, as soon as he began to dream of entering politics after all, he would have realized how dependent he was upon the sponsorship of anti-Bryan Democrats such as Harvey. It was surely not a coincidence that it was in a document designed to win the backing of extremely conservative editors and businessmen in New York that Wilson came closest to an unqualified endorsement of *laissez-faire*, describing the constitutional protection of 'the right of freedom of contract' as 'that most precious of all the possessions of a free people'.[27] The truth seems to be that Wilson's real interest remained in the structure and nature of politics rather in issues of policy, or even questions of political philosophy. (Although his views in the 1906–12 period might seem to manifest a consistent commitment to Jeffersonian principles, he had earlier described himself as 'a Federalist', and was later to favor the nationalization of public utilities, including the railroads.)[28] The form of Wilson's oratory, that commonly evoked abstract ideals and made effective use of imagery, gave an impression of consistency, but this did not extend to the content of his policies. These took shape piecemeal, as he learnt more about the facts and arguments bearing on particular issues, and in response to what he perceived to be public sentiment, with respect to which he had an instinct for the center ground. If flexibility is an essential element in successful political leadership, it was not one that Wilson lacked.

Governor of New Jersey

There was opposition to Wilson's nomination at the New Jersey Democratic party convention in September 1910 from progressives suspicious of Smith and what they saw as the Wall Street interests behind him, and from delegates supporting a rival candidate who was a popular party figure. However, Smith carried the day, aided by the two arguments that seem to have weighed most with him – that Wilson was the candidate most likely to win the governorship for the Democrats, and that he was a potential president. That someone with no previous experience in politics could rise so quickly owed much to the widespread public distrust of professional politicians and their 'machines' during the progressive era; four years earlier, Charles Evans Hughes, a rather academic lawyer with much less interest in the political game than Wilson, had been induced into the governorship of New York by a Republican party anxious to cleanse its reputation after some spectacular scandals.[29] Wilson surprised the professionals by accepting the nomination in person at the convention and won over many progressives by a speech in which he declared that, if elected, he would enter office 'with absolutely no pledge of any kind to prevent me from serving the people of the State with singleness of purpose'. Although Harvey had watered down Wilson's original draft of the platform, it remained a progressive one, calling for a regulatory public utilities commission, the equalization of taxation between individuals and corporations, the outlawing of corrupt election practices and the establishment of workmen's compensation. On the stump, Wilson quickly became an effective performer, but the most important event in the campaign was his response to a public letter from George L. Record, the leading figure among the progressive insurgents who had long been fighting the regular Republican machine in the state. In his reply to Record's list of specific questions, Wilson unequivocally endorsed all the reforms in the Democratic platform, including those such as the direct election of senators and state primary elections about which he had previously sounded hesitant. More dramatic was his wholehearted concurrence in Record's thorough analysis of 'the boss system', through which the public utility corporations gained privileged treatment by doing favors to party leaders, and his declaration that 'I should deem myself forever disgraced should I in even the slightest degree cooperate in any such system or any such transactions as you describe.' 'That letter will elect Wilson governor', Record is reputed to have said, and it no doubt contributed to the margin of eleven percentage points by which Wilson defeated his Republican opponent in November. It was a good year for the Democrats across the country, and they won a majority in the House of Representatives for the first time since 1892. This boded well for their chances of capturing the White House in 1912, and Wilson's triumph made him a leading contender for the presidential nomination.[30]

In New Jersey, the Democrats' victory was sufficiently sweeping to give them a majority not only in the Assembly but also in the joint session of the two houses of the legislature that would select the next US Senator. In this unexpected situation, Smith embarrassed Wilson by saying that he would like to return to the Senate himself. Recognizing that this would be regarded as a test of the independence from machine politics he had repeatedly claimed during the campaign, Wilson felt that he had to oppose Smith and support James Martine, the undistinguished victor in a primary election held earlier in the year when few had expected the Democratic senatorial nomination to mean much. He explained to Harvey that he owed his victory to 'the "progressives" of both parties, who are determined to live no longer under either of the political organizations that have controlled the two parties of the state', and that they 'will again draw off in disgust if we disappoint their expectations'. His hopes for the presidency were at stake: 'It is a national as well as a state question. If the independent Republicans who in this State voted for me are not to be attracted to us they will assuredly turn again, in desperation, to Mr Roosevelt, and the chance of a generation will be lost to the Democracy.' Although a governor had no official involvement in the election of a senator, Wilson moved to make his view prevail with energy and determination, augmenting private pressure on local Democratic organizations and assemblymen with public statements and speeches. Smith accused Wilson of 'foul play' as well as 'a gratuitous attack upon one who has befriended him', but his support melted away and Martine was elected by an overwhelming majority.[31]

In this contest Wilson collaborated with the former Democratic assemblyman who was managing Martine's campaign – a 31-year-old Irish-American lawyer named Joseph P. Tumulty. The boldness and political skill with which Wilson fought for principle won Tumulty's heart, and it proved to be the beginning of a long and important relationship. In January 1911 Wilson appointed Tumulty as his private secretary to 'guide' him in the tangled world of New Jersey politics – which, in practice meant that Tumulty took charge of patronage issues. Loyal, shrewd and immensely admiring of his chief, Tumulty was to move with him to the White House and to become someone upon whose political knowledge and judgment Wilson was to rely greatly. Tumulty, with his roots in the poor wards of Jersey City, also provided a link to a much wider range of people than Wilson had been accustomed to meeting as a college professor. This was all the more necessary because Wilson was not naturally gregarious and attached great importance to retaining his private space; he did not want to share his lunch and dinner table with political associates but with family and friends who could be relied on not to discuss public business. It was easier for him to maintain this pattern because he continued as governor to live in Princeton, driving each day the eleven miles to Trenton, the state capital.[32]

Following the defeat of Smith, Wilson continued to display strong, progressive leadership with bipartisan appeal. With respect to legislation, he took a much fuller and more active role than governors had customarily done. Having sought advice from Record among others on the formulation of a program, he helped to draft bills, consulted intensively with committees and individual legislators, and mobilized opinion through public statements and speeches. Unprecedently, he attended meetings of the Democratic caucus and, in accommodating himself to the style of the new social world he had entered, even went so far as to dance a cakewalk with a Republican state senator whose vote was crucial. The first measure he promoted, a bill to establish a comprehensive primary election system, was fiercely resisted by the local party machines, which provided further favorable publicity when Wilson ordered from his office a boss who had accused him of using his patronage powers in its support. 'It is all very well to get applause and credit for such things,' Wilson wrote rather defensively to his friend Mary Peck, but 'I cannot help feeling a bit vulgar after them.' The primary law passed the Assembly shortly thereafter, and was followed by the other major bills Wilson pushed for – on corrupt election practices, workmen's compensation, and the establishment of a regulatory public utilities commission with sweeping powers. The measures had been largely drafted by the reformers, mostly Republicans, who had been agitating for them for years, and there was truth as well as modesty in Wilson's observation that he came to office 'in the fulness of time, when opinion was ripe on all these matters'. But he was also right to say that 'by never losing sight of the business for an hour, but keeping up all sorts of (legitimate) pressure all the time', he had 'kept the mighty forces from being diverted or blocked at any point'. In any case, it had been a remarkable achievement. 'I got everything I strove for, – and more besides', he exulted.[33]

Such success was obviously helpful to the presidential ambitions which had done much to tempt Wilson into the political arena. He was evidently also conscious of the advantages of having repositioned himself politically. Shortly after his election to the governorship, he asked a supporter who proposed organizing a nationwide movement not to have Harvey as its public sponsor because the editor's Wall Street connexions had given rise to 'real suspicion upon my methods and connections among those whose confidence it would be most necessary to win'. Although Bryan had suffered three heavy defeats in presidential elections, he remained the Democrats' leading figure, and his populist, anticorporation attitudes resonated in the areas where the party was strongest, in the West and the South. Believing that 'no Democrat can win whom Mr Bryan does *not* approve', Wilson seems to have set out to capture the support of 'the Great Commoner'. In fact, it was Bryan who initiated direct contact between the two men by writing to say that Wilson's stand over the senatorship had assuaged some of the doubts raised by 'the fact that you were against us in 1896', and to ask if Wilson endorsed the platform Bryan had run on in 1908. Wilson provided this reassurance and also, at Bryan's urging, recommended to the New Jersey legislature ratification of the Income Tax amendment to the US Constitution. In May 1911 he made a striking volte-face by coming out in favor of the proposals for giving direct power to the voters that had become, in the words of Bryan's brother, 'the acid test of a man's democracy in these days'. Conservatives attached at least as much importance to these measures, seeing them as a threat to property rights which opened the way to socialism. Wilson had previously defended the virtues of representative government on Burkean grounds but he now argued that the initiative, referendum and recall were necessary to counter the covert control of legislatures by 'organized wealth' (though he still opposed the recall of judges). He took this position in a speech in Kansas City at the beginning of an 8,000-mile tour through the West that was obviously designed to test sentiment and garner support. His speeches denouncing machine politics and 'the money power' were sufficiently well received to encourage the opening in July of a campaign headquarters in New York under the direction of William F. McCombs, a lawyer and former student of Wilson's, and William Gibbs McAdoo, a businessman who had built the first tunnel under the Hudson River; funds for the campaign came in good part from Wilson's Princeton friends and supporters, particularly Dodge. With his candidacy gaining much favor in the press, and especially in educational and religious circles, Wilson had established himself by the autumn of 1911 as the frontrunner for the Democratic nomination. As such he attracted the support of an unobtrusive Texan with a private income and progressive views who was looking to play a behind-the-scenes role in national politics; in October 1911, Edward House wrote to Wilson what would prove to be the first of many letters.[34]

After this flying start in politics, both Wilson's governorship and his presidential bid ran into difficulties in the winter and spring of 1911–12. Having secured control of the New Jersey party organization, Wilson campaigned hard for the return of a Democratic majority in the legislative elections that autumn. Holding to his vision of popularly accountable government, in which the electorate rendered a judgment on the fidelity and effectiveness with which an administration had discharged the responsibility entrusted to it, he was confident of success. 'You voted for the forecast. Are you going to confirm the reality?' he asked. 'If you don't vote to return a Democratic Legislature on November 7 you lied when you voted for me last fall.' By presenting the issue as a verdict on his own performance in this way, Wilson maximized the damage to his prestige when the Republicans secured a majority in both houses. The result was less of a rebuff than it seemed as the Democrats' candidates had secured a larger total vote than the Republicans', and the party would have won a majority had it not lost the county controlled by the Smith machine, which Wilson believed had deliberately sought to damage his presidential prospects as an act of revenge. In striking contrast to his behavior a year earlier, Wilson made no real effort to work with the new legislature, and by the end of a session in which he had issued a record number of vetoes (several in stinging language) his relationship with the Republican majority had become one of mutual recrimination. 'This has been a petty and barren legislature', he wrote to Mrs Peck. 'Small men have ignorantly striven to put *me* in a hole by discrediting themselves!'[35]

Soon Wilson's drive for the presidency, too, was faltering. The apparently Bryanite character of his recent speeches disturbed his original constituency among Democrats in the northeast. In response, Wilson backtracked somewhat by saying that the desirability of the initiative, referendum and recall depended on local conditions, and that the banking issue was a complicated one that he needed to study further. He returned to ground on which all Democrats could stand by declaring that 'the tariff question is at the heart of every other economic question we have to deal with' and by devoting a whole speech to the issue. He was still running, however, as 'a progressive Democrat' and so experienced some embarrassment when his earlier conservative attitudes were highlighted, as they were by various developments during the winter and spring. One was the publication of his 1907 letter to A.F. Joline, a conservative Princeton trustee, expressing the wish that Bryan could be knocked 'into a cocked hat'. A second arose from the perhaps inevitable break with Harvey. After Wilson had admitted in response to a direct question that Harvey's support now caused him some embarrassment, Harvey publicized this in a manner designed to portray Wilson as someone who sacrificed friendship to political ambition. However, Wilson surmounted these two incidents fairly smoothly, taking the occasion of a Jackson Day dinner to praise Bryan for his 'steadfast vision' and for basing his career upon 'principle' rather than 'calculation'. For his part, Bryan assured his followers that the break with Harvey showed that 'Mr Wilson is the best modern example of Saul of Tarsus.' More damaging was the use made, particularly by the chain of newspapers owned by William Randolph Hearst who was bitterly opposed to Wilson's candidacy, of passages from his *History of the American People* in which Wilson had written extremely disparagingly of recent immigrants from southern and eastern Europe. Although Wilson retained the support of organized labor and could point to his longstanding opposition to immigration restriction, there was a deluge of pained protests from ethnic organizations and spokesmen.[36]

This was all the more serious because of the emergence of two candidates much more formidable than the lackluster governor of Ohio who had hitherto been Wilson's main rival. Champ Clark of Missouri, Speaker of the House of Representatives, had a progressive record, and Bryan declared himself neutral as between Clark and Wilson. Representative Oscar Underwood of Alabama, the able majority leader, was very attractive to Southern conservatives. Both men, as veteran politicians, possessed the network of contacts with party organizations across the country that the Wilson campaign notably lacked. Wilson's strength was his apparent appeal to the general public, and this came under question when he lost primary elections to Clark by large margins in Illinois, Massachusetts and California during April and May. 'It begins to look', Wilson wrote dispiritedly to Dodge, 'as if I must merely sit on the side lines and talk, as a mere critic of the game I understand so intimately, – throw all my training away and *do* nothing.' A big win in New Jersey and victories in Texas and Minnesota, together with strong press support, kept Wilson in the field but the odds seemed heavily against his nomination when the Democratic delegates gathered in Baltimore in June.[37]

In an era when American party conventions constituted genuine political theater (rather than tightly controlled television productions), 1912 was a vintage season. The Republican convention in Chicago saw the climax of the bitter battle between President William Taft and his predecessor, Theodore Roosevelt. Roosevelt had easily won most of the primaries that had been held, but Taft was renominated after the convention had awarded him the great majority of contested delegate votes. Denouncing this 'saturnalia of larceny and fraud', Roosevelt led his forces out of the convention and made it clear he would run as a third-party candidate.[38] The prospective split in the Republican vote suggested that any Democrat was likely to be elected, thereby weakening the force of the argument that only Wilson could win. However, he scored a point when, disregarding McCombs' advice, he alone of the candidates unequivocally supported Bryan's protest against the choice of the conservative Alton B. Parker as temporary chairman of the Democratic convention. But Clark entered the convention with the most pledged delegates, and he secured more than half the total votes cast when New York's delegation, which was controlled by the boss of Tammany Hall, backed him on the tenth ballot. This did not give him the nomination because the party's rules required a two-thirds majority (which Wilson, when frontrunner, had privately condemned as undemocratic). Not since 1844, however, had anyone securing a simple majority failed to be nominated and, at McCombs' urging, Wilson sent a telegram releasing his delegates: 'Now we can see Rydal again', Ellen said consolingly. However, Wilson swiftly countermanded his message when McAdoo telephoned that the Underwood delegates were holding firm and that all was not lost. The next day, Bryan, who had been stridently attacking the sinister influence of Wall Street throughout the convention, announced that Nebraska would vote for Wilson rather than Clark so long as the latter had the support of New York. Dramatic as this switch was, and helpful to Wilson's cause, it was not decisive. Much more crucial was Underwood's refusal to withdraw, and the later transfer to Wilson of the Indiana and Illinois delegations, all of which were the result of deals done by Wilson's managers. Eventually, after five days of voting and 46 ballots, a two-thirds majority was mustered for the man who had been presented to the convention as 'the seer and philosopher of Princeton, the Princeton schoolmaster, Woodrow Wilson'.[39]

Notes

1 Wilson to Ellen Wilson, 10 August 1902, 19 July 1902. *PWW*, 14 (1972), pp. 70, 27.

2 On this comparison, see, for example, Arthur S. Link, *Wilson: the Road to the White House*, Princeton, NJ, pp. 90–91; Henry Wilkinson Bragdon, *Woodrow Wilson: The Academic Years*, Cambridge, MA, 1967, pp. 382–3.

3 The former interpretation is best presented in Alexander L. George and Juliette L. George, *Woodrow Wilson and Colonel House: A Personality Study*, New York, 1956, the latter in

John Milton Cooper, Jr, *The Warrior and the Priest: Woodrow Wilson and Theodore Roosevelt*, Cambridge, MA, 1983, and Arthur S. Link et al. (eds), *The Papers of Woodrow Wilson*, Princeton, NJ, 1966–94. Edward W. Weinstein, *Woodrow Wilson: A Medical and Psychological Biography*, Princeton, NJ, 1981, presents an interpretation that combines medical and psychological factors.

4 Wilson to Ellen Wilson, 19 July 1902, *PWW*, vol. 14, p. 27; a Commemorative Address, 21 October 1896, *PWW*, vol. 10, pp. 11–31; an Inaugural Address, 25 October 1902; address to Princeton Alumni of New York, 9 December 1902, *PWW*, vol. 14, pp. 170–85, 268–76; Report to the Board of Trustees, 14 December 1905, *PWW*, vol. 16, pp. 259–60.

5 Report to the Board of Trustees, 21 October 1902; address to Princeton Alumni of New York, 9 December 1902, *PWW*, vol. 14, pp. 150–61, 275; Wilson to Ellen Wilson, 17, 26 April 1904, *PWW*, vol. 15, pp. 264, 296; Ellen Wilson to Anna Harris, 12 February 1907, *PWW*, vol. 17, p. 35; Bragdon, *Woodrow Wilson*, pp. 294–308, 360–61; Ray Stannard Baker, *Woodrow Wilson: Life and Letters*, London, 1928, vol. 2, pp. 133–73; Link, *The Road to the White House*, pp. 44–5.

6 Supplementary Report to the Board of Trustees, c. 13 December 1906, *PWW*, vol. 16, pp. 519–25; report to the Board of Trustees, c. 6 June 1907; Wilson's address to the Board of Trustees, c. 10 June 1907; B. Henry to Wilson, with enclosures, 29 July 1907; Wilson to B. Henry, 6 August 1907; Cleveland H. Dodge to Wilson, 28 September 1907; W.S. Myers diary, 30 September 1907; T.H. Hunt to Wilson, 8 October 1907; M.T. Pyne to A.C. Imbrie, 23 October 1907; D.B. Jones to Wilson, 12 November 1907; Wilson to M.W. Jacobus, 23 October 1907; M.W. Jacobus to Wilson, 25 October, 5 November 1907, *PWW*, vol. 17, pp. 176–86, 199–203, 301–7, 338–9, 405–6, 408, 424, 453–4, 495–7, 450–1, 458–60, 468–9.

7 Cooper, *The Warrior and the Priest*, pp. 97–9. On the effects on Wilson's personality and attitudes of his health problems in 1896 and 1906, see Bragdon, *Woodrow Wilson*, pp. 225, 313.

8 Speech to Princeton Alumni in East Orange, New Jersey, 10 November 1905; memorandum on the Clubs at Princeton, 17 February 1916, *PWW*, vol. 16, pp. 214, 218, 314–15.

9 E.g. Editorial in the *Daily Princetonian*, 2 October 1907; A.H. Joline to the *Princeton Alumni Weekly*, 9 October 1907; A.F. West to Wilson, 10 July 1907, *PWW*, vol. 17, pp. 411, 428–31, 270–71.

10 For example, in responding to the Gore and McLemore resolutions in February 1916. See Chapter 5, pp. 120–1.

11 Address to Princeton Alumni of New York, 9 December 1902, *PWW*, vol. 14, pp. 269–70.

12 Wilson to M.T. Pyne, 25 December 1909, *PWW*, vol. 628–31; editorial note on Board of Trustees meeting, 13 January 1910; M.T. Pyne to W.C. Procter, 15 January 1910, to Wilson Farrand, 25 January 1910; Wilson to C.H. McCormick, 25, 26 May 1910; Wilson to T.D. Jones, 30 May 1910, *PWW*, vol. 20, pp. 6–9, 17–19, 56–7, 472–3, 483–5; Baker, *Woodrow Wilson*, vol. 2, pp. 275–360; Link, *The Road to the White House*, pp. 59–90.

13 Baker, *Woodrow Wilson*, vol. 2, pp. 264–6, 334; Link, *The Road to the White House*, pp. 55–6; E.E. Schattschneider, *The Semisovereign People: A Realist's View of Democracy in America*, Hinsdale, IL, 1960, pp. 1–19.

14 E.g. Address to the Princeton Club of Chicago, 12 March 1908; Address to Western Association of Princeton Clubs, Pittsburgh, 2 May 1908, *PWW*, vol. 18, pp. 23–34, 281–85.

15 Wilson to M.W. Jacobus, 6 November 1907; Jacobus to Wilson, 25 October 1907; D.B. Jones to Wilson, 12 November 1907, *PWW*, vol. 17, pp. 470–1, 458–9, 495–7; H.B. Brougham to Wilson, 31 January, 4 February 1910, Wilson to H.B. Brougham, 1 February 1910; *New York Times* editorial, 3 February 1910; news reports of Pittsburgh speech, 17, 20 April 1910, *PWW*, vol. 20, pp. 65, 76–8, 69–71, 74–6, 363–8, 373–6.

16 'Mr Cleveland as President', 15 January 1897, *PWW*, vol. 10, pp. 102–19; address to the Society of the Virginians, New York, 30 November 1904, *PWW*, vol. 15, pp. 545–9; Wilson to A.H. Joline, 29 April 1907, *PWW*, vol. 17, p. 124; Link, *The Road to the White House*, pp. 98–102.

17 Link, *The Road to the White House*, pp. 116–20, 140–52; Wilson to Ellen Wilson, 6 July 1908; Wilson to M.A.H. Peck, 2 November 1908, *PWW*, vol. 18, pp. 351–2, 478–80; Wilson to M.A.H. Peck, 5 September 1909, *PWW*, vol. 19, p. 358; Wilson to Ellen Wilson, 20 February 1910, with editorial note; Ellen Wilson to Wilson, 28 February 1910; Wilson to D.B. Jones, 27 June 1910; two telegrams from D.B. Jones to Wilson, 30 June 1910; D.B. Jones to Wilson, 30 June 1910; C.H. Dodge to Wilson, 30 June 1910; E.W. Sheldon to Wilson, 30 June 1910; *Newark Evening News*, 15 July 1910, *PWW*, vol. 20, pp. 144–8, 189, 543–4, 550–52, 581.

18 For example, Link, *The Road to the White House*, pp. 23–7, 32–4, 95–132; Bragdon, *Woodrow Wilson*, pp. 337–52.

19 Address on Thomas Jefferson, 16 April 1906; address in Chattanooga, Tennessee, 27 October 1906, *PWW*, vol. 16, pp. 362–9, 475–6; address to New York Press Club, 9 September 1912; address in Sioux City, Iowa, 17 September 1912; speech in Sioux Falls, South Dakota, 17 September 1912, *PWW*, vol. 25, pp. 124, 152–3, 158–61.

20 R.C. Childs to Wilson, 14 October 1909, *PWW*, vol. 19, pp. 419–20. On Wilson's move to a more conservative position on the Constitution after the 1880s, see Daniel D. Stid, *The President as Statesman: Woodrow Wilson and the Constitution*, Lawrence, KS, 1998, pp. 35–65.

21 Remarks at the National Democratic Club, New York, c. 13 April 1908, *PWW*, vol. 18, pp. 263–9; address to the Civic League of St Louis, 9 March 1909, *PWW*, vol. 19, pp. 81–97; Wilson to James Calloway, 30 October 1907, *PWW*, vol. 17, p. 461; Kendrick A. Clements, *Woodrow Wilson: World Statesman*, Boston, MA, 1987, p. 51; Stid, *The President as Statesman*, pp. 69, 72.

22 Address to the Society of the Virginians, New York, 30 November 1904, *PWW*, vol. 15, p. 547; address on Thomas Jefferson, 16 April 1906, *PWW*, vol. 16, p. 365; address in Detroit, 19 September 1912, *PWW*, vol. 25, p. 196.

23 Senator A.J. Beveridge to John C. Shaffer, 27 March 1906, quoted in John Braeman, *Albert*

J. Beveridge: American Nationalist, Chicago, IL, 1971, pp. 99–100. See also Carl H. Chrislock, The Progressive Era in Minnesota, 1899–1918, St Paul, MN, 1971, p. 22.

24 Address to the Cleveland Chamber of Commerce, 6 November 1907; 'Grover Cleveland: Man of Integrity', 17 March 1907, PWW, vol. 17, pp. 500, 73–8; 'Mr Cleveland as President', 15 January 1897, PWW, vol. 10, pp. 102–19; Wilson to Mary A.H. Peck, 2 November 1908, PWW, vol. 18, pp. 479–80; 'The Ministry and the Individual', 2 November 1909, PWW, vol. 19, pp. 476–7.

25 Wilson to Mary A.H. Peck, 24 October 1909, PWW, vol. 19, pp. 442–3; Pittsburgh Gazette-Times, 17 April 1910, PWW, vol. 20, p. 365; Pittsburgh Post, 10 April 1912, PWW, vol. 24, p. 310.

26 Cooper, The Warrior and the Priest, pp. 121–2; Bragdon, Woodrow Wilson, p. 337.

27 'A Credo', 6 August 1907, PWW, vol. 17, pp. 335–8. On the provenance of this document, see Link, The Road to the White House, pp. 110–12.

28 Wilson to A.B. Hart, 3 June 1889, PWW, vol. 6, p. 243; V.C. McCormick diary, 1–3 July 1919, PWW, vol. 61, p. 366.

29 Robert F. Wesser, Charles Evans Hughes: Politics and Reform in New York, 1905–1910, Ithaca, NY, 1967, pp. 25–8, 49–69.

30 Speech accepting the New Jersey gubernatorial nomination, 15 September 1910; A Proposed Democratic State Platform, 9 August 1910; G.B.M. Harvey to Wilson, 9 September 1910; Platform of the New Jersey Democratic Party, 15 September 1910; George L. Record to Wilson, 17 October 1910; Wilson to George L. Record, 24 October 1910; interview in the Newark Evening News, 17 September 1910, PWW, vol. 21, pp. 91–4, 43–6, 87–8, 94–6, 338–47, 406–11, 126–7. For a full account of Wilson's nomination and election as Governor of New Jersey, see Link, The Road to the White House, pp. 153–203.

31 Wilson to G.B.M. Harvey, 15 November 1910; a statement by James Smith, Jr, 9 December 1910, PWW, vol. 22, pp. 46–8, 166–7.

32 Wilson to O.G. Villard, 2 January 1911, PWW, vol. 22, pp. 288–9; John M. Blum, Joe Tumulty and the Wilson Era, Boston, MA, 1951; Stockton Axson, 'Brother Woodrow': A Memoir of Woodrow Wilson, Princeton, NJ, 1993, pp. 80–82. On the manner in which Tumulty used patronage to strengthen Wilson's hold over both the legislature and the New Jersey Democratic party, see Stid, The President as Statesman, pp. 77–8.

33 Wilson to Mary A.H. Peck, 26 March, 9 April, 23 April 1911, PWW, vol. 22, pp. 518, 531–2, 581–3; Link, The Road to the White House, pp. 239–75.

34 H.S. Breckinridge to Wilson, 17 December 1910; Wilson to H.S. Breckinridge, 21 December 1910; Wilson to Mary A.H. Peck, 9 April 1911; W.J. Bryan to Wilson, January 5, 1911, March 1911; to the New Jersey legislature, 20 March 1911, PWW, vol. 22, pp. 213–14, 236–7, 545, 307, 465, 511–12; news report of address in Kansas City, 6 May 1911; E.M. House to Wilson, 16 October 1911, PWW, vol. 23, pp. 5–9, 458–9; C.H. Dodge to Wilson, 5 September 1912, PWW, vol. 25, pp. 109–11n; Link, The Road to the White House, pp. 311–38, 391–3, 402–4; Stid, The President as Statesman, pp. 72–3.

35 Campaign speeches in Morristown, Dover and Madison, New Jersey, 16 October 1911, *PWW*, vol. 23, pp. 449–50; Stid, *The President as Statesman*, p. 78; Wilson to C.H. Grast, 10 November 1911, *PWW*, vol. 23, pp. 546–7; Wilson to Mary A.H. Peck, 1 April 1911, *PWW*, vol. 24, p. 271; Link, *The Road to the White House*, pp. 280–307.

36 Interview in *New York World*, 24 December 1912; address to National Democratic Club of New York, 3 January 1912, *PWW*, vol. 23, pp. 607–14, 637–50; address at Jackson Day dinner, 8 January 1912, *PWW*, vol. 24, p. 10; Link, *Wilson: The Road to the White House*, pp. 338–44, 352–87.

37 Wilson to C.H. Dodge, 16 May 1912, *PWW*, vol. 24, p. 402; Link, *The Road to the White House*, pp, 398–430.

38 George E. Mowry, *Theodore Roosevelt and the Progressive Movement*, New York, 1960, pp. 237–55.

39 Wilson to E.M. House, 24 October 1911, *PWW*, vol. 23, p. 480; Link, *The Road to the White House*, pp. 431–65.

Chapter 4

A Progressive President

The New Freedom

Wilson's campaign for the presidency was shaped by what was to become one of the great rivalries of American history.[1] When Theodore Roosevelt was nominated by the newly formed Progressive party in August 1912, it quickly became apparent that the real contest was between him and Wilson. 'I think I might as well give up so far as being a candidate is concerned', the hapless President Taft wrote to his wife. 'There are so many people in the country who don't like me.'[2] By contrast, Roosevelt, who gave the new party its nickname when he said that he was feeling like a bull moose, had enthused his followers by a 'confession of faith' in which he called for a wide range of political and economic reforms. Both his rhetoric and his program reflected the social democratic character that progressivism had acquired as it moved beyond the condemnation of specific acts of corruption or exploitation to a more comprehensive critique of 'the system'. Declaring that both the old parties 'represent government of the needy many by the professional politicians in the interests of the rich few', Roosevelt called for presidential primaries, the popular review of court decisions on constitutional questions, a powerful commission to regulate corporations, a national system of insurance against sickness, unemployment and old age, minimum wage and maximum hours legislation and the abolition of child labor. He thereby augmented the charismatic appeal of his own personality with the enthusiastic support of committed reformers and the idealistic young. Among those who seconded Roosevelt's nomination was the revered and nonpolitical figure of Jane Addams, head of Hull House in Chicago, the most famous of the social settlements that had done much to imbue hundreds of young middle-class men and (especially) women with the conviction that the problems engendered by the related processes of industrialization, urbanization and mass immigration required an active and creative response by both society and government.[3]

Wilson had looked to a similar constituency and his platform contained many of the same planks. He, too, called for presidential primaries, the direct election of US senators, conservation of natural resources, and laws to better the conditions and hours of labor. Privately, he recognized that he was unlikely to win a straight personality contest with Roosevelt:

> He appeals to their imagination; I do not. He is a real, vivid person, whom they have seen and shouted themselves hoarse over and voted for, millions strong; I am a vague, conjectural personality, more made up of opinions and academic prepossessions than of human traits and red corpuscles.

Wilson's advantage, of course, was that he had the support of an established party, but he sought to combine this with fashioning a distinctive appeal to progressive opinion. Democratic tradition was honored and party unity served by emphasizing the tariff issue, which he did in his acceptance speech. But in portraying Republican tariff-making as the favoring of powerful interests in return for campaign contributions, he linked it to the formation of 'the trusts' that had 'gained all but complete control of the larger enterprises of the country', and thus highlighted an area in which Roosevelt was vulnerable – the omission from the Progressive party platform of any reference to antitrust legislation. This had been at the insistence of George W. Perkins, the Wall Street financier and businessman who was not only managing but also largely funding the new party's campaign. Roosevelt defended the omission with typical aggression by saying that reliance on the antitrust law was 'a sign not of progress, but of toryism and reaction', and that a commission to regulate the activities of corporations would be more effective: 'we propose to penalize conduct and not size'.[4]

Wilson's attack on this position was given greater sharpness and depth by the advice of Louis D. Brandeis, with whom he had a long conversation in late August and subsequently corresponded. Brandeis, a lawyer who had specialized in anticorporation cases, believed that small businesses were economically as well as socially better than big ones and that the enforcement of fair competition would enable them to flourish, except in those few activities that were 'natural monopolies' and should therefore be publicly owned and operated. Brandeis's influence was apparent in the distinction Wilson thereafter made between his own program for 'regulated competition' and Roosevelt's for 'regulated monopoly'. The latter, he charged, was both chimerical and a threat to democracy and freedom. For 'once the government regulates the monopoly, then monopoly will have to see to it that it regulates the government', so that 'if America is not to have free enterprise, then she can have freedom of no sort whatever'. In taking this line, Wilson denounced both paternalism and bureaucracy in a way that seemed to echo the antigovernment note that had been a staple of Democratic party rhetoric since the days of Jefferson and Jackson. 'The minute you are taken care of by the government, you are wards, not independent men', he declared. 'What I fear is a government of experts' and being 'scientifically taken care of by a small number of gentlemen who are the only men who understand the job'.[5]

Such flourishes, like Roosevelt's counter-claim that Wilson upheld 'the *laissez-faire* doctrine of the English political economists threequarters of a century ago', gave a misleading impression of the extent to which the policies of the two men actually differed. On the central issue of monopoly, there was a real intellectual disagreement between the theorists upon whom the two were respectively relying – Brandeis and Charles Van Hise – over whether large corporations owed their dominance to market power or to efficiencies of scale, and this fundamental division was to bedevil policymaking into the 1930s and beyond. But Wilson, unlike Brandeis, declared himself to be 'for big business' though 'against trusts', while Roosevelt called for the antitrust law to 'be kept on the statute books and strengthened so as to make it genuinely and thoroughly effective against every big concern tending to monopoly or guilty of antisocial practises'. In specific terms, both men favored action not against size *per se* but against unfair business practices. It is small wonder that the progressive editor William Allen White later wrote that between Roosevelt's 'New Nationalism' and Wilson's 'New Freedom' 'was that fantastic imaginary gulf that always has existed between Tweedledum and Tweedledee'.[6]

Although White's witticism captured a truth with regard to corporation control, there were broader differences between the approaches of Roosevelt and Wilson which reflected both party traditions and their personal perspectives. Roosevelt and other Progressive party spokesmen frequently compared the new party's birth to the creation of the Republican party by opponents of slavery in the 1850s, thereby evoking a Yankee-Protestant faith in highminded public authority. By contrast, the anti-elitism that ran through Wilson's speeches reflected the culture of the Democratic party. It also chimed in with the theme of social renewal from below that he had adopted during the Princeton controversies, and which he often linked with the example of Lincoln. 'What this country needs above all', he declared, 'is a body of laws which will look after the men who are on the make rather than the men who are already made.' In his intensive and unscripted speechmaking, Wilson naturally made heavy use of earlier thoughts, even to the extent of retailing favorite stories and limericks. More significant was the articulation of his ideas about the nature of leadership in a democracy. 'By leading I do not mean telling other people what they have got to do', he explained. 'I mean finding out what the interests of the community are agreed to be, and then trying my level best to find the methods of solution by common counsel.' Of course, being in a contest with Roosevelt gave Wilson a special reason for discounting the heroic model. 'A man borrows greatness, doesn't possess it', he insisted. 'He is as big as the thoughts and the impulses that he has received from the common life of the people.'[7]

Such themes gave Wilson's speeches in this first national campaign a unified and distinctive character, and they have been described as among 'the greatest platform accomplishments of American political history'. Audiences were attracted and impressed as much by the fluency and elegance of Wilson's extemporaneous diction as by the substance of his message. Samuel Gompers, the long-serving president of the American Federation of Labor (AFL), recalled 'his beautiful English, the perfect enunciation and modulation of his speaking voice'. He also projected an image of grace and dignity. When in mid-October Roosevelt was shot by a fanatic, Wilson announced that he would cut short his own campaigning unless his opponent was able to go on the stump again, and in fulfilling his immediate engagements said he did so 'with a very great reluctance, because my thought is constantly of that gallant gentleman lying in the hospital at Chicago'.[8]

By this stage newspaper polls suggested that he could be confident about the outcome of the election. In the event, the divided opposition enabled him to win a sweeping victory in the electoral college after he had carried 40 states to Roosevelt's six and Taft's two. However, he had gained only 42 percent of the popular vote – a smaller share than Bryan in 1908. This was not only because the combined total for Roosevelt and Taft far exceeded his but also because the Socialist candidate, Eugene V. Debs, with 6 percent of the vote, had done more than twice as well as previously. In the congressional elections, the Democrats won substantial majorities in both houses. This was important to Wilson, who had argued strongly for undivided government as he closed his campaign, but it reflected the failure of the Progressive party to develop any strength at the congressional or state level to compare with that of Roosevelt as a presidential candidate. The figures suggested that many Americans had voted both for Roosevelt and for Democratic congressional candidates. With the future of the Progressive party looking shaky, Wilson could hope to gain the support of such people in a straight fight with a Republican. But the results also showed that he would need to do so to have any hope of a second term.[9]

Following his election, Wilson's first task was to construct a cabinet. In this delicate and important business, he relied greatly on the advice of House, who had a much wider range of acquaintance than he did. During the campaign, House had won Wilson's complete trust through his discretion, good judgment and loyalty – arranging, for example, for a former Texas Ranger to act as Wilson's bodyguard after the attempt on Roosevelt's life. Despite misgivings, Wilson was persuaded that offering the premier position, Secretary of State, to Bryan was 'a purely political necessity'. Once he had been assured that his refusal to serve alcohol constituted no bar, Bryan accepted with pleasure. House declined Wilson's offer to appoint him to any of the other departments, preferring what he called 'a freelance' role. McAdoo, who had emerged ascendant in the feud that had developed with McCombs, was given the Treasury. A problem arose over Brandeis, who was a hero to progressives such as La Follette and Bryan but was hated and distrusted in Northeastern Republican circles and opposed even by Democrats in his home state of Massachusetts. Wilson considered appointing him as Attorney-General, and then as Secretary of Commerce, but eventually took House's advice and passed him over. He then chose more conservative figures for these positions, and approved House's attempt to quiet the anxieties on Wall Street by private reassurances that Wilson would not approve any measure 'in the least degree demagogic'. Wilson was determined to find a cabinet position for the North Carolina editor, Josephus Daniels, who had directed the publicity for his campaign, and somewhat inconguously this near-pacifist (and prohibitionist) was made Secretary of the Navy. Underwood, whom Wilson respected and whose cooperation would be essential, seems to have secured the appointment of his fellow-congressman, Albert S. Burleson, as Postmaster-General. Gompers, who had backed Wilson in the election, pointed out that William B. Wilson, a trade union leader with congressional experience, was well qualified to be the first Secretary of Labor. Wilson accepted House's recommendations for the Departments of the Interior and of Agriculture, and Tumulty's for the War Department.[10]

The success of the administration would depend in good part upon the quality of these appointments. At first, in accordance with his professed allegiance to 'common counsel', Wilson held cabinet meetings twice a week, but after accounts of the proceedings appeared in the press (through the indiscretion of Franklin Lane, the Secretary of the Interior) they became less frequent and rarely a forum for serious discussion. But if members of the cabinet came to feel excluded from important decisions (particularly in the realm of foreign policy), they enjoyed great authority as heads of their departments. Such departments more or less constituted the executive branch in this era, when there was neither a host of special agencies nor a large White House staff. Although Wilson was prepared to offer advice to cabinet members about matters relating to their departments, he was notably respectful of their authority within their own spheres.

This readiness to delegate reflected not only a clear sense of priorities but also his mental characteristics and working habits. He was fond of saying that he had a 'one-track mind', and he clearly did not want to have his mind cluttered with myriad details about a variety of problems. He needed to conserve both his time and his energy, all the more so because when he did take personal charge of a matter he did so in such a direct and detailed way – commonly typing important speeches and diplomatic notes himself. He preferred to work on paper, and his appointments were scheduled very precisely and tightly. Having learned the danger to his health of overwork, and being prone at the best of times to intestinal disorders, he built periods of leisure into his routine, invariably taking off the late afternoon for a car ride or game of golf. The latter activity had been encouraged by Cary Grayson, the young naval doctor who had been assigned as his personal physician, and Wilson quickly became devoted to it. 'Each stroke requires your whole attention and seems the most important thing in life', he explained to a friend. 'While you are playing golf you *cannot* worry and be preoccupied with affairs.'[11]

Wilson's attempts to control the demands made upon him did not, of course, imply a limited view of the presidency. On the contrary, he made it plain even before he was inaugurated how highly he regarded the role of this 'great office' within the American system when he explained his opposition to a proposed constitutional amendment to limit presidents to a single term of four or six years. 'The President is held responsible for what happens in Washington in every large matter', he observed. 'He must be prime minister, as much concerned with the guidance of legislation as with the just and orderly execution of law; and he is the spokesman of the nation in everything, even the most momentous and most delicate dealings of the government with foreign nations.' He was thus entitled to 'all the power he can get from the support and convictions and opinions of his fellow countrymen': 'No one will fear a President except those whom he can make fear the elections.' As the political scientist Daniel Stid has pointed out, there was a tension in Wilson's conception of the presidency, which he seems never to have consciously recognized, between party and national leadership. Retaining from his early admiration of the British system a belief in party government, Wilson also saw the president as having the responsibility of representing and speaking for the nation as a whole. As he assumed office, he confronted a related but more precise dilemma – whether to govern through the Democratic party and its machinery or to seek to build a transparty coalition of progressives. In his inaugural address he appeared to be hovering between the two approaches. He began by announcing that 'there has been a change of government', citing the Democrats' control of both houses of Congress and the presidency. But he closed by asserting that 'here muster, not the forces of party, but the forces of humanity' and calling for the support of 'all honest men, all patriotic, all forward-looking men'.[12]

For Wilson, there was no contradiction between these statements. The Democratic party was in power, but he hoped that progressive Republicans and independents would support it. Thus, when signing the Federal Reserve Act, he expressed 'real gratification' that so many Republicans had voted for it, saying that 'all great measures under our system of government are party measures, for the party of the majority is responsible for their origination and their passage; but this cannot be called a partisan measure'.[13] In any case, when he set about the tasks of government he soon made it clear that he did so as 'the responsible leader of the party in power'. As he had done in New Jersey, he sought to apply the British model of a party elected to carry out a program by means of a legislative agenda presented by the executive. To his mind, this was the remedy for the ills of the American system denounced by progressives, as well as the way to overcome popular cynicism about politics. He had boasted when campaigning for the presidency of the fidelity with which he had tried to fulfill 'every promise that I made' in New Jersey, and he adopted the same methods in Washington that had been so successful in Trenton. Most dramatically, having called Congress into a special session to revise the tariff, he presented the case for such a measure in person, thereby overturning the tradition of more than a century. Jefferson had abandoned the practice of addressing Congress on the grounds that it resembled too much the speech from the throne of British monarchs, and since his day presidents had sent written messages. Wilson's move met initial hostility from Democrats who revered Jefferson's memory, but he presented it deftly as a way of showing that the President was 'a human being trying to cooperate with other human beings in a common service', rather than 'a mere department of the government, hailing Congress from some isolated island of jealous power'. He conferred personally with Democratic legislators, breaking another precedent by going to the Capitol for the purpose, and also having a direct phone-line installed between it and the White House. Yet, although Wilson was fond of saying that he relied only on persuasion, he backed Underwood's use of private caucus meetings to agree a party line to which members were expected to adhere, and also came to employ the enormous patronage resources of the executive to reward loyalty.[14]

This use of patronage involved a retreat from principles that Wilson had previously proclaimed. There were two fundamental issues. One was whether patronage should be used to strengthen reform elements in the Democratic party, which had generally favored Wilson's nomination, against the political machines that had mostly opposed it. Before taking office, he had said that he would choose 'progressives, and only progressives'. Since by far the greatest number of jobs were postmasterships across the country, most patronage was dispensed through Burleson, who later recounted how he had persuaded Wilson that gaining support for his legislative program necessitated respecting the wishes of senators and congressmen whatever their views or connections. Although Burleson's version of events was doubtless heightened for effect, this was in fact the policy Wilson came to follow, even to the extent by 1914 of accommodating the New Jersey machine and Tammany Hall in New York (over the objections of McAdoo among others). The second issue was the extent to which merit rather than political considerations should determine appointments. This was the cause that Civil Service reformers had been promoting for over 30 years with increasing success. Wilson, like Roosevelt and Taft, had been a strong advocate of it. But there were many in the Democratic party who remained deeply attached to the 'spoils system' that the party's great hero Andrew Jackson had openly championed. Bryan was one such, and in the State Department he set back the nascent development of a professional foreign service by replacing qualified ministers, particularly in Latin America, with party hacks. In a letter that was (embarrassingly) made public, he enquired of his newly installed Receiver of the Dominican customs, 'what positions you have at your disposal with which to reward deserving Democrats?' The demand for jobs was aggravated by the length of time the party had been out of office. 'The wild asses of the desert are athirst and hungry; they have broken into the green corn', one senator quoted from scripture. In response to the pressure, Wilson acquiesced in the opening up for political appointments of thousands of positions in the Post Office and Treasury. 'Our Texas Democracy', one party worker wrote, 'is in thorough accord with the reform ideas of Mr Wilson but I have not yet come across any sort of a Texas Democrat who favors letting the Republicans continue to hold the offices.'[15]

A number of the Republicans who lost official positions in the Southern states were African-Americans, and they were not replaced by black Democrats. This was a disappointment to those black leaders and their white allies who had supported Wilson in the election and helped him to secure more black votes than any previous Democratic presidential candidate. Such people were further disillusioned when the new administration started to segregate federal employees by race. Nothing indicated more clearly how the Democratic party of this era was still an institution dominated by white Southerners. Not only was the congressional leadership largely Southern but half the cabinet were Southerners by birth if not residence, including Burleson and McAdoo whose departments employed by far the largest numbers of blacks and who took the lead in instituting separate offices, toilets and lunchrooms for the two races. But the policy was discussed in cabinet before it was implemented, and Wilson defended it against the protests of Northern liberals and black spokesmen as being 'distinctly to the advantage of the colored people themselves'. He developed this argument to a black delegation led by W.M. Trotter, explaining that the system was designed to 'prevent friction'. But when Trotter pressed the protest, and stated that he and others who had advocated Wilson's election felt betrayed, the President lost his temper and accused Trotter of 'blackmail'. The truth was that in his racial attitudes Wilson remained a Southerner. As such, he was comparatively liberal in that he did favor Negro advance, as he showed by nominating African-Americans to some significant offices in the face of objections from senators such as James K. Vardaman of Mississippi, who wanted to subordinate the race completely and permanently.[16]

In this period, however, race was not an important issue in national politics. Center stage in the summer of 1913 was the tariff. The Democrats were committed to its reduction, and had apparently won public support for their argument that the high rates imposed by Republican legislation were responsible both for the growth of trusts and the rise in the cost of living. A draft bill had been prepared by the House Ways and Means Committee under Underwood's chairmanship even before Wilson took office. This draft, however, retained duties on some agricultural products, and Wilson, fearing that this would lead to the usual 'log-rolling' in which duties were traded upwards, threatened to veto the bill unless these products were added to the 'free list', though he was prepared to accept a phased transition in the case of sugar. Once the bill had been amended as Wilson wished, Underwood swiftly steered it through the House of Representatives, maintaining party discipline through the caucus system. Passage by the Senate was more problematic as defections by those pledged to support tariffs on sugar and wool threatened the Democrats' narrow majority, and progressive Republicans such as La Follette had been alienated by Wilson's making the bill a party measure and excluding them from the work of the finance committee. Wilson responded with a public statement denouncing the lavishly financed activities of the lobbyists who were seeking to encourage these defections. When a Senate investigation revealed how much had been spent by the beet-sugar industry, all but two of the Democratic senators came into line. After attempts by progressive Republicans to raise the levels of the federal income tax that the bill introduced for the first time had been defeated, an agreed measure that greatly extended the free list and significantly reduced the average level of duties was passed by both houses and signed by Wilson in October.[17]

By this time, Wilson had long been engaged in another struggle, endeavoring to achieve a comprehensive reform of the banking and currency system. This was a much more complicated issue than the tariff, and one on which, as he complained, there were 'almost as many judgments as men'. A fundamental problem was that the requirements of an advanced and integrated national economy ran counter to sentiments deepseated in the political culture, such as the almost religious belief in competition and hostility to the financial power of New York. This last was highlighted by a congressional inquiry into the 'money trust' in 1912–13 that revealed that J.P. Morgan and allied investment bankers in Wall Street held directorates in corporations across the country whose aggregate capitalization amounted to over 22 billion dollars. However, the weakness of a banking structure with thousands of independent units and no agency to coordinate interest rates or control the money supply had been demonstrated by periodic financial panics, the most recent of which in 1907 had precipitated a severe recession. It had also given rise to a plan for a central bank, with regional branches, put forward by the Republican Senator Nelson Aldrich but drawn up in Wall Street. Democrats united in rejecting this plan but differed in their grounds of opposition in ways that made the formulation of an alternative solution difficult. Carter Glass, chairman of the House banking committee, wanted a decentralized system of privately run and independent reserve banks. McAdoo proposed a central bank under the control of the Treasury. To Bryan, the essential point was that the nation's currency should be issued by the government, not private banks. Wilson played a key role in constructing a compromise that the three could accept – a number of regional reserve banks capped by a Federal Reserve Board appointed by the government. When the bill was published, it was attacked both by agrarian radicals as 'a perfectly organized financial trust' and by bankers as 'a vast engine of political domination over the great forces of profitable American industry and internal commerce'. But Bryan's explicit support brought most of the agrarian Democrats into line, and the favorable response of business organizations, and of the press generally, helped the administration to face down the banker opposition, which was in any case divided. Obstruction by three strategically placed senators delayed matters for some weeks but Wilson managed to contain his 'exasperation', and he held firm when a last-minute proposal by Frank Vanderlip of the National City Bank for a government-operated central bank attracted a flurry of support across the political spectrum. The Federal Reserve Act as it was eventually passed had weaknesses that were not remedied until the 1930s, notably the limited authority of the Federal Reserve Board and the overrestrictive requirements of backing for the currency. Yet it established the framework within which central authority in this vital area could be exercised, and a structure that reconciled the claims of banker independence and public accountability. It was a remarkable legislative achievement, and Wilson was entitled to the gratification he expressed as he signed the bill just before Christmas, 1913.[18]

Wilson sought to capitalize on the general acceptance of the Federal Reserve Act by seeking a similar consensus on the emotionally charged issue of antitrust legislation. In another address to Congress early in 1914, he claimed that 'the antagonism between business and government is over', and that all were agreed that the 'methods of monopoly' and 'hurtful restraints of trade' were 'indefensible and intolerable'. He therefore proposed a bill that defined such practices, imposed criminal penalties on those found guilty of them, and prohibited holding companies and interlocking directorates. He also advocated the creation of a commission to investigate corporate activities and to recommend ways in which undesirable combinations might be dissolved without damaging financial consequences. When bills along these lines were introduced into the House of Representatives, controversy initially focused on the strenuous attempt by Gompers and the AFL to include an explicit and complete exemption of labor unions from antitrust legislation. Wilson firmly resisted this campaign, accepting only an amendment stating that labor, farm and cooperative organizations were not themselves illegal. Although this hardly altered the existing situation and, as events were to show, did not end the use of court injunctions in labor disputes, Gompers hailed it as labor's 'Magna Carta'. Meanwhile, Wilson had been persuaded by Brandeis and others that the criminalization of a whole series of defined trade practices could never be sufficient to prevent monopoly but would have the undesirable effect of outlawing the attempts being made by small businessmen to eliminate 'cut-throat' competition by means of trade associations.

Accordingly, while the legislation was being considered by the Senate, Wilson supported an amendment giving the new commission a general power to check unfair trade practices. The establishment of this strong Federal Trade Commission now became the main feature of Wilson's anti-trust program, the more so as the specification of illegal practices in the other bill was weakened, and the criminal penalties eliminated, before it was enacted into law in October 1914.[19]

This change in approach has been seen by some historians as marking a significant shift in Wilson's political ideology. His 1912 campaign speeches attacking both monopoly and big government are taken to indicate that he had a classical economist's faith in the free market, and thought that such a market could be restored by a few well-designed laws enforced through the courts. This interpretation follows that of contemporary critics, supporters of Roosevelt's Progressive party, who saw Wilson as representative of the traditional Democratic attachment to individual and states' rights and, in his celebration of competition and opportunity, of the characteristic viewpoint of small businessmen. That he had a principled adherence to the ideal of a limited and neutral government seemed to be confirmed by some of the stands he took during his early years in the White House – in particular, his opposition to a number of measures that enjoyed much support in Congress. These included a national child labor law, a publicly financed rural credits scheme, the AFL's campaign for total exemption of labor unions' activities from the anti-trust act, a literacy test to restrict immigration, and a bill to improve the conditions of American seamen. Yet it is hard to reconcile the view that Wilson was committed at this time to 'the *laissez-faire* ideal' with much that he did and said. He had pushed for a powerful regulatory commission for public utilities in New Jersey, and in his inaugural address as President had explicitly supported 'sanitary laws, pure food laws, and laws determining conditions of labor which individuals are powerless to determine for themselves', in calling for government to be 'put at the service of humanity, in safeguarding the health of the nation, the health of its men and its women and its children, as well as their rights in the struggle for existence'. Consistently with this declaration, he had supported the Seamen's Bill until appraised of international complications and, notwithstanding these, signed it in March 1915. He evidently had no strong feelings either way on immigration restriction but felt bound by pledges he had made to ethnic groups during the election to oppose the literacy test. Yielding to the campaigns by labor and farm groups for what were generally regarded as special favors would have damaged his standing with mainstream public opinion. As at other points in his career, his positions on policy issues at this time are much more readily explained by pragmatic considerations than by any ideological conviction.[20]

Another area in which Wilson's rhetoric can give a misleading impression is with respect to his style of leadership. He frequently stressed the collegial character of this, lauding the Federal Reserve Act as the product of 'team work', and telling reporters that 'I haven't had a tariff program. I haven't had a currency program. I have conferred with these men who handle these things, and asked the questions, and then gotten back what they sent to me – the best of our common counsel.' Even to his most intimate friends, he insisted that newspaper stories of his 'bending Congress to my indomitable individual will' were 'silly': 'I do not know how to wield a big stick, but I do know how to put my mind at the service of others for the accomplishment of a common purpose.' As his use of the phrase 'big stick' indicated, Wilson was anxious, as he had been in the campaign, to distinguish his approach from Roosevelt's alleged dictatorial tendencies. Roosevelt had certainly worked less closely with Congress, partly no doubt because of his ideological differences with his party's Old Guard leadership. But Wilson's modest presentation of his role discounted the crucial part he had played in shaping all three of the major pieces of legislation he had called for – in securing the elimination of protection for agricultural products, conceiving the federal structure of the new reserve system, and coming to support a powerful trade commission. He had also shown great strength in resisting pressure, on such issues as the sugar and wool schedules or the Vanderlip proposal, that would almost certainly have prevailed without firmness on his part. He had unquestionably acted as a leader, not simply as a chairman or facilitator.[21]

In any case, Wilson undoubtedly merited the praise he received for the remarkable legislative record of the 63rd Congress. His triumph seems to have induced in him a mixture of feelings. In a late-night conversation with House, he expressed doubts about running for a second term, saying that he would not be able in the future 'to accomplish anything like what he had accomplished in a legislative way', and that 'he feared the country would expect him to continue as he had up to now, which would be impossible'. But he also evidently felt that he had demonstrated the possibility within the American system of the kind of efficient, accountable, democratic government he had argued for since his youth. 'He thinks our form of government can be changed by personal leadership', House noted. 'But I thought the Constitution should be altered, for no matter how great a leader a man was, I could see situations that would block him unless the Constitution was modified.'[22]

A Democratic foreign policy

'It would be the irony of fate if my administration had to deal chiefly with foreign affairs.' Wilson's reported remark to a friend shortly before going to Washington has been much quoted because of the heaviness of the 'irony' fate had in store for the man who had to lead America through World War I. Even before this, however, Wilson seems to have devoted the greater part of his time and attention to foreign policy matters. This may suggest that the irony that Wilson referred to was not as unwelcome to him as is usually assumed. Domestic affairs had dominated the election campaign, as they did the minds of most congressmen and of Americans generally. But the President's authority was much less trammeled in foreign affairs – indeed, Wilson had written that he had 'virtually the power to control them absolutely'. Throughout his time in the White House, he was to react fiercely to any attempt by Congress to substitute its own judgment for his in this area. It is true that Wilson had not made much study of international affairs, and had visited Europe (apart from Britain) only briefly and no other continents at all. But he approached the conduct of foreign policy with some assumptions and beliefs that were perhaps more deeply rooted than his views on domestic economic and social issues, as well with some more general predispositions and values that were to prove equally relevant.[23]

Fundamental was a belief in the virtue and power of his own country. Like most Americans he had no doubt that the political and social system of the United States was superior to that of other countries and, more than most, he believed in the nation's historic mission to lead the world on to a higher plane. It was to do this chiefly by example, and an aspect of this example should be a foreign policy designed to serve broad human interests rather than narrow selfish ones. 'Every time you let the Stars and Stripes free to the wind', he told a graduating class of naval officers, it meant 'that you are on an errand which other navies have sometimes for-gotten; not an errand of conquest, but an errand of service'. Wilson also was very impressed by the scale of American power, and thought that this in itself impelled a more active involvement with world affairs than had been traditional. Although he had been uncertain at the time whether the United States should take the Philippines after the war of 1898, he had come to see its doing so as marking the country's 'full maturity' and the end of its 'isolation'. He recognized that America's new power was the product of the nation's tremendous economic advance, and believed that this advance had in itself widened the scope of the nation's interests. 'Our industries have expanded to such a point that they will burst their jackets, if they cannot find a free outlet to the markets of the world', he declared in his acceptance speech. 'Our domestic markets no longer suffice.' However, he said this in arguing for tariff reduction and the building up of America's shrunken merchant marine, not for the exercise of diplomatic muscle to promote the 'open-door world' for American economic interests that some historians have seen as the overriding goal of US foreign policy. On the contrary, he insisted that 'if American enterprise in foreign countries, particularly in those foreign countries which are not strong enough to resist us, takes the shape of imposing upon and exploiting the mass of the people of that country, it ought to be checked and not encouraged'.[24]

There was another aspect to Wilson's idealism, one that was perhaps a legacy of his adolescent romanticism. As the United States fought to gain control of its new possessions, he expressed satisfaction that 'this country has some young men who prefer dying in the ditches of the Philippines to spending their lives behind the counters of a dry goods store in our eastern cities'. Wilson was aged forty-two when he said this, but thirteen years later he startled House by remarking that 'he did not share the views of so many of our present day statesmen that war was so much to be deprecated' and that 'he thought there was no more glorious way to die than in battle'. These sentiments were of a piece with Wilson's love of Shakespeare's *Henry V*; he was particularly fond of the couplet, 'But if it be a sin to covet honor, I am the most offending soul alive', quoting it (slightly wrongly) in both private correspondence and public utterances. However, in conducting foreign policy, Wilson conceived it as his duty not to express his personal feelings but to represent the wishes of the American people, and he was confident of his ability to discern what these were. 'When I wish to know the true sentiment of my country', he told a Swiss visitor in 1917, 'I lock myself in my study and sink into the depths of my consciousness as a citizen, and there I am sure to find it.' It was perhaps this that caused Wilson's longest-serving Secretary of State, Robert Lansing, to complain that 'intuition rather than reason played the chief part in the way in which he reached conclusions and judgments'.[25]

If Wilson's attitudes to foreign policy were subject to a variety of sometimes conflicting impulses, so were those of the Democratic party as a whole. The party of Andrew Jackson, in which Southerners played such a prominent part, was not likely to be insensitive to the demands of national honor, but in the early twentieth century the antimilitarist tradition that could be traced back to the party's other great hero, Thomas Jefferson, was more marked. It had been in the Republican party that support had developed since the 1880s for the strengthening of the US navy, the construction of an isthmian canal, and a generally more energetic and expansionist foreign policy. The fact that proponents of this more active diplomacy often favored some degree of cooperation with Great Britain only increased the antagonism to it within Democratic ranks, where Anglo-phobia was strong among Irish-Americans and some agrarian radicals. The Democratic party had opposed the acquisition of the Philippines and other overseas territories in 1898 as a violation of the principles of the Declaration of Independence. Bryan had led that assault and his pacifist, anti-imperialist viewpoint was the dominant one within the party when Wilson took office.

The differences between the approaches to foreign policy of Wilson and Bryan would emerge in time, but for the first two years of the administration the two men cooperated without friction and in a notably friendly manner. This was mostly due to the extent to which they came to agree on matters – a process eased partly by Bryan's willingness to modify his views as he became more aware of the practical complexities of problems, and partly by a division of reponsibilities. Thus Wilson left to Bryan the negotiation of bilateral 'cooling-off' treaties in which the parties agreed to submit any disputes to a commission of inquiry and not to resort to war for six months or a year; 30 such treaties were eventually signed, and Bryan presented the diplomats concerned with paperweights in the form of miniature plowshares made out of an old army sword. One attitude which Wilson and Bryan shared was a suspicion of professional diplomats, whom they regarded as conservative and snobbish. Consequently, Wilson did not object to Bryan's purge of Republican appointees in the State Department. Wilson initially hoped to choose distinguished educators and writers as ambassadors, rather than the wealthy campaign contributors who were the norm, but he found it difficult to persuade those he approached to accept, in good part because the salaries paid fell so far short of the expenses that would be incurred. He did persuade Walter Hines Page, the editor of the journal, *World's Work*, who had been one of the earliest and most active of his supporters during the campaign, to accept the London embassy, but it was only because of Cleveland Dodge's great generosity that Page was able to remain in this post beyond a year. Wilson eventually settled on James W. Gerard, a financial backer of the Democratic party in New York, as Ambassador to Germany.[26]

Like several later American presidents, Wilson began by seeking to show how different his foreign policy was going to be from that of his predecessors. Within days of taking office, he had withdrawn support for the participation by American bankers in an international consortium to make a large loan to China. The Taft administration's attempt in this way to use private American capital to buttress its policy objectives – the preservation of China from the formal or informal imperialism of other powers – was a prime example of what the Democrats had condemned as 'dollar diplomacy', and Wilson's move was hailed in progressive circles as a blow against profiteering exploitation. But the lack of American financial assistance rendered the government of the new Chinese republic (which Wilson was quick to recognize) vulnerable to Japanese expansionism, and by 1917 the administration was attempting to organize a new consortium. Repudiation of Republican actions was also involved in the treaty that Bryan negotiated with Colombia, by which the United States undertook to pay 25 million dollars and expressed regret for its part in the process by which the province of Panama had broken away in 1903, thereby opening the way for the United States to build the canal. This initiative, too, proved unsuccessful, though because of domestic rather than foreign difficulties. The treaty infuriated Roosevelt, who had boasted in his recently published *Autobiography* of 'taking' Panama, and the ex-President's friends in the Senate, led by Henry Cabot Lodge, prevented its ever being ratified.[27]

Wilson showed that his concept of national honor involved fair dealing with other countries even at the expense of more substantial American interests when he pressed for the abolition of the preferential rates for American shipping in the newly opened Panama Canal. Although this involved the repeal of a measure signed by Taft, Wilson had support for his stand in this case from internationalist-minded Republicans such as Lodge and Senator Elihu Root. The chief opposition came from Democratic leaders in the House of Representatives, responding to the energetic lobbying of American shipping interests, particularly those trading between the east and west coasts of the United States who enjoyed a total exemption from tolls under the existing law. Once he had been convinced that this discrimination was a violation of the Anglo-American treaty in which Britain had ceded a share in control of the canal, Wilson pushed for its repeal wholeheartedly. 'I ask this of you in support of the foreign policy of the administration', he told Congress. 'I shall not know how to deal with other matters of even greater delicacy and nearer consequence if you do not grant it to me in ungrudging measure.' To reporters, he explained that the law had caused other countries to doubt the reliability of American pledges. To these strong words, Wilson added the ruthless use of patronage to bring Democratic congressmen into line. His bold leadership, which was crowned with success in June 1914, greatly enhanced the President's standing abroad, particularly in London.[28]

In this case, a stand on principle and the readiness to face down domestic pressure groups won respect abroad and served the broader national interest. As we have seen with regard to China, this approach was less adequate in more complex situations. The greatest difficulties arose with regard to the Caribbean and Central America, particularly Mexico. This had become an area in which the time-honored policy of the Monroe Doctrine, warning European powers that imperialistic incursions into the Western Hemisphere were unacceptable to the United States, had acquired a more serious strategic significance with the construction of the Panama Canal and the reliance upon it of the US navy for moving its strength from one ocean to the other. Although there was no serious disposition on the part of any of the other great powers to challenge American hegemony in the Caribbean basin, they still wanted to protect the rights of their citizens against mistreatment at the hands of unscrupulous or incompetent regimes in Latin America. Following an Anglo-German naval blockade of Venezuela for this purpose, Roosevelt had proclaimed a so-called 'Corollary' to the Monroe Doctrine in which he stated that the United States assumed the right 'to the exercise of an international police power' in the Western Hemisphere when 'chronic wrongdoing, or an impotence which results in a general loosening of the ties of civilized society', required 'intervention by some civilized nation'. Under Roosevelt and Taft, the United States took over the customs house in Santo Domingo and sent the marines into Nicaragua; under Wilson, it intervened militarily in Haiti, Santo Domingo, Nicaragua, and twice in Mexico.[29]

The interventions resulted from events in the countries concerned, particularly the Mexican revolution, but they also reflect the attitudes with which Wilson and Bryan approached policymaking in this area. Their anti-imperialism by no means implied isolationism, and certainly not in a part of the world where they were determined to maintain American hegemony but felt that it brought responsibilities. 'Those Latin republics are our political children, so to speak', Bryan declared. 'It is written that much is required of them to whom much is given, and this country will fall short of its duty if it does not do more than any other country in the work of fellowship and brotherhood.' He was seeking approval for a treaty with Nicaragua by which the United States would pay three million dollars for an exclusive option on a transoceanic canal route, gain a naval base on the Pacific coast, and be given the right to intervene to maintain the country's independence and good order. This last provision, modeled on that which had made Cuba an American protectorate in 1901, had been inserted at the request of the Nicaraguan government, but it nevertheless caused the treaty to be rejected by the Senate, with Republican anti-imperialists such as William E. Borah of Idaho and George W. Norris of

Nebraska leading the attack on it. As an alternative means of alleviating the financial plight of Nicaragua and other Central American states, Bryan suggested that the United States should essentially underwrite their governments' bonds, but this proposal was rejected by Wilson as too 'novel and radical' to be acceptable to American opinion. Bryan then felt obliged to adopt the Republican solution of arranging a loan to Nicaragua from private American bankers. This only increased the hostility in the Senate to the Nicaraguan treaty, and even after the intervention clauses had been removed, there was much delay before it was finally ratified in February 1916. Thereafter, however, to ensure that the authorized payment was not misappropriated, the United States used naval as well as diplomatic pressure to produce a government that would cooperate with American officials in restoring solvency. By this time, American military force had already been employed in a more active way to take direct control of both Haiti and Santo Domingo, in both cases as the result of a process that had started with an attempt to oversee the management of the customs revenue and proceeded by way of somewhat naïve attempts to secure freely elected and uncorrupt governments.[30]

Mexico was a different proposition. Taking control of it militarily, American planners estimated, would require a force of at least 300,000 men, which rendered such an enterprise politically out of the question. And yet, throughout Wilson's first term, Mexico was as subject to internal instability and disorder as the smaller states in the region. The Mexican revolution had begun in 1911 with the overthrow of the long rule of Porfirio Diaz, whose policies had attracted much foreign investment, particularly from the United States. A few weeks before Wilson entered the White House, the revolutionary president had been deposed and murdered in a coup led by General Victoriano Huerta. This coup had been covertly encouraged by the US Ambassador, without the knowledge of Washington but in accordance with the anti-revolutionary sentiment of the large American community in Mexico City. Shocked at the methods by which Huerta had come to power, Wilson resisted pressure from officials in the State Department to recognize his government – a stand that gained additional justification when Huerta's effective control of the country could be questioned after revolutionary leaders under Venustiano Carranza launched a military movement against him, calling themselves the Constitutionalists. Initially, Wilson hoped that the withholding of recognition, combined with an arms embargo, would induce Huerta to accede to Washington's demand that he schedule elections at which he himself would not be a candidate, but in October 1913 Huerta assumed dictatorial powers and dissolved the Congress. Convinced that Huerta's intransigence was due to the support of European powers, particularly Britain, and that their policy was motivated by concern for their economic interests in Mexico, Wilson drafted a note expressing this view and asserting America's 'paramount influence in the Western Hemisphere'. Although he was dissuaded from sending this note, press reports of his attitude led the British to give assurances of cooperation with American policy. In a note to the powers in late November, Wilson indicated that he was prepared to use force if necessary to compel Huerta to stand down. In February 1914 he recognized the belligerent status of the Constitutionalists, allowing them openly to buy arms. He had thus sacrificed his insistence on a peaceful transfer of power to his determination to prevail in a public contest of wills with Huerta in which he evidently felt his own prestige, as well as that of his country, was at stake. Along with this shift of policy, he adopted a new interpretation of the requirements for Mexican self-government, now saying that the root cause of instability was the land question, and that liberty could be achieved only through a social and economic revolution.[31]

Notwithstanding Wilson's new policy, Huerta's position appeared to grow stronger in the spring of 1914, in part because the Constitutionalists were weakened by rivalry between Carranza and his ambitious lieutenant, Francisco Villa. Frustrated, Wilson seized upon an incident at Tampico in April as an opportunity to bring American power to bear. After some American sailors had been arrested by a junior Mexican officer, the commanding US admiral demanded a 21-gun salute from the Mexicans as well as an apology. An apology from Huerta himself seemed satisfactory to Bryan and Daniels, but Wilson pressed the demand for a gun salute. When the Mexicans refused to make this without the explicit promise of a 'reciprocal' salute, Wilson secured congressional approval to use force 'to obtain from General Huerta and his adherents the fullest recognition of the rights and dignity of the United States', and started preparations for a full naval blockade of Mexico, the occupation of Tampico and Veracruz, and a possible march on Mexico City. To forestall the delivery of arms to Huerta from a recently arrived ship Veracruz was quickly seized, but only after fighting in which nineteen Americans and over a hundred Mexicans lost their lives. Regardless of their internal divisions, Mexicans reacted angrily to what they perceived as American aggression, and Carranza talked of war. Wilson had no wish to be drawn into a full-scale war, especially as most public opinion in the United States as well as Europe regarded the issues at stake as trivial and as resting on an archaic sense of honor. He quickly accepted an offer by Argentina, Brazil and Chile to mediate the dispute. In the meantime, however, the Americans retained control of

Veracruz, cutting off Huerta's supplies, and in the negotiations remained adamant that only Huerta's retirement in favor of the Constitutionalists could resolve the issues. In July, Huerta resigned and a month later Carranza entered Mexico City in triumph, having uncompromisingly rejected all American efforts to influence the form and manner in which power was transferred.[32]

This was by no means the end of the story. Villa made a bid for power that initially seemed likely to succeed, and during the ensuing conflict foreigners in Mexico City suffered much hardship. This, and attacks on church institutions and personnel by the anti-clerical revolutionaries, led to demands, particularly from Catholic spokesmen, Roosevelt and some Republicans, that Wilson do more to restore order in Mexico. The administration sought to bring unity to the various revolutionary factions, initially unilaterally and later in collaboration with other Latin American governments. However, Wilson frequently expressed sympathy with the basic aims of the revolution and insisted that social reforms needed to be enacted before elections could be held. By October 1915, Carranza's forces had clearly prevailed and his government was granted recognition by the United States and the major Latin American countries. When protests continued about affairs in Mexico, Wilson gave emphatic expression to the principle of self-determination: 'If the Mexicans want to raise hell, let them raise hell. We have got nothing to do with it. It is their government, it is their hell. And after they have raised enough of it, it will sit so badly on their stomachs that they will want something else.'[33]

In 1916, however, the issue was not to be Mexico's right to determine its own government in its own way but the conflict between its sovereign prerogatives and the duty of the American government to safeguard the lives of its citizens. This issue was raised by the activities of Villa, whose defeated forces now constituted little more than a bandit gang in northern Mexico. Blaming the United States for his plight, and perhaps hoping that provoking military intervention would embarrass Carranza, Villa began attacking Americans, killing eighteen in Mexico in January and in March leading a raid on Columbus, New Mexico, in which seventeen more Americans lost their lives. Although Wilson had responded calmly to the first event, placing the responsibility on Carranza to punish the perpetrators, the second outrage obviously demanded a direct response, and Tumulty warned the President that failure to 'get' Villa would doom his chances for re-election. However, Carranza refused to give permission for the US army to enter Mexico, and Wilson was determined to avoid war; the immediate crisis was resolved when the local commander cooperated with an American Punitive Expedition that crossed the border on March

15th. But Villa proved elusive, and within a couple of weeks the American force, led by General J.J. Pershing, had penetrated 350 miles into Mexico. Later, Wilson felt that he should have ordered Pershing back north at this point. He said this when the crisis had brought the two countries to the verge of war. Weeks of mounting tension, with increasingly insistent demands by Carranza that the Americans withdraw, a serious clash between Pershing's force and Mexican civilians, more border raids, and the calling out of the entire National Guard, had reached its climax in a battle between an American unit and Carranza's troops at Carrizal, Chihuahua, on June 21st, in which 14 Americans were killed and another 25 taken prisoner. 'The break seems to have come in Mexico; and all my patience seems to have gone to nothing', Wilson wrote to House, as he sent an ultimatum demanding the release of the prisoners and drafted an address to Congress requesting authority to use force 'in any way that may be necessary to guard our frontier effectively'.[34]

In the event, both countries backed away from the brink. Instead of taking further offense at the peremptory tone of the American ultimatum, Carranza released the prisoners without seeking to use them as a bargaining counter. By this time, it had become clear that only a small segment of American opinion was in a bellicose mood, and in a speech given without notes Wilson scorned the idea that 'any act of violence by a powerful nation like this against a weak and distracted neighbor would reflect distinction upon the annals of the United States', or the notion that the clear duty of self-defense should be carried to the point of 'dictation in the affairs of another people'. When Carranza proposed mediation or direct negotiations, Wilson suggested that the two countries should establish a joint high commission to resolve the issues between them. He did not, however, follow military advice to withdraw the Punitive Expedition immediately, probably for domestic political reasons rather than as a means of diplomatic leverage. The commission's deliberations proved lengthy and unproductive because the Americans insisted that any agreement must cover the protection of the rights and property of foreigners in Mexico as well as the security of the border and the withdrawal of American forces. The deadlock may well have served Wilson's purpose during the election campaign as it de-escalated the crisis without sacrificing America's position in any way. When the Commission abandoned its work in early 1917, its members advised that Pershing's force be withdrawn, and Wilson had decided on this course before the crisis in German–American relations made it imperative.[35]

In the summer of 1914, when explaining his belief that there were 'no conceivable circumstances which would make it right for us to direct by force or by threat of force the internal processes of what is a profound revolution', Wilson had remarked that 'all the world has been shocked ever since the time of the revolution in France that Europe should have undertaken to nullify what was done there, no matter what the excesses then committed'.[36] There seems little doubt that his experiences with regard to Mexico deepened his conviction that outside intervention in such situations was not only wrong in principle but likely in practice to be both counterproductive and the source of intractable difficulties and serious embarrassments. As we shall see, these attitudes were to shape his response to pressure for military intervention to affect the outcome of the revolution and civil war into which Russia was plunged in 1917.

Building a Democratic majority

As in New Jersey three years earlier, Wilson found in 1914 that legislative achievement and fulfilling one's campaign promises did not necessarily bring a party the electoral reward that his theory of democratic government suggested it should. In the congressional elections of 1914, the Democrats comfortably retained control of the Senate but their majority in the House of Representatives was reduced from 147 to 25.[37] Wilson was undoubtedly disappointed by the result, telling House that 'it seemed hardly worth while to work as hard as he had worked during the past two years and to have it so scantily appreciated'. A few days later, however, his natural optimism returned and he pointed to the gains that the Democrats had made in the West, 'the heart of America'. 'That gives me vital comfort and a very lively hope', he wrote. 'A different part of America now decides, not the part which has usually arrogated to itself a selfish leadership and patronage of the rest.' The Democrats' success in the West had been largely at the expense of the Bull Moose Progressive party, for whom the elections were a real disaster, leaving it with only scattered pockets of strength and a doubtful future.[38]

Analysts of the election results generally concluded that the Republican gains had been mainly due to two factors – economic discontent and the return to their former allegiance of many who had followed Roosevelt into the Progressive party two years earlier. The former reflected the sharp recession that had begun in 1913 and had been aggravated by the effects of the European war. This made Wilson anxious to restore business confidence, and in a public letter to McAdoo two weeks after the election he indicated that his reform program was essentially completed, asserting that it had 'in very large measure' corrected the 'fundamental wrongs' that had given rise to 'agitation' over the previous decade. In the future, there would be no cause for conflicts between different 'groups and classes': 'Our task is henceforth to work, not for any single interest, but for all the interests of the country as a united whole.' From the spring of 1915, economic activity did revive, spurred by a massive increase in Allied purchasing of munitions and other supplies. By 1916 GNP was growing at a rate of almost 8 percent in real terms, providing favourable conditions for an incumbent president seeking re-election.[39]

The collapse of the Progressive vote, however, presented a real threat to Wilson's prospects of a second term. Roosevelt, who had campaigned hard for his new party, privately despaired of its future after the 1914 elections and started aligning himself with the Republicans by stressing issues of foreign policy and national defense. If he succeeded in carrying the bulk of his supporters with him into an alliance with the Republican party, Wilson's chances of re-election would be slim, given that he had received only 42 percent of the popular vote in 1912. The President thus needed to win over a sizeable proportion of former Bull Moose voters, which would not be easy since the great majority of Roosevelt's supporters had, like their chief, come from the Republican party. On the other hand, leadership of that party was now in the hands of those who had remained loyal to Taft in 1912, most of whom were seen by Progressives as 'standpat' conservatives or reactionaries. Wilson sought to exploit this situation in a speech in early 1915 by arguing that 'the independent progressive voter finds a great deal more company in the Democratic ranks than in the Republican ranks', because 'only about one-third' of the Republican party was 'progressive', as opposed to 'about two thirds' of the Democratic party. He also claimed that all the things that 'the progressive Republicans proposed that were practical, the Democrats either have done or are immediately proposing to do'.[40]

It has been argued that Wilson's attempt to woo former Progressives over the next two years, and especially in 1916, led him to adopt the 'New Nationalist' philosophy that Roosevelt had espoused in 1912, and to abandon the antistatist approach of the 'New Freedom'.[41] But, as before, such an analysis exaggerates the extent to which Wilson's positions at any one time possessed the clear ideological coherence this view attributes to his campaign slogan. Early 1915 did see Wilson fighting hard for a measure that its opponents denounced as 'state socialism' – a bill to establish a government-owned corporation to own and operate a merchant shipping fleet. Wilson, too, cast the issue at stake in broad terms, as part of the struggle against 'reaction', 'privilege' and 'the control of special interests over this government'. In fact, the Ship Purchase Bill was a unique measure, which had been devised (before the 1914 elections) as a way of dealing with the shortage of international shipping caused by the European war; the fact that the proposed corporation would probably purchase the ships of German registry interned in American ports contributed further emotion to the hostility to it of pro-Ally Republicans, and the bill was eventually defeated through a Senate filibuster aided by some Democratic defectors. The scheme had been devised by McAdoo, but Wilson's keen support of it reflected his own long-held belief that a revival of the American merchant marine was in the nation's interest, and in 1916 he did secure passage of a bill establishing a Shipping Board for this purpose (though this time forbidding the purchase of ships of belligerent nationality). His approach to this issue demonstrated that he had no ideological objections to an expansion of the government's economic role, but it did not presage a wider program to this end.[42]

Another bitterly fought battle a year after that on the Ship Purchase Bill provided further evidence that the real division in American politics at this time was between progressives and conservatives, rather than between different forms of progressivism. Wilson precipitated this battle by nominating Louis Brandeis in January 1916 to fill a vacancy on the Supreme Court. Conservatives were outraged; Taft, for example, describing Brandeis as 'a muckraker, an emotionalist for his own purposes, a socialist, prompted by jealousy, a hypocrite'. By contrast, the nomination delighted progressives of all kinds, including those, such as the editors of the *New Republic*, who by no means shared Brandeis' faith in competition and enthusiasm for small business. Brandeis was the first Jew ever to be nominated to the Court, and there was a marked element of antisemitism in the extraordinary campaign that was mounted to prevent Senate confirmation of his appointment, with seven former presidents of the American Bar Association affirming that Brandeis was 'not fit' to be a member of the Supreme Court. The issue was certainly in doubt until Wilson threw his full weight into the fight, employing both flattery and patronage pressure on wavering Democratic senators, and in a public letter lauding Brandeis in the highest terms, and saying that the aspersions upon him derived from those who 'hated' him because he had opposed their 'selfish interests'. The nomination was confirmed by the Senate after a strict party vote in the Judiciary Committee – a much rarer occurrence in those days than in recent years.[43]

Wilson's admiration for Brandeis dated back to their first meeting in 1912, but other actions of his in 1916 did represent some clear shifts from earlier positions. This was very decidedly true of his support for the creation of a tariff commission, an idea he had ridiculed in 1912 when it formed part of the Bull Moose program. He justified his change of mind by referring to the effects of the European war, but, because it was seen as opening the way to the restitution of protection removed by the Underwood Act, the establishment of an advisory commission in the 1916 Revenue Act was warmly welcomed by manufacturers and their work-forces, especially in the Northeast. The same Revenue Act imposed duties on imported chemical products. Even more strikingly, Wilson in early 1916 approved the inclusion in a bill setting up banks to make long-term loans to farmers' cooperatives of a provision for federal underwriting that he had earlier opposed as 'class' legislation. He now justified this special treatment by saying that farmers 'have occupied hitherto a singular position of disadvantage' in securing credit. In the same session, he signed bills to assist road-building and permitting bonded warehouses to issue receipts that could be used as collateral for loans, later justifying all these as necessary 'to put the farmer upon the same footing as the other industrial workers of the country'.[44]

During the summer of 1916, with his re-election campaign looming, Wilson took advantage of opportunities to reinforce his appeal to two of his target constituencies. The Progressive party finally disbanded in June after Roosevelt had refused to accept its nomination and then urged his followers to support Charles Evans Hughes, the Republican candidate. It was quickly evident that not all of them would do so, particularly not those who had been attracted by the social welfare legislation in the Bull Moose program, and the Democratic platform sought to attract such people by including an extended statement of the 'enlightened measures of social and industrial justice' to which the party was committed. Not long afterwards, the President put pressure on the Senate to pass a bill that had been approved by the House of Representatives in February forbidding the shipment in interstate commerce of the products of child labor. The bill had languished in the Senate due to the opposition of Southerners who feared it would open the door to other federal measures outlawing the cheap labor that was their region's competitive advantage. Wilson had not hitherto had anything to do with the bill, having earlier taken the position that under the Constitution the prohibition of child labor was a matter for the states. However, his role in securing the legislation was crucial and gained him much praise from the reformers who had campaigned for it. In August, the President and the country faced the threat of a national railroad strike as the labor unions demanded an eight-hour day with an overtime rate of time and a half. Wilson summoned the two sides to the White House and proposed a settlement involving immediate acceptance of the eight-hour day (though not of the overtime demand) and the establishment of a committee of inquiry to be appointed by him. When the railroad managers rejected this, insististing on arbitration, Wilson secured the passage through Congress in two days of legislation imposing his solution. This measure, known as the Adamson Act, won praise from progressive commentators as well as organized labor. As the bill was going through Congress, Wilson delivered his speech accepting the Democratic nomination, in which he claimed that 'we have in four years come very near to carrying out the platform of the Progressive party, as well as our own; for we are also progressives'.[45]

However, the Adamson Act gave Hughes' campaign the focus it had hitherto lacked. 'Transcending every other issue', he declared, 'is the issue that has just presented itself – whether the Government shall yield to force.' In response, Wilson maintained that the legislation had been in the national interest, and reflected the judgment, 'sustained now by abundant experience', that 'a man does better work within eight hours than he does within a more extended day'. A few days later, he praised those Republicans who had four years earlier rebelled against their party's enslavement to special interests, and claimed again that he was 'a progressive': 'I do not spell it with a capital P, but I think my pace is just as fast as those who do.' In the run-up to the election, Wilson gained the articulate and active support of the great majority of prominent progressives, including many former supporters of the Bull Moose party. Thoroughly committed also to his cause were the spokesmen for the other constituencies he had cultivated – organized labor and farmers. Particularly significant and influential among the organizations representing the latter was the Non-Partisan League, a new and rapidly growing movement in the Northern Plains states and Middle West that represented the tradition of American agrarian radicalism.[46]

These constituencies were to prove crucial in securing Wilson a second term in the White House. The election was so close that its outcome was not known until two days after the voting, when California's full returns came in. As had been the case since 1896, the Republicans were dominant in the Northeast and Middle West, with Hughes carrying all but Ohio of the populous states in that segment of the country. Wilson, like other Democratic candidates, could rely on the Southern and border states but he also carried nearly the whole of the trans-Mississippi West. Bryan's experience had shown, however, that the South and West were not sufficient by themselves, so Ohio, where Wilson had enjoyed ardent backing from organized labor, was vital to his narrow margin of 23 votes in the electoral college. He had gained 49 percent of the popular vote to Hughes' 46 percent, and it was estimated that he had received support from about a fifth of those who had voted for Roosevelt in 1912, though this varied greatly from state to state.[47]

Although Wilson's electoral college majority was much smaller than in 1912, his share of the popular vote was over 7 percent higher, and indeed larger than that of any Democrat since 1876. Wilson so much dominated his party by now that he could also take credit for the Democrats' narrow victory in the congressional elections. It was an impressive political achievement by the lifelong student of politics. Not the least part of that achievement, however, had been the widespread approval he had gained for his shaping of America's response to the cataclysmic war that had engulfed Europe two and a half years earlier.

Notes

1 For a full and insightful account of this rivalry, see John Milton Cooper, Jr, *The Warrior and the Priest: Woodrow Wilson and Theodore Roosevelt*, Cambridge, MA, 1983.

2 Henry F. Pringle, *The Life and Times of William Howard Taft*, New York, 1939, p. 817.

3 Address, 6 August 1912; Progressive National Platform, Theodore Roosevelt, *Progressive Principles*, London, 1913, pp. 115–73, 314–30; George E. Mowry, *Theodore Roosevelt and the Progressive Movement*, New York, 1960, pp. 264–6. For a contemporary analysis of the evolution of 'the old reform' into 'modern progressivism', see Herbert Croly, *Progressive Democracy*, New York, 1914, pp. 5–11.

4 Wilson to M.A. Hulbert, 25 August 1912; acceptance speech, 7 August, 1912, *PWW*, vol. 25, pp. 55–6, 3–18; Roosevelt, *Progressive Principles*, pp. 141, 152.

5 Campaign speeches in Minneapolis, 18 September 1912, Buffalo, 2 September 1912, *PWW*, vol. 25, pp. 167–8, 73, 78.

6 Theodore Roosevelt, *Progressive Principles*, pp. 209, 148; campaign speech in Sioux City, 17 September 1912, *PWW*, vol. 25, pp. 148–56; William Allen White, *Woodrow Wilson: The Man, his Times and his Task*, Boston, 1924, p. 264. On later divisions among policymakers on this issue, see Ellis W. Hawley, *The New Deal and the Problem of Monopoly*, Princeton, NJ, 1966.

7 Campaign addresses in Scranton, PA, 23 September 1912, Buffalo, 2 September 1912, Atlantic City, 10 September 1912, *PWW*, vol. 25, pp. 228, 77, 131. For an analysis of the difference between Wilson's conception of leadership and Roosevelt's, see Cooper, *The Warrior and the Priest*, pp. 172–4, 213–15.

8 August Heckscher, *Woodrow Wilson*, New York, 1991, p. 258; Samuel Gompers, *Seventy Years of Life and Labor: An Autobiography*, London, 1925, vol. 1, pp. 545–6; *New York Times*, 16 October 1912; Speech in Dover, DE 17 October 1912, *PWW*, vol. 25, pp. 419, 424–5.

9 Campaign speeches in West Chester, PA, 28 October 1912, Montclair, NJ, 29 October 1912; message to Democratic rallies 2 November 1912, *PWW*, vol. 25, pp. 465–6, 468–71, 503–4. On the way the results showed 'that there was little to the Progressive party save Roosevelt', see Mowry, *Roosevelt and the Progressive Movement*, pp. 281–3.

10 House diary, 16 October 1912, 16 November 1912, 19 December 1912, *PWW*, vol. 25, pp. 423–4, 550, 614; House diary, 8 January 1913, 13 February 1914, House to Wilson, 9 January 1913, *PWW*, vol. 27, pp. 20–24, 109–11, 26–7; Arthur S. Link, *Wilson: The New Freedom*, Princeton, NJ, 1956, pp. 4–23.

11 Wilson to Edith Gittings Reid, 15 August 1912, *PWW*, vol. 28, p. 161; Link, *The New Freedom*, pp. 70–77; Heckscher, *Woodrow Wilson*, pp. 277–83; Kendrick A. Clements, *Woodrow Wilson: World Statesman*, Boston, MA, 1987, pp. 92–3.

12 Wilson to A. Mitchell Palmer, 5 February 1913; inaugural address, 4 March 1913, *PWW*, vol. 27, pp. 98–101, 148–52; Daniel Stid, *The President as Statesman: Woodrow Wilson and the Constitution*, Lawrence, KS, 1998, especially pp. 177–8; Link, *The New Freedom*, pp. 145–7, 152–3.

13 Remarks Upon Signing the Federal Reserve Bill, 23 December 1913, *PWW*, vol. 29, p. 64.

14 Address to Joint Session of Congress, 23 June 1913, *PWW*, vol. 27, p. 573; campaign address in Buffalo, 2 September 1912, *PWW*, vol. 25, p. 69; address to Joint Session of Congress, 8 April 1913, *PWW*, vol. 27, pp. 269–72; Link, *The New Freedom*, pp. 152–7; Stid, *The President as Statesman*, pp. 90–102.

15 Remarks to New Jersey electors, 13 January 1913, *PWW*, vol. 27, p. 40; Link, *The New Freedom*, pp. 103–10, 158–75, quotations on pp. 105, 173.

16 Arthur S. Link, *Wilson: The Road to the White House*, Princeton, NJ, 1947, pp. 501–5; Daniels diary, 11 April 1912, *PWW*, vol. 27, pp. 290–91; Wilson to H.A. Bridgman, 8 September 1913, *PWW*, vol. 28, pp. 265–6; reports of meeting with National Independence Equal Rights League delegation, 12 November 1914, *PWW*, vol. 31, pp. 298–309; Link, *The New Freedom*, pp. 243–52. Perhaps the most notable nomination was that of the black Oklahoman Adam E. Patterson to head the office of the register of the Treasury; the nomination was withdrawn when some Southern senators threatened to obstruct the tariff and currency bills. Clements, *Woodrow Wilson*, p. 98.

17 Link, *The New Freedom*, pp. 177–97.

18 Wilson to Mary A. Hulbert, 22 June 1913, *PWW*, vol. 27, p. 556; Wilson to Mary A. Hulbert, 28 September 1913, *PWW*, vol. 28, pp. 336–7; remarks on signing the Federal Reserve Bill 23 December 1913, *PWW*, vol. 29, pp. 63–6; Link, *The New Freedom*, pp. 199–240, quotations on pp. 219, 216; Robert H. Wiebe, *Businessmen and Reform: A Study of the Progressive Movement*, Cambridge, MA, 1962, pp. 129–37.

19 Remarks on signing the Federal Reserve Bill, 23 December 1913; address to Joint Session of Congress, 20 January 1914, *PWW*, vol. 29, pp. 63–6, 153–8; Link, *The New Freedom*, pp. 423–44.

20 Link, *The New Freedom*, pp. 241–3, 254–7, 261–76, 423–7, 435–44 (quotation on p. 242); Clements, *Woodrow Wilson*, pp. 120–21; inaugural address, 4 March 1913, *PWW*, vol. 27, pp. 150–51.

21 Remarks on signing the Federal Reserve Bill, 23 December 1913, *PWW*, vol. 29, pp. 63–4; press conference, 3 November 1913; Wilson to Mary H. Hulbert, 21 September 1913, *PWW*, vol. 28, pp. 487, 311.

22 House diary, 28 September 1914, *PWW*, vol. 31, pp. 91–6; Stid, *The President as Statesman*, pp. 1, 94–5.

23 Ray Stannard Baker, *Woodrow Wilson: Life and Letters*, vol. 4, London, 1932, p. 55; John Milton Cooper, '"An Irony of Fate": Woodrow Wilson's Pre-World War I Diplomacy', *Diplomatic History*, 3:4 (Fall 1979): 426; *Constitutional Government in the United States* 24 March 1908, *PWW*, vol. 18, p. 120.

24 A Commencement Address, 5 June 1914, *PWW*, vol. 30, p. 146; memorandum, 'What Ought We To Do?' c. 1 August 1898, *PWW*, vol. 10, pp. 574–6; 'The Ideals of America', 26 December 1901, *PWW*, vol. 12, p. 226; Acceptance speech 7 August 1912, *PWW*, vol. 25, pp. 16–17; address in Philadelphia, 4 July 1914, *PWW*, vol. 30, pp. 251–2. The classic statement of the 'open-door' interpretation of US foreign policy is William Appleman Williams, *The Tragedy of American Diplomacy*, New York, 1962; for a critique, see J.A. Thompson, 'William Appleman Williams and the American "Empire"', *Journal of American Studies*, 7 (1973): 91–104.

25 Report of a speech on patriotism, 14 December 1899, *PWW*, vol. 11, p. 299; House diary, 14 February 1913, *PWW*, vol. 27, p. 113; Wilson to M.A. Hulbert, 21 September, 1913; remarks upon signing the Tariff Bill, 3 October 1913, *PWW*, vol. 28, pp. 311, 351–2; memorandum by W.E. Rappard, 1 November 1917, *PWW*, vol. 44, p. 485; Link, *The New Freedom*, pp. 67–8.

26 Link, *The New Freedom*, pp. 280–83, 97–107, 279.

27 Ibid., pp. 283–8, 320–24.

28 Address to Congress on Panama Canal Tolls, 5 March 1914; press conference, 26 March 1914, *PWW*, vol. 29, pp. 312–13, 378–80; Link, *The New Freedom*, pp. 304–14.

29 Roosevelt message to Congress, 6 December 1904, quoted in Julius W. Pratt, *America and World Leadership, 1900–1921*, London, 1967, pp. 28–9.

30 Link, *The New Freedom*, pp. 331–46, quotation on p. 335; Bryan to Wilson with enclosure, c. 20 July 1913, 16 August 1913; Wilson to Bryan, 18 August 1913, *PWW*, vol. 28, pp. 47–8, 175–7, 184–5; Wilson to Bryan, 20 March, 1914, *PWW*, vol. 29, p. 360; Arthur S. Link, *Wilson: The Struggle for Neutrality*, Princeton, NJ, 1960, pp. 495–550.

31 Link, *The New Freedom*, pp. 347–91; draft of a circular note to the Powers, 24 October 1913; Wilson to Bryan, with enclosure, 23 November 1913, *PWW*, vol. 28, pp. 431–3, 585–6; Sir C.A. Spring Rice to Sir E. Grey, 7 February 1914; S.G. Blythe, 'Mexico: The Record of a Conversation with President Wilson, 27 April 1914, *Saturday Evening Post*, 23 May 1914, *PWW*, vol. 29, pp. 229, 516–24.

32 Link, *The New Freedom*, pp. 392–416; address to Congress on the Mexican Crisis, 20 April 1914, *PWW*, vol. 29, pp. 471–4.

33 Link, *The Struggle for Neutrality*, pp. 232–66, 456–94, 629–44; Arthur S. Link, *Wilson: Confusions and Crises, 1915–1916*, Princeton, NJ, 1964, pp. 195–200; Jackson Day address in Indianapolis, 8 January 1915, *PWW*, vol. 32, pp. 38–9; Wilson telegram to R. Lansing, 8 August 1915, *PWW*, vol. 34, pp. 132–3; after-lunch talk to the Democratic National Committee, 8 December 1915, *PWW*, vol. 35, pp. 314–15.

34 Link, *Wilson: Confusions and Crises*, pp. 200–21, 280–314; Tumulty to Wilson, 15 March 1916; House diary, 17 March 1916, *PWW*, vol. 36, pp. 317, 335; Wilson to House, 22 June 1916; draft of an address to Congress, 26 June 1916, *PWW*, vol. 37, pp. 280–81, 298–304.

35 Link, *Wilson: Confusions and Crises*, pp. 314–18; Arthur S. Link, *Wilson: Campaigns for Progressivism and Peace, 1916–1917*, Princeton, NJ, 1965, pp. 51–5, 120–23, 328–39; remarks to New York Press Club, 30 June 1916, *PWW*, vol. 37, pp. 333–4.

36 Wilson to L.M. Garrison, 8 August 1914, *PWW*, vol. 30, p. 362. (Wilson's admiration of Burke evidently did not involve endorsing his passionately held views on this question.)

37 Not, as wrongly stated by Arthur Link and historians who have followed him, from 73 to 25. Link, *The New Freedom*, p. 468; Cooper, *The Warrior and the Priest*, p. 250.

38 House diary, 4 November 1914; Wilson to Nancy S. Toy, 9 November 1914, *PWW*, vol. 31, pp. 265, 290.

39 Wilson to W.G. McAdoo, 17 November 1914, *PWW*, vol. 31, pp. 324–7; US Bureau of the Census, *Historical Statistics of the United States*, Washington, DC, 1973, p. 224.

40 Jackson Day address in Indianapolis, 8 January 1915, *PWW*, vol. 32, pp. 29–41.

41 Link, *The New Freedom*, pp. 322–3.

42 Link, *Struggle for Neutrality*, pp. 86–91, 138, 143–61; Wilson to Nancy S. Toy, 31 January 1915, *PWW*, vol. 32, pp. 165–6; Link, *Confusions and Crises*, pp. 339–41.

43 Link, *Confusions and Crises*, pp. 323–7, 356–62, quotations on pp. 325, 356; Wilson to Senator C.A. Culberson, 5 May 1916, *PWW*, vol. 36, pp. 609–11; John A. Thompson, *Reformers and War: American Progressive Publicists and the First World War*, Cambridge, 1987, p. 38.

44 Link, *Confusions and Crises*, pp. 341–50; Wilson to Carter Glass, 12 May 1914, *PWW*, vol. 30, p. 24; remarks upon signing the Rural Credits Bill, 17 July 1916, *PWW*, vol. 37, p. 427; campaign address to farmers at Shadow Lawn, 21 October 1916, *PWW*, vol. 38, pp. 502.

45 Link, *Campaigns for Progressivism and Peace*, pp. 39–40, 56–60, 83–92, 94, quotations on pp. 40, 94.

46 Ibid., pp. 100–6, 124–30, quotations on pp. 103, 104, 106.

47 Ibid., pp. 160–64; Cooper, *The Warrior and the Priest*, pp. 255–7.

Chapter 5

Responding to the War in Europe, 1914–17

The initial stance

As the European crisis sparked by the assassination of Archduke Franz Ferdinand in Sarajevo escalated into full-scale war between the great powers, the President of the United States was sitting by the bedside of his dying wife. Ellen had been slow to recover from a fall she had in March 1914 and by June it was clear that she was seriously ill. In mid-July Bright's disease, a degeneration of the kidneys, was diagnosed. Her death on August 6th devastated Wilson, who had held out hope of her recovery almost to the end. He poured out his sorrow in a torrent of letters to friends and in talk with such confidants as House and Dr Grayson. As late as November, he told House he 'was not fit to be President because he could not think straight any longer, and had no heart in the things he was doing'.[1]

To present-day readers, the fact that a president of the United States was so possessed by anxiety and grief that he could hardly attend to public affairs might well seem a crucial factor in the run-up to a world war. An undistracted White House, it might be thought, would have made some positive and energetic move to avert the catastrophe building up in Europe. However, this was not really how things were in 1914. It is true that earlier that summer House had been in Europe seeking to ease tensions between England and Germany and to draw these countries, together with France and the United States, into a disarmament plan. In Berlin and London he had had conversations with, among others, the Kaiser and the British prime minister and Foreign Secretary. But he had been able to offer no more to the cause of European peace than the good offices of the United States and his own services as a mediator. Even the prospect of American participation in a disarmament agreement was of little significance to the European powers, since the country's army was tiny by international standards and the coal-fired battleships of its more formidable navy lacked the range to fight effectively far from their bases.

The reality was that America was not yet a player in the game of world politics. This was not because it lacked the capacity. It was in the 1880s that the United States overtook Great Britain as the world's leading producer of manufactured goods, and by 1913 its proportion of world manufacturing output was 32 percent, more than twice that of its nearest rival (Germany).[2] In the twentieth century, steel production was, in Churchill's words, 'a rather decisive index of conventional military power'.[3] In 1913 Germany produced more steel than Britain, Russia and France combined (which must help to explain its military performance in the following years) – but America's output was almost double Germany's. By this measure, the United States was already a superpower. In addition, the country's farms produced more than could be consumed by its population of a hundred million, and it was virtually self-sufficient in raw materials.

However, America's economic and financial might had not yet been deployed in sustained and substantial efforts to affect the course of events overseas. This is not to say that consciousness of the country's growing strength had not had any effect upon its foreign policy or the attitudes of Americans. As we have seen, the United States had come to assume a hegemonic role in the Caribbean and Central America since the 1890s. After acquiring the Philippines in 1898, it had also played some sort of role in Far Eastern diplomacy, contributing a small force to the international Punitive Expedition to Beijing in 1900–1, mediating an end to the Russo-Japanese war of 1904–5, and calling for the maintenance of an 'Open Door' in China for all foreign investors and traders and also for the preservation of China's integrity and independence. But the assertion of US interest in East Asia was neither as consistent nor as forceful as it was in the Caribbean and Central America, and it did not meet with the same acquiescence from other powers.

The main arena of great power politics at this time, however, was unquestionably Europe and here the United States remained firmly committed to its traditional stance of noninvolvement. Theodore Roosevelt as president had sent delegates to the Algeciras Conference that resolved the Franco-German dispute over Morocco in 1906, but he made it plain that they could undertake no commitment, and even this degree of involvement proved to be unique. It was not repeated in the second Moroccan crisis of 1911, and during the Balkan wars of 1912–13 Taft remarked that the United States was 'involved neither directly nor indirectly with the causes or questions incident to ... these hostilities' and 'maintained in regard to them an attitude of absolute neutrality and of complete political disinterestedness'.[4]

In taking this position, Taft was simply restating what had been an axiom of American foreign policy since the early years of the republic. In his Farewell Address, George Washington had instructed his countrymen that 'the great rule of conduct for us in regard to foreign nations is, in extending our commercial relations to have with them as little *political* connection as possible'. Washington's main argument was that because of its 'detached and distant situation', the United States had no need to 'entangle our peace and prosperity in the toils of European Ambition, Rivalship, Humor or Caprice'.[5] As Washington's phraseology indicated, the policy of noninvolvement had an ideological as well as a pragmatic basis. From the classical republican and English Country Whig traditions of political thought, Americans had inherited a belief that standing armies were a threat to domestic liberty as well as a burden on taxpayers; free societies should rely on a citizen militia for defense. This idea became incorporated into the broad distinction between the 'New World' and the 'Old' that was fundamental to the ideology of American nationalism as it developed after the Revolution. The whole business of power politics, including professional diplomacy and espionage as well as war, came to be associated with the European social order – the means by which an essentially feudal ruling class justified both its privileges and the whole oppressive apparatus of states and empires. When such oppression was challenged by peoples who seemed to be following the example of 1776, there was usually some feeling that the United States ought to render them assistance, but the policy of noninvolvement was upheld by the argument that this would endanger republican liberty at home. In the 1820s, as Latin America fought for independence and Greece rebelled against Turkish rule, John Quincy Adams eloquently defended America's position:

> She well knows that by enlisting under banners other than her own, were they even the banners of foreign independence, she would involve her-self beyond the power of extrication, in all the wars of interest and intrigue, of individual avarice, envy and ambition, which assume the colors and usurp the standards of freedom. The fundamental maxims of her policy would insensibly change from liberty to force.[6]

There were, however, countervailing factors. Indeed, what has been called the tendency to define America as 'a kind of non-Europe' can itself be seen as testimony to the importance of the transatlantic relationship.[7] In the most literal sense, the vast majority of Americans (and an even higher proportion of the electorate) were children of Europe since it was from that continent that they or their forebears had come. From its English colonial past the nation had derived not only its language but also its law and the basic character of its political institutions. Moreover, political independence did not bring with it cultural independence. Like Wilson, most educated Americans in the nineteenth century were brought up on the classics of English literature and were as likely to read contemporary English writers as American ones. Even to many who had never crossed the Atlantic, the landscape of 'the old country' occupied a significant place in their imaginations. And if by the early twentieth century, the culture and mores of the United States diverged from those of Britain rather more than they had a generation or two earlier, this was due not only to the development of a more self-confident national style but also to the rising influence of those Americans whose background was in other parts of Europe. Although the concept of 'Western civilization' had not yet become a standard phrase, the assumption that it existed and that the United States was part of it was taken for granted – as was the assumption that it represented the most advanced stage of human progress.

All these elements entered into the responses of Americans to the war of 1914. Since it had been widely believed that moral and material progress had made full-scale war between Western countries a thing of the past, many expressed a sense of shock when it broke out. 'If civilized Europe were holding back India, for example, it would be comprehensible', observed *Harper's Weekly*. 'But for Germans and French, with a whole complex and delicate civilization in common, to be using huge death engines to mow down men and cities is so unthinkable that we go about in a daze, hoping to awake from the most horrid of nightmares.'[8] Naturally enough, however, Americans were also inclined to congratulate themselves on their exemption from the conflict. 'We never appreciated as keenly as now the foresight exercised by our forefathers in migrating from Europe', one Midwestern newspaper remarked.[9] From this point of view, the war could easily be seen as an atavistic throwback, an indication that Europe had not, after all, yet become a properly modern society. 'There will be some accounts to be settled after peace is declared', the sociologist Franklin H. Giddings insisted. 'And the biggest one will be that which Enlightenment has against Medievalism.'[10]

While the war was widely seen as confirming the dichotomy between the 'old world' and the 'new', there were significant variations in the way in which the evils of the former were perceived. Giddings, who blamed the war on hereditary monarchs and emperors, clearly had in mind Central and Eastern Europe rather than republican France and parliamentary Britain. In 1914 the majority of Americans saw these countries as fighting a defensive battle against German aggression and felt sympathetic to their cause. Over the next two years, this clear-cut picture became blurred by a sense that the causes of the war were much more complex and that the Allies' objectives were not purely defensive or altruistic. But this more impartial perspective was also compatible with seeing the war as the product of a system of power politics that served the interests of a ruling class, though in this case with the emphasis more on imperialistic and trade rivalries (in which Britain and France were as implicated as any).

Despite this trend of opinion, there remained many passionate partisans of the Allied cause throughout the period of American neutrality. Academic and publicists (including Giddings) were prominent among them, as were lawyers and investment bankers, particularly those associated with the leading Wall Street firm, J.P. Morgan & Co. Although the attitudes of the latter have often been attributed to their role in financing Allied war purchases in the United States, sentiment in this case preceded interest and the willingness of the Morgan partners to underwrite the risky (and largely unsuccessful) Anglo-French Loan of 1915 demonstrated the extent to which they were moved by considerations other than profit. Close associations with Britain and a shared culture that made such upper-middle-class WASPs responsive to appeals for Americans to 'do their bit' in the fight for civilization were the proximate explanations for this sort of commitment, but it is difficult to escape the feeling that the emotional drive owed something to uneasiness about changes in the character of the United States itself.[11] On the eve of American intervention in 1917, Walter Hines Page, the magazine editor who had become US ambassador in London, wrote to his son that 'the most important end of the thing for us' was the effect 'on our own country', which he hoped would include making 'us less promiscuously hospitable to every kind of immigrant' and killing 'the Irish and German influence'.[12]

Certainly, reactions to the war in Europe had brought to Americans what one historian has called 'a belated realization of what it meant to be a nation of immigrants', as 'millions of American citizens sided with the countries from which they or their ancestors had come'.[13] The most striking example was the large and well-established German-American community, the great majority of whom supported the cause of the Fatherland unreservedly. The outbreak of war saw thousands of reservists ready to fight in the Kaiser's armies (though they were prevented from doing so by British control of the seas), millions of dollars were contributed for German war-bonds and war relief, and a major propaganda and lobbying campaign was mounted to influence American policy and public opinion. Other ethnic groups that tended to favor the Central Powers were Jewish-Americans (out of hostility to Tsarist Russia), Swedish-Americans (who had a historic hatred of Russia and friendship towards Germany) and, to a lesser extent, Irish-Americans (out of antagonism to Britain). Pro-Allied feeling was present among some ethnic groups, particularly those hostile to the Austro-Hungarian empire, but the most significant emotional tie on this side was that of many old-stock Americans with Britain – though some felt a sentimental attachment to France, the sister-republic and old ally in the Revolutionary War.

It was against this background that Wilson shaped the official response of the United States to the European war. There is no question that in deciding the difficult issues that arose and in setting the objectives of his policy he was always very conscious of American opinion. In talking to the Associated Press in April 1915, he explained that 'when I am almost overcome by perplexities, what I try to remember is what the people at home are thinking about. I try to put myself in the place of the man who does not know all the things that I know and ask myself what he would like the policy of this country to be.'[14] Although this might seem no more than a piece of democratic piety, it reflected Wilson's longstanding view about the essentially interpretative character of leadership. Equally important, it accorded with his personal political interest. As we have seen, Wilson needed to broaden the base of his support if he was to be reelected in 1916. He must have been very conscious that his personal standing would be much affected by the manner in which he conducted American foreign policy at this critical time. He needed to do so in a way that received broad approval from the American people. As he was later to explain to the British ambassador,

> no action could be taken or at least usefully taken unless it received the support of the great majority. It was not so much a question of what was the right thing to do from the abstract view-point as what was the possible thing to do from the point of view of the popular condition of mind.[15]

Although public opinion was strongly divided over many issues connected to the war, he must try to find a position that could command a consensus.

At the same time, he had to take account of the attitudes of the European belligerents, since policies that did not do so were likely to meet with frustration and become discredited. In other words, Wilson faced the problem that has confronted all his successors as the United States has come to play an active role in international affairs: how to establish a viable relationship between American opinion and the outside world. Those who make US foreign policy always have to seek a way of doing this since a policy that fails to respect the external realities will be unsuccessful while a policy that does not possess domestic support cannot, under the American system, long be sustained. But, given the nature both of public opinion in that largely self-contained and confident society and of the diverse and intractable world environment, it has been a supremely difficult task, and few have managed to accomplish it for long. Wilson's attempt to bridge the internal and external realities was also, of course, to fail in the end – substantially abroad and then comprehensively at home. But the origins and objects of his policy can best be understood in terms of this problem.

His first move was to affirm and emphasize the neutrality of the United States in the European conflict. That the nation would not join in the war was hardly a matter for decision. Not even the most extreme pro-Ally partisan publicly recommended such an abandonment of the hallowed tradition of noninvolvement when no national interest appeared to require it. But Wilson erected neutrality into more than a technical status. Five days after returning to Washington from Ellen's funeral in Georgia, he composed 'an appeal to the American people' in which he called on them to be 'impartial in thought as well as in action'. Only if America displayed 'the fine poise of undisturbed judgment, the dignity of self-control' would she be able properly to perform her 'duty as the one great nation at peace, the one people holding itself ready to play a part of impartial mediation and speak the counsels of peace and accommodation, not as a partisan, but as a friend'. However, Wilson made it clear that it was not only out of concern for America's international role that he sought to discourage his countrymen from taking sides in the European conflict. He also feared the domestic effects of the naturally divided sympathies of a people 'drawn from many nations, and chiefly from the nations now at war'.[16] On learning that cinema audiences were demonstrating when scenes of the war were being shown, he drafted a message to be displayed on the screen beforehand:

> It would be a patriotic act in the interest of the neutrality of the nation and the peace of mankind if the audience in this theatre would refrain during the showing of pictures connected with the present war from expressing either approval or disapproval.
>
> Woodrow Wilson.[17]

As such statements indicated, Wilson sought to override the divisive sentiments aroused by the war by appealing to a higher loyalty to America. He evidently felt that this made it all the more necessary that official policy should be clearly based upon the nation's own interests as a neutral in the conflict. Of course, the effect of America's actions upon the fortunes of the belligerents could hardly be excluded from the minds of Wilson and his advisors as they considered what to do in particular circumstances. With the exception of Bryan, whose passionate desire that the fighting should be brought to an end as soon as possible was uncontaminated by partiality for either side, Wilson's advisers were all pro-Ally in their sympathies, to various degrees and for somewhat different reasons. The most extreme in this regard was Walter Hines Page in London who felt that 'all that holds the world together is the friendship and kinship of our country and this'.[18] Page objected when he was instructed to press the British government to conduct their naval blockade of Germany in a way that respected the legal right of neutrals to trade in noncontraband goods. In reply, Wilson explained that

> more and more, from day to day, the elements (I mean the several racial elements) of our population seem to grow restless and catch more and more the fever of the contest. We are trying to keep all possible spaces cool, and the only means by which we can do so is to make it demonstrably clear that we are doing everything that it is possible to do to define and defend neutral rights.[19]

Yet Wilson himself sought to avoid pushing the dispute with Britain to the point of confrontation. Rather than despatching an official protest drafted in September 1914 by the Counselor of the State Department, Robert Lansing, the President and House sought an agreement through private negotiations in Washington and London. These were unsuccessful and the British further tightened their controls over the next six months until they amounted to a more or less complete embargo on both direct and indirect trade with Germany. As part of the enforcement measures, the Royal Navy mined a large part of the North Sea in November 1914 and announced that neutral ships could only traverse the area safely if they submitted to guidance by Admiralty pilots. The US government expressed no objection to this move, and the official notes that were sent in December 1914 and March 1915 refusing to accept the legality of the rules set out in successive Orders-in-Council were couched in a friendly manner and contained no threat of any retaliatory sanctions.

The failure to resist Allied violations of international law more strenuously has been seen by some, both at the time and since, as a departure from neutrality that paved the way to America's eventual involvement in the war. 'The Wilson administration permitted, and in some cases encouraged, systematic British violation of American neutral rights on a scale unprecedented at the height of the Napoleonic Wars', the historian John W. Coogan writes. The American response to the blockade 'was simple unneutrality'. Coogan attributes this to the President's own Anglophilia: 'William Wordsworth, Walter Bagehot, and the other paragons of liberal idealism who shaped Wilson's romantic view of English civilization in the final analysis deserve more credit for the success of the economic campaign than Grey, Churchill, or anyone else in the British government in 1914.'[20] It is true that in the early weeks of the war Wilson in private expressed sympathy with the Allies and fears about the consequences for the United States of a German victory – following one such conversation, the British ambassador assured London that 'I am sure we can at the right moment depend upon an understanding heart here.'[21] Yet Sir Cecil Spring Rice's confidence in this respect was shortlived, and there is little to suggest that a desire to help the Allies win the war played much part in shaping Wilson's conduct of American neutrality. 'If I permitted myself to be a partisan in this present struggle, I would be unworthy to represent you', he told the Associated Press in April 1915.[22] Moreover, Wilson's own feelings about the war evolved in a more neutral direction as the danger of a quick German victory faded and further consideration of the way the conflict had started tended to distribute the blame more widely.[23] In an off-the-record interview with a *New York Times* journalist in December 1914, he said that the best outcome would be 'a deadlock' that would demonstrate to all the belligerents 'the futility of employing force in the attempt to resolve their differences'.[24]

If, unlike Page, Wilson retained detachment from the Allies' cause, how are we to explain his effective acquiescence in their violations of the legal rights of American traders? Writers of the 'Realist' school have attributed it to a recognition that America's own security was served by British command of the seas.[25] But this consideration was never articulated by Wilson and there is no reason to believe that he dissented from the general assumption that the United States was quite capable of defending itself against any attack without assistance.[26] The historian E.R. May has given the credit for the fact that Anglo-American relations never came to a critical point to the British Foreign Secretary, Sir Edward Grey, and his concern 'to preserve the friendship of the United States at almost any cost'.[27] Against this, Coogan has pointed out that, for all his readiness to exchange highminded liberal sentiments with Ambassador Page and Colonel House, Grey was committed to the defeat of Germany and actually took the lead in measures to tighten the blockade.[28] Yet if Grey was undeflected by American representations, he did not disregard real American interests. The prosperity of the South depended upon the export of cotton, and Grey resisted strong French pressure to put this commodity on the contraband list. When he eventually conceded the point in August 1915, the British government simultaneously undertook to purchase sufficient cotton to maintain the price.

In this context, Wilson's response to the British blockade represented an almost inevitable response to the realities of the situation, of which he showed a shrewd appreciation in a letter to Bryan in March 1915. On the one hand, the American interests at stake were not substantial in material terms. The increase in exports to the Allies more than compensated for the decline in trade with the Central Powers, which was also being reduced by the action of Germany herself. On the other hand, the British were determined to tighten the blockade which was, indeed, the principal way in which they hoped to bring Germany to its knees: 'We are face to face with *something they are going to do*, and they are going to do it no matter what representations we make.'[29] Wilson had correctly appraised the mood in London – six months earlier, the First Lord of the Admiralty, Winston Churchill, had told Grey that there should be no concessions on the blockade 'until it is certain that persistence will actually and imminently bring the United States into the field against us'.[30] At this stage of the war, when the war trade was comparatively modest and not dependent on American credit, the commercial and financial sanctions that gave Wilson potential leverage over the British in 1916 were not available. War with them was, of course, inconceivable. It would have run counter not only to the American people's preponderantly pro-Ally sympathies but also to their much deeper and more universal desire to avoid involvement.

The primacy of this last concern was also reflected in Wilson's initial attitude to two other issues that the war raised for American policy – whether the nation should strengthen its own armed forces and the possibility of mediation. Ever conscious that the size of their budgets depended upon congressional and public opinion, senior officers in the army and navy departments sought to take advantage of the shock created by the outbreak of the war in Europe. They provided assistance to the authors of sensational magazine and newspaper articles that claimed that 'defenseless America' was as open to invasion as Belgium had been. After the Progressive party's débâcle in the 1914 elections, Theodore Roosevelt threw his weight behind a campaign that not only accorded with his life-long conviction that the nation should 'carry a big stick' but also offered a possible route for him back to the Republican party. Roosevelt's close friend, the patrician Republican Senator Henry Cabot Lodge and his son-in-law, Representative Augustus P. Gardner (also of Massachusetts), demanded a special congressional inquiry into the state of the nation's defenses. A high-profile lobby organization, the National Security League, was formed to rally public opinion behind the movement for 'preparedness'.

For Wilson to have backed this cause would have involved him in an uphill battle in Congress where the great majority of Democrats were against large expenditures on the navy and army. Also, as he pointed out to House when the latter urged the establishment of 'a reserve army', 'the labor people would object'. In any case, the President was unpersuaded of the need, arguing to House that 'no matter how the great war ended, there would be complete exhaustion, and, even if Germany won, she would not be in a condition to seriously menace our country for many years to come'.[31] In his annual message to Congress in December, Wilson declared that there was no 'reason to fear that from any quarter our independence or the integrity of our territory is threatened'. For America to abandon her 'ancient principles of action' by building up a standing, or even a reserve, army at this time

> would mean merely that we had been thrown off our balance by a war with which we have nothing to do, whose causes cannot touch us, whose very existence affords us opportunities of friendship and disinterested service which should make us ashamed of any thought of hostility or fearful preparation for trouble.[32]

As we have seen, Wilson had likewise invoked America's special responsibility to help restore peace to Europe in his call for a strict neutrality. At the very beginning of the war he formally offered his services as a mediator to all the belligerent powers, and in the following weeks Bryan energetically tried to get both sides to state their peace terms. Soon after these well-publicized efforts came to nothing, Bryan left Washington to make speeches for Democratic candidates in the forthcoming elections, and Wilson took advantage of his absence to transfer management of the business to House, who was not only utterly discreet but also much more conscious than Bryan of the geopolitical aspects of the war. Believing that a limited Allied victory that did not leave Russia in a dominant position would be the best basis for a lasting peace, House was inclined to act in cooperation with the British. In early 1915 he went to Europe on a confidential mission to pursue the possibility of mediation. But he made it clear to those he talked with that Wilson and he desired only to bring the belligerents together, not to suggest terms of peace. When Grey said to him that if the United States were prepared to take an active part in 'the making of a programme of forcible security for the future – in that event England might consent to end the war in a drawn contest and trust to the subsequent discussion and world-wide agreement to secure safety for the future', House emphatically repudiated the suggestion: it would be contrary to 'not only the unwritten law of our country but also our fixed policy not to become involved in European affairs'.[33]

After six months of war, then, it seemed that the traditional pattern of America's relations with Europe had been disturbed neither by the great increase in US power since the early nineteenth century nor by the unprecedented scale and character of the conflict. Indeed, the most salient recent development appeared to be the increased awareness of the implications of America's ethnic heterogeneity, and the net effect of this had been to provide a further justification for the long-hallowed policy of noninvolvement. As Wilson reportedly said to the German ambassador, 'We definitely have to be neutral, since otherwise our mixed populations would wage war on each other.'[34]

The impact of the U-boat

Notwithstanding this affirmation, and the concern that gave rise to it, less than three years later Wilson was asking Congress to declare war on Germany. In the intervening period, he had not only twice gone to the brink of war but had also broken with the tradition of noninvolvement by committing the United States to participation in a postwar league of nations. As some historians have recognized, the years 1915–16 witnessed something like 'a revolution' in American foreign policy.[35] How are we to account for it?

The proximate cause was unquestionably the German use of submarines against merchant vessels. It was this that raised the serious possibility of American entry into the war, and it was in the context of that possibility that Wilson came to accept commitments to the future maintenance of peace that he had previously shunned. At first glance, it is not easy to understand why the U-boat campaign against Allied commercial shipping provoked such a response on the part of the United States. No one at the time saw it as endangering America's security, or even as something that would enable Germany to achieve victory in the war. More at risk, it might seem, was America's prosperity as this came to depend increasingly upon exports to the Allies, which increased almost fourfold during the period of neutrality. But, in reality, this trade did not need the protection of the US government. Because it had become so important to their war effort, the Allies would have been bound in any case to continue to purchase American munitions and other supplies and to attempt to transport them safely across the Atlantic (as, of course, the British did in the face of much more formidable U-boats in 1939–41). It is true that American shipowners might well have decided the business was not worth the risk but, as the US oceangoing marine was very small, this would have made little practical difference.

More to the point, perhaps, was that the torpedoing of merchant ships by submarines, especially without warning, was clearly illegal. Under established international law, a warship imposing a blockade had to observe the rules of 'visit and search' when stopping either belligerent or neutral vessels; enemy merchantmen could be captured but could only be fought and sunk if they put up resistance. The US government emphatically insisted that

> American citizens act within their indisputable rights in taking their ships and in traveling wherever their legitimate business calls them upon the high seas, and exercise those rights in what should be the well justified confidence that their lives will not be endangered by acts done in clear violation of universally acknowledged international obligations.[36]

As we have seen, upholding the rights of Americans under international law was something Wilson seems to have seen as an essential aspect of a truly neutral policy. That had been the basis on which he and Bryan had firmly resisted moves in Congress, responding to a vociferous campaign spearheaded by German-Americans, for an embargo on the sale of arms. It had also been what had led him to compel the reluctant Ambassador Page to deliver protests against the illegalities of the British blockade. But, in those negotiations, the US government, while reserving its position and seeking redress in particular cases, had not threatened to break relations when the Allies failed to bring their practices into line with its demands. Why did it resist German violations of American rights so much more strongly?

The answer commonly given to this question is that much more was at stake. 'Debating the legality to destroy life and the legality to destroy property are very different things', Lansing observed.[37] In a note to Germany, Wilson declared that 'the Government of the United States is contending for something much greater than mere rights of property or privileges of commerce. It is contending for nothing less high and sacred than the rights of humanity.'[38] But, as critics of the administration's policy pointed out, the only reason why the Allied blockade did not endanger life was that neutrals adjusted their behavior to it. British mines were potentially as lethal as a U-boat's torpedoes. If Americans did not risk their lives sailing in the North Sea outside the authorized lanes, why should they do so in the English Channel and that part of the western Atlantic that the German government declared to be a 'zone of war'? It might well seem that the policy equivalent of the administration's effective acquiescence in the illegalities of the Allied blockade would be an official warning to American citizens against traveling in the war-zone on a ship of a belligerent country. The inclusion of this measure in the Neutrality Laws of the 1930s reflected a retrospective judgment that such a concession of American rights was a small price to pay to avoid involvement in a major foreign war.

However, Wilson firmly resisted this course of action even though it was passionately advocated by Bryan within the cabinet and later attracted much support in Congress. Why he did so is, like many problems of historical explanation, better understood through a narrative than through abstract analysis. When the Germans first announced their U-boat campaign in February 1915, it was not regarded as a very serious threat by either the British or the Americans; the sinking of commercial vessels without warning seemed unthinkable and, in any case, the German navy's few oceangoing submarines could reach the Atlantic sea-lanes only by means of a painfully slow journey around the north of Scotland. In a note which was regarded in Washington as parallel to one to the British protesting against their use of neutral flags as a *ruse de guerre*, the United States declared that it would hold the German government to 'a strict accountability' for its navy's acts and that it would take all necessary steps 'to safeguard American lives and property and to secure to American citizens the full enjoyment of their acknowledged rights on the high seas'. This wording did not make it entirely clear whether the US government had in mind only the safety of American ships or also that of Americans taking passage on belligerent ships. In their reply, the German government both strenuously justified the U-boat campaign as a reprisal for the Allied 'food blockade' and stressed that it was directed only against enemy vessels (though American ships might be endangered by the British use of neutral flags).[39]

The US government was forced to confront the ambiguity of its position in late March when a small British liner, the *Falaba*, was sunk *en route* to West Africa and an American engineer, Leon Thrasher, was among those who lost their lives. The case set off a fierce debate within the administration. Lansing drafted a note demanding that the German government disavow the act, punish the U-boat commander, and make reparation for Thrasher's death. On the other side, Bryan argued that an American citizen pursuing his business interests in a risky situation should not expect his country to protect him. Wilson was at first inclined to send a note condemning the use of submarines against merchant vessels as inherently inhumane but was apparently impressed by Bryan's insistence that the American people would 'be slow to admit the right of a citizen to involve his country in war when by exercising ordinary care he could have avoided danger'. A month after the sinking, Wilson observed that 'perhaps it is not necessary to make formal representations in the matter at all'.[40] Arthur Link has concluded that 'at this juncture the possibilities of an American adjustment to the submarine war were by no means remote'.[41]

Less than two weeks later, on 7 May 1915, the premier British liner, the *Lusitania*, was sunk by a U-boat with the loss of 1,200 lives, including 128 Americans. It requires an effort of historical imagination, after the horrors of the twentieth century, to understand how appalling this event seemed. The American public experienced a sense of shock comparable to that which followed the assassination of President Kennedy in 1963. According to the journalist and historian Mark Sullivan, people years after could 'remember the surroundings in which they read it, the emotions they had, their actions the rest of the day'.[42] It was, after all, little more than three years since the sinking of the *Titanic*, but this time the disaster was the result of a deliberate human act – 'murder on the high seas' was a common description.[43] The denunciations of German barbarism by editorialists and commentators, particularly in the east, were no doubt heightened by the pre-existing pro-Ally sentiments of many of them. The underlying feeling of such people that the United States ought really to be in the war found expression in demands for a strong American response to the *Lusitania* sinking. 'It is inconceivable that we can refrain from taking action in this matter', Theodore Roosevelt declared, 'for we owe it not only to humanity but to our own self-respect.'[44]

For Wilson, this public crisis coincided with an emotional period in his personal life. Three days before the *Lusitania* had been torpedoed, he had proposed to Edith Bolling Galt, a handsome widow in her early forties whom he had met in March through his cousin, Helen Bones, who had herself been his companion in the White House since Ellen's death. Although Mrs Galt quietly rebuffed what she saw as the President's precipitate proposal, her response was warm enough to encourage him. In the next few days, he deluged her with a series of letters in which Shakespearean sonnets were mingled with passionate declarations of his love and need. On the Friday on which news of the *Lusitania* sinking came in, Wilson evidently found the tension unbearable. Before the secret service men knew what he was doing, he walked out of the main door of the White House and, disregarding a light rain, paced the streets, as he wrote to Edith, 'to get my mind and purpose in hand'. Over the following weekend, he ostentatiously followed his usual routine in public, but he also wrote four more notes to Edith urgently pressing his suit, and on Monday morning she came to the White House before he set off for Philadelphia where he was to give an address to newly naturalized citizens. At seven o'clock the following morning he was writing to Edith again:

> I do not know just what I said at Philadelphia (as I rode along the street in the dusk I found myself a little confused as to whether I was in Philadelphia or New York!) because my heart was in such a whirl from that wonderful interview of yesterday and the poignant appeal and sweetness of the little note you left with me.[45]

Among the things that Wilson, speaking as usual without a text, had said in Philadelphia was that

> The example of America must be a special example. The example of America must be the example, not merely of peace because it will not fight, but of peace because peace is the healing and elevating influence of the world, and strife is not. There is such a thing as a man being too proud to fight. There is such a thing as a nation being so right that it does not need to convince others by force that it is right.[46]

The sentiments were very Wilsonian, echoing his mother's injunction to him as an undergraduate not to lower himself by engaging in fisticuffs with Northern boys, and stressing the values of dignity and self-control. But at the time the remarks naturally aroused great anger in Allied countries and fierce criticism in America from people who saw them as signaling a weak response to the *Lusitania* sinking. To the press the following day, Wilson insisted that this was not so: 'I was expressing a personal attitude that was all. I did not really have in mind any specific thing. I did not regard that as a proper occasion to give any intimation of policy on any special matter.'[47]

It was during these fraught days that Wilson decided how to respond to the situation, and in so doing defined US policy on the U-boat issue. He discussed the matter with no advisers or members of Congress, though he did receive a few written communications. In a cable from London, House stressed that failure to take a strong stand, backed if necessary by entry into the war, would diminish America's future influence over the peace: 'We are being weighed in the balance, and our position amongst the nations is being assessed by mankind.'[48] From the State Department came two short notes from Bryan and some hawkish memoranda from Lansing. On the morning of Tuesday, 11 May, Wilson read to the cabinet the draft he had himself written of a note to Germany. In it, he reverted to the line he had thought of taking over the *Falaba* – that it was a 'practical impossibility' to employ submarines against commerce 'without an inevitable violation of many sacred principles of justice and humanity'. Professing confidence that the German government accepted 'the rule that the lives of noncombatants, whether they be of neutral citizenship or citizens of one of the nations at war, cannot lawfully or rightfully be put in jeopardy by the capture or destruction of an unarmed merchantman', the note demanded that it disavow the acts complained of, 'make reparation so far as reparation is possible for injuries that are without measure', and take immediate steps to prevent any recurrence.[49]

The demands could scarcely have been more uncompromising, but the note was studiously vague about what would follow if the German government failed to comply with them. When the possibility of a break in diplomatic relations was raised during the cabinet discussion, the President stressed that this need not lead to war (which Lansing had assured him). Nevertheless, Bryan remained deeply troubled and, in response to his pleas, Wilson drafted an off-the-record statement for the press, affirming the administration's confidence that the issue would be settled peacefully, possibly by arbitration. But when Tumulty learnt about this proposed 'tip' to reporters, he was appalled, and persuaded the President not to issue it on the grounds that it would undermine the effect of his strong note both in Berlin and with American public opinion.[50] Disappointed, Bryan pressed his previous recommendation that Americans be officially warned against traveling on belligerent vessels, arguing that this would be in line with the usual practice of advising them to leave foreign countries in which there was disorder: 'The bystander is always in danger when there is shooting upon the street and no government would feel justified in refusing to warn noncombatants away from the dangerous place, merely because the citizens ordinarily have the right to go upon the streets.'[51] After initially favoring the latter suggestion, Wilson decided that either of these moves would reduce the force of his note to Germany. When the German reply sought to justify the *Lusitania* sinking on the grounds that the ship was armed and carrying troops and ammunition (only the last was true), Wilson drafted a second note reiterating the demands of the first. Rather than sign this note, Bryan resigned as Secretary of State.

Shortly before Bryan's resignation, Wilson had written to him that 'I wish with all my heart that I saw a way to carry out the double wish of our people, to maintain a firm front in respect of what we demand of Germany and yet do nothing that might by any possibility involve us in the war.'[52] The difference between the two men was that whereas Bryan was unequivocal that the latter objective should have clear priority, Wilson had in effect subordinated it to the first. The course he had chosen to follow over the *Lusitania* had made American entry into the war a real possibility as it had not been before. Why had he taken this momentous step? There are some indications that American credibility abroad weighed with him. He read House's cable to the cabinet and made the point to Bryan that 'everything that affects the opinion of the world regarding us affects our influence for good'.[53] But it seems that domestic opinion was his chief concern. The reaction to the sinking of the *Lusitania* (and to his own remarks in Philadelphia) appeared to indicate that the American public would be satisfied with nothing less than a strong response. And the almost unanimous praise with which the first *Lusitania* note was greeted in the United States showed that Wilson had interpreted the sentiment of his fellow-countrymen accurately. 'American public opinion has coalesced about this note and the extremists on both sides have been silenced', the intellectual weekly, the *New Republic* observed.[54] Wilson had skilfully positioned himself on the middle ground, between the belligerency of Theodore Roosevelt and the pacifism of Bryan.

But in responding so sensitively to the internal realities, Wilson had taken a chance with the external ones. As Bryan warned, the position the President had adopted was a precarious one because it depended upon Germany's acceding to his demands.[55] If Germany were defiant and the dispute escalated, it would be much more difficult for Wilson to avoid going to war now that he had put the nation's prestige (and his own) on the line. In the last analysis, Wilson's course over the *Lusitania* rested on a confidence that he could force Germany to back down. Several elements may have contributed to this confidence – a genuine belief that the Germans, too, would have been shocked by the *Lusitania* sinking, an assumption that the U-boat campaign was more in the nature of a gesture than a serious weapon of war, a sense of American power and of the recognition of this in Berlin, and possibly even the subconscious influence of his euphoric state of mind that summer (and particularly that weekend). In any case, Wilson clearly hoped he would be able to fulfill 'the double wish of our people'. Writing to a supportive friend in late July, he echoed the terms of his earlier letter to Bryan but with a significant addition: 'The opinion of the country seems to demand two inconsistent things, firmness and the avoidance of war, but I am hoping that perhaps they are not in necessary contradiction and that firmness may bring peace.'[56]

Wilson attempted to persuade Berlin to back down through a series of private as well as public communications. In talks with the German ambassador in Washington, Count Johann von Bernstorff, he held out the prospect that, once this dispute was settled, the United States would turn its attention to the Allied blockade and possibly impose an arms embargo; moreover, he himself, as head of the leading neutral nation would make an effort to bring the war to an end on terms reasonably favorable to Germany. But he also warned that a break in diplomatic relations would lead to increased American material and financial aid to the Allies. This pressure had some effect. Notwithstanding its self-justifying public stance, the German government secretly issued new orders to the U-boat commanders stressing the importance of not attacking neutral ships or large liners of any nationality.

This step away from the brink was followed by one from Wilson. In the third *Lusitania* note of 21 July he modified the position he had taken in the first that the use of submarines against merchant shipping inevitably involved violations of both international law and basic principles of humanity. By observing that 'the events of the past two months' had shown that such a campaign could be conducted 'in substantial accord with the accepted practices of regulated warfare', he both reduced and somewhat blurred what he was demanding of Germany.[57] A week later, Bernstorff suggested to Berlin that it make no formal reply to this note but resolve the matter through private negotiations. 'Mr Wilson was carried away by his emotions about the sinking of the *Lusitania*', he explained. 'Stimulated by this emotion, he has taken such an inflexible position that he cannot retreat without making himself impossible in the eyes of public opinion here.' But Bernstorff stressed that neither the President nor 'the overwhelming majority of the American people' wanted 'to wage war against us or to become a partisan of England. About this matter one should not be fooled by the eastern press in the United States'.[58]

By this time, there were, indeed, many indications that the passing fury over the *Lusitania* had not altered the basic desire of the great majority of Americans not to become involved in the war. As 'a sample of, I might almost say, all the letters I am receiving nowadays', Wilson sent on to House one from a Democratic Congressman stressing that 'the mass of the people want peace' and questioning whether 'the metropolitan press' spoke for the country. Although in reply House argued that 'the press of the country generally voices the views of the people better than individuals who write largely for the purpose of influencing your action', Wilson was evidently not persuaded by this.[59] To both Edith and House, he was emphatic that

> the two things that are clear to me are that the people of this country rely upon me to keep them out of war and that the worst thing that could possibly happen to the world would be for the United States to be drawn actively into this contest – to become one of the belligerents and lose all chance of moderating the results of the war by her counsel as an outsider.[60]

Wilson wrote this as he was faced by a new crisis caused by the sinking of another large British liner, the *Arabic*, on 19 August with the loss of

44 lives, including two Americans. She had been outward bound from Liverpool so, as Wilson pointed out to Edith, there could in this case be 'no plea of destroying arms and ammunition that were intended to be used against sacred German lives'. Although House was a little shocked by the President's evident reluctance to face the prospect of war, Wilson knew that he could not ignore this 'brutal defiance of the opinion and power of the United States'. Warned by House that further notes would be regarded with 'derision' abroad, the President proceeded by combining off-the-record press briefings that relations would be broken with private negotiations between Lansing (now Secretary of State) and Bernstorff. In the event, he found himself pushing at an open door. With the army Chief of Staff, General von Falkenhayn, emphatic that the moral and financial effect of an American entry into the war outweighed the gains of the submarine campaign, the Chancellor, Bethmann Hollweg was able to get the Kaiser to overrule the navy. The US government was assured that the U-boats had been ordered not to sink any liners without providing for the safety of their passengers, a 'pledge' that Bernstorff, at Lansing's insistence, made public. Accepting defeat, at least for the time being, the German Admiralty responded to this restriction by secretly calling off all submarine operations in the Atlantic and the English Channel. Although unaware of this move, Wilson seems to have become confident that Germany would yield to his demands. Brushing aside pleas that the U-boat commander had thought the *Arabic* was about to ram him, he and Lansing again threatened a break in relations in order to secure a public disavowal of the sinking and the promise of an indemnity.[61]

This conclusion left Wilson apparently triumphant. With Germany's public abandonment and repudiation of the use of submarines against passenger ships, his handling of the crisis that began with the *Lusitania* sinking was lauded in the American press. 'Without mobilizing a regiment or assembling a fleet', boasted one New York paper, 'by sheer dogged, unswerving persistence in advocating the right, he has compelled the surrender of the proudest, the most arrogant, the best armed of nations, and he has done it in completest self-abnegation, but in fullest, most patriotic devotion to American ideals.'[62] But Wilson was well aware how fragile the triumph was. At the time of the *Arabic* sinking, he had confessed to Edith that he felt 'special anxiety' as 'the shadow of war' lay across the page he was writing – though he had hastened to assure her that a break in diplomatic relations need not '*necessarily*' have this outcome.[63] The danger of a conflict that the great majority of Americans did not want had been averted only by the actions of the German government. By securing 'peace with honor' he had placed himself in a strong position for his reelection campaign, but he never lost sight of the fact that Berlin could at any time force him to choose between these values – and he recognized that either choice would divide the American people and lose him support.

Consciousness of this danger was the dominating background of Wilson's policy for the rest of the period of neutrality. It impelled him to take steps that moved the United States significantly nearer to a full and active participation in international politics. In the first place, he reversed his position over 'preparedness'. The timing here makes it clear that this was a direct consequence of the submarine dispute. Although the President did not publicly make the case for increases in the size of America's armed forces until November 1915, he had indicated an abrupt change of mind on this issue within two weeks of the *Lusitania* sinking, and in July he requested the Secretaries of War and the Navy to draw up detailed programs to be presented to Congress. The crisis had given a great boost to the public campaign for preparedness, with East Coast businessmen as well as college students eagerly enrolling for reserve officer training in summer camps at Plattsburg, New York, and elsewhere. But Wilson's conversion to the cause shocked many in his own party. No one was more distressed than Bryan, who since his resignation had been campaigning for measures to keep America out of the war. If these were adopted, he maintained, there would be no danger: 'this nation does not need burglars' tools unless it intends to make burglary its business'. Faced with determined opposition to his program in Congress, Wilson took his case to the country in a series of speeches in early 1916.[64]

In this effort to rally public support, Wilson indicated fairly clearly the reasons for his change of position and also foreshadowed some of the ways in which he would later justify greater departures from traditional policies. Attempting to answer his critics' question 'preparedness for what?' he emphatically repudiated any ambition to pursue a course of national aggrandizement: 'There is not a foot of territory belonging to any other nation which this nation covets or desires.'[65] He also reiterated his commitment to neutrality, arguing that this was not based on a selfish desire to keep out of trouble but on the conviction that it was how the United States could best serve the world. But whereas 'a year ago, it did seem as if America might rest secure without very great anxiety and take it for granted that she would not be drawn into this terrible maelstrom ... now no man can confidently say whether the United States will be drawn into the struggle or not'.[66] This, Wilson repeatedly stressed, was because of 'the double obligation you have laid upon me' – of which he was 'constantly reminded ... by means of every voice that comes to me out of the body of the nation' – 'to keep us out of this war' and 'to keep the honor of the nation unstained'. 'Do you not see', he pleaded, 'that a time may come when it is impossible to do both of these things?'[67] The actions of other countries might make it necessary to defend the Monroe Doctrine or 'to use the force of the United States to vindicate the right of American citizens everywhere to enjoy the protection of international law'. Specifically, these were the rights to travel and to trade across the world, but Wilson linked these mundane privileges to more elevated and universal principles and to America's historic mission – 'that flag stands for the rights of mankind, no matter where they be', it was the nation's 'spiritual interests' rather than 'her material interests' that were at stake. Above all, he stressed the importance of America's 'self-respect' and 'honor': 'the real man believes that his honor is dearer than his life; and a nation is merely all of us put together'. If what he was proposing was 'not done, and thoroughly done, and done very soon, it may turn out that you have laid upon me an impossible task, and that I should have to suffer the mortification and you the disappointment of having the combination of peace with honor prove to be impossible'.[68]

Wilson's tour, which attracted large audiences, was generally judged a success.[69] On his return to Washington, he supplemented his strengthened position with a readiness to compromise with congressional critics. He dropped the controversial proposal for a reserve 'Continental Army' of 400,000 men, even though doing so led to the resignation of the Secretary of War, Lindley M. Garrison. (As successor, Wilson chose Newton D. Baker, an able lawyer who had gained a nationwide reputation as a progressive Mayor of Cleveland, Ohio.) Following this concession, a bill passed both houses that substantially increased the regular army and also provided for a greatly enlarged National Guard under more effective federal control. Even more impressive was the Navy Act of 1916 which authorized a building program (sixteen capital ships over three years) larger than any ever previously undertaken by any nation.

Such measures made the United States more evidently a military power, but this did not ensure that Wilson would be able to fulfill 'the double obligation'. As he warned an audience in St Louis, 'one reckless commander of a submarine, choosing to put his private interpretation upon what his government wishes him to do, might set the world on fire'.[70] Such dangers would remain as long as the war continued. The second major effect of the crisis of 1915 on US policy was that it added urgency and force to Wilson's efforts to bring the war to an end. In the attempt to achieve this goal, he departed from the tradition of nonentanglement in a very dramatic way – by committing the United States to participation in a postwar league of nations.

The connection between the goal and the commitment was originally made in London. As early as the winter of 1914–15 Grey had more than once suggested that, if the United States were prepared to help guarantee the settlement, Britain would be more ready to accept a peace that did not involve crushing German power. As we have seen, House had at that time rebuffed the suggestion, but in their continuing correspondence Grey referred to the idea of a league of nations as 'the pearl of great price, if it can be found'.[71] When in September 1915 House suggested that the President might now call for a peace 'upon the broad basis of the elimination of militarism and navalism and a return, as nearly as possible to the status quo', Grey replied by asking directly: 'How much are the United States prepared to do in this direction? Would the President propose that there should be a League of Nations binding themselves to side against any Power which ... refused, in case of dispute, to adopt some other method of settlement than that of war?'[72]

Grey's letter seems to have been designed to fend off an American peace move, but it prompted a very different response to that of his previous inquiries along the same lines. This was clearly because the submarine dispute had in the meantime raised the possibility of American involvement in the war. To House himself the prospect was not unwelcome, but he wanted the United States to fight for a better world order rather than simply in defense of technical neutral rights. He therefore concocted an elaborate plan whereby Wilson would call for peace when the Allies thought the moment was opportune and then force Germany, if necessary by war, to accept reasonable terms. When he sketched this idea to Grey, the latter again inquired what the United States would do to guarantee the subsequent settlement. Although conscious that it meant 'a reversal of the foreign policy of this Government', House urged Wilson to reply positively: 'It seems to me that we must throw the influence of this nation in behalf of a plan by which international obligations must be kept, and in behalf of some plan by which the peace of the world may be maintained. We should do this not only for the sake of civilization, but for our own welfare, for who may say when we may be involved in such a holocaust as is now devastating Europe ... This is the part I think you are destined to play in this world tragedy, and it is the noblest part that has ever come to a son of man.'

Wilson laconically approved House's draft message to Grey. There seems no doubt that this was because House had persuaded him that his scheme stood a good chance of bringing the war to an end in the near future. When in early 1916 House went to Europe to promote his plan, he continued to encourage the President's hopes even though none of the conversations he had in London, Paris, and Berlin gave real grounds for believing that any of the belligerent governments were prepared to meet their enemies half way. Grey did allow himself to initial a memorandum embodying House's plan but mostly, it seems, because House pressed so hard. The Allies did not want peace at this time, and the only element in the plan that was attractive to them – the prospect of American entry into the war on their side – lacked credibility in the light of reports from Washington on the strength of anti-interventionist sentiment in the United States. Such skepticism could only have been deepened when Wilson qualified this commitment by inserting the word, 'probably' into the text of the memorandum at this point before approving it.[73]

This amendment indicated a significant difference between Wilson's point of view and that of House. Whereas House saw himself as paving the way for a full and imminent American involvement in European affairs, Wilson sought both to postpone and to limit the commitment. He made this clear in the (rather disregarded) guidelines he wrote for House's mission: 'We have nothing to do with local settlements – territorial questions, indemnities, and the like – but are concerned only in the future peace of the world and the guarantees to be given for that.' Like later presidents, Wilson was seeking to translate the great power of the United States into diplomatic influence without actually deploying it. Grey's urging had led him to believe that the Allies would value an American guarantee of the peace very highly, and from the detached perspective of Washington it must have seemed that they would rationally prefer this alternative to the hazardous and expensive project of fighting on for a total victory. And, once one side had agreed to a peace that established a league of nations, 'it will clearly be our duty to use our utmost moral force to oblige the other to parley, and I do not see how they could stand in the opinion of the world if they refused'.[74]

Wilson's desire to bring an early end to the war was spurred on by House's reports that, with new and more powerful U-boats coming into service, the pressure in Germany for an unrestricted submarine campaign was likely to become irresistible. Ironically, however, the importance he attached to House's project caused him to abandon an attempt to defuse the submarine controversy. The Allies had begun providing their merchant vessels and liners with a gun for self-defense. In these circumstances, it seemed unreasonable to demand that the frail U-boats of those days expose themselves before attacking such ships. With Wilson's approval, Lansing proposed to the Entente governments a *modus vivendi* whereby the Allies would disarm their merchantmen and the Germans would undertake to abide by the law of visit and search – suggesting that otherwise the United States might treat armed merchantmen as auxiliary cruisers and deny them clearance from its ports. It seemed to the British government that such an agreement would simply serve to facilitate the German campaign and they responded indignantly. When House made it clear from London that the success of his mission was at stake, Wilson instructed Lansing to state that the United States would not press the proposal or deny clearance to defensively armed merchant ships.

Unfortunately, the terms of the proposed *modus vivendi* had by this time become known to both to the German government and the American public. The former had taken the opportunity to announce that their submarines would in future treat armed merchantmen as warships, and hence fair game for attacks without warning. In Congress, support quickly grew for a resolution introduced by a Democratic Representative, McLemore of Texas, warning American citizens not to travel on such ships. When the chairman of the Senate Foreign Relations Committee, William J. Stone of Missouri, wrote to Wilson that he would find it difficult 'to consent to plunge this nation into the vortex of this world war' because of the 'foolhardiness' of 'our own people recklessly risking their lives on armed belligerent ships', the President's response struck the same note as his preparedness speeches earlier in the month:

> For my own part, I cannot consent to any abridgement of the rights of American citizens in any respect. The honor and self-respect of the nation is involved. We covet peace, and shall preserve it at any cost but the loss of honor … What we are contending for in this matter is of the very essence of the things that have made America a sovereign nation. She cannot yield them without conceding her own impotency as a nation and making virtual surrender of her independent position among the nations of the world.[75]

The extravagance of this language is striking, particularly about rights that twenty years later the great majority of Americans showed themselves quite prepared to sacrifice for the sake of peace through the neutrality legislation of 1935–37. It reflected Wilson's determination to defeat what he saw as a challenge to his own control of foreign policy. The letter's most hyperbolic sentences had been supplied by Tumulty who told Wilson that the congressional revolt, which Bryan had played an active role in promoting, was an attempt to discredit his leadership. But the only reason that presidential prerogatives were at stake was because Wilson had alarmed the Democratic leaders in private conferences by his apparent readiness to risk war for what they saw as insubstantial reasons. Why had he been so unyielding? Domestic politics may provide part of the explanation. A recent speech by Senator Elihu Root, a former Secretary of

State, had attacked Wilson for being 'brave in words and irresolute in action' – and this was presumably the line Republicans were planning to take in the forthcoming election.[76] But Wilson's chief concern seems to have been with what would later be called 'credibility' on the diplomatic front. On the one hand, he was seeking to induce the Allies to agree to an early peace by offering an American guarantee of their future security. House was constantly pointing out that the valuation of this offer would depend upon how willing the United States seemed to be to fight for its own rights. On the other hand, Wilson was hoping to avoid war by deterring Germany from the kind of conduct that would leave him no other option. Any sign of weakness, he insisted to Stone, would be fatal: 'Once accept a single abatement of right and many other humiliations would certainly follow.'[77] Like Franklin Roosevelt in 1939–41, Wilson argued that the less isolationist course was actually the best way to keep the United States out of the war.

The letter to Stone was effective both at home and abroad. In the face of the President's resounding bang of the patriotic drum, support for the McLemore Resolution (and a similar one in the Senate) ebbed away. In Berlin, it hardened Bethmann Hollweg's resolve to resist pressure from the navy, now backed by von Falkenhayn as army Chief of Staff, for completely unrestricted submarine warfare. But the Chancellor did consent to U-boat commanders being instructed to attack without warning all enemy freighters in the war-zone, as well as armed merchantmen everywhere. It was not long before reports reached Washington of the sinking of unarmed British ships and also some neutral (Dutch) ones.

The inevitable crisis was precipitated by the torpedoing on 24 March of a cross-Channel passenger ship, the *Sussex*, with four Americans among the injured. In the face of this apparently clear violation of the *Arabic* pledge, Lansing and House urged Wilson to break off diplomatic relations at once. Caught between his hawkish advisers and the doves in Congress, the President temporized. He insisted on checking the facts of the case, and the Germans initially denied responsibility (the U-boat commander had thought his target was a minelayer). After receiving conclusive evidence that the *Sussex* had been attacked, Wilson recognized that he had again to face the prospect of war but he decided to give Germany one more chance to back down. He composed a note arguing that the *Sussex* case, which 'unhappily does not stand alone', vindicated the American government's original position that the use of submarines against commerce was by its nature bound to contravene 'the principles of humanity' as well as international law. The note concluded with an explicit threat to break relations unless the German government abandoned forthwith 'its present methods of submarine warfare against passenger and freight-carrying vessels'.[78] But this apparently uncompromising public ultimatum was accompanied by some gentler private diplomacy. House assured Bernstorff that if Germany suspended U-boat warfare Wilson would move for peace and also act against British infractions of international law. The ambassador explained to Berlin that 'Wilson's main wish is not, as is often said, to help England, but rather to bring about peace and to be reelected. At the moment he believes that the English would simply ridicule his suggestions of peace if he had won nothing from us with his notes.'[79] When Bethmann Hollweg, judging a complete suspension of U-boat warfare to be a political impossibility in Germany, inquired whether a campaign conducted according to the rules of visit and search would be acceptable, he was assured that it would. With even the head of the Admiralty desirous of avoiding war with the United States at this time, the Germans then replied that henceforth their submarines would operate within such limits but in the expectation that Washington would also compel the British to observe international law. Wilson accepted the 'pledge' but not the qualification: 'Responsibility in such matters is single, not joint or conditional; absolute, not relative.'[80]

Holding the middle ground

As with the *Arabic*, the outcome of the *Sussex* crisis represented a precarious triumph for Wilson. The new German pledge was wider in its scope (not limited to passenger liners) but also more clearly provisional. The Germans forebore to reply publicly to Wilson's riposte to their note but Bethmann Hollweg emphasized privately to the US ambassador that the pressure for a resumption of all-out submarine warfare would soon become irresistible if nothing were done to inforce international law against England.[81] Wilson was well aware of the instability of the situation but his preferred solution remained to bring about an end to the war, which would not only terminate all his difficulties with neutral rights but also give a great boost to his reelection campaign. He therefore sought urgently to activate the agreement House had made with Grey in February. (He had tried to do so during the *Sussex* crisis, naïvely writing to Grey that it was necessary to avoid the danger of America's being dragged into the war.)[82] In the face of Grey's steady resistance to the idea of a peace initiative, Wilson through House attempted to use both stick and carrot. The stick was that otherwise the United States would have to force Britain, too, to amend its maritime practices. The carrot was the promise of full American involvement in an international organization to keep the peace and provide security to all countries. To add credibility to this commitment, Wilson decided to make it public.

By chance, a most appropriate forum was available in the imminent meeting in Washington of the League to Enforce Peace, which had been founded in June 1915. Even before the war, there had been a flourishing peace movement in the United States. Although few Americans paid close attention to foreign affairs, in the confident atmosphere of the progressive era war was widely regarded as an anachronism and many groups actively promoted measures to prevent its occurrence. However, there were significant differences of opinion about the means for doing this between the more conservative and the more progressive wings of the movement. The former assumed that the interests of states would inevitably conflict, and that the incidence of war could be reduced only if the role of international legal institutions and processes was both enlarged and more effectively enforced. The latter believed that the peoples of different countries would not wish to fight each other and that wars were the consequence of imperialistic policies generated by various forms of special interest – not least, arms manufacturers. The outbreak of the European war greatly increased the level of interest in these issues and many more people became involved in peace organizations of various kinds. But the preexisting differences of outlook persisted and were, indeed, often aggravated by being associated with deeply felt disagreements over the causes of the war between those who attributed it to barbaric German aggression and those who saw it as a conflict between rival imperialisms.

The progressive viewpoint was represented, for example, by the Woman's Peace Party, founded by Jane Addams and other leading social reformers in early 1915. Its comprehensive program called for an immediate armistice, international agreements on disarmament and government ownership of all munitions manufacture, democratic control of foreign policy and self-determination as well as machinery for arbitration and a 'Concert of Nations' to supersede the balance-of-power system. The last goals were common ground in that no one in the peace movement questioned the desirability of more organized international cooperation to resolve conflicts without war, but there was less agreement over the form this should take. The League to Enforce Peace stood for a comparatively conservative approach. Its specific and limited program was that a league of all the great powers (including the United States) should agree that disputes between them would be submitted either to judicial arbitration or to formal conciliation (whichever was more appropriate), and that economic and military sanctions would be brought to bear upon any members failing to follow these procedures. The organization's leaders, most of whom were pro-Ally Republicans, emphasized that this was a program for the future and that they were not seeking an end to the present war. Bryan, whose priorities were entirely different, denounced the enforcement provisions in the League's proposals as a false attempt to fight militarism with militarism.[83]

A wish to avoid involvement in such controversies may well have contributed to Wilson's originally declining the invitation to address the League to Enforce Peace, though he gave as a reason his preoccupation with the *Sussex* crisis. In any case, there is no doubt that his later change of mind was inspired by the desire to encourage the Allies to accept an American peace initiative. As he prepared to draft his speech, Wilson asked House 'to formulate what you would say, in my place, if you were seeking to make the proposal as nearly what you deem Grey and his colleagues to have agreed upon in principle as it is possible to make it ... The only inducement we can hold out to the Allies is one which will actually remove the menace of Militarism'.[84] But, as with all his major addresses during the war, Wilson's speech to the League to Enforce Peace on 27 May 1916, was aimed at more than one audience.

One intended audience, certainly, was the Allies. In deference to their clear indications that they would not welcome a peace move at this time, Wilson referred to such an initiative only in vague and conditional terms. Mistakenly believing, on the basis of Grey's reiterated inquiries, that the Allied governments generally placed great value on an American underwriting of European security, he declared that the United States was 'willing to become a partner in any feasible association of nations' formed 'to prevent any war begun either contrary to treaty covenants or without warning and full submission of the causes to the opinion of the world – a virtual guarantee of territorial integrity and political independence'. He also affirmed the American commitment to principles that Allied statesmen commonly said they were fighting for – the rights of small states and the need for protection against aggression. All this, however, was to a large extent vitiated by Wilson's attribution of the war to the whole system of secret diplomacy rather than to German ambition, and by his insistence that the United States was not concerned 'with its causes and its objects' (thereby apparently retreating from House's endorsement of several specific Allied war aims in the secret memorandum he had drawn up with Grey). The upshot was that it was only the more liberal sections of British and French opinion that responded favorably to the speech.

The phrases in the speech that caused offense in London and Paris reflected Wilson's concern with his domestic audience. He was, after all, proposing a break with the hallowed policy of nonentanglement and he was at pains to emphasize the extent to which he remained committed to the nation's traditions and principles. Thus, he reaffirmed American neutrality: 'we are in no sense or degree parties to the present quarrel'. If America was to exercise her power overseas, it would be for her own purposes. Remarkably, the first object of the 'universal association of the nations' Wilson called for would be to maintain the freedom of the seas. Moreover, although 'we have nothing material of any kind to ask for ourselves', Americans held certain 'fundamental' beliefs, among them 'that every people has a right to choose the sovereignty under which they shall live'. But the President urged his countrymen to accept that the war had shown that the old stance of noninvolvement was no longer practicable: 'Our own rights as a nation, the liberties, the privileges, and the property of our people has been profoundly affected. We are not mere disconnected lookers-on ... We are participants, whether we would or not, in the life of the world.' It followed that the United States had a real interest in seeing peace restored and given 'an aspect of permanence'.

The isolationist tradition had been challenged by American leaders before, particularly by Republicans like Lodge and Theodore Roosevelt. But Wilson's approach was significantly different from theirs. It was not only that he had avoided their virtually open endorsement of the Allied cause. He also suggested that the United States should not so much join the existing international system as create a different one: 'the peace of the world must henceforth depend upon a new and more wholesome diplomacy'. Wilson had immediately in mind here an idea he had derived from House – that 'nations must in the future be governed by the same high code of honor that we demand of individuals'. But this thought was associated with a broader condemnation of power politics – 'henceforth alliance must not be set up against alliance, understanding against understanding, but ... there must be a common agreement for a common object, and ... at the heart of that common object must lie the inviolable rights of peoples and of mankind'.[85] Such rhetoric appealed both to deep-rooted American suspicion of Old World diplomatic intrigue and to the anti-imperialistic idealism of most progressives. Significantly, Wilson sought with some success to use his new commitment to reconcile such people to his preparedness program.[86]

American public opinion was, of course, particularly important to Wilson as he faced reelection. Well aware of the minority status of the Democratic party, he sought to broaden his support by capturing the middle ground. But the question was, where did this lie? With Republicans attacking him for failing to uphold American rights, Wilson began by adopting an emphatically patriotic posture. Carrying a flag, he marched at the head of a 'preparedness parade' in Washington, DC. In an address on the newly instituted Flag Day he called for the crushing of internal 'disloyalty', and pledged himself to 'vindicate the glory and honor of the United States'.[87] He arranged for the Democratic convention to sing many patriotic songs and loudly cheer all mention of America and the flag. But while the delegates dutifully followed these instructions, their spontaneous demonstrations expressed other emotions. When the keynote speaker, a former governor of New York, recounted a series of occasions on which previous American leaders had behaved with restraint in the face of provocations, they responded with enormous enthusiasm. Although the convention, which rose affectionately when Bryan entered the press box, may not have been representative of the country as a whole, its clearly pacific temper did suggest that Wilson had once again slightly misjudged the national mood.[88] It was easy for those whose social milieu was among the upper classes of the eastern seaboard to underestimate the strength of most Americans' desire to keep out of the war (and overestimate their concern with the rights of that tiny proportion of the population who traveled overseas). Wilson was less prone to this tendency than House or Lansing, but he was not immune from it, as he had shown in the summer of 1915 and also later that year when he apparently shared Lansing's view that the administration would face criticism from the returning Congress for failing to secure a German disavowal of the *Lusitania* sinking – rather than, as was to be the case, for risking war for insufficient cause.[89]

External developments, too, were serving to render more remote the possibility of American intervention on the side of the Allies, which had been raised by the *Lusitania* crisis and envisaged in the House–Grey agreement. It was not only that the *Sussex* pledge had resolved the submarine dispute, at least for the time being. Relations with Britain and the Allies deteriorated considerably through the summer of 1916. The execution of the leaders of the Easter Rising in Dublin completely alienated the Irish-American community and also aroused anti-British sentiment more widely. A Paris conference in June that drew up plans for continued economic cooperation between the Allies after the war may not have attracted as much attention at the time as it has since from New Left historians, but it did draw unfavorable comment from Lansing and in the Senate.[90] As far as Wilson himself was concerned, however, by far the most important factor was the increasingly unambiguous hostility of the Allied governments to a peace initiative by him. He had ensured that the Democratic platform included his commitment to American participation in a postwar league of nations and hoped, as he wrote to House, that this would give it 'immensely increased importance ... with all parties to the war'.[91] But, in response to House's repeated urgings, Grey made it crystal clear at the end of August that the Allies were not prepared to consider peace until they had won some military victories, and that the evident determination of American public opinion 'at all costs to keep out of war' had devalued the promise to enter a league of nations, the appeal of which had in any case been reduced by Wilson's declared indifference to the causes and objects of the war and stress on the freedom of the seas.[92]

Wilson's frustration in the face of what appeared to him (following House's misleading reports) to be backsliding found expression in irritation at Allied blockade practices. The British replied tardily and unresponsively to an American protest against their interception of American mail to neutral countries, and in mid-July published a 'blacklist' of US and Latin American firms suspected of trading with the enemy with whom British subjects were forbidden to have any dealings. 'I am, I must admit, about at the end of my patience with Great Britain and the Allies. This black list business is the last straw', Wilson wrote to House. 'I am seriously considering asking Congress to authorize me to prohibit loans and restrict exportations to the Allies.'[93] When a note of protest to the British government remained unanswered, the administration secured congressional resolutions empowering the President to restrict trade with countries discriminating against American firms or illegally interfering with the movement of American goods or ships.[94]

This move produced an agitated response in London. The initial reaction was indignation and there was talk of reprisals. However, an interdepartmental committee, on which the young Treasury economist John Maynard Keynes played an active role, reported to the cabinet that the dependence on American supplies 'was so vital and complete in every respect that it was folly even to consider reprisals'.[95] Britain and France were by this time importing almost four times as much from the United States as they had before the war. Since there had been no increase in their reciprocal exports, a massive trade deficit had developed that could be met only by borrowing and the sale of gold and financial assets.[96] In 1914 Bryan, declaring money to be 'the worst of all contrabands because it commands everything else', had announced that the administration regarded loans to the belligerents as inconsistent with neutrality. This policy was soon interpreted as allowing private commercial credits, and in September 1915 it was abandoned when Wilson tacitly permitted the floating of a large public loan by the Allies in the American market.[97] He had done so at the strong urging of McAdoo and Lansing, both of whom had emphasized the extent to which American prosperity had become dependent on the continued flourishing of the export trade. In 1916, over 11 percent of American GNP was exported, more than twice the prewar proportion.[98] The assumption that the US government could not afford to obstruct this trade gave comfort to British policymakers: 'their only weapons against us are too big for them to use', a Foreign Office paper concluded.[99]

The Allies' confidence in this respect was reinforced by the belief, encouraged by Lansing, that the securing of retaliatory powers should be viewed as an election ploy that Wilson had no intention of acting upon. Although Wilson was not prepared to play politics with foreign policy in the crude way that Lansing thought (and recommended), in his campaign speeches he did seek to exploit the unpopularity of the belligerent attitudes of Theodore Roosevelt and other Republicans.[100] 'If the Republican party should succeed', he warned, 'one very large branch of it would insist upon what its leader has insisted upon, a complete reversal of policy ... that reversal of policy can only be a reversal from peace to war'. Charging that the intention of such people was 'to promote the interests of one side in the present war in Europe', Wilson expressed an emphatically neutral view of the conflict's origins to an audience of clubwomen in Cincinnati:

> Have you ever heard what started the present war? If you have, I wish you would publish it, because nobody else has. So far as I can gather, nothing in particular started it, but everything in general. There had been growing up in Europe a mutual suspicion, an interchange of conjectures about what this government and that government was going to do, an interlacing of alliances and understandings, a complex web of intrigue and spying, that presently was sure to entangle the whole of the family of mankind on that side of the water in its meshes.[101]

It was on the grounds of neutrality rather than pacifism that Wilson sought to distance himself from Roosevelt, Lodge, and their followers. Conscious that the diplomatic value of his commitment to a postwar league of nations depended upon the credibility of the undertaking to enforce its provisions, he insisted that 'America is always ready to fight for things that are American'. She would not fight 'for the ambitions of this group of nations as compared with the ambitions of that group of nations', but 'let us once be convinced that we are called into a great combination to fight for the rights of mankind, and America will unite her force and spill her blood for the great things which she has always believed in and followed'.[102]

Notwithstanding such caveats, Wilson was clearly benefiting from his implication that the Republicans would be more likely to take America into the war, and Democratic party workers and speakers hammered away on this theme, particularly in the Middle West. It was a difficult issue for the Republican candidate, Charles Evans Hughes, a former governor of New York who had resigned from the Supreme Court to run for president. Not only did his party contain people with strongly divergent views about the war but he was also aware that many in the German-American community, seeing Wilson as pro-British, were inclined to vote against the President (to Bernstorff's dismay). Hughes attempted to square the circle by maintaining that a firmer defense of American rights against both sets of belligerents would better preserve neutrality, but he incautiously also said that he was in 'complete accord' with Roosevelt after one of the latter's bellicose speeches.[103]

It was obvious that the race was a close one and Wilson recognized that he might well lose it. At House's suggestion, he planned if he did so to leave the White House at once rather than wait until his term formally ended in March 1917. He wrote to Lansing that, in order to avoid having a lame-duck administration handle the nation's foreign policy at such an unprecedently critical time, he proposed to appoint Hughes Secretary of State, in which position (under the law as it then stood) he would succeed to the presidency on the resignation of Wilson and the vice-president.[104] Wilson actually went to bed on election night believing that he would be putting this plan into effect. As we have seen, his narrow victory resulted from his association with progressive reform at home as well as with peace abroad. But, since there are several indications that the appeal of progressivism to the electorate at large was waning in these years, the latter issue was almost certainly the more important.[105] Certainly, that was how it seemed to many contemporary observers. 'The elections have clearly shown that the great mass of the Americans desire nothing so much as to keep out of the war', the British ambassador reported. 'It is undoubtedly the cause of the President's re-election.'[106]

Yet, although Wilson had received the enthusiastic support during the election of Bryan and other pacifists, he had not adopted their position that the cause of non-involvement was worth the sacrifice of American rights. In full-page advertisements on the eve of poll, the issue had been posed as:

> Wilson and Peace with Honor?
>
> or
>
> Hughes with Roosevelt and War?

There had been no retreat from the claim made on behalf of Wilson by a bombastic orator at the Democratic convention that without orphaning a single American child, without widowing a single American mother, without firing a single gun, without the shedding of a single drop of blood, he wrung from the most militant spirit that ever brooded above a battlefield an acknowledgement of American rights and an agreement to American demands.[107]

The American people had been encouraged in their desire to believe that the exercise of power in the world could be cost-free.

So, rather than resolving the dilemma Wilson had faced since the summer of 1915, the role of peace sentiment in his election victory served to sharpen it. His response, firstly, was to soft-pedal the submarine issue. When a British armed merchantman, the *Marina*, was torpedoed without warning and six American crewmen were among those who lost their lives, the President 'astonished' House by saying that he did 'not believe the American people would wish to go to war no matter how many Americans were lost at sea'. He also stated (wrongly) that 'our understanding with Germany' covered only passenger ships. Further incidents, including the torpedoing without warning of a British liner, the *Arabia* (also armed), led Lansing in early December to urge the breaking-off of diplomatic relations. But Wilson did not even acknowledge Lansing's letter. Three weeks before the election he had received a message from the German government warning him that they might soon feel compelled to revoke the conditional *Sussex* pledge, and urging him to act quickly if he wanted to offer his services to bring the conflict to an end. Germany had not previously welcomed the idea of Wilson's mediation but there had been a change of policy in the late summer when her military situation seemed bleak. It was the Kaiser who, against Bethmann's better judgment, played up the threat of unrestricted submarine warfare to spur Wilson into action, but the danger was nonetheless real enough. The German admiralty was now pressing steadily for such a campaign and the powerful new army chiefs, Hindenburg and Ludendorff, had withheld their support for it in August only because they did not wish at that moment, when Rumania had just entered the war on the Allied side, to risk a break with the European neutrals, Holland and Denmark.[108]

Within days of his election victory, Wilson told House that he desired 'to write a note to the belligerents demanding that the war cease'. House was not keen on the idea. The situation was quite different from the one he had envisaged a year before. Then he had planned that the United States, in secret association with the Allies, would force Germany to accede to a moderate settlement. Now, an American initiative would be welcomed by Germany and resisted by the Allies. Lansing, too, was alarmed by the possibility of the United States ending up on the wrong side in what he saw as essentially a conflict between autocracy and democracy. In his view, a peace at this point was not only impossible but undesirable and American entry on the side of the Allies only a matter of time. But it was just this prospect that was impelling Wilson's move – as House recorded, 'his argument is that unless we do this now, we must inevitably drift into war with Germany upon the submarine issue'. In response to House's objections, he raised the possibility of 'a separate understanding with the Allies by which we would agree to throw our weight in their favor in any peace settlement brought about by their consent to mediation'. It was Lansing's pressure for a break with Germany over recent sinkings, House thought, that had led Wilson to summon him to Washington. He sought to deflect the President by downplaying the sense of crisis.[109]

The next few weeks were to prove, however, that Wilson's perspective differed considerably from that of his chief foreign-policy aides. Events were to give him an opportunity to put real pressure on the Allies, and he seized it unhesitatingly. The enormous trade deficit was running down the British Treasury's reserves of dollar assets and gold at an alarming rate – at this time, almost two-fifths of the money being raised for the war had to be found in North America. The foreseeable need for large-scale American credits led the Chancellor of the Exchequer to warn the cabinet that 'by next June or earlier, the President of the American Republic will be in a position, if he wishes, to dictate his own terms to us'. As an expedient, the House of Morgan suggested that short-term British and French Treasury Notes should be sold to American banks. But the Federal Reserve Board, which had already been worrying about the extent to which the American economy had become dependent upon the necessarily temporary war trade, drafted a statement cautioning its member banks against purchasing too many such bonds. When the Board's chairman sought Wilson's approval, the President suggested the warning be strengthened and addressed to private investors as well as banks. The Board's statement caused a flight from sterling, and the role in the affair of the 'highest authority' was gloomily reported to London by Spring Rice: 'The object of course is to force us to accept President's mediation by cutting off supplies.'[110]

Wilson drafted a peace note in late November but the pleas of House and Lansing, and then the fall of the Asquith government in Britain, caused him to delay sending it. He rejected House's suggestion that he attempt to revive the agreement with Grey: 'We cannot go back to those old plans. We must shape new ones.' He was then disconcerted to hear that Germany had made a direct offer of peace negotiations to the Allied governments. Ironically, this move, too, was the product of a desire to avoid war between Germany and the United States (as well as of pressure from Austria-Hungary). With Rumania defeated, the German High Command was now unequivocally supporting the navy's demand for unrestricted submarine warfare. Even if the overture were rejected, Bethmann hoped the demonstration of Germany's willingness for peace might soften the American reaction to such a campaign. With the Allies apparently about to dismiss the German approach summarily, Wilson hastened to dispatch his own note to all the belligerent governments on 18 December 1916, stressing that it was an entirely independent initiative which he had been planning to make for some time.[111]

Although Wilson had originally intended to propose a conference, the note as sent simply called for the countries at war to state their terms of peace. In a sentence that House rightly predicted would infuriate the Allies, the President observed that 'the objects which the statesmen of the belligerents on both sides have in mind in this war are virtually the same, as stated in general terms to their own people and to the world'. Insofar as these aims were the establishment of security for all, including 'weak peoples and small states', America stood 'ready, and even eager, to cooperate in the accomplishment of these ends when the war is over'. But it felt justified in intervening now because 'the life of the entire world has been profoundly affected' by the conflict, and the situation of neutral states, already difficult, threatened to become 'altogether intolerable'. At the close of the year which had witnessed Verdun and the Somme, there were of course grounds other than national interest on which to make a plea for peace, and Wilson eloquently invoked these:

> If the contest must continue to proceed towards undefined ends by slow attrition until the one group of belligerents or the other is exhausted, if million after million of human lives must continue to be offered up until on the one side or the other there are no more to offer, if resentments must be kindled that can never cool and despairs engendered from which there can be no recovery, hopes of peace and of the willing concert of free peoples will be rendered vain and idle.[112]

Neither set of belligerents wanted to respond to Wilson's request. Although the Central Powers would have been happy for a settlement at this time, they wished to achieve it through direct negotiations with their adversaries and without the mediation of an American president whom they still saw as pro-British. As politely as possible, they indicated this in their reply. The Allies' position was more difficult. Committed to war aims that presupposed military victory, they were determined to go on fighting but the British government at least also knew that, as Balfour the new Foreign Secretary observed, 'the United States had it in their power to compel peace'. However, in the aftermath of Wilson's note, more encouraging reports reached them from Washington. Distressed by the fear of a breach with the Allies, Lansing told the press that Wilson's was not 'a peace note' but an attempt to clarify the purposes of the conflict at a time when the United States was 'drawing nearer to the verge of war ourselves'. Although Wilson swiftly forced Lansing to repudiate the implication that American belligerency was imminent, the Secretary of State continued to reassure the British and French ambassadors that the United States would understand if they announced extensive war aims. The Allies followed this advice and their reply to Wilson in early January outlined territorial adjustments that could obviously only be achieved if the Central Powers were defeated.[113]

But Wilson had no intention of abandoning his peace offensive at this point. He pursued a twin-track approach of both public and private diplomacy. In an address to the Senate on 22 January 1917, he coined another of the phrases with which he has been associated ever since by declaring:

> It must be a peace without victory ... Victory would mean peace forced upon the loser, a victor's terms imposed upon the vanquished. It would be accepted in humiliation, under duress, at an intolerable sacrifice, and would leave a sting, a resentment, a bitter memory upon which terms of peace would rest, not permanently, but only as upon quicksand. Only a peace between equals can last.[114]

This sentiment, according to Arthur Link, represented Wilson's 'deep convictions' about the war.[115] As early as December 1914, it will be recalled, he had said that only a stalemate would discredit war as a means of attaining national ambitions.[116] Yet that had been an off-the-record conversation and Wilson had not articulated the thought publicly or made it an object of policy until now. At this time, when he had an urgent political interest in bringing the war to an end, the chief merit of 'a peace without victory' may have been less its durability than its accessibility – for it was clearly the only possible sort of *early* peace.

Again, Wilson was aiming at several audiences in his speech. One was, of course, the governments of the belligerent powers. He attempted to maximize the leverage he could gain from his readiness to bring the United States into a postwar league of nations. Firstly, he stressed the value of American participation: 'no covenant of cooperative peace that does not include the peoples of the New World can suffice to keep the future safe against war'. Secondly, however, he indicated that the commitment was not unconditional: 'there is only one sort of peace that the peoples of America could join in guaranteeing'. He had made the offer to underwrite European security, first privately and then publicly, in order to induce the Allies to agree to a compromise peace; now, he threatened to withdraw the offer if they failed to do so.

But this implied that noninvolvement remained a perfectly viable policy for the United States. If its abandonment was not a necessity, as Wilson had earlier argued, then Americans would have to be persuaded that it was nonetheless desirable. For the domestic audience, Wilson went to remarkable lengths to present his policy as in accordance with the nation's traditions. As essential conditions of a lasting peace, he specified 'the principle that governments derive all their just powers from the consent of the governed', 'the freedom of the seas', and 'moderation of armaments'. Moreover, he was suggesting that 'all nations henceforth avoid entangling alliances', for 'there is no entangling alliance in a concert of power'. Indeed, 'I am proposing, as it were, that the nations should with one accord adopt the doctrine of President Monroe as the doctrine of the world.' 'These', he concluded, 'are American principles, American policies. We could stand for no others.' But, in a classic statement of the universalistic claims of the national ideology, he went on to declare that 'they are also the principles and policies of forward-looking men and women everywhere, of every modern nation, of every enlightened community. They are the principles of mankind and must prevail.'

This peroration also signaled Wilson's third intended audience, which was the most immediate target of this piece of public diplomacy. 'The real people I was speaking to was neither the Senate nor foreign governments', he explained to a correspondent, 'but the *people* of the countries now at war.' He had delayed giving the speech until it had been transmitted in code to US embassies in Europe so that they could ensure its full publication locally, and in the text he remarked that

> I would fain believe that I am in effect speaking for the silent mass of mankind everywhere who have as yet had no place or opportunity to speak their real hearts out concerning the death and ruin they see to have come already upon the persons and the homes they hold most dear.

By appealing to the war-weariness of their populations, Wilson hoped to add to the pressure on the belligerent governments to make peace.[117]

Meanwhile House had been in regular private contact with Ambassador Bernstorff, who was also anxious to see the war end before the submarine issue brought another crisis in German–American relations and who suggested that Germany's peace terms were moderate. Through House, Wilson pressed for something more definite and official: 'if Germany really wants peace she can get it, and get it soon, *if she will but confide in me and let me have a chance* ... with something reasonable to suggest as from them, I can bring things about'.[118] The President seems to have been both confident of his power over the Allies and prepared to use it. On 31 January Bernstorff sent a document to House in New York formally welcoming Wilson's attempt to bring about a peace conference and confidentially setting out Germany's terms. On the same day, he called at the State Department to hand over an announcement of unrestricted submarine warfare.[119]

Notes

1 Arthur S. Link, *Wilson: The New Freedom*, Princeton, NJ, 1956, pp. 459–65.

2 Paul Bairoch, 'International Industrialization Levels from 1750 to 1980', *Journal of European Economic History*, 11 (1982): 269–333.

3 Peter Boyle (ed.), *The Churchill–Eisenhower Correspondence, 1953–1955*, Chapel Hill NC, and London, 1990, p. 179.

4 Annual Message of the President, 3 December 1912, Department of State, *Foreign Relations of the United States, 1912* [hereafter *FRUS*], Washington, DC, 1919, p. xx.

5 Farewell address, 19 September 1796, John C. Fitzpatrick (ed.), *The Writings of George Washington*, Washington, DC, 1931–44, vol. 35, pp. 231–6.

6 Worthington C. Ford (ed.), *The Writings of John Quincy Adams*, New York, 1913–17, vol. 7, p. 115.

7 Daniel J. Boorstin, *America and the Image of Europe: Reflections on American Thought*, Cleveland, OH, and New York, 1960, pp. 19–20. For a fuller development of this theme, see Cushing Strout, *The American Image of the Old World*, New York, 1963.

8 *Harper's Weekly*, 59, 12 September 1914: 241. For other comments of this kind, see John A. Thompson, *Reformers and War: American Progressive Publicists and the First World War*, Cambridge, 1987, pp. 85–9.

9 *Wabash Plain-Dealer*, quoted in Eric F. Goldman, *Rendezvous with Destiny: A History of Modern American Reform*, Rev. edn, New York, 1956, p. 180.

10 *The Independent*, 79, 10 August 1914, 195.

11 Literally 'WASP' stands for White, Anglo-Saxon Protestant, but the term is usually applied to those within this category who were in the upper echelons of American society.

12 Burton J. Hendrick, *The Life and Letters of Walter H. Page*, London, 1929, vol. II, pp. 217–21.

13 Maldwyn A. Jones, *The Old World Ties of American Ethnic Groups*, London, 1974, p. 4.

14 *PWW*, vol. 33, Princeton, NJ, 1980, p. 41. Link also emphasizes the influence of American public opinion upon Wilson. See Arthur S. Link, *Wilson: The Struggle for Neutrality 1914–1915*, Princeton, NJ, 1960, p. 49.

15 Sir Cecil Spring Rice to A.J. Balfour, 4 January 1918, *PWW*, vol. 45, p. 455.

16 'An Appeal to the American People', 18 August 1914, *PWW*, vol. 30, pp. 393–4.

17 Link, *Struggle for Neutrality*, pp. 66–7.

18 W.H. Page to Wilson, 4 November 1914, *PWW*, vol. 31, p. 263.

19 Wilson to W.H. Page, 28 October 1914, ibid., p. 243.

20 John W. Coogan, *The End of Neutrality: The United States, Britain, and Maritime Rights 1899–1915*, Ithaca, NY, and London, 1981, pp. 209–10, 247.

21 Sir Cecil Spring Rice to Sir Edward Grey, 8 September 1914, *PWW*, vol. 31, pp. 13–14; House diary, 30 August 1914. *PWW*, vol. 30, pp. 462–3.

22 *PWW*, vol. 33, p. 41.

23 Link, *Struggle for Neutrality*, pp. 51–3.

24 Memorandum by Herbert B. Brougham, 14 December 1914, *PWW*, vol. 31, p. 458.

25 See, for example, Edward H. Buehrig, *Woodrow Wilson and the Balance of Power*, Bloomington, IN, 1955, p. 103.

26 Robert E. Osgood, *Ideals and Self-Interest in America's Foreign Relations: The Great Transformation of the Twentieth Century*, Chicago, IL, 1953, especially pp. 174–5.

27 Ernest R. May, *The World War and American Isolation, 1914–1917*, Cambridge, MA, 1959, p. 33.

28 Coogan, *End of Neutrality*, pp. 217–19.

29 Wilson to Bryan, 24 March 1915, *PWW*, vol. 32, pp. 424–5.

30 Churchill to Grey, 27 October 1914. Quoted in Coogan, *End of Neutrality*, pp. 195–6.

31 House diary, 4 November 1914, *PWW*, vol. 31, p. 265.

32 Annual Message to Congress, 8 December 1914, *PWW*, vol. 31, pp. 421–3.

33 Link, *Struggle for Neutrality*, pp. 218–19; House diary, 10 February 1915, Charles Seymour, *The Intimate Papers of Colonel House*, London, 1926, vol. I, p. 375.

34 Link, *Struggle for Neutrality*, p. 31. Three years later, Wilson recalled that at this time

> his chief preoccupation was not external but internal. There was imminent danger of civil discord, the country was divided into groups which did not understand one another, which were of different origin and which at any moment might fly at each other's throats … That was his main preoccupation during the first year of the war.

> (Sir Cecil Spring Rice to A.J. Balfour, 4 January 1918, *PWW*, vol. 45, p. 455)

35 For example, Reinhard R. Doerries, *Imperial Challenge: Ambassador Count Bernstorff and German–American Relations, 1908–1917*, Chapel Hill, NC, 1989, pp. 131–2, 308.

36 Secretary of State to US Ambassador in Germany, 13 May 1915, *FRUS, 1915, Supplement: The World War* Washington, DC, 1928, p. 395.

37 Memorandum, 7 April 1915, quoted in Link, *Struggle for Neutrality*, p. 362.

38 Secretary of State to US Ambassador in Germany, 9 June 1915. *FRUS, 1915, Supplement*, p. 437.

39 Secretary of State to US Ambassador in Germany, 10 February 1915; US Ambassador in Germany to Secretary of State, 17 February 1915, *FRUS, 1915, Supplement*, pp. 98–100, 112–15.

40 *FRUS: The Lansing Papers, 1914–1920*, Washington, DC, 1939, vol. I, pp. 365–80.

41 Link, *The Struggle for Neutrality*, p. 367.

42 Mark Sullivan, *Our Times*, vol. 5, *Over Here, 1914–1918*, New York, 1933, p. 120.

43 E.g. *The Nation*, 13 May 1915: 527; *Metropolitan Magazine*, 42 (June 1915): 527 p. 3.

44 Quoted in Osgood, *Ideals and Self-Interest in America's Foreign Relations*, p. 140.

45 Heckscher, *Woodrow Wilson*, pp. 347–52, 365; Link, *Struggle for Neutrality*, pp. 379–81; *PWW*, vol. 33, pp. 108–12, 117–19, 124–29, 132–3, 136–8, 146–7, 160–61.

46 An address in Philadelphia to Newly Naturalized Citizens, 10 May 1915, *PWW*, vol. 33, p. 149.

47 Remarks at a press conference, 11 May 1915, ibid., p. 153.

48 E.M. House to Wilson, 9 May 1915, ibid., p. 134.

49 A draft of the First *Lusitania* note, 11 May 1915, ibid., pp. 155–8.

50 Link, *Struggle for Neutrality*, pp. 384–9.

51 W.J. Bryan to Wilson, 3 June 1915, *PWW*, vol. 33, pp. 323–4.

52 Wilson to Bryan, 7 June 1915, ibid., p. 349.

53 Wilson to Bryan, 10 May 1915, ibid., p. 139.

54 Quoted in Link, *Struggle for Neutrality*, pp. 396–7 According to Link, the *Lusitania* note 'evoked warmer and more overwhelming approbation than anything the President had said or done since issuing his appeal for neutrality in August 1914'.

55 Bryan to Wilson, 5 June 1915, *PWW*, vol. 33, p. 342.

56 Wilson to Melancthon Williams Jacobus, 20 July 1915, ibid., vol. 33, p. 535.

57 Link, *Struggle for Neutrality*, pp. 412–13, 405–9, 445–50; *PWW*, vol. 33, pp. 279–84, 316–20; *FRUS, 1915, Supplement*, pp. 480–82.

58 Ambassador von Bernstorff to the Foreign Office, 28 July 1915, quoted in Link, *Struggle for Neutrality*, pp. 451–3.

59 Link, *Struggle for Neutrality*, pp. 439–41; *PWW*, vol. 33, pp. 494–5, 506, 511.

60 Wilson to Edith Bolling Galt, 19 August 1915; Wilson to House, 21 August 1915, *PWW*, vol. 34, pp. 261, 271.

61 Wilson to Edith Bolling Galt, 19 August 1915, ibid., pp. 257–8; Link, *Struggle for Neutrality*, pp. 565–85, 653–79.

62 *New York Evening Post*, 2 September 1915, quoted in Link, *Struggle for Neutrality*, p. 586.

63 Wilson to Edith Bolling Galt, 20 August 1915, *PWW*, vol. 34, p. 260.

64 Link, *Struggle for Neutrality*, pp. 590–93; *Wilson: Confusions and Crises 1915–1916*, Princeton, NJ, 1964, pp. 15–48.

65 Address in Cleveland, 29 January 1916. Also address in Topeka, Kansas, 2 February 1916, *PWW*, vol. 36, pp. 47, 92.

66 Address in Chicago, 31 January 1916. Also address in Topeka, Kansas, 2 February 1916, ibid., pp. 64–6, 93.

67 Address in Cleveland, 29 January 1916. Also address in Chicago, 31 January 1916, in Topeka, 2 February 1916, ibid., pp. 47, 66, 92.

68 Addresses in Topeka, 2 February 1916, in Cleveland, 29 January 1916, in Chicago, 31 January 1916, ibid., 92–5, 47, 72–3.

69 Link, *Confusions and Crises*, pp. 49–50.

70 *PWW*, vol. 36, p. 116.

71 Sir Edward Grey to E.M. House, 10 August 1915, *PWW*, vol. 34, p. 372.

72 Link, *Confusions and Crises*, pp. 102–3. To a greater extent than Wilson and House realized, Grey's desire for a postwar league of nations represented his personal feelings rather than an agreed British policy. See Keith Robbins, *Sir Edward Grey: A Biography of Lord Grey of Fallodon*, London, 1971, pp. 319–20.

73 Link, *Confusions and Crises*, pp. 101–41.

74 Wilson to E.M. House, 24, 16 December 1915, *PWW*, vol. 35, pp. 387–8.

75 W.J. Stone to Wilson, 24 February 1916; Wilson to W.J. Stone, 24 February 1916, *PWW*, vol. 36, pp. 209–11, 213–14.

76 Tumulty to Wilson, 24, 16 February 1916, ibid., pp. 211–13, 186–7n.

77 Wilson to Stone, 24 February 1916, ibid., p. 214.

78 Secretary of State to US Ambassador in Germany, 18 April 1916, *FRUS, 1916, Supplement: The World War*, Washington, DC, 1929, pp. 232–4.

79 Bernstorff to the Foreign Office, 23 April 1916, quoted in Link, *Confusions and Crises*, p. 263.

80 Secretary of State to US Ambassador in Germany, 8 May 1916, *FRUS, 1916, Supplement: The World War*, p. 263.

81 Link, *Confusions and Crises*, pp. 278–9.

82 Ibid., pp. 237–8.

83 For more detailed discussions, see Thomas J. Knock, *To End All Wars: Woodrow Wilson and the Quest for a New World Order*, Princeton, NJ, 1992, especially Chapter 4, and William C. Widenor, *Henry Cabot Lodge and the Search for an American Foreign Policy*, Berkeley, CA, 1980, pp. 221–31.

84 Wilson to E.M. House, 18 May 1916, *PWW*, vol. 37, pp. 68–9.

85 Address in Washington to the League to Enforce Peace, 27 May 1916, ibid., pp. 113–16.

86 Knock, *To End All Wars*, pp. 66–7; Thompson, *Reformers and War*, pp. 134–6, 169–71.

87 A Flag Day address, 14 June 1916, *PWW*, vol. 37, pp. 221–5

88 Arthur S. Link, *Wilson: Campaigns for Progressivism and Peace, 1916–17*, Princeton, NJ, 1965, pp. 42–8.

89 Link, *Confusions and Crises*, pp. 62–72.

90 Lansing to Wilson, 23 June 1916, Senator W.J. Stone to Wilson, 10 July 1916, *PWW*, vol. 37, pp. 287–8, 397. The Paris conference is seen as having a major influence on US policy

in Carl P. Parrini, *Heir to Empire: United States Economic Diplomacy, 1916–1923*, Pittsburgh, PA, 1969, especially pp. 15–39.

91   Wilson to House, 2 July 1916, *PWW*, vol. 37, p. 345.

92   Viscount Grey of Fallodon to House, 28 August 1916, *PWW*, vol. 38, pp. 89–92; Link, *Campaigns*, pp. 10–23, 32–38.

93   Wilson to House, 24 July 1916, *PWW*, vol. 37, pp. 466–7.

94   Link, *Campaigns*, pp. 65–71.

95   Ibid., pp. 73–7, 178–80; John Milton Cooper, Jr, 'The Command of Gold Reversed: American Loans to Britain, 1915–1917', *Pacific Historical Review*, 45 (May 1976): 218–20. As the mandarin Spring Rice was to put it, the Allies 'would be quarrelling with their victuals if they resented the manners of their grocer', Spring Rice to Grey, 5 December 1918, Stephen Gwynn (ed.), *The Letters and Friendships of Sir Cecil Spring Rice*, London, 1929, vol. 2, p. 359.

96   US Bureau of the Census, *Historical Statistics of the United States*, Washington, DC, 1973, pp. 903, 906.

97   Link, *The Struggle for Neutrality*, pp. 62–4, 132–6, 616–28.

98   *Historical Statistics*, p. 887.

99   Link, *Campaigns*, pp. 180–2.

100   Ibid., pp. 76–80, 106–8.

101   Campaign address, 7 October 1916; luncheon address to women in Cincinnati, 26 October 1916, *PWW*, vol. 38, pp. 364–5, 531.

102   Campaign address, 14 October 1916. See also address to the Commercial Club of Omaha, 5 October 1916; Nonpartisan Address in Cincinnati, 26 October 1916, ibid., pp. 436–7, 347–8, 541.

103   Link, *Campaigns*, pp. 100, 108–12, 135–40.

104   Ibid., pp. 153–6.

105   On the declining appeal of progressivism, see Thompson, *Reformers and War*, pp. 112–16.

106   Link, *Campaigns*, p. 162.

107   Ibid., pp. 111, 45–6.

108   Ibid., pp. 186–7, 193, 165–75; House diary, 2 November 1916, *PWW*, vol. 38, pp. 607–8; Lansing to Wilson, 8 December 1916, *PWW*, vol. 40, pp. 190–91.

109   House diary, 14 November, 15 November 1916, *PWW*, vol. 38, pp. 646–7, 656–60; Link, *Campaigns*, pp. 187–90, 199–200.

110   Link, *Campaigns*, pp. 179–84, 200–6; Spring Rice to the Foreign Office, 3 December 1916, *PWW*, vol. 40, pp. 136–7; Cooper, 'The Command of Gold Reversed', pp. 220–26.

111   Link, *Campaigns*, pp. 197–200, 206–17.

112   Note to Belligerent Governments, 18 December 1916, *FRUS, 1916, Supplement: The World War*, pp. 98–9; Link, *Campaigns*, pp. 197–9, 209, 215–19.

113   Link, *Campaigns*, pp. 221–39.

114   Address to the Senate, 22 January 1917, *PWW*, vol. 40, p. 536.

115   Arthur S. Link, *Woodrow Wilson: Revolution, War, and Peace*, Arlington Heights, IL, 1979, pp. 22–7.

116 See above, p.104.
117 Address to the Senate, 22 January 1917, *PWW*, vol. 40, pp. 533–9; Link, *Campaigns*, pp. 250, 253–5, 271. Quotation on p. 271.
118 Wilson to House, 24 January 1917, *PWW*, vol. 41, p. 3.
119 Link, *Campaigns*, pp. 249–50, 255–61, 277–80, 284–90.

Chapter 6

A War President

Leading America to war

Two decisions, taken within a few months of each other in 1916–17, were to have profound effects on the subsequent history of the twentieth century. The first was the decision of the German government to unleash a full-scale submarine campaign against commercial shipping, including that of neutral countries sailing to Allied ports. This was an essential precondition of the second decision, that of the United States to declare war on Germany. Had this not happened, it is hard to see how hopes of an Allied victory could have survived the combination of Britain's financial difficulties, the morale problems of the French army, Italian military failure and the collapse of the Russian front during 1917. Counterfactual history is not a sufficiently exact science to enable one to say whether the Central Powers would have then been able to dictate their own terms, or if a negotiated, compromise settlement would at last have been agreed, but it is inconceivable that Germany would have suffered the kind of defeat she did in 1918 or the kind of terms imposed by the Treaty of Versailles. Since these experiences and the resentments they bred contributed so largely to Hitler's rise to power, it is almost certain that Europe would have been spared at least some of the horrors of the 1930s and 1940s.

This is not the place to explore at length the reasons for the German decision, which was the culmination of an internal debate that had been going on for almost two years. During that time, the navy's demands for an all-out submarine campaign, backed by right-wing forces in the press and the Reichstag, had been resisted by the Chancellor, who feared the reaction of neutrals, particularly the United States. But by late 1916, the dominant power in Germany lay with the Army High Command of Hindenburg and Ludendorff, whose public prestige was reflected in a Reichstag resolution in October that the Chancellor should be guided by them in any decision regarding 'a ruthless U-boat war'. Following the defeat of Rumania in early December, the generals favored such a campaign, and Bethmann was forced to concede that unrestricted operations against armed merchantmen should be launched if his peace overture failed. In early January, the US government was informed of this decision. By then, however, the German Admiralty had produced a long memorandum arguing that this halfway step was not enough but that an all-out campaign would force Britain to sue for peace within five months. Possessing new, more powerful U-boats, they calculated that they could sink so much tonnage within that period that the British would no longer be able to import sufficient wheat to feed their population. Although this memorandum's underestimation of the effects of American belligerency was pointed out by the Vice-Chancellor, Karl Helfferich, Bethmann lacked the political strength to counter its appeal and, at a conference with the Kaiser on 9 January 1917, he gave way to the demands of the Navy and the High Command.

As for the American decision, which resulted in the United States for the first time in its history projecting its power into the maelstrom of world politics, it has been subject to the tendency to assume that great events must have great causes. During the nineteen months that the country was at war, the US government not only raised an army of almost four million men and transported more than half of them to France but raised the level of its spending by a factor of 25. (The cost of the war to the United States exceeded the previous total of all federal expenditures since the establishment of the Constitution.)[1] Such a major effort, it is natural to think, must have been the product of a clear threat to an important national interest. The most vital interest is national security, and it is often asserted that the real object of American belligerency was to preserve, or restore, the European balance of power.[2] This explanation can only be valid, however, if those who took the decision believed both that America's own security did depend upon the balance of power in Europe and that the maintenance of that balance was seriously at risk in the spring of 1917.

With regard to the first proposition, it is true that in the early twentieth century the naval historian, A.T. Mahan, and a few other publicists had touted the idea that a German victory in a European war would present a threat to the United States, and also that this argument was quite often used by both House and Lansing during the period of American neutrality. In conversation with the British ambassador in September 1914 Wilson himself had seemed to subscribe to it, but a few weeks later he told House that 'he did not believe there was the slightest danger to this country from foreign invasion, even if the Germans were successful', and over the next two years he frequently indicated his realization that the war was weakening all the belligerents and enhancing the relative power of the United States.[3] In the public debate over preparedness, as Robert Osgood pointed out in his thorough study of this issue, both sides assumed that the country had the capacity to defend itself unaided against any foreign attack, and that this was all that national security required.[4] In line with this assumption, the measures adopted to strengthen the army and navy, like the war plans of both services, envisaged resisting an assault on the Western Hemisphere rather than projecting power to Europe.[5]

Whereas there were certainly some Americans who had expressed anxiety about the consequences for national security of a German victory, there is no evidence that any saw such a victory as imminent in the spring of 1917, or thought that only US intervention could prevent it. Once the Germans had failed in the first weeks of the war to crush France before Russia was fully mobilized, the great majority of American commentators on the European conflict seem to have envisaged only two possible results – an Allied victory or a stalemate. In February 1917, Frank H. Simonds, the most authoritative of such commentators, reported after a visit to the battlefields in France that the British army was superior to its foe in *matériel* and morale and was finally advancing after two years of holding the line. Nor did Americans see the unrestricted submarine campaign as a winning weapon. Figures published at the beginning of March showed only slight increases in Allied tonnage losses. Indeed, some of the strongest supporters of intervention, including Lodge, feared that the British navy would defeat the campaign before it had produced the desired effect of bringing the United States into the war.[6] Lacking any sort of foreign intelligence service, Wilson and the administration were no better informed about the seriousness of the threat the U-boats constituted – or, indeed, about any other aspects of the military situation.[7]

Certainly, there was no indication of any concern with the fate of the Allies in the way the US government responded to the submarine campaign. On 3 February 1917 Wilson broke off diplomatic relations with Germany, but in reporting this to Congress he said that 'only actual overt acts' would lead him to go further and made it clear that he had in mind attacks on 'American ships and American lives'.[8] Three weeks later, to counter the apprehension of shipowners, he sought authority from Congress to put naval guns on merchantmen, stating that 'there may be no recourse but to *armed* neutrality'. Such a course of action might have protected American shipping but it would hardly have had a decisive effect upon the balance of power in Europe.

The adoption of armed neutrality was, however, explicitly designed to keep goods moving across the Atlantic. Recommending it, Wilson pointed out that 'many of our ships are timidly keeping to their home ports', and that, as a result, there was 'a very serious congestion of our commerce'. Although Wilson himself asserted that his concern was with 'fundamental human rights' rather than 'material interests merely', some historians have seen in the importance of the trade that now contributed so much to American prosperity the ultimate reason why the United States could not simply accept the German warning that neutral ships should stay out of the war-zone.[9] However, it remained the case that comparatively few oceangoing freighters flew the American flag. Two-thirds of Britain's imports were brought in by her own merchant navy, and American ships carried only a fraction of the remainder. Even without them, the British would still have had the means, as they clearly had the will, to transport goods across the Atlantic. Moreover, if the timidity of neutral shipping had led to some diminution in the volume of exports, this would not necessarily have been bad for the American economy. There were, as the Federal Reserve Board had recognized, dangers in its becoming too dependent on the essentially temporary war trade. And Wilson himself had not only endorsed this view implicitly by approving the restriction of credit but had explicitly argued that the boom America was enjoying could not be attributed to Allied orders.[10]

Indeed, it is not the prosperity of the nation as a whole so much as that of special interests within it that has most commonly been seen as providing the economic motivation for American intervention. American steel-manufacturers and munitions-makers, as well as the banking firm of J.P. Morgan, had been making great profits from the war trade, as the Nye Committee of the 1930s was to confirm. When Senator George Norris of Nebraska declared that 'we are going into war upon the command of gold', he was arguing that such monied interests had been able to manufacture sentiment through their control of the press.[11] But the previous two years had clearly shown that bellicose comment in East Coast newspapers could not shape the opinion of the country – or of Congress. Nor was the administration likely to be sympathetic to the interests of the Morgan partners, who had openly backed the Republicans in the recent election.[12] Indeed, in the progressive era, it would be a liability for any politician to appear to be doing the bidding of Wall Street – as Norris's comment implicitly showed.

When neither a concern with national security nor economic interest seems to explain why a state goes to war, it is natural to ask what other foreign policy objectives its government was pursuing. In this case, no one at the time or since has doubted that 'the government' meant Woodrow Wilson – that, as Churchill later wrote, the fateful action of the greatest power in the world at this crucial time depended 'upon the workings of this man's mind and spirit'.[13] Most students of the subject have concluded that it was what one has called Wilson's 'dream of peace' that led him to war.[14] In the learned judgment of Arthur Link, 'the most important reason for Wilson's decision was his conviction that American belligerency now offered the surest hope for early peace and the reconstruction of the international community'.[15] There are two elements in this thesis. The less persuasive is that Wilson was driven, as he had been in advocating a peace without victory, by the desire to bring the war to an end as soon as possible. But since Wilson's peace offensive had been designed to fend off the danger of American belligerency, this argument posits a dramatic reversal of his priorities. And there is no reason at all to believe that the failure to achieve peace at this time would have led him to declare war had it not been for the assault on American rights in the submarine campaign. A connection with the latter is the strength of the second version of the thesis, which revolves around the issue of credibility. A promise to underwrite European security had not only been a key diplomatic asset in Wilson's eyes, it was also to be the bedrock of the lasting peace he envisaged. If the stern words and ultimata he had addressed to Germany over the previous two years were now shown to be hollow, such a promise would be of little value. In Patrick Devlin's words, 'what weight could anyone attach to guarantees given by a nation that quaked at the thunder of the guns?'[16]

Belligerency would also enhance Wilson's ability to shape the postwar order by making him a full participant in the peace conference. This was a privilege that neither side had been happy to grant him as a mediator, although Lloyd George now professed that 'we want him to come into the war not so much for help with the war as for help with peace'. In a message through Page in early February, the new British prime minister insisted that Wilson's personal presence at the peace conference was 'necessary', and declared that only the United States 'wants nothing but justice and an ordered freedom and guarantees for the future'.[17] In an interview with Jane Addams and other delegates from peace societies at the end of the month, Wilson made the point that as head of a nation participating in the war he would have a seat at the peace table, but that otherwise he could at best 'call through a crack in the door'.[18]

These were considerations that must have weighed with Wilson, but before we elevate them into the decisive factor we should see whether the evidence suggests that they had priority in his mind and that his actions can best be explained in terms of them. Certainly, his initial response to the German announcement of unrestricted submarine warfare did not give the impression that maximizing his international influence was his chief concern. The genuineness of his hopes that his peace campaign was on the verge of success was manifested by his remark to House that 'he felt as if the world had suddenly reversed itself; that after going from east to west, it had begun to go from west to east and that he could not get his balance'. At the same time he insisted 'that he would not allow it to lead to war if it could possibly be avoided', and he startled the cabinet by saying that if 'in order to keep the white race or part of it strong to meet the yellow race – Japan, for instance, in alliance with Russia, dominating China – it was wise to do nothing, he would do nothing, and would submit to anything and any imputation of weakness or cowardice'.[19]

This was only one of the reasons Wilson gave at different times for his reluctance to take America into the war – the need for an uninvolved power to lead the belligerents to peace and the effects on the nation's domestic life were others – but the basic reason was surely his knowledge of the strength of noninterventionist sentiment among his countrymen, so recently demonstrated in the election campaign. Although House believed he and Lansing had persuaded the President that the German announcement could only be met by breaking off diplomatic relations, Wilson did not commit himself to this step until he had consulted a group of Democratic senators, most of whom represented Southern and Western states.[20]

However, the alternative options he presented to the senators were to give a final warning to the Germans before breaking off relations or to wait until an overt act had been committed against American rights. He did not suggest accepting the situation and warning American ships to keep out of the war-zone. It seems doubtful that in excluding this option he was primarily thinking of a future league of nations and the import-ance to that of American credibility. Announcing the break to Congress, Wilson declared that there was 'no alternative consistent with the dignity and honor of the United States'. Apart from any consideration of the effect on his future influence abroad of backing down completely from the *Sussex* ultimatum, he knew that doing so would open him up to tremen-dous political attack at home. If most Americans did not want to go to war, neither did they wish to see their country humiliated.

For almost two years, Wilson had been able to satisfy their 'double wish' by giving them 'peace with honor'. Through February and early March 1917 he desperately sought ways to continue to do so. In the first place, he declared that he could not 'bring myself to believe' that the

Germans would in fact do what they said they would and that 'only actual overt acts on their part can make me believe it even now'.[21] Secondly, he indicated, both through press leaks and through his own inaction, that attacks on belligerent merchantmen without warning did not qualify as such acts – tacitly, he thus gave up the ground over which earlier controversies had been fought.[22] When the new Austro-Hungarian Foreign Minister, Count Czernin, sent a message that his government would favor an early 'peace without victory' if the empire was not threatened with dismemberment, Wilson earnestly sought such an assurance from the Allies.[23] In deciding to respond to the pressure from nervous shipowners by asking Congress for authority to arm merchantmen, Wilson seems to have been hoping that this would deter the Germans from attacking American vessels – which they had not yet done.

In the end, though, as Wilson had always known, he could not deliver 'peace with honor' without the cooperation of the Germans. On this occasion, there were no signs of the 'give' in Berlin that had defused previous crises. In late February, the British government passed to Washington the decoded text of an intercepted telegram sent by Foreign Minister Zimmermann to the German minister in Mexico City in mid-January. This astonishingly inept message proposed that, in the event of war between Germany and the United States, Mexico should ally with Germany and receive in return not only financial support but also her lost territory in Texas, New Mexico and Arizona. The publication of this telegram aroused anti-German fury and indignation even in the most isolationist parts of the country, but for Wilson its chief significance may have been that it showed that the Berlin authorities were now prepared for war with the United States. In early March, the German Admiralty announced that the period of grace for neutral ships had expired, and on the 18th news reached Washington that three American merchant vessels had been sunk, with the loss of fifteen lives.[24]

This was really the end of the road for 'peace with honor'. If forced to choose between these values, it was by now amply clear that the country would divide, with passionate minorities on either side and a majority in the middle with inevitably mixed feelings.[25] Although this majority would be inclined to follow the administration's lead, it would be much harder to sustain a consensus behind either war or submission than it had been when Wilson had seemed able to deliver the best of both worlds. At first, Wilson tried to see if there remained a viable middle way. He called in at the Navy Department, urging that everything possible be done to protect American shipping and telling Daniels that he still hoped to avoid war.[26] But he already knew that effective defense against submarines required the sort of offensive action that would be virtually indistinguishable from undeclared war.[27]

There was no doubt about the way Washington opinion came down. Theodore Roosevelt's demand for an immediate declaration of war was predictable but Lansing, too, pulled no punches either in conference or on paper in urging the same course. He pleaded with House to come down from New York to 'put your shoulder to the wheel'. On 20 March, Wilson held a meeting of the full cabinet in which every member, including Daniels who was well known for his pacifist tendencies, said that war was now the only course. Following the meeting, Wilson issued the call for a special session of Congress that marked his decision to ask for a declaration of war.[28]

After the event, Wilson himself suggested that his delay in coming to this point had been largely tactical. To Cleveland Dodge he wrote that 'it was necessary for me by very slow stages indeed and with the most genuine purpose to avoid war to lead the country on to a single way of thinking'.[29] Wilson had never been a pacifist, but there is no reason to doubt the authenticity of his reluctance to lead his countrymen into what he had recently described as 'this vast, gruesome contest of systemized destruction'.[30] At the moment of his decision for war, he said to more than one person that he had been driven to the conclusion that there was now 'no alternative'.[31] If he had found another course compatible with the nation's honor and his own standing, he would surely have taken it. Yet his attitude was not that of someone like Bryan, who held antiwar rallies across the country to the end. Indeed, the President took various actions during these weeks to weaken the anti-interventionist cause, including the publication of the Zimmermann telegram and a fierce attack on senators filibustering the Armed Ships Bill as 'a little group of wilful men, representing no opinion but their own'.[32] As he in fact made clear in his letter to Dodge, and on other occasions, what Wilson really wanted to avoid was leading a divided nation into war.[33] It was his greater awareness of, and concern with, the range of domestic opinion that distinguished him, now as earlier, from men like House and Lansing. In laying before the cabinet the question of how to respond to the sinking of American ships, he 'spoke of the situation in this country, of the indignation and bitterness in the East and the apparent apathy of the Middle West.'[34]

Like other American presidents contemplating committing their country to a costly or hazardous enterprise (for example, Kennedy during the Cuban missile crisis), Wilson's main concern in the final crisis was how what he did could be presented in a way that would command broad support.[35] In the cabinet meeting, Lansing had conceded that 'to go to war solely because American ships had been sunk and Americans killed would cause debate', and urged that the war should be presented as one of democracy against autocracy – something which the overthrow of the Tsar in Russia the previous week had made much easier to do. 'The President said', Lansing recorded,

> that he did not see how he could speak of a war for Democracy or of Russia's revolution in addressing Congress. I replied that . . . he could do so indirectly by attacking the character of the autocratic government of Germany as manifested by its deeds of inhumanity, by its broken promises, and by its plots and conspiracies against this country. To this the President only answered, 'Possibly'.

A few days later Wilson received a letter from Tumulty, based upon his study of newspaper opinion across the country, advising that

> if we are driven into war by the course of Germany, *we must remain masters of our own destiny*. If we take up arms against Germany, it should be on an issue exclusively between that Empire and this Republic; and that the United States must retain control of that issue from beginning to end.

House suggested that Wilson should emphasize that the conflict was with the government of Germany, not the people.[36]

Having gathered such advice and other materials, Wilson retired to his study to type his address to Congress, with the staff of the White House walking on tiptoe to give him the quiet he demanded.[37] On the evening of Monday, 2 April, he went to the Capitol to make the case for war. He began by emphasizing the completely unrestrained character of the U-boat campaign. It had 'ruthlessly sent to the bottom without warning and without thought of help or mercy for those on board, the vessels of friendly neutrals along with those of belligerents', even 'hospital ships and ships carrying relief to the sorely bereaved and stricken people of Belgium'. It was 'a war against all nations', each of whom had to decide how it would respond. He had hoped that armed neutrality would suffice but this, 'it now appears, is impracticable' because the way to counter submarines was to attack them before they showed their hostile intention, and American sailors therefore needed the protection of belligerent status if they were not to be treated as pirates. He reiterated that 'there is one choice we cannot make, we are incapable of making: we will not choose the path of submission and suffer the most sacred rights of our nation and our people to be ignored or violated'. So he called upon Congress 'to formally accept the status of belligerent which has thus been thrust upon it'. He broadened the issue by declaring that the object of American policy remained, as it had been when he addressed the Senate in January, 'to vindicate the principles of peace and justice in the life of the world' – but now he adopted Lansing's argument that the threat to these principles came from autocratic governments, particularly that of Imperial Germany. America would thus fight 'for the ultimate peace of the world and for the liberation of its peoples, the German people included'. This was the theme he returned to in the elevated and beautifully cadenced peroration:

> It is a fearful thing to lead this great peaceful people into war, into the most terrible and disastrous of all wars, civilization itself seeming to be in the balance. But the right is more precious than peace, and we shall fight for the things which we have always carried nearest our hearts, – for democracy, for the right of those who submit to authority to have a voice in their own governments, for the rights and liberties of small nations, for a universal dominion of right by such a concert of free peoples as shall bring peace and safety to all nations and make the world itself at last free. To such a task we can dedicate our lives and our fortunes, everything that we are and everything that we have, with the pride of those who know that the day has come when America is privileged to spend her blood and her might for the principles that gave her birth and happiness and the peace which she has treasured. God helping her, she can do no other.[38]

Congress rose to Wilson as he finished, and Lodge shook his hand warmly in congratulation. Lansing in his memoirs wrote of this as Wilson's greatest triumph:

> From the moment that he entered the auditorium up to the time that he passed out into the corridors of the Capitol he was master of the situation. His personality was dominant. His vibrant voice, modulated to the solemnity of the occasion and expressive of the grave import of his words, was firm and distinct ... His control of language and of his audience was a marvelous exhibition of his genius as an orator. One who heard that impressive address and saw the dignity and sternness of the speaker as he stood on the rostrum, recognized him as a leader of men of whom there was no greater within the boundaries of the United States.[39]

The type of leadership Wilson had demonstrated, however, accorded with the Burkean conception he had described in his 1890 lecture on the subject – 'to follow, not to force, the public inclination'. His ear had 'rung with the voices of the people' as he had attempted to chart a course that would bring the greatest national unity.[40] His war message contained something for most of the main elements in American opinion – the stress on the attacks on American rights and the hostility of the German government for isolationist nationalists such as Senator William Borah; the portrayal of the war as one of democracy against autocracy for pro-Allied interventionists; the insistence on the continuity in his thinking with his January address to the Senate for progressive idealists. In this context, his remark to Jane Addams and her colleagues that belligerency would give him a seat at the peace table seems to be an aspect of this consensus-building rather than a unique insight into his own motivation. There is neither any evidence nor any reason for believing that a personal commitment to establishing a league of nations played any significant part in leading Wilson to ask Congress for a declaration of war.[41] There were only the briefest and most indirect references in his war message to the project, which had already been the object of serious attack in the Senate from both Borah and Lodge. In his pursuit of national unity, Wilson had evoked the broader and vaguer causes of peace, freedom, and democracy. There is thus a sense in which the decision to go to war is better seen as America's than as Wilson's. Wilson, though, had taken responsibility for it and in doing so had articulated a vision of a new world order, at once democratic and harmonious, which was deeply appealing to Americans but rather less in tune with the external realities.

Mobilizing the nation

Wilson's speech won much warm praise but it by no means stilled dissent either across the country or in Congress. Although the war resolution passed by 82 votes to six in the Senate, and 373 votes to 50 in the House, the number of votes cast against it contrasts with the virtual unanimity in 1941. The most bitter opponents were those such as La Follette and Norris who maintained that the United States, by acquiescing in the British blockade and resisting Germany's retaliation, and by providing munitions and money to the Allies, had never been truly neutral. Both these progressive Republican senators represented states with substantial German-American populations (Wisconsin and Nebraska, respectively), but it was clear that support for the war was weak throughout the West, and to a lesser extent, the South – the very areas that had given Wilson his narrow victory in 1916. In urging that Germany be given one last warning, Senator McCumber from North Dakota observed that 'if we declare war against Germany today, we shall run counter to the sentiment and wishes of a very considerable portion of our people, as is evidenced by the vast number of antiwar telegrams, resolutions, and petitions'.[42] His Republican colleague, Smoot of Utah, noted in his diary that 'this war is a very unpopular one'.[43]

Nevertheless, the great majority of senators and representatives (including Smoot and McCumber) voted for the war resolution. Overwhelmingly, the reason given for doing so was the need to protect the nation's honor and the rights and lives of its citizens against Germany's attacks on them. Several picked up the point that the enemy was the autocratic, militaristic regime of the Hohenzollerns rather than the German people. Different views were expressed about the relationship of America's war with that of the Allies. Lodge urged the closest possible cooperation with 'the other nations who are fighting for the same end', but Borah declared that 'I seek or accept no alliances; I obligate this Government to no other power. I make war alone for my countrymen and their rights; for my country and its honor.'[44]

For all their disagreement over this issue, Lodge and Borah were both Republicans and militant nationalists. National honor had less resonance for progressive idealists, who had generally been among Wilson's keenest supporters in the election campaign and had responded enthusiastically to his address to the Senate. Wilson sought to appeal to this constituency by stressing the exalted motives that had led America to war. 'There is not a single selfish element, so far as I can see, in the cause we are fighting for', he declared. 'We have gone in with no special grievance of our own, because we have always said that we were the friends and servants of mankind. We look for no profit ... We will accept no advantage out of this war.' When some Republicans sought to make hay with this suggestion that the United States had no 'special grievance' against Germany, Wilson drew a distinction between the reasons why America had entered the war and what it was fighting for. Germany's 'very serious and long-continued wrongs' against the nation and its citizens constituted the former, but the latter was the kind of peace Wilson had outlined in his address to the Senate: 'We have entered the war for our own reasons and with our own objects clearly stated, and shall forget neither the reasons nor the objects.'[45]

Both elements in this formulation of Wilson's accorded with Tumulty's advice that America's war should be kept distinct from the preexisting European conflict.[46] Whether it was her rights or her ideals that she was fighting for, America's purposes were her own. In taking this position, the President was maintaining a more unequivocally nationalist line than such Republicans as Roosevelt and Lodge who saw their country as joining Britain and France, shamefully late, in a common cause. As during the period of neutrality, Wilson held on to important aspects of the isolationist tradition even as he was leading the United States into commitments and actions that broke with it – specifically, the ideological contrast between the purity of the New World and the corruption of the Old, and the practice of unilateral diplomacy. Not only did the United States sign no treaty with the other states fighting Germany but Wilson was very concerned to avoid even informal use of the term 'our allies', complaining to Herbert Hoover when it appeared on Food Administration posters:

> I would be very much obliged if you would issue instructions that 'Our Associates in the War' is to be substituted. I have been very careful about this myself because we have no allies and I think I am right in believing that the people of the country are very jealous of any intimation that there are formal alliances.[47]

The President was reluctant to allow American participation in inter-Allied conferences and councils and, when he did so, insisted that any decisions be confined to technical and military, rather than political, matters. He emphasized to House that 'England and France *have not the same views with regard to peace that we have* by any means.'[48] As we shall see, he felt no obligation to consult Allied governments before issuing his own public declarations of American policy.

The respect in which the insistence on American independence came under most pressure from the Allies, however, was the military. It was far from clear at the beginning what form America's war effort would take. While members of the cabinet had been united in the meeting on 20 March in urging a declaration of war, they had disagreed over whether the United States should send an army to Europe.[49] Most congressmen apparently neither desired not anticipated such a step.[50] In the Senate debate, Lodge observed that 'we can not send a great army across the ocean, for we have no army to send'. Since the US Army, with a total strength of less than 130,000, ranked seventeenth in the world, he had a point. Reflecting current British and French views, Lodge urged that the United States concentrate on furnishing the Allies with supplies and 'large credits'.[51] In his war message, Wilson, too, had identified these, together with naval action against submarines, as urgent specific tasks. But he had also called for an increase in the armed forces of 'at least five hundred thousand men' to be 'chosen upon the basis of universal liability to service'.[52] It has been argued that Wilson was already determined to send a large army to Europe because this would enable him 'to dominate' the peace conference.[53] But there is no evidence to support this interpretation, which seems to be another example of the tendency to see all Wilson's actions during the war as governed by a single, long-term goal. He made it clear, both implicitly and explicitly, that the nature of the peace was not now his priority. Some contemporaries pointed out, as have historians, that Wilson's potential leverage over the Allies was greater at this time than it would ever be again.[54] Yet he never seems to have even contemplated exploiting their critical need for American support by making the extent of such support conditional upon the Entente powers bringing their objectives into line with the principles he had set forth. In his letter to House emphasizing the discrepancy between the two, he simply stated that 'we cannot force them now'.[55] Quarreling with the Allies would hardly be the way either to build domestic support for the war or to bring it to a swift and successful conclusion. For Wilson at this point, as for all war leaders, the most important objective was victory.

It was this goal that led him to send an army to Europe, which was less a single decision than an incremental process. The first step was the bold and controversial one of conscription. In taking it, Wilson was following the advice of the General Staff, who could point to the experience of Britain which had been forced to resort to conscription the previous year. Although there were many to whom such compulsion was antithetical to all that America stood for (some said a conscript was the equivalent of a convict, if not a slave), Wilson was not one of them. The principle of universal liability to service could be justified in progressive terms as promoting democratic equality as well as efficiency. Wilson also seems to have hoped that this demonstration of wholehearted commitment would have an 'immediate moral effect' in Berlin, writing to one correspondent that 'the more businesslike determination we use now the less likelihood there is that our men will have to be sacrificed in any great numbers'.[56] At this stage, Wilson remained uncommitted to any particular military strategy. When missions from Britain and France came to Washington in late April, he told them 'he was ready to make whatever decisions were most useful for the cause of the Allies'. In the aftermath of the failure of the Nivelle offensive, Marshal Joffre and the other Allied representatives pleaded that some American troops be sent to the Western Front as soon as possible. While insisting that they form an independent command rather than being amalgamated as small units in the French or British army, Wilson and Baker agreed to this suggestion.[57] General Pershing (recently returned from Mexico) was appointed Commander of the American Expeditionary Force, and by the end of May was in France, together with a division of regulars. In early June, ten million young men across the country registered for military service and eventually over two and a half million were called up and the American army reached a strength of nearly four million.[58]

The request for troops in no way diminished the Allies' demands for help in other ways. Washington soon learnt that the U-boats were in fact sinking merchant ships at an alarming and accelerating rate. The US navy hurriedly sent all the destroyers it could spare across the Atlantic, and with the introduction of the convoy system monthly figures of tonnage sunk began to fall after June.[59] The most vital American contribution, however, was money. Even before the United States entered the war, the Federal Reserve Board not only reversed its position on the purchase of Allied Treasury Notes but gave a green light to foreign loans generally.[60] But by now the size of the problem was beyond the capacity of the private capital market. In April, Congress approved intergovernmental loans to the Allies of $3 billion but in late June the US Treasury at first refused to meet an overdraft of $400 million the British government had run up with J.P. Morgan & Co. This caused a panic in London, with the British Foreign Secretary Balfour cabling House that 'we seem on the edge of a financial disaster which would be worse than a defeat in the field'. It was this dependence, rather than the as yet nebulous prospect of a large American army in Europe, that Wilson saw as giving him leverage over the Allies in the future. 'When the war is over we can force them to our way of thinking', he assured House, 'because they will, among other things, be financially in our hands.'[61]

Eventually loans totaling $11.2 billion were made to the various Allied governments – the infamous 'war debts' that were to cause so much ill-feeling in the interwar period. When added to the $24.3 billion that was spent directly on the US war effort, it amounted to a colossal sum. Wilson had originally hoped that it would be possible to finance the war largely by taxation and the rates of both direct and indirect taxes did rise sharply, especially in 1918. Two-thirds of the cost, however, was met by the sale of bonds, known as 'Liberty Loans'.[62] Nearly all of these dollars were used to purchase goods and services in the United States. Sustaining the country's own military effort without diminishing the flow of essential food and other supplies to the Allies made great demands even on the giant American economy. Special agencies were set up to increase and direct production, including a Food Administration, a Fuel Administration, a War Industries Board and a War Shipping Board. Transportation proved a big problem. A War Trade Board attempted to impose priorities in the use of the precious commodity of shipping space. In December, a Railroad Administration was established to take over the nation's railroads which had proved unable to cope with the extra pressures. Most of these agencies were manned by business executives from the private sector who offered their services out of patriotism and in some cases for a nominal salary – the so-called 'dollar-a-year men'. The top positions went to people

of whose loyalty Wilson was confident – either former associates and supporters or nonpartisan figures (of whom the Food Administrator, Herbert
Hoover, a successful mining engineer who had made a reputation as
administrator of Belgian relief, was at this point one). He kept his cabinet
intact, disregarding House's advice to replace Daniels and Baker because
of their poor public reputations.[63]

Nothing better demonstrated the importance Wilson attached to personal loyalty than his appointment of the journalist George Creel as chairman of the Committee on Public Information (CPI). The 40-year-old Creel,
who had helped in the President's re-election campaign, lacked administrative experience and enjoyed no great standing in his profession.
However, he was energetic and competent and had liberal instincts.
Although his agency had responsibility for censorship, he placed the
weight very deliberately on positive publicity, launching what he called
'the world's greatest adventure in advertising'. The agency called on the
services not only of public figures and journalists but of scholars, photog-
raphers and cartoonists, as the country was flooded with material supporting the war effort. Tens of thousands of speakers, known as 'Four-
Minute Men', gave short pep talks to audiences in movie houses, theaters,
and other places. Special films were produced by a Motion Picture
Division. CPI agents in Europe distributed Wilson's speeches and photo-
graphs of him. Creel, who had made his name with crusading 'muckraking' articles and was never one for nuanced judgments, threw himself
into the work with enthusiasm. His initial inclination was to emphasize
the ideals for which America was fighting but, as the war went on and the
sacrifices it involved increased, much of the propaganda became cruder
with the 'Hun' enemy being demonized.

The same progression marked the more negative side of the mobilization of opinion – the suppression of dissent. The Espionage Act of July
1917 imposed stiff penalties for anyone obstructing recruitment or promoting disloyalty in the armed services. It also gave the Postmaster General
authority to exclude from the mail material he considered seditious.
Burleson exercised this power principally against the press of the Socialist
party, which had come out against the war, but in September 1918 he
caused a furore by withholding mailing privileges from an issue of the
venerable liberal weekly, the *Nation*. Wilson overruled Burleson in this
case, but on the whole he gave him his head, as he did the Attorney-General,
Gregory, who launched several prosecutions under the Espionage Act and
the even tougher Sedition Act of 1918. It was a local US attorney, however,
who was responsible for the prosecution of the Socialist party's most
famous leader, Eugene Debs, in June 1918. Debs was sentenced to ten years

in prison for speeches in which he had opposed the draft and attacked the war as a capitalist one. Federal legislation against antiwar activity was supplemented by state laws and local ordinances, and also the action of private organizations and vigilante groups. People suspected of a lack of patriotic fervor were forced to kiss the flag, tarred and feathered, whipped or – in a few cases – killed. After the lynching of a young German baker in Illinois had been given international publicity by the Germans, Wilson issued an eloquent public condemnation of 'the mob spirit' as a betrayal of the democracy for which America's 'heroic boys' were fighting.[64]

Wilson had, apparently, foreseen that war would foster illiberalism at home, but he had insisted that it would not change the goals of his foreign policy.[65] In his War Message, he had maintained that 'I have exactly the same things in mind now that I had in mind when I addressed the Senate on the twenty-second of January last.'[66] But, notwithstanding this claim to continuity, the move from neutrality to belligerency produced significant shifts in the views Wilson expressed both about the war and the peace. One was with respect to the causes of the war. In October 1916, as we have seen, he had attributed it to the whole European system of power politics, with its imperialism and secret diplomacy – 'nothing in particular started it, but everything in general'.[67] A year later, while still admitting that 'its roots run deep into all the obscure soils of history', he declared flatly that 'the war was started by Germany' because she was 'determined that the political power of the world shall belong to her'.[68] A second change was over the desirability of a compromise peace based upon the status quo ante. He had argued that this alone would discredit war with the populations of all the belligerent countries and provide the only basis for a lasting settlement. In May 1917 the Soviet that had been set up in Petrograd following the revolution urged socialists everywhere to demand 'peace without annexations or indemnities on the basis of the self-determination of peoples'.[69] This might have seemed an exact paraphrase of the 'peace without victory' Wilson had called for in January, but he now responded that the formula would *not* produce a lasting peace because

> it was the status quo ante out of which this iniquitous war issued forth, the power of the Imperial German Government within the Empire and its widespread domination and influence outside of that Empire. That *status* must be altered in such fashion as to prevent any such hideous thing from ever happening again.[70]

Related to this was a change, which has generally gone unnoticed, in the nature of the projected league of nations. When he had first publicly committed himself to the idea in May 1916, Wilson had spoken of 'an universal association of the nations', and in his address to the Senate he had said that he was 'proposing that all nations henceforth avoid entangling alliances' by uniting in 'a concert of power'.[71] But in his War Message, Wilson had declared that 'a steadfast concert for peace can never be maintained except by a partnership of democratic nations. No autocratic government could be trusted to keep faith within it or observe its covenants.'[72] The implication was that either all governments must become democratic or some would be excluded.[73]

These changes were all quite easily explicable, of course. Once in a war, it was natural to blame the enemy for starting it, to fight for victory rather than a draw, and to insist upon the iniquity and unacceptability of the enemy government. At the most basic level, Wilson was unwavering in his commitment to the liberal values of the national tradition and this, together with the exalted and generally abstract character of his rhetoric and the earnest dignity of his demeanor, enabled him to carry the majority of his countrymen with him as he shifted his position. But those whose own attitudes, whether pacifist or belligerent, underwent no such change were less impressed. Theodore Roosevelt responded indignantly when his old friend and supporter, the Kansas editor William Allen White, expressed admiration for Wilson's war message. The former president conceded that it was possible to justify going to war in the spring of 1917 because Germany had assaulted America's own rights and interests more outrageously than before:

> But what is impossible, what represents really nauseous hypocrisy, is to say that we have gone to war to make the world safe for democracy, in April, when sixty days previously we had been announcing that we wished a 'Peace without victory,' and had no concern with the 'causes or objects' of the war. I do not regard any speech as a great speech when it is obviously hypocritical and in bad faith.[74]

The change in Wilson's position emerged most clearly in his response to the various moves for peace that were made in the course of 1917. In April 1917, the secretary of the Second International, at the initiative of the Danish and Dutch socialists, proposed a conference (in the neutral capital of Stockholm) of socialists from all countries to consider 'the international situation'. Wilson clearly regarded this as a threat to the war effort, particularly in Russia, and after some hesitation agreed with Lansing that the administration should prevent American socialists from attending by denying them passports. This stance was much criticized by liberal opinion at home as well as by foreign socialists but Wilson responded in a fierce Flag Day address that 'the military masters' of Germany were now using men, in Germany and without, as their spokesmen whom they have hitherto despised and oppressed, using them for their own destruction – socialists, the leaders of labor, the thinkers they have hitherto sought to silence. Let them once succeed and these men, now their tools, will be ground to powder beneath the weight of the great military empire they will have set up.[75]

In August, a plea for peace came from a less easily disregarded source and in terms very similar to those Wilson himself had employed the previous winter. The Pope sent a message to the heads of the belligerent states appealing to them all to accept 'a just and lasting peace' that would provide for disarmament, 'the institution of arbitration', freedom of the seas, no indemnities and the reciprocal restitution of occupied territory. The message stressed the horrors of war and that European civilization, 'so glorious and flourishing', would be destroyed by its continuation.[76] In a politely worded reply, Wilson reiterated that the *status quo ante* could not provide the basis of 'a stable and enduring peace' as it would simply enable the power that had started the war in pursuit of world domination an opportunity to recuperate its strength. 'This power is not the German people', he again maintained. 'It is the ruthless master of the German people.' But 'we cannot take the word of the present rulers of Germany as a guarantee of anything that is to endure, unless explicitly supported by such conclusive evidence of the will and purpose of the German people themselves as the other peoples of the world would be justified in accepting.'[77]

House had pleaded with Wilson to 'answer the Pope's proposal in some such way as to leave the door open', to 'take the peace negotiations out of the hands of the Pope and hold them in your own' and to seize 'this great opportunity'. House knew that his advice was running contrary to that of Lansing and others in Washington and, when Wilson sent him a brief outline of what he was intending to say, the Colonel wrote in his diary that he feared the President was about to 'make a colossal blunder'. In view of House's doubts about Wilson's peace offensive in 1916, the reversal of positions was ironic, but it was not so much that the adviser was working from an out-of-date script as that he was worried about what the future might hold. Priding himself on the extent to which he was 'saturated with information from the other side', House cited the dangers of collapse not only in Russia but also in France, the continuing submarine problem and the unpopularity of the war in America to make the case that 'we will never again be in such a position as now to dictate a just peace'. [78]

In looking for reasons why Wilson did not on this occasion take

House's advice, we must begin by noting that he knew that the Allies had no intention of agreeing to a peace. Like Lansing, they regarded the Pope's appeal as serving, whether wittingly or not, the interests of the Central Powers.[79] Wilson had earlier explained to House that he did not want 'directly to contradict' the Allies in anything he said.[80] If he appeared to be pressing for peace, such public disagreement would be hard to avoid. However, it is doubtful that Wilson himself was still seeking an early end to the war.[81] He could hardly have made it plainer that he was not prepared to negotiate with the existing German government, and there is nothing to suggest that he was persuaded by House's argument that a public commitment to moderate peace terms 'would probably bring about such an upheaval in Germany as we desire.'[82] In private letters to friendly journalists in the autumn, the President deprecated 'all discussion of peace at this time', pointing out that 'the Germans have in effect realized their program of Hamburg to Bagdad' and would be left 'in possession of all that they ever expected to get'. Speaking to a newly formed League for National Unity in early October, he stressed that the war should end only when Germany was beaten.[83] From this perspective, the Pope's message had not been so much an opportunity as a threat because, like the socialist peace moves, it constituted a potential rallying point for antiwar opinion in the United States.

In countering that threat, Wilson not only stressed the impossibility of doing a deal with Germany's present rulers but also his continuing commitment to a moderate peace. In his reply to the Pope, he declared that 'punitive damages, the dismemberment of empires, the establishment of selfish and exclusive economic leagues' would be 'worse than futile', and that a lasting peace could only be 'based upon justice and fairness and the common rights of mankind'. As he had said earlier to the Russians, once victory had been won, 'we can afford then to be generous'. But to achieve this, it was essential to 'stand together'. Speaking to the AFL, the President claimed to have the same objectives as his critics: 'What I am opposed to is not the feeling of the pacifists, but their stupidity ... I want peace, but I know how to get it, and they do not.'[84]

Balancing the claims of war and peace

To make good this boast, Wilson knew he had two battles to fight. One was against that German government to whose defeat he was now clearly committed. The other would be against those of his 'associates' in the war whose own plans and ambitions were incompatible with the kind of peace he had outlined in his address to the Senate and reply to the Pope. The requirements of the first conflict were in tension with those of the second in that, as we have seen, Wilson felt he could not put pressure on his part-ners in the complex and hazardous enterprise of war.[85] Beyond this, it would obviously be more difficult, both psychologically and in balance-of-power terms, to make a 'peace without victory' after one side had in fact been victorious. But, for Wilson, the two were linked in that his stake in a peace based on liberal principles rather than imperialistic ambitions had grown enormously now that he had made it the principal justification for the sacrifices demanded by America's own war effort. His actions in 1917–18 were governed by his need to win both the war and the peace and, in so far as he could, to get the requirements of one objective to serve the other also. In the process, his policy positions on specific issues and also his priorities underwent significant modifications.

Although the Allied governments were reassured by the uncompro-mising tenor of Wilson's reply to the Pope, they deliberately refrained from publicly saying 'ditto' as he had hoped. (Interestingly, it was not only the President's phrases about the peace but also his insistence on the un-acceptability of the existing German government that the British Foreign Office did not wish to endorse.)[86] Shortly afterwards, Wilson quietly began preparations for the postwar battle by asking House to assemble a group to

> ascertain as fully and precisely as possible just what the several parties to this war on our side of it will be inclined to insist upon as part of the final peace arrangements, in order that we may formulate our own pos-ition either for or against them and begin to gather the influences we wish to employ, or, at the least, ascertain what influences we can use: in brief, prepare our case with a full knowledge of the position of all the litigants.[87]

This project, which became known as 'The Inquiry' and was paid for out of the President's discretionary funds, consisted of a team of academics, mostly historians and geographers, working discreetly in New York. As director, House chose his brother-in-law, Sidney Mezes, president of the City College in New York, and as secretary the 28-year-old journalist Walter Lippmann who had become close to the administration as an editor of the liberal weekly, the *New Republic*.

In the same month, Wilson received a long personal letter from Lloyd George. In this, the British prime minister pointed out that 'the Germans at the end of 1917 as at the end of each of the previous years' campaign, find themselves in possession of more and not less Allied territory', and argued that the 'comparative failure' of the Allies was due to their lack of a truly unified strategy. As well as touting his ideas for attacks in the south and east as well as the west, he strongly urged American participation in a stronger system of inter-allied cooperation.[88] Meanwhile, McAdoo urged the practical advantages of American representation on the body that determined supply priorities, including the hope that it might reduce the enormous financial burden on the US Treasury.[89] Under such pressure, Wilson modified his insistence on American independence by agreeing to send House as his representative to an inter-Allied conference and that joint councils should be established to coordinate military strategy and supply. But, as House noted, the President had 'no intention of loosening his hold on the situation' by allowing American policy to be determined in such forums.[90] At the end of October, House set off again for Europe, for the first time in an official capacity, and accompanied by both military and civilian aides.

By the time the Allied leaders gathered in Paris in late November, their cause had suffered further heavy blows. A German–Austrian offensive broke through the Italian lines at Caporetto and although Venice did not fall (contrary to House's pessimistic prediction), over a quarter of a million Italian troops were taken prisoner in this massive defeat.[91] Shortly afterwards, the Bolsheviks seized power in Russia. The weakness of the Russian war effort following the February revolution had been cited by Lloyd George as the chief reason for the Allies' military failure in 1917 but at least the Provisional Government had attempted to keep an army in the field. The Bolsheviks sought an immediate end to the war and called on the working people of all the belligerent countries to support this demand. To show that the war was being fought for imperialistic purposes, they published from the Foreign Ministry files the secret treaties in which the Entente powers had promised each other specific territorial gains from the defeated Central Empires. Soon afterwards, they arranged a truce and at Brest-Litovsk began negotiations with the Germans for an armistice.

In the face of these setbacks, the recently established Allied Supreme War Council agreed that the United States should send 24 divisions to France by the end of June – 'Is such a program *possible*?' Wilson asked as he forwarded the request to Baker.[92] If the Russians left the war, the Germans would be able to concentrate their forces on the Western Front. The serious implications of this inspired various Allied efforts to maintain an eastern front. One approach was to provide assistance to anti-Bolshevik elements in the south of Russia and the Ukraine that were apparently willing to continue the war against Germany. The British and French organized such an effort, for which Lansing persuaded Wilson to authorize some covert and indirect financial assistance.[93] The President and House, however, placed much greater hopes on the potential effects of public diplomacy. Ever since the February revolution, the Provisional Government had called for a liberalization of Allied war aims, and pro-war liberals in the West had insisted that Russians would continue fighting only if they were persuaded that it was genuinely a war for democracy and peace. House had pressed this view on Wilson, whose message to the Provisional Government in May and reply to the Pope had been designed to provide such reassurance. Following the Bolshevik revolution and the publication of the secret treaties, House, with Wilson's approval, proposed that the inter-Allied conference declare that they were not fighting for aggression or indemnity but to enable nations to lead their lives as seemed to them best. But even this anodyne formulation was unacceptable; as House reported, 'England passively was willing, France indifferently against it, Italy actively so.' Apparently believing that unilateral American action was now inevitable, House cabled the President not to make any statement concerning foreign affairs until he returned.[94]

Wilson responded that to 'omit foreign affairs' from his forthcoming Annual Message to Congress would be 'resented and do much harm'. In this address, he again made clear his opposition to calls for peace before victory was achieved, and that 'we shall regard the war as won only when the German people say to us, through properly accredited representatives, that they are ready to agree to a settlement based upon justice and the reparation of the wrongs their rulers have done' – and among those wrongs he specified not only Belgium but German domination of Middle Europe. But he also reiterated that the subsequent settlement must be based 'on generosity and justice, to the exclusion of all selfish claims to advantage even on the part of the victors'. He used the peace agitation of the socialists to claim that this ideal represented the aspirations of ordinary people in every country:

> You catch, with me, the voices of humanity that are in the air. They grow daily more audible, more articulate, more persuasive, and they come from the hearts of men everywhere. They insist that the war shall not end in vindictive action of any kind; that no nation shall be robbed or punished because the irresponsible rulers of a single country have themselves done deep and abominable wrong.

The combination of belligerence and moderation in this speech was expressed in microcosm towards Austria-Hungary. In response to pleas from Italy, Wilson asked Congress to declare war against that empire (as he had not done in April) on the grounds that it had become 'simply the vassal of the German Government'. But, in the face of fierce demands from

Theodore Roosevelt that the United States 'insist on liberty for the subject races' of the Central Empires, the President declared that 'we do not wish in any way to impair or to rearrange the Austro-Hungarian Empire'.[95]

On House's return to Washington, Wilson quickly decided to formulate American war aims more fully and requested a memorandum from 'the Inquiry' on the questions a peace conference would have to settle. The resultant document, of which Lippmann was the principal author, had a strikingly realpolitik tenor, being organized in terms of the assets and liabilities of the United States in its fight to prevent the Prussian autocracy becoming 'the master of the continent' by consolidating its control of central Europe. Thus, it argued that Austria-Hungary could be weaned away from Berlin by first stirring up nationalist discontent within the empire and then 'refusing to accept the extreme logic of this discontent, which would be the dismemberment of Austria-Hungary'. In comparable fashion, Germany could be pressured 'to democratize' by the threat that otherwise it would be commercially excluded from 'the outer world' after the war. The memorandum recommended that the United States indicate some interest in Alsace-Lorraine 'for the sake of the morale of France'. It concluded with a suggested statement of nine territorial peace terms and one on the emergence of 'a league of nations for common protection' among the countries resisting 'Germany's effort to dominate the world', to which that country's inclusion after the war 'will depend upon whether the German government is in fact representative of the German democracy'.[96]

On the typescript of this memorandum, Wilson drafted in shorthand what were to become several of the Fourteen Points. In doing so, he reduced the recommendations to brief declarations, deliberately excluding most of the argumentative justification. On the first Saturday morning of 1918, he and House worked through these points, 'first outlining general terms, such as open diplomacy, freedom of the seas, establishment of equality of trade conditions, guarantees for the reduction of national armaments, adjustment of colonial claims, general associations of nations for the conservation of peace'. They then discussed the 'territorial adjustments'. 'We actually got down to work at half past ten and finished remaking the map of the world, as we would have it, at half past twelve o'clock', House recorded in his diary.

As House noted with some anxiety, this 'entrance into European affairs to the extent of declaring *territorial* aims' constituted a further step away from traditional American policy.[97] The discontinuity was lessened by the fact that the Fourteen Points were mostly just specific applications of principles Wilson had set out in his address to the Senate – such as 'government by consent of the governed' and that 'every great people' should have access to the sea. He now more clearly interpreted the former principle as meaning national self-determination – a recognition of European realities that may also have been a response to the energetic propagation of this ideal by the Bolsheviks. However, he avoided explicitly endorsing the principle as such, simply calling for several frontiers to be drawn along 'clearly recognizable lines of nationality' and, more cautiously, for 'opportunity of autonomous development' to be given to the nationalities within the Austro-Hungarian and Turkish empires.[98] Nevertheless, the overall conception of a liberal peace presented in the Fourteen Points was significantly different from the idea of a settlement based on the status quo – which had seemed to be the implication of such phrases as 'a peace without victory' and 'no annexations, no indemnities'. It allowed for some accommodation of the revisionist aspirations of the countries fighting the Central Empires – as well as implying some opposition to them, notably with respect to what Italy had been promised as reward for entering the war in 1915. In staking out the ground he would stand on at the peace conference, Wilson was distancing himself from the more imperialistic provisions of the secret treaties but, with House at his elbow, he also sought to do so in a way that minimized disagreements with America's associates in the war.[99]

Lansing was given the opportunity to suggest some minor textual changes but the rest of the cabinet were not even informed of the President's intention to make a speech before he addressed Congress on 8 January 1918. Wilson justified this high-handedness on the grounds that he wished to avoid prior newspaper speculation about what he might say that would distract attention from his actual words. He also apparently felt a sense of urgency on account of the Russian situation, which he expressly gave as the reason for now making this more specific statement of what he presented as the war aims of 'the adversaries of the Central Powers'. The negotiations at Brest-Litovsk had been suspended after the Germans had made it clear that, in the absence of a general peace, they would not give up any of the territory they held. Wilson used this circumstance both to anathematize the German 'military leaders' again, and to praise the Russian people for supposedly refusing 'to compound their ideals or desert others that they themselves may be safe'. To the territorial points in the Inquiry memorandum, Wilson and House added one calling for 'the evacuation of all Russian territory', and declaring that 'the treatment accorded to Russia by her sister nations in the months to come will be the acid test of their good will, of their comprehension of her needs as distinguished from their own interests, and of their intelligent and unselfish sympathy'. Within days, the CPI office in Petrograd had pro-duced and distributed hundreds of thousands of poster copies of the President's speech in Russian.[100]

This desperate attempt to maintain an eastern front was only the most immediate way in which the Fourteen Points address was intended to aid the war effort. Some eminent scholars suggest that Wilson was still, as a year earlier, seeking to bring the war to an early end through a negotiated, compromise peace – acting 'more like a mediator than a belligerent', in Arthur Link's words.[101] But the new British ambassador, Lord Reading, reported from Washington in February that 'there is not the slightest sign of weakening in their determination to continue to the end'.[102] And Wilson had himself given Reading's predecessor his reasons for believing that a public statement of moderate war aims would help the cause at this critical juncture. One was the hope of weakening the German people's loy-alty to their government and will to fight. In the speech Wilson reiterated that 'we have no jealousy of German greatness, and there is nothing in this program that impairs it', and contrasted 'that military and imperialistic minority that has so far dominated their whole policy' with 'the liberal leaders and parties of Germany', whom he saw as responsible for the Reichstag resolution of the previous July that had repudiated 'forced acquisitions of territory and political, economic, or financial oppressions'. But the purpose on which Wilson laid most stress was the need to coun-teract what he saw as the likely appeal of the Bolshevik peace propaganda within the Allied countries.[103] The Inquiry memorandum had assured the President that a declaration of America's war aims would rally liberal opinion in Britain and France 'and therefore restore their national unity of purpose'. There were clear signs of war-weariness in both countries, prompted in Britain by the conservative Lord Lansdowne's plea for an end to the war and the publication of a Labour Party Memorandum on War Aims. With the demands for military manpower necessitating the cooper-ation of labor leaders, Lloyd George delivered an address to the Trades Union Congress on 5 January in which he set out British war aims in a manner 'so nearly akin' to the Fourteen Points that Wilson at first thought that 'it would be impossible for him to make the contemplated address before Congress'. House provided reassurance that Wilson's address 'would so smother the Lloyd George speech that the latter would be for-gotten and that he, the President, would once more become the spokesman for the Entente and, indeed, the spokesman for the liberals of the world'.[104]

House's flattering prediction was to be largely borne out. In Europe, the Fourteen Points were greeted enthusiastically in liberal and left-wing circles and met with little overt criticism (except in Italy). Although the speech had been primarily inspired by foreign policy considerations, the Inquiry memorandum had also argued that 'a powerful liberal offensive on the part of the United States will immensely stimulate American pride and interest in the war, and will assure the administration the support of that great mass of the American people who desire an idealistic solution'. This last assumption reflected Lippmann's progressive optimism. Wilson's speech was much applauded at home and succeeded particularly in reinforcing the allegiance of many liberals to the President and, to a lesser extent, the war.[105] But already it was far from clear that progressive idealism was the dominant mood of the country.

Certainly, it was not from the left that the fiercest criticism of the administration came in the winter of 1917–18. Despite their praise for the President's war message and their passionate commitment to the fight against Germany, neither Theodore Roosevelt nor Lodge had abated their hostility to Wilson. For his part, Wilson had told House before America entered the war that he regarded calls for 'a coalition cabinet' on the British model as 'the *Junkerthum* trying to creep in under cover of the patriotic feeling of the moment'.[106] Baker's rejection of Roosevelt's plan to lead a division of volunteers to the Western Front further embittered 'the Colonel' and his friends. Despite the lip-service paid on all sides to the principle that politics should be 'adjourned' during the war, Roosevelt was soon denouncing the administration in newspaper articles and speeches for bungling the war effort.[107] When Congress assembled in December, such criticisms were amplified. A committee chaired by the Democratic Senator Chamberlain of Oregon aggressively investigated the failures of the War Department in procuring ordnance, particularly machine guns, and in safeguarding the health of the draftees in the hastily-built cantonments where they were being trained. The severest winter weather for decades aggravated the situation and produced a crisis in the supply of coal. Giving priority to the bunkering of ships that otherwise were confined to port, the Fuel Administrator, Harry A. Garfield, ordered all factories except a few munitions plants to close for a week and for no fuel to be burned by businesses on Mondays until late March. Thereupon, as House noted, 'bedlam broke loose', with even Democratic newspapers abusing the hapless Garfield (a former colleague of Wilson's at Princeton).[108]

The administration faced down the storm. Baker out-argued his critics in the Senate hearings, and when Chamberlain charged that there was 'inefficiency in every bureau and in every department of the government', the President himself issued a stinging rebuttal.[109] As his opponents promoted bills to set up a war council and an all-powerful director of munitions, Wilson turned the tables on them by securing the passage of a measure to give *him* sweeping authority to reorganize the executive branch. 'Senator after senator has appealed to me most earnestly to "Cut the red tape"', he observed artlessly. 'I am asking for the scissors.'[110] This skillful exploitation of the patriotic inclination to support the President during a war and of his own personal standing fed the growing resentment in Congress, particularly the Senate, of Wilson's 'autocratic' style.

The upshot was, however, a great improvement in the efficiency of the government. The War Department was transformed when General Peyton March took over as Army Chief of Staff in early March. The War Industries Board at last became an effective organization under the direction of Bernard Baruch, a successful Wall Street speculator who was devoted to Wilson. Baruch, McAdoo (who was now in charge of the nation's railroads as well as the Treasury), Baker, Daniels, Hoover, Garfield, and the heads of the Shipping and War Trade Boards now met regularly on Wednesday mornings in the White House, in what came to be known as 'the war cabinet'. As one of the participants recollected, the President chaired these meetings with grace as well as efficiency, being at the door of his study to greet each member by name as they entered, ensuring they were all comfortably seated, passing round cigars. The collegiality of academic life rather than modern business management was Wilson's model, as he indicated when he rejected the idea of setting up procedures to monitor how well each department was meeting its schedules on the grounds that the consequent 'irritation' would be counterproductive: 'Inasmuch as I deal with sensibilities every day, I know how much, as a rule, they play in efficiency itself, and I do not think it would be wise to risk ruffling them all the time.' Wilson's own workload had been greatly increased by the war (as the number of volumes of his published *Papers* devoted to these months attests), but he seemed to stand the strain well, maintaining both his health and his regular games of golf.[111]

If management of the war effort was essentially a collective enterprise, Wilson himself retained firm control of high policy. Responding to complex, dramatic, and swiftly changing circumstances in the manner that best promoted his own goals was too important and delicate a matter to be delegated. On 24 January both the new German Chancellor, Hertling, and the Austrian Foreign Minister, Czernin, replied publicly to the Fourteen Points address. Their speeches had been coordinated, with each addressing the specific points that concerned their own country, but Czernin's evinced Vienna's eagerness for an end to the war. In his own reply, given in another speech to Congress on 11 February Wilson exploited the difference in tone to draw a sharp contrast between Hertling's wish to return to 'the method of the Congress of Vienna', with its bilateral deals between governments, and what he took to be Czernin's understanding of 'the fundamental elements of peace' in the modern, democratic age. On this occasion, Wilson spoke not of specific terms but of the four 'principles' that such a settlement should embody. In one of these, he endorsed national self-determination more explicitly than he had in the Fourteen Points address but in a carefully qualified way:

> all well defined national aspirations shall be accorded the utmost satis-faction that can be accorded them without introducing new or perpetu-ating old elements of discord and antagonism that would be likely in time to break the peace of Europe and consequently of the world.

This qualification no doubt represented Wilson's increasing awareness that the hallowed American axiom, 'government with the consent of the governed', had potentially explosive implications in the ethnic checker-board of central and eastern Europe, as well as his concern not to give the Vienna government the impression that he was bent on dismantling the Austro-Hungarian empire.[112] But it also indicated how Wilson ranked the different values that he thought should shape the settlement; where they conflicted, the claims of peaceful order would take priority over those of 'liberty'. Of course, Wilson believed that in the modern world only governments that rested on popular consent would be stable, but a little later he went further in disclaiming ideological evangelism by dis-tinguishing between 'free governments' and democracy. 'I am not fighting for democracy except for the peoples that want democracy', he told foreign correspondents in Washington. 'If they don't want it, that is none of my business.'[113]

As well as reiterating the moderation of America's war aims, Wilson in his speech to Congress reasserted the nation's determination and whole-hearted commitment to the cause.[114] He doubtless hoped that the shadow of American power would compensate for the collapse of the Eastern Front. He was already under strong pressure from the Allies for the Japanese to be given permission to send troops to Siberia in an effort to reconstitute an anti-German presence in the east. With American public and congressional opinion deeply suspicious of Japanese aggrandizement, Wilson agreed with House that approving such an enterprise would dis-credit his anti-imperialist principles at home as well as abroad. After the failure of Trotsky's 'no war–no peace' strategy, the Bolsheviks finally accepted Germany's peace terms at the beginning of March. In the Treaty of Brest-Litovsk, European Russia was reduced approximately to its pre-Peter the Great dimensions.

Wilson was to interpret this as showing that Germany's 'military leaders, who are her real rulers' sought to build an empire in the east that would dominate the whole of Eurasia. In the face of such an attitude, he declared that there was 'but one response possible from us: Force, Force to the utmost, Force without stint or limit, the righteous and triumphant Force which shall make Right the Law of the world, and cast every selfish dominion down in the dust'.[115] But the timing of this bellicose speech, delivered in Baltimore on 6 April suggests it was prompted less by the terms of the Brest-Litovsk treaty than by the need to prepare the American public for a greater military effort. On 21 March Ludendorff, having transferred forces from the east, launched an assault in the west, initially against the British lines. As the British reeled back, Lloyd George, in a hectic series of telegrams to Washington, pleaded for American reinforcements to be sent quickly and for them to be 'brigaded' with the Allied armies: 'It rests with America to win or lose the decisive battle of the war.'[116] Although Wilson in Washington did not succumb to the panic apparently prevailing in London, he was very conscious that his political opponents were seeking to present the crisis as further evidence that the American army had not been made ready in time. In this situation, the President's reluctance to merge the American war effort with that of the Allies diminished, though not to the extent that he was prepared to accede to British requests that he overrule Pershing's obstinate determination to maintain the independence of his army. It was readily agreed that a Supreme Commander, the French General Foch, be appointed to coordinate strategy, a rather shaky compromise was reached over the 'brigading' issue and, with the British promising to provide the necessary shipping, the US War Department undertook to send 480,000 US troops to France over the next four months. In the event, the figure was to be almost double that number, and by early July Pershing had more than a million men under his command. The Americans became actively engaged in the fighting in early June when, at Château-Thierry and Belleau Wood, they played an important part in checking a German offensive that threatened Paris and they continued to be heavily involved on the Aisne–Marne Front through July. At the end of that month, Wilson approved a War Department plan to build the AEF up to 80 divisions (about three and a half million men) for the 1919 campaign (the Supreme War Council had requested 100 divisions).[117]

At this critical stage of the war, Wilson shifted his position on two issues – military intervention in Russia and the future of the Austro-

Hungarian empire. On the first, there were two stages to the process. Following Lansing, the President drew a sharp distinction between the proposed Japanese intervention in Siberia and sending western forces to the north Russian ports of Murmansk and Archangel, where there were substantial quantities of Allied military supplies. His opposition to the latter idea, which seemed at one time to meet with Trotsky's approval, was never so strong, and in early June he agreed to American participation in such an expedition provided that Foch authorized the consequent diversion of troops and shipping from the Western Front. Far from diminishing Allied pressure for intervention in Siberia, this concession only served to increase it. An additional justification was furnished by the position of the so-called Czech Legion, a body of over 50,000 former Austro-Hungarian prisoners of war who now wanted to fight for their own nation's freedom on the Western Front but had become embroiled with Bolshevik forces along the trans-Siberian railway. The Bolshevik forces included some German and Austrian former prisoners of war whose numbers and role were greatly exaggerated in reports reaching Washington. The Supreme War Council now insisted that it was vital to prevent Germany, with either reactionary or Bolshevik collaborators, from gaining control of Russia's resources, and that this would require a force of 100,000, who would necessarily be mostly Japanese. While privately indicating that he did not read the situation in this way, Wilson did agree in early July to the sending to Vladivostok (which had just been captured by the Czechs) of a force of 14,000, equally composed of Americans and Japanese. Shortly afterwards, he drafted on his own typewriter an aide-mémoire that was circulated to the Allies and then given, in slightly modified form, to the press. This emphasized that the intervention was solely to help the Czechs, guard military stores and 'render such aid as may be acceptable to the Russians in the organization of their own self-defense'.[118]

In later years, Soviet historians portrayed this intervention as the first move in the Cold War, and Wilson's motivation in sending troops to Russia became the subject of a highly charged historiographical controversy. There is little doubt that the President had become increasingly antipathetic to the Bolsheviks, but this feeling seems to have played a comparatively small part in his troubled consideration of the issue.[119] He fully shared the judgment of his military chiefs that American resources of men and shipping should not be diverted from the much more important and accessible Western Front. In resisting Allied pressure, he took his stand on the impropriety of uninvited military expeditions to a friendly country – a principle no doubt reinforced by his Mexican experience which had taught him that such intervention was likely to produce a nationalist backlash that would strengthen the very political forces it was designed to weaken. In addition, he was well aware that any association with what might be seen as pro-Tsarist forces would outrage progressive opinion in America. And, for both foreign policy and domestic political reasons, he was unwilling to give Japan a green light in Siberia. His eventual acquiescence seems to been an attempt to limit both the scale and the scope of Japanese intervention as well as a response to the demands of Allied unity and the moral claims of the Czechs. But the outcome of these complex and conflicting considerations was an ill-defined mission whose support of the Czechs inevitably made it appear to be taking sides in the developing civil war in Russia.

It was all the more difficult to refuse the Czechs' pleas because the United States had begun to support their claims to independence. At the end of May, the State Department expressed the 'earnest sympathy' of the American government with 'the nationalistic aspirations of the Czecho-Slovaks and Jugo-Slavs for freedom', and a month later it declared that 'all branches of the Slav race should be completely freed from German and Austrian rule'. In early September, the United States recognized the Czechoslovak National Council as a *de facto* belligerent government, and by October, when the Austrian government requested an armistice on the basis of the Fourteen Points, Wilson himself drafted the official note that made explicit the change in his position: he was

> no longer at liberty to accept the mere 'autonomy' of these peoples [the Czechoslovaks and Jugoslavs] as a basis of peace, but is obliged to insist that they, and not he, shall be the judges of what action on the part of the Austro-Hungarian government will satisfy their aspirations and their conception of their rights and destiny as members of the family of nations.[120]

The change in policy followed the ending of hopes that Austro-Hungary could be weaned from Germany and induced to make peace. Allied attempts to achieve this goal through clandestine contacts had been dealt a fatal blow in April when the French premier Clemenceau published a letter in which the Austrian emperor had appeared to endorse France's claim to Alsace-Lorraine. Lansing pointed out to Wilson that, 'from the standpoint of winning the war', there was now a strong case for encouraging the nationalities' hopes for independence. Wilson accepted the logic of this analysis, but with some reluctance. He told Sir William Wiseman, the young British official who had become House's confidant, that 'it was a thousand pities that Clemenceau had acted as he did', and that 'he disliked most intensely' the idea of 'setting the Austrian people against their own government by plots and intrigues. We were not good at that work, and generally made a mess of it, but he saw no other way. He intended to support the Czechs, Poles, and Jugo-Slavs.'[121]

Developments during the summer increased the President's commitment to his new course. The American press and public became increasingly conscious of, and sympathetic to, the aspirations of the Czechoslovaks and Jugoslavs, stimulated by the presence in the United States of the Czech leader, Thomas Masaryk. The exploits of the Czechs in Russia excited much admiration, and in August a speech by Lodge indicated that the Republicans were likely to make recognition of the nationalities a campaign issue.[122] Masaryk, a fellow professor, made a very favorable impression on Wilson who assured him in September that it was 'my earnest endeavor to be of as much service as possible to the Czecho-Slovak peoples'.[123] The esteem was mutual and Wilson's name was to be much honored in independent Czechoslovakia as a liberator and the apostle of self-determination.[124] In fact, the President's endorsement of claims to national independence continued to be dependent upon the particular political and diplomatic circumstances of each case and, as we have seen, even with respect to the Austro-Hungarian empire his stance had for long been notably cautious. Indeed, it is striking that Wilson adopted each of the two causes with which his name is most commonly identified as a result of pressures from Europe. Just as it had been Grey's pleas that had led him in 1915–16 to commit the United States to participation in a league of nations, so his espousal of the principle of national self-determination was a response, first to Bolshevik propaganda, and then to wartime exigencies and developments on the ground.[125]

The Austrian peace note reflected the turn in the tide on the Western Front during the summer; from August, it was the Allies who were on the offensive, with the AEF playing a full part in the fighting. The engagement of American troops, and the consequent casualty lists, raised the war spirit in the United States to new heights. Leading Republicans took advantage of the bellicosity of the public mood to express views about the peace that implicitly challenged the President's approach. Lodge called for Germany's 'unconditional surrender' and a peace dictated in Berlin, while Roosevelt declared that 'to substitute internationalism for nationalism means to do away with patriotism'. In part these outbursts were opening shots in the forthcoming congressional elections but they also reflected authentic and deeply felt convictions. Believing that Germany alone was responsible for the slaughter of the last four years, Roosevelt and Lodge wanted a punitive peace, and regarded schemes for reforming the whole nature of international relations as both utopian and cover for an immoral pacifism. They were consciously allying themselves with conservatives and nationalists in the Allied countries against Wilson and his liberal supporters.[126]

In a major address at the end of September, Wilson met the challenge by declaring that the new diplomacy was a product of forces beyond the control of any government. After four years, during which the whole world had been drawn into the conflict, 'the common will of mankind has been substituted for the particular purposes of individual states', and 'statesmen must follow the clarified common thought or be broken'. Peace could not be obtained through 'any kind of bargain or compromise' with the discredited governments of the Central Empires, but after their defeat the settlement must be based on 'impartial justice', with 'no discrimination between those to whom we wish to be just and those to whom we do not wish to be just'. The 'indispensable instrumentality' of 'a secure and lasting peace' was 'a League of Nations formed under covenants that will be efficacious'; under its auspices, there would be no place for alliances, 'special, selfish economic combinations' or secret agreements and treaties. Wilson argued strongly that such a League of Nations must be included in the peace settlement itself. He resisted the frequently made suggestion that it be formed immediately, as in that case 'it would be merely a new alliance confined to the nations associated against a common enemy'. It must not be left until later because 'there will be parties to the peace whose promises have proved untrustworthy, and means must be found in connection with the peace settlement itself to remove that source of insecurity'. He did not explain how this argument fitted with his implication elsewhere that the existing German government would not survive the war, but it is likely that the real reason why he was so insistent on incorporating the league in the peace treaty is that this would make it more difficult for the Senate to reject it – a problem of which he was already very conscious.[127]

Wilson ended his speech by urging Allied leaders to speak openly if they thought he was 'in any degree mistaken' in his judgment of the best way to secure 'a satisfactory settlement'. None rose to the challenge; reservations or dissent were expressed by silence, as they were at home where the address was very warmly received, particularly by liberals, Democrats and pro-League Republicans such as Taft. The most dramatic response, however, came from the German government which shortly afterwards sent a note to Wilson asking for an armistice, and accepting 'as a basis for the peace negotiations, the program laid down by the President of the United States in his message to Congress of January 8, 1918, and in his subsequent pronouncements, particularly in his address of September 27,

1918'. The initiative for this move had come from the High Command following dramatic Allied successes on the Western Front.[128]

Upon receiving the German note, Wilson immediately drafted a reply seeking explicit assurance that the German government accepted the terms he had set out in his speeches and that their forces would withdraw at once from all invaded territory. This response was in sharp contrast to his instant refusal of a request for peace parleys from the Austrian government three weeks earlier. The speed and unilateral nature of that action had been deplored by House who had attributed it to Tumulty's influence and domestic political considerations. House again wanted Wilson to consult with the Allies before replying to the German note but, on this occasion, the President also flew in the face of Tumulty's insistence that anything short of 'an absolute and unqualified rejection' of the German approach 'would destroy your leadership, which means so much at this time'. In the Senate, Democrats as well as Republicans declared that this was no time to be talking of peace and that the Fourteen Points would be inadequate as the basis for an armistice. The Democratic Senator Ashurst of Arizona called at the White House to warn the President face to face that 'if your reply should fail to come up to the American spirit, you are destroyed'. When Wilson responded that 'so far as my being destroyed is concerned, I am willing if I can serve the country to go into a cellar and read poetry the remainder of my life', Ashurst 'told him that his failure to demand unconditional surrender would leave him leisure in which to read poetry, and that he would read it in a cellar to escape the cyclone of the people's wrath'. [129]

Why did Wilson at this time adopt such a defiant stance towards American public opinion when he was generally so sensitive to it? Partly, no doubt, because he felt that the bellicosity of the public mood was not only unattractive but also shortsighted; he told Ashurst that he was 'now playing for a hundred years hence'. As a young man, he had written of the statesman's need 'to distinguish the firm and progressive popular *thought* from the momentary and whimsical popular *mood*, the transitory or mistaken popular passion'. But it was unlike Wilson to leave an exposed flank for his political opponents to attack, and he had gratified the demand for no truck with the enemy in his brusque dismissal of the Austrian overture. His equally quick decision to engage in dialogue with the German government surely reflected a realization that the terms of its note offered an opportunity to enhance his influence over the peace. He had over the summer received several reports of the strong opposition within the Allied governments both to the views he had expressed and to the whole idea that the President of the United States should determine the nature of the European settlement.[130] House had recently warned him that 'as the Allies succeed, your influence will diminish', and that he should seek to commit them 'to as much of your program as is possible' while they still needed American military assistance. That Wilson recognized the realism of this advice was shown when he wrote to House in late October that

> our whole weight should be thrown for an armistice which will prevent a renewal of hostilities by Germany but that will be as moderate and reasonable as possible within those limits, because it is certain that too much success or security on the part of the Allies will make a genuine peace settlement exceedingly difficult if not impossible.[131]

The German note and President's reply gave a new status to the Fourteen Points and Wilson's other statements about the peace and, not surprisingly, opened them to more explicit criticism than they had hitherto received. At home, Theodore Roosevelt called on the Senate and the American people to 'emphatically repudiate the so-called Fourteen Points and the various similar utterances of the President'. More politely, the Allied governments reminded the President that there had been no discussion among the Associated Powers of the 'points at issue', and stressed the danger that an armistice might simply give the German army a breathing space to regroup.[132]

The German approach had placed Wilson in a diplomatically advantageous position which he was not prepared to surrender by immediately bringing the Allies into the dialogue, but he evidently felt the stress of playing a lone hand when the stakes were so high. He and House agreed that 'the question of going to war with Germany was easy compared to it', and he struck members of his War Cabinet as 'more nervous than usual' when the form of a note to Germany was under discussion.[133] As the correspondence continued, Wilson responded to the pressures at home and abroad by extending his demands on Berlin. He indicated that the detailed terms for an armistice were matters for the 'military advisers' of the Associated Governments to determine, and that they had to be such as 'to make a renewal of hostilities on the part of Germany impossible'. In his second note (14 October), he also observed that among the points he had set out and that Germany had now accepted as the basis of peace was his call, in a speech on the Fourth of July, for 'the destruction of every arbitrary power anywhere that can separately, secretly, and of its single choice disturb the peace of the world; or, if it cannot be presently destroyed, at least its reduction to virtual impotency'. Wilson now stated flatly that 'the power that has hitherto controlled the German nation is of the sort here described', and in a further note on 23 October declared that if the

American government had to deal with 'the military masters and the monarchical autocrats of Germany ... it must demand, not peace negotiations, but surrender'.[134] This tougher stance did much to defuse criticism both at home and abroad as well as contributing to the pressures that led to the Kaiser's forced abdication on 9 November. Once again, Wilson had found in the distinction between the German government and its people a way of expressing belligerence without abandoning the ideal of a moderate peace.

Shortly after the dispatch of his final note to Germany, Wilson appealed for the return of a Democratic Congress on the grounds that 'unity of command is as necessary now in civil action as it is upon the field of battle' and that a Republican victory 'would certainly be interpreted on the other side of the water as a repudiation of my leadership'. This statement obviously made the Republicans' success ten days later in winning control of both houses of Congress more damaging to the President's prestige than it would otherwise have been, and several of his close associates, including Mrs Wilson as well as House, judged it to have been a blunder – as have most historians. Yet a very similar appeal had been made in 1900 by President McKinley and his supporters (including Theodore Roosevelt). Nor was Wilson the first in 1918 to politicize the nation's foreign policy – only the previous day, Roosevelt had declared that a peace based on the Fourteen Points 'would represent not the unconditional surrender of Germany but the conditional surrender of the United States'.[135]

However, Wilson's move was not an impulsive riposte; it was something he had planned to do several weeks earlier. It accorded, of course, with his lifelong belief in party government as well as being a response to the pleas for his endorsement from Democratic candidates across the country. But it also seems to have reflected an increasing sense of his own status in world affairs. In conversation with the sympathetic Morgan partner, Thomas Lamont, the President recounted stories of how French schoolgirls and Liverpool dockers had deferred to the invocation of his name.[136] And he evidently wanted to use his enhanced authority to strike back at his chief opponents. It was only upon an adviser's suggestion that he omitted a direct reference to Lodge in Tumulty's original draft of the appeal.[137] The personal animosity was, of course, entirely mutual – more than two years earlier, Lodge had written to Roosevelt that he had 'never expected to hate anyone in politics with the hatred I feel towards Wilson'.[138] The natural clash of ambitious rivals with well-developed egos had gained an extra emotional dimension from the strong feelings aroused by the war in Europe.[139]

Although certainly disappointed by the election results, Wilson was not downcast. He remained determined to shape the peace, and confident that he could do so. To secure agreement with the Allies over the Armistice, House had gone again to Europe, whence he communicated with Wilson by cable in a private code so elementary that the British Secret Service found it comically easy to crack.[140] With regard to the military terms of the Armistice, Wilson initially expressed misgivings at the provision for Allied bridgeheads across the Rhine, but he did not press the point. Instead, he and House concentrated on securing agreement that the Fourteen Points and Wilson's other public statements should form the basis of peace. When Clemenceau and Lloyd George, observing that they had not been consulted over the Fourteen Points, professed uncertainty over their meaning, House produced a memorandum (prepared by Walter Lippmann and another journalist, Frank Cobb) that sought to spell out their implications, stressing the ideals of national self-determination and the protection of minorities. Wilson agreed to this document as a 'satisfactory interpretation' of the general principles involved, though 'merely illustrative' and not binding in its details. The point that caused the most trouble was the second, concerning freedom of the seas. Wilson, describing this as one of the 'essentially American terms' in the program, insisted that he would not take part in the peace negotiations unless it was accepted. Through House, he threatened to publicize the matter and also warned that, failing agreement, the United States would use its greater resources to outbuild the Royal Navy. For his part, Lloyd George maintained that, if he accepted the principle, he would be out of office in a week.[141]

The eventual compromise was that the Allied governments declared their willingness to make peace on the terms 'laid down in the President's address to Congress of 8 January 1918, and the principles of settlement enunciated in his subsequent addresses', subject to two qualifications. The first was that they reserved their position on the interpretation of the phrase, 'freedom of the seas', and the second that the restoration of invaded territory for which Wilson had called should include compensation for all damage done to Allied civilians and their property. House assured the President that 'we have won a great diplomatic victory ... in the face of a hostile and influential junta in the United States and the thoroughly unsympathetic personnel constituting the Entente governments'. But in observing that he doubted if the other governments 'quite realize how far they are now committed to the American peace program', House gave grounds for questioning the extent of his achievement.[142] For, with German power irretrievably broken, there could henceforth be no effective challenge to the victors' interpretation of the terms of the armistice. It remained to be seen how far Wilson's ability to shape the peace had really been enhanced by this formal endorsement of his various points and principles.

Notes

1 US Bureau of the Census, *Historical Statistics of the United States*, Washington, DC, 1973, p. 1104; Robert H. Ferrell, *Woodrow Wilson and World War I, 1917–1921*, New York, 1985, pp. 84–7.

2 See, for example, Arthur M. Schlesinger, Jr, *Cycles of American History*, London, 1987, p. 53; Arthur A. Stein, 'Domestic Constraints, Extended Deterrence and the Incoherence of Grand Strategy', in Richard Rosecrance and Arthur A. Stein (eds), *The Domestic Bases of Grand Strategy*, Ithaca NY, and London, 1993, p. 97; John Lewis Gaddis, *We Now Know: Rethinking Cold War History*, Oxford, 1997, p. 5.

3 For example, Address to Businessmen, Detroit, 10 July 1916, Luncheon Address to Women in Cincinnati, 26 October 1916, *PWW*, vol. 37, p. 384, vol. 38, pp. 527–9. For the 1914 comments, see Spring Rice to Sir Edward Grey, 8 September 1914, *PWW*, vol. 31, pp, 13–14; House diary, 8 November 1914, Charles E. Seymour, *The Intimate Papers of Colonel House*, London, 1926, vol. I, p. 305.

4 Robert E. Osgood, *Ideals and Self-Interest in America's Foreign Relations: The Great Transformation of the Twentieth Century*, Chicago, IL, 1953, pp. 209–11, 221–2.

5 For the war plans, see J.A.S. Grenville, 'Diplomacy and War Plans in the United States', in Paul M. Kennedy (ed.), *The War Plans of the Great Powers, 1880–1914*, London, 1979, pp. 35–7; David M. Esposito, *The Legacy of Woodrow Wilson: American War Aims in World War I*, Westport, CT, 1996, pp. 45–56.

6 Osgood, *Ideals and Self-Interest*, pp. 253–4; Ernest R. May, *The World War and American Isolation, 1914–1917*, Cambridge, MA, 1959, p. 426; Arthur S. Link, *Wilson: Campaigns for Progressivism and Peace, 1916–17*, Princeton, N.J., 1965, pp. 302–3; *New Republic*, 10 (17 February 1917): p.57.

7 For more details on this point, see Link, *Campaigns*, pp. 410–11.

8 Address to Congress, 3 February 1917, *PWW*, vol. 41, pp. 108–12.

9 Address to Congress, 26 February 1917, *PWW*, vol. 41, pp. 283–7; Richard M. Abrams, *The Burdens of Progress, 1900–1929*, Glenview, IL, 1978, pp. 101, 107–8.

10 Luncheon address in Cincinnati, 26 October 1916, *PWW*, vol. 40, p. 528.

11 *Congressional Record*, 65th Congress, 1st session, Senate, pp. 213–14.

12 John Milton Cooper, Jr, 'The Command of Gold Reversed: American Loans to Britain, 1915–1917', *Pacific Historical Review*, 45 (May 1976): 223.

13 Winston S. Churchill, *The World Crisis, 1916–1918*, London, 1927, Part I, p. 229.

14 May, *World War and American Isolation*, p. 432.

15 Link, *Campaigns*, p. 414.

16 Patrick Devlin, *Too Proud to Fight: Woodrow Wilson's Neutrality*, London, 1974, p. 680.

17 W.H. Page to the President and Secretary of State, 11 February 1917, 6 February 1917, *PWW*, vol. 41, pp. 211–14, 136–7.

18 Jane Addams, *Peace and Bread in Time of War*, New York, 1922, pp. 63–4.

19 House diary, 1 February 1917, *PWW*, vol. 41, p. 87; Link, *Campaigns*, p. 296.

20 House diary, 1 February 1917, *PWW*, vol. 41, p. 87; Link, *Campaigns*, pp. 293–8.

21 Address to Congress, 3 February 1917, *PWW*, vol. 41, p. 111.

22 Link, *Campaigns*, pp. 301, 309–10.

23 Ibid., pp. 314–17.

24 Ibid., pp. 342–6, 353–9, 372, 396–7.

25 For evidence of the state of public opinion at this time, including the Congressional debate on armed neutrality, see ibid., pp. 291–3, 349–50, 354, 359–61. 415–19.

26 Diary of Josephus Daniels, 19 March 1917, *PWW*, vol. 41, p. 430.

27 Link, *Campaigns*, pp. 373–7; May, *World War and American Isolation*, p. 428.

28 Link, *Campaigns*, pp. 396–408.

29 Wilson to Cleveland H. Dodge, 4 April 1917, *PWW*, vol. 41, pp. 542–3.

30 An Unpublished Prolegomenon to a Peace Note, c. 25 November 1916, *PWW*, vol. 40, p. 67.

31 Link, *Campaigns*, pp. 398–400, House diary, 27 March 1917. *Intimate Papers*, vol. II, p. 467.

32 A Statement, 4 March 1917, *PWW*, vol. 41, pp. 318–19.

33 In his second inaugural address, (5 March 1917) he had laid great stress on the importance of national unity: 'it is imperative that we should stand together' (*PWW*, vol. 41, pp. 332–5). Two years later, returning from the peace conference in Paris, he explained to Mrs Wilson's secretary that

> he didn't go into the war until he was sure he had the country behind him, that he felt he could not have gone one minute sooner, for the American people were not ready. I asked him later if he was like so many, ready ahead, and he said, 'No, I was like the majority of my countrymen, and followed with them.' He said he used to ask the members of the Cabinet at the meetings every week what they heard, and they said the Americans would follow him, and he said, 'I couldn't have them follow, they had to go into it with a whoop.'

> (Diary of Edith Benham, 2 July 1919, *PWW*, vol. 61, pp. 370–71)

34 Lansing memorandum, 20 March 1917, *PWW*, vol. 41, 438. The division of opinion to which Wilson referred had been illustrated in the vote in the House of Representatives on an amendment to the Armed Ships Bill that would have forbidden armed American ships from carrying munitions or belligerent nationals to a belligerent country. This amendment was supported by 47 percent of the members from the Middle West and 64 percent from the Far West, and was lost by 293 votes to 125 in a division on 1 March. Link, *Campaigns*, p. 354n.

35 For Kennedy's concern with the way his actions could be presented and might be perceived, see Ernest R. May and Philip D. Zelikow (eds), *The Kennedy Tapes: Inside the White House During the Cuban Missile Crisis*, Cambridge, MA, 1997, especially pp. 493–9, 512–18, 528–30.

36 Lansing Memorandum, 20 March 1917; Tumulty to Wilson, 24 March 1917; House diary, 28 March 1917, *PWW*, vol. 41, pp. 440–41, 462–4, 497–8.

37 Link, *Campaigns*, pp. 420–21.

38 Address to Congress, 2 April 1917, *PWW*, vol. 41, pp. 519–27.

39 *War Memoirs of Robert Lansing*, London, 1935, p. 243.

40 'Leaders of Men', 17 June 1890, *PWW*, vol. 6, pp. 658–70. See above, Chapter 2, pp. 37–8.

41 For a contrary view, see Thomas J. Knock, *To End All Wars: Woodrow Wilson and the Quest for a New World Order*, Princeton, NJ, 1992, pp. 118–21.

42 *Congressional Record*, 65th Congress, 1st session, pp. 210–14, 223–34.

43 Quoted in Ferrell, *Wilson and World War I*, p. 8.

44 *Congressional Record*, 65th Congress, 1st session, pp. 200–54; Osgood, *Ideals and Self-Interest*, pp. 259–61.

45 An Appeal to the American People, 15 April 1917; remarks at the dedication of the Red Cross Building, 12 May 1917; Representative James T. Heflin to Wilson, 17 May 1917; Wilson to Heflin, 22 May 1917, *PWW*, vol. 42, pp. 72, 282, 323–4, 370–71.

46 See above, p. 149.

47 Wilson to Herbert Hoover, 10 December 1917, *PWW*, vol. 45, pp. 256–7.

48 Wilson to House, 21 July 1917, *PWW*, vol. 43, pp. 237–8 (emphasis in original).

49 Lansing memorandum, 20 March, 1917, *PWW*, vol. 41, pp. 436–44.

50 One newspaper survey found a two-to-one sentiment in Congress against sending any troops to Europe. Walter Millis, *Road to War: America 1914–1917*, Boston, MA, 1935, p. 435. In response to an army request for $3 billion of military equipment a few days after the declaration of war, the chairman of the Senate Finance Committee exclaimed, 'Good Lord! You're not going to send soldiers over there are you?' Frederick Palmer, *Newton D. Baker: America at War*, New York, 1931, vol. 1, p. 120.

51 *Congressional Record*, 65th Congress, 1st session, pp. 207–8; Ferrell, *Wilson and World War I*, p. 14; Esposito, *Legacy of Wilson*, pp. 92–3; Palmer, *Baker*, vol. 1, pp. 108–9.

52 Address to Congress, 2 April 1917, *PWW*, vol. 41, pp. 521–2.

53 Esposito, *Legacy of Wilson*, pp. 100, 123–4.

54 Thompson, *Reformers and War*, pp. 157–8; Victor S. Mamatey, *The United States and East Central Europe 1914–1918: A Study in Wilsonian Diplomacy and Propaganda*, Princeton, NJ, 1957, p. 90.

55 Wilson to House, 21 July 1917, *PWW*, vol. 43, p. 238.

56 Wilson to E.W. Pou, 13 April, 1917, *PWW*, vol. 42, p. 52.

57 *PWW*, vol. 42, pp. 173–6, 182–94; Palmer, *Baker*, vol. 1, pp. 150–56, 170–75.

58 Ferrell, *Wilson and World War I*, pp. 17–18.

59 Ibid., pp. 34–9.

60 Link, *Campaigns*, pp. 379–82.

61 A.J. Balfour to Sir William Wiseman, 28 June 1917; Wilson to House, 21 July 1917, *PWW*, vol. 43, pp. 38–9, 238.

62 Ferrell, *Wilson and World War I*, pp. 86–90; Wilson's address to Congress, 2 April 1917, *PWW*, vol. 41, p. 522.

63 House diary, 27 March 1917, *PWW*, vol. 41, p. 483.

64 'A Statement to the American People', 26 July 1918, *PWW*, vol. 49, pp. 97–8. Wilson has been much criticized for the tardiness of this statement, but in fact he had more briefly condemned 'the mob spirit' in his address to the American Federation of Labor in November 1917 (*PWW*, vol. 45, p. 16). For an example of such criticism, and details on the vigilante activity, see H.C. Peterson and Gilbert C. Fite, *Opponents of War, 1917–1918*, Madison WI, 1957, pp. 194–207.

65 This is if one accepts, as Link gives reasons for doing, the authenticity of the newspaper editor Frank Cobb's account of the interview he had with Wilson in March 1917. Arthur S. Link, 'That Cobb Interview', *Journal of American History*, 72 (1985): 7–17.

66 Address to Congress, 2 April 1917, *PWW*, vol. 41, p. 523.

67 Address to Women in Cincinnati, 26 October 1916, *PWW*, vol. 38, p. 531. See above, Chapter 5, p. 128.

68 Address to the American Federation of Labor, 12 November 1917, *PWW*, vol. 45, pp. 12–14. I was alerted to this contrast by Devlin, *Too Proud to Fight*, pp. 683–4.

69 Arno J. Mayer, *Political Origins of the New Diplomacy, 1917–1918*, New Haven, CT, 1959, pp. 194–5.

70 To the Provisional Government of Russia, 22 May 1917, *PWW*, vol. 42, p. 366.

71 Address to the League to Enforce Peace, 27 May 1916; address to the Senate, 22 January 1917, *PWW*, vol. 37, p. 116; vol. 40, p. 539.

72 Address to Congress, 2 April 1917, *PWW*, vol. 41, p. 524.

73 That Wilson anticipated the latter eventuality was made clear publicly a few weeks later when he said that after the war 'the free peoples of the world must draw together in some common covenant, some genuine and practical cooperation that will in effect combine their force to secure peace and justice in the dealings of nations with one another'. In conversation with the Belgian Foreign Minister in August, Wilson suggested that 'a pact for mutual defense' would be 'much more practical than a "League of Nations", which would be very difficult to organize since all countries, the smallest ones as well as the largest, would wish to take part there on the same footing'. To the Provisional Government of Russia, 22 May 1917; Baron Moncheur to Baron Charles de Broqueville, 14 August 1917, *PWW*, vol. 42, p. 367; vol. 43, pp. 467–8.

74 Theodore Roosevelt to W.A. White, 3 August 1917, quoted in Osgood, *Ideals and Self-Interest*, pp. 271–2.

75 Wilson to Lansing, 11 May 1917; Lansing to Wilson, 19 May 1917; Flag Day address, 14 June 1917, *PWW*, vol. 42, pp. 274, 350, 501–3.

76 Pope Benedict XV to the Rulers of the Belligerent Peoples, 1 August 1917, enclosed in W.H. Page to Lansing, 15 August 1917, *PWW*, vol. 43, pp. 482–5.

77 Wilson to His Holiness the Pope, 27 August 1917, *PWW*, vol. 44, pp. 57–9.

78 House to Wilson, 15, 17 August 1917, Wilson to House, 16 August 1917; House diary, 15, 18 August 1917, *PWW*, vol. 43, pp. 471–2, 508–9, 488–9, 486–7, 521.

79 Lansing to Wilson, 20 August 1917, 21 August 1917, ibid., pp. 523–5, vol. 44, pp. 18–22.

80 Wilson to House, 1 June 1917, *PWW*, vol. 42, p. 433.

81 For a contrary view, see Arthur S. Link, *Woodrow Wilson: Revolution, War, and Peace*, Arlington Heights, IL, 1979, pp. 79–81.

82 House to Wilson, 17 August 1917, *PWW*, vol. 43, pp. 508–9.

83 Wilson to H.B. Brougham, 29 September 1917, to David Lawrence, 5 October 1917; *New York Times*, 9 October 1917, *PWW*, vol. 44, pp. 279, 309, 325–7. Wilson also discussed with House making a speech 'to say that our people must not be deceived by Germany's apparent willingness to give up Belgium and Alsace-Lorraine, for it would leave her impregnable in both Austria and Turkey and her dream of Mittle-Europa would be realized'. House diary, 13 October 1917, *PWW*, vol. 44, p. 379.

84 Wilson to His Holiness the Pope, 27 August 1917, *PWW*, vol. 44, p. 59; to the Provisional Government, 22 May 1917, *PWW*, vol. 42, p. 367; address to the American Federation of Labor, 12 November 1917, *PWW*, vol. 45, p. 14.

85 In sending House a draft of his reply to the Pope, Wilson explained that 'I have not thought it wise to say more or to be more specific because it might provoke dissenting voices from France or Italy if I should – if I should say, for example, that their territorial claims did not interest us', Wilson to House, 23 August 1917, *PWW*, vol. 44, p. 33.

86 Sterling J. Kernek, 'Distractions of Peace During War: The Lloyd George Government's Reactions to Woodrow Wilson, December 1916–November 1918', *Transactions of the American Philosophical Society*, new series, 65: 2 (Philadelphia, PA, 1975): 59–60; Wilson to House, 23 August 1917, *PWW*, vol. 44, p. 33.

87 Wilson to House, 2 September 1917, *PWW*, vol. 44, pp. 120–21.

88 David Lloyd George to Wilson, 3 September 1917 (received by Wilson, 20 September), ibid., pp. 125–30.

89 W.G. McAdoo to Wilson, 13, 29 September 1917, ibid., pp. 195–8, 280–84.

90 House diary, 13 October 1917, *PWW*, vol. 44, p. 380.

91 For House's prediction, see House to Wilson, 14 November 1917, *PWW*, vol. 45, p. 47.

92 Wilson to N.D. Baker, 4 December 1917 (emphasis in original), ibid., p. 208.

93 George F. Kennan, *Russia Leaves the War*, New York, 1967, pp. 173–8; David S. Foglesong, *America's First Secret War Against Bolshevism: US Intervention in the Russian Civil War, 1917–1920*, Chapel Hill, NC and London, 1995, pp. 79–105.

94 House to Wilson, 30 November 1917, 2 December 1917, 1 December 1917; Wilson to House, 1 December 1917; House diary, 18 December 1917, *PWW*, vol. 45, pp. 166, 176, 184–5, 177, 323.

95 Wilson to House, 3 December 1917; Annual Message on the State of the Union, 4

December 1917, ibid., pp. 187, 194–200. For Roosevelt's support of the nationalities, see Mamatey, *The United States and East Central Europe*, pp. 133–5, 156–7, 162–3.

96 House diary, 18 December 1917; memorandum by S.E. Mezes, D.H. Miller and W. Lippmann, 'The Present Situation: The War Aims and Peace Terms It Suggests', 22 December, 1917, *PWW*, vol. 45, pp. 323–4, 459–75; Ronald Steel, *Walter Lippmann and the American Century*, London, 1981, pp. 133–6. In his Annual Message, Wilson himself had indicated that if a postwar Germany retained 'ambitious and intriguing masters', it might be excluded both from 'the partnership of nations which must henceforth guarantee the world's peace' and from 'free economic intercourse', *PWW*, vol. 45, p. 198.

97 House diary, 9 January 1918, *PWW*, vol. 45, pp. 550–59 (emphasis in original).

98 Address to the Senate, 22 January 1917; address to Congress, 8 January 1918, *PWW*, vol. 40, p. 537; vol. 45, pp. 534–9.

99 Thus, House noted how he and Wilson managed to draft a paragraph on 'the colonial question' that 'was acceptable to us both, and we hoped would be to Great Britain'. At House's suggestion, Wilson used the word 'must' over points where there was general agreement and 'should' where there was a controversy. House diary, 9 January 1918, *PWW*, vol. 45, p. 552.

100 Address to Congress, 8 January 1918, *PWW*, vol. 45, pp. 534–7; Kennan, *Russia Leaves the War*, p. 263.

101 Link, *Wilson: Revolution, War, and Peace*, pp. 79–85; August Heckscher, *Woodrow Wilson: A Biography*, New York, 1991, pp. 468–73.

102 Lord Reading to A.J. Balfour, 26 February 1918, *PWW*, vol. 46, pp. 466–7. Wilson's speeches led the German government to send out confidential peace-feelers through various intermediaries, but he did not respond to any of these. Klaus Schwabe, *Woodrow Wilson, Revolutionary Germany, and Peacemaking, 1918–1919: Missionary Diplomacy and the Realities of Power*, Chapel Hill, NC, 1985, pp. 24–7.

103 Sir Cecil Spring Rice to A.J. Balfour, 4 January 1918; address to Congress, 8 January 1918, *PWW*, vol. 45, pp. 455–6, 534–9; Mayer, *Political Origins*, p. 133.

104 Inquiry memorandum, *PWW*, vol. 45, pp. 467–8; Mayer, *Political Origins*, pp. 282–5, 313–28; House diary, 9 January 1918, *PWW*, vol. 45, pp. 556–7. The similarity of the two speeches testifies to the extent to which the two statesmen were responding to the same pressures as well as to House's efforts to minimize the areas of disagreement. However, Lloyd George took a much less sympathetic attitude to Russia. For a paraphrase of Lloyd George's speech, see *PWW*, vol. 45, pp. 487–8.

105 Knock, *To End All Wars*, pp. 145–7; Inquiry memorandum, *PWW*, vol. 45, p. 468.

106 Wilson to House, 12 February 1917, *PWW*, vol. 41, p. 201.

107 Wilson used the phrase, 'politics is adjourned' in an address to Congress, 27 May 1918, *PWW*, vol. 48, p. 164.

108 House diary, 17 January 1918, *PWW*, vol. 46, p. 23.

109 Press release, 21 January 1918, ibid., pp. 55–6.

110 Wilson to L.S. Overman, 21 March 1918, *PWW*, vol. 47, p. 94.

111 Heckscher, *Woodrow Wilson*, pp. 467–8; Kendrick A. Clements, *Woodrow Wilson: World*

Statesman, Boston, MA, 1987, p. 93; Wilson to H.B. Swope, 21 March 1918, *PWW*, vol. 47, p. 93.

112 To Spring Rice in January, Wilson had observed of national self-determination that

> in point of logic, of pure logic, this principle which was good in itself would lead to the complete independence of various small nationalities now forming part of various Empires. Pushed to its extreme, the principle would mean the disruption of existing governments, to an undefinable extent. Logic was a good and powerful thing, but apart from the consideration of existing circumstances might well lead to very dangerous results.
>
> (Spring Rice to A.J. Balfour, 4 January 1918, *PWW*, vol. 45, p. 456)

113 Address to a Joint Session of Congress, 11 February 1918; remarks to foreign correspondents, 8 April 1918, *PWW*, vol. 46, pp. 318–24; vol. 47, p. 288.

114 Though House persuaded him to cut out the specific boast that 'behind the million and a half men now in training or ready for the line of battle there are ten million more'. House diary, 8 February 1918; revised draft of address to Joint Session of Congress, 8–10 February 1918, *PWW*, vol. 46, pp. 290–97.

115 An address in Baltimore, 6 April 1918, *PWW*, vol. 47, pp. 267–70.

116 David Lloyd George to Lord Reading, 14 April 1918; also 28 March, 29 March, 2 April, 9 April, 1918, *PWW*, vol. 47, pp. 338–41, 181–3, 203–5, 229–30, 307.

117 Ferrell, *Wilson and World War I*, pp. 69–77, 53.

118 Reading to Wilson with enclosures, 3 July 1918; Reading to Balfour, 3 July 1918; Sir William Wiseman to A.C. Murray, 4 July 1918; Lansing memorandum, 6 July 1918; Wilson to Frank L. Polk with enclosure, 17 July 1918; press release, c. 3 August 1918, *PWW*, vol. 48, pp. 493–501, 511–14, 523–5, 542–3, 639–43, vol. 49, pp. 170–72.

119 'I have been sweating blood over the question of what it is right and feasible (*possible*) to do in Russia.' Wilson to House, 8 July 1918, *PWW*, vol. 48, p. 550.

120 Mamatey, *The United States and East Central Europe*, pp. 260–61, 269–70, 309, 334; Lansing to the Swedish Minister, 19 October 1918, *Foreign Relations of the United States* [hereafter *FRUS*], *1918. Supplement 1 The World War*, vol. 1 (1933), p. 368.

121 Lansing to Wilson, 10 May 1918; Sir William Wiseman to Sir Eric Drummond, 30 May 1918, *PWW*, vol. 47, pp. 589–91; vol. 48, pp. 205–6.

122 Mamatey, *The United States and East Central Europe*, pp. 258, 301–2, 308–9.

123 Wilson to Thomas G. Masaryk, 10 September 1918, *PWW*, vol. 49, pp. 511–12.

124 Professor Mamatey has observed that a visitor to interwar Prague 'would detrain at the Wilson Station. Coming out of the station, he would face the Wilson Square and the Wilson Park, with a statue of President Woodrow Wilson in its center' (*The United States and East Central Europe*, p. vii).

125 A point made by Michla Pomerance in his thorough review of the whole issue. 'The United States and Self-determination: Perspectives on the Wilsonian Conception', *American Journal of International Law*, 70 (1976): 1–27, at p. 2.

126 Knock, *To End All Wars*, pp. 167–9; Seward W. Livermore, *Politics is Adjourned: Woodrow Wilson and the War Congress, 1916–1918*, Middletown, CT, 1966, pp. 210–12; William C. Widenor, *Henry Cabot Lodge and the Search for an American Foreign Policy*, Berkeley and Los Angeles, CA, 1980, pp. 270–87; Arno J. Mayer, *Politics and Diplomacy of Peacemaking: Containment and Counterrevolution at Versailles, 1918–1919*, New York, 1967, p. 55.

127 An address in the Metropolitan Opera House, 27 September 1918, *PWW*, vol. 51, pp. 127–33. Wilson had indicated his awareness of possible problems with the Senate over the League of Nations as early as March. See Wilson to House, 22 March, 1918; memorandum by W.H. Taft on conference of leaders of the League to Enforce Peace with the President, c. 29 March 1918, *PWW*, vol. 47, pp. 105, 200–1.

128 Knock, *To End All Wars*, pp. 163–6; F. Oberlin to Wilson with enclosure, 6 October 1918, *PWW*, vol. 51, pp. 252–3; Schwabe, *Woodrow Wilson, Revolutionary Germany, and Peacemaking*, p. 31.

129 Draft of a Note to the German government, 7 October 1918; House diary, 16 September 1918; House telegram to Wilson, 6 October 1918; Tumulty to Wilson, 8 October 1918 (two letters); Diary of H.F. Ashurst, 14 October 1918, *PWW*, vol. 51, pp. 255–7, 23, 254, 265–9, 338–40.

130 'Leaders of Men', 17 June 1890, *PWW*, vol. 6, p. 659; Knock, *To End All Wars*, pp. 161–2.

131 House to Wilson, 3 September 1918; Diary of H.F. Ashurst, 14 October 1918; Wilson telegram to House, 28 October 1918, *PWW*, vol. 49, pp. 428–9; vol. 51, pp. 339, 473.

132 Ray Stannard Baker, *Woodrow Wilson: Life and Letters*, vol. 8, pp. 476, 478–9; Lord Robert Cecil to the British Embassy, Washington, 9 October 1918, *PWW*, vol. 51, pp. 288–9.

133 House diary, 9 October 1918, *PWW*, vol. 51, p. 276; Baker, *Wilson*, vol. 8, pp. 505–6.

134 Lansing to F. Oederlin, 14, 23 October 1918. *FRUS, 1918*, Supplement 1, vol. 1, pp. 358–9, 381–3.

135 An Appeal for a Democratic Congress, 19 October 1918, *PWW*, vol. 51, pp. 381–2; Knock, *To End All Wars*, p. 178; Roosevelt to Senators Lodge, Poindexter and Johnson, 24 October 1918, Elting E. Morison et al. (eds), *The Letters of Theodore Roosevelt*, vol. 8, Cambridge, MA, 1954, p. 1380.

136 Lamont memorandum, 4 October 1918, *PWW*, vol. 51, p. 225.

137 The adviser who recommended the omission was Homer S. Cummings, acting chairman of the Democratic National Committee. See his memorandum, 18 October 1918, also Tumulty's draft c. 1 October 1918, and Wilson's draft, c. 17 October 1918, *PWW*, vol. 51, pp. 380–81, 304–6, 353–5.

138 Lodge to Roosevelt, 1 March 1915, quoted in William Widenor, *Henry Cabot Lodge*, p. 208.

139 To an English friend, Roosevelt claimed in mid-November that

I was able to render substantial service to the allies during the last month by being probably the chief factor in preventing Wilson from doing what he fully intended to do, namely, double-cross the allies, appear as an umpire between them and the Central Powers and get a negotiated peace which would put him personally on a pinnacle of glory in the sight of every sinister pro-German and every vapid and fatuous doctrinaire sentimentalist throughout the world.

(Roosevelt to Arthur Hamilton Lee, 19 November 1918, *Letters of Theodore Roosevelt*, vol. 8, p. 1397)

140 Christopher Andrew, *For the President's Eyes Only: Secret Intelligence and the American Presidency from Washington to Bush*, New York 1995, p. 41.
141 P.C. March to Pershing, 27 October 1918; House to Wilson, 29 October 1918, 30 October 1918(3), 3 November 1918; Wilson to House, 30 October 1918(2), 31 October 1918, 4 November 1918, *PWW*, vol. 51, pp. 471–2, 495–504, 511–13, 515–17, 533, 569–70, 575; Arthur Walworth, *America's Moment: 1918: American Diplomacy at the End of World War I*, New York, 1977, p. 64. Wilson defined the other 'essentially American terms' as those concerning open covenants, equality of trade conditions, and the League of Nations.
142 House to Wilson, 4, 5 November 1918, *PWW*, vol. 51, pp. 580–82, 594–5.

Chapter 7

The Appearance of Power: Wilson in Paris

Expectations, resources and objectives

Wilson's participation in the Paris peace conference was a unique episode in the history of the US presidency. No previous president had gone overseas while in office, and indeed some authorities thought that such a move should entail the assumption of power by the vice-president.[1] Nor has any subsequent president left the country for anything like as long. Wilson was away for over six months, spending only two weeks in the United States between 3 December 1918 and 8 July 1919.[2]

This characteristically bold break with precedent indicated the extent to which by this time international affairs, and America's role in them, dominated the President's attention. His descent upon Europe constituted the climactic moment of his career and, as we saw in Chapter 1, has done much to shape the images of Wilson that have lived on in historical memory. And Wilson has figured largely in the voluminous and often passionate historiography of the peace conference. Although he has had his defenders and champions, assessments of his performance in Paris have been generally negative. Why has this been so, and how far are such criticisms justified?

The first point to make is that disappointment in what Wilson achieved was inevitable because so much was expected of him. It was indeed anticipated by some of his followers and, at moments, by the President himself. 'Poor Wilson!', his young admirer Raymond Fosdick wrote in his diary after penning the description of the President's triumphant arrival in Paris quoted earlier. 'The French think that with almost a magic touch he will bring about the day of political and industrial justice.' Fosdick's slightly eccentric interpretation of what the Parisian crowds sought from the American leader may have reflected an experience he had on the day he left New York. Mingling on the early-morning ferry with sweatshop workers, he had asked one how long he worked each day. 'Fourteen hours', the man replied. 'But do you see that boat?' (pointing to the President's ship), 'there's a man aboard her that is going to Europe to change all that.' When this story was retailed to him, Wilson remarked that 'it frightened him to think how much the common people of the world expect of him'.[3]

Millennial expectations flourish in the euphoria following victorious wars, particularly when these have been long and hardfought. People feel that they deserve compensation and reward for the suffering they have endured, and the mentality of war tends to simplify matters, so that it seems as if the enemy is the one problem and source of trouble in the world, and that with his defeat the way should be open for the fulfillment of all wishes and dreams. That so many of such hopes became focused at this time on Wilson was not due only to the endorsement of his wartime speeches in the Armistice, or the loftiness of their rhetoric. It was also because he embodied America. Long a legendary land of freedom and opportunity to many ordinary Europeans, the United States now also appeared to be, in the words of a German staff officer, 'the power to which, as far as anyone can tell, the future on this earth belongs'.[4] And the President's own personality, his academic background and dignified demeanor, seems to have contributed to the confidence that this 'professor' would bring wisdom as well as disinterestedness to the deliberations.

The expectations were impossible to fulfill: not only were they huge but they were also conflicting. While there was a general longing for a lasting peace that would prevent any repetition of the horrors of the last four years, there was no agreement about the kind of settlement that would produce such a result. The ambitions of the victorious nations were not easily reconcilable and they were certainly incompatible with the way Germans saw the terms of the armistice. Few expected the conference to be harmonious, and much American opinion cast the anticipated battles as a manichaean conflict between the old order and the new, between the selfish, imperialistic ambitions of traditional diplomacy and the ideal of a 'democratic peace'. Wilson himself promoted this view as he traveled to Europe on the *George Washington* (ironically a former German luxury liner that had been seized and renamed by the Americans during the war). He told some newspaper correspondents that 'the representatives of France, Great Britain and Italy are determined to get everything out of Germany that they can', and to members of the Inquiry (who had been included in the American delegation) he said, 'tell me what's right and I'll fight for it'.[5] Anticipating the battles ahead, the President had remarked before he left Washington that he wanted 'to go into the Peace Conference armed with as many weapons as my pockets will hold so as to compel justice'.[6]

Wilson seems to have been confident that he had possession of such 'weapons'. In the first place, the Allies owed their victory to the United States. 'It is not too much to say that at Château Thierry we saved the world', he declared to the members of the Inquiry, 'and I do not intend to let those Europeans forget it. They were beaten when we came in and they know it.' Of course, with Germany conclusively defeated, the immediate need for America's military assistance no longer existed but the President evidently believed that, as Grey had indicated in 1914–16, the European powers set great store by an ongoing American commitment to their security. Accordingly, he felt that the threat not to make such a commitment would be a winning card in the negotiations. To the journalists, he said that he would tell the European leaders right at the beginning that 'it must not be a peace of loot or spoliation', and that 'if that is the kind of peace they demand, I will withdraw personally and with my commissioners return home and in due course take up the details of a separate peace'.[7]

Secondly, there was America's economic and financial power. The great increase in the nation's exports during the war had transformed its international account, changing a net debt of $3.7 billion in 1914 to a almost identical net credit by 1919. In addition, the US government had lent over $8 billion to foreign states, nearly half of it to Great Britain. As we have seen, Wilson had long anticipated that the fact that the Allies after the war would be 'financially in our hands' would enable the United States to 'force them to our way of thinking'. Nor had the need of the war-disrupted economies for American aid come to an end with the armistice, and Wilson appointed Hoover to oversee the provision of food relief to central and eastern Europe in particular. The President also evidently believed that incidental consequences of the mobilization of American resources for the war effort held potential as diplomatic bargaining chips. We have seen how he employed the threat of a sustained naval-building program in the negotiations over the pre-armistice agreement, while his remark about wishing to hold weapons in his pockets was made in connection with the possibility of using the war-enhanced American merchant marine and shipbuilding capacity to make up for the shipping losses of the Allies, particularly Britain.[8]

Economic and financial strength, like military capacity, are generally acknowledged to give a state power in the international arena. Some political scientists argue that to these 'hard', tangible factors should be added the 'soft' power that can be the product of cultural authority or ideological appeal.[9] With this, too, Wilson evidently felt himself endowed. He made little secret of his belief that 'the peoples of all the Allies are with me in the sentiments that I have expressed', and that 'if necessary I can reach the peoples of Europe over the heads of their rulers'. Wilson was by no means alone in making this assumption, which accorded with the common American view that only elites were interested in the game of power politics and imperialism. It was encouraged by the reports of Ray Stannard Baker, a sympathetic journalist who had been sent by House to assess the degree of support for Wilson's peace program in the Allied countries. Recording the hostility of the Entente governments to the Fourteen Points, House himself noted that 'the plain people generally both in America and in Europe are, I think, with the President'. The ovations Wilson received upon his arrival in France, Britain, and Italy can only have increased his confidence. They certainly caused Lansing to change his mind over the wisdom of the President's decision to leave Washington to take part personally in the peace conference.[10]

Wilson believed not only that 'the men whom we were about to deal with did not represent their own people' but also that their divergent ambitions would enable him to play them off against each other. As 'the only disinterested people at the peace conference', the Americans would be courted for their support by the leaders of other countries. He told the members of the Inquiry that 'there was much hostility between Italy and France and some between France and England but that all were anxious to cooperate with us'.[11]

William Bullitt, who recorded this remark, later denounced Wilson bitterly for accepting a peace that departed so far from the principles he had proclaimed. Such criticisms by Wilson's erstwhile liberal supporters were to be eagerly exploited by his Republican opponents in the later Senate debate, and were augmented in due course by those of Lansing who had felt sidelined in Paris. Failure to take advice is one of the charges against Wilson, as is lack of detailed knowledge and of negotiating skill and determination. When resigning, Bullitt lamented that the President 'did not fight our fight to the finish', and in the book he wrote with Sigmund Freud a decade later he attributed Wilson's 'moral collapse' to his psychological frailties.[12]

Bullitt's analysis, like that of Keynes and many later critics, was based on the premise that Wilson held a strong hand in the negotiations and so should have achieved more. Yet, on closer examination, the 'weapons' at the President's disposal look much less formidable than such critics assume or than he seems to have anticipated. In the first place, the debts the Allies had incurred did not in themselves generate any particular diplomatic leverage. They could only have done so if the United States had been prepared to offer the possibility of their being reduced (or even written off entirely) if the debtor nations acceded to American wishes, for example on the size and terms of German reparations. But scaling down the Allies' debts was not something that Wilson could do, even if he had been so inclined. Soon after arriving in Paris he received a telegram from Carter Glass, who had just taken over from McAdoo as Secretary of the Treasury, expressing 'grave concern' about 'the possibility that the debts may be forgiven or exchanged for debts not as good' and stressing that 'Congress believes these loans are good and should be collected'. Having come from the House of Representatives, Glass wrote with authority about the attitudes of Congress which, of course, under the Constitution held the purse-strings. Such attitudes also severely constrained the extent to which further financial aid could be offered to European nations. The combination of American agricultural surpluses and heavy emphasis on the danger of Bolshevism spreading through central Europe persuaded Congress to appropriate $100 million in January 1919, but this sum covered only a small proportion of the costs of Hoover's relief operation. In addition, the administration was able to offer limited further credits from the unexpended portion of the $10 billion that had been appropriated during the war, but the Treasury was insistent that these be used only for purchases in the United States; there was no question of larger loans for broader purposes along the lines of the Marshall Plan after World War II. In these circumstances, America's great economic resources represented only a limited diplomatic asset.[13]

The second weapon that Wilson was presumed to have had was the power of public opinion. 'If you had made your fight in the open, instead of behind closed doors', Bullitt wrote in his resignation letter, 'you would have carried with you the public opinion of the world, which was yours.'[14] But it was surely an illusion to believe that ordinary people everywhere would have supported Wilson against their own governments and national ambitions if he had called on them to do so. The appeal of a peace based on the Fourteen Points was by no means universal. Wilson's core constituency, in Europe as in America, was the liberal left of the political spectrum – the *Manchester Guardian* hailed him as 'the only statesman of the first rank who has concerned himself seriously to think out any policy at all'. But this element was losing ground to a surgent right in all the Allied countries. In the British general election of December 1918, Asquith and his chief lieutenants lost their seats and most of the Labour party's leading figures were also defeated. The landslide victory of the Conservative-dominated Lloyd George coalition followed a campaign in which some of its spokesmen had called for 'hanging the Kaiser' and squeezing 'the German lemon until the pips squeak'. Shortly afterwards, the French socialists, who had explicitly adopted Wilson's program and done much to orchestrate the demonstrations in his favor, were crushed in the Chamber of Deputies by Clemenceau, who stoutly defended the old diplomacy and referred ambiguously to the American President's *noble candeur*. In Italy, Wilson's foremost supporter, the Reformist Socialist, Leonida Bissolati, found himself humiliated as he tried vainly to stem the tide of annexationist sentiment that was being fanned by populist nationalists like Benito Mussolini. And the Republicans' victory in the congressional elections suggested that their demand for unconditional surrender and a tough peace had caught a popular mood in the United States, too. Only in Germany was there something like unanimous support for the Fourteen Points. As the historian Arno Mayer has pointed out, since 1917 the varying strength of Wilsonianism in the different countries had been obversely related to military success – which hardly boded well for its realization.[15]

During the pre-armistice negotiations, Wilson had told House that he would not agree to a settlement that did not embody his principles, and House had warned the Allies that the President might make a separate peace with Germany. Such a threat was Wilson's ultimate weapon, and Bullitt (with Freud) maintains that if he had had the virility to employ it in Paris, 'he might possibly have obtained the "just and lasting peace" he had promised to the world'.[16] But after the armistice, it would matter less if the United States were to make a separate peace (as it eventually did). In these circumstances, threatening to do so was a high-risk tactic that could easily backfire. Indeed, in a paradoxical way, articulating the threat could diminish its potency. For its effectiveness now depended solely upon the value that the other states placed upon an American guarantee of the settlement, and this would in turn depend in part upon the credibility such a guarantee possessed. Given the evident reluctance of the American military as well as public and congressional opinion to assume long-run commitments outside the Western Hemisphere, European statesmen were already inclined to put their trust in other, more traditional, forms of security.[17] A move that emphasized the conditional nature of American involvement would thus be at least as likely to weaken as to strengthen their willingness to adopt Wilson's ideas. And if the President, having threatened to withdraw, then felt compelled to do so, he would have utterly failed to achieve his goals.

And so, what were these goals? To the journalists on the *George Washington*, the President declared that 'a statement that I once made that this should be a "peace without victory" holds more strongly today than ever'. It was such remarks that led all those who hoped for a generous settlement with Germany (including, of course, Germans) to put their faith in him. In truth, Wilson's position was not quite as it had been in January 1917. The Fourteen Points themselves contained provisions, such as the return of Alsace-Lorraine to France and the grant to an independent Poland of 'free and secure access to the sea', that presupposed a defeated Germany. And whereas Wilson had initially called for a 'universal association of the nations', he indicated before he reached France that he now felt that Germany needed 'to pass through a probationary period before being admitted to the League of Nations'. But the President also explicitly reiterated his opposition to indemnities that went beyond the simple reparation of damages, and the fighting tone of his shipboard conversations seemed to portend a firm resistance to any of the victors' claims that could not be sustained by 'the highest principles of justice'.[18]

However, this was not quite the picture presented by Lloyd George to the Imperial War Cabinet after he and Balfour, the Foreign Secretary, had talked with Wilson in London. The Prime Minister reported that the President had given the impression that the League of Nations 'was the only thing that he really cared much about'. Since Wilson had evidently also expressed strong views on a number of other issues, it is possible that Lloyd George was seeking to disarm those of his colleagues, such as the Australian prime minister, William Hughes, who were hostile to Wilson and what they saw as his pretensions. However, there is no question that Wilson had stressed his desire that the League should be 'the first subject discussed at the peace conference'. This sense of priority is very understandable. The League, together with open diplomacy, freedom of the seas and equality of trade conditions, was among those of the Fourteen Points that Wilson had described to House as the 'essentially American terms in the program'.[19] These were all things that Wilson had called for before American entry into the war and his subsequent expression of views about European territorial issues. They all implied some repudiation of what was seen as the old order of imperialism and balance-of-power diplomacy, but the League was the real embodiment of the new system that would replace it.

It was also, as it had been since his endorsement of the idea in 1916, the means by which Wilson sought to involve the United States in world politics in a continuous, active way, thereby ending the isolationist tradition. In a broad perspective, this enterprise was the most significant aspect of his presidency, and explanations of why Wilson pursued this objective merge with more general interpretations of the motives and purposes of US foreign policy in the twentieth century. 'Realist' writers view it as an implicit recognition that America's own security now demanded an orderly world, and that this required a positive contribution towards maintaining the balance of power. However, there is no evidence that

Wilson saw the situation in these terms. On the contrary, he seems to have shared the confidence of most Americans in their country's military security, pointing out to the conference when it opened that 'with her great territory and her extensive sea borders, it is less likely that the United States should suffer from the attacks of enemies than that many of the other nations here should suffer'.[20]

The 'revisionist' interpretation that became influential in the 1960s and 1970s sees US policy as proactive rather than defensive in inspiration. In one of the most notable works of this school, N. Gordon Levin argued that Wilson set the framework for later policymakers in seeking to establish 'a peaceful liberal capitalist world order under international law, safe both from traditional imperialism and revolutionary socialism, within whose stable liberal confines a missionary America could find moral and economic pre-eminence'. Levin sees this drive as deriving from the traditional sense of an American mission, the nation's commitment to 'liberal-capitalist values', and its concrete interest in securing overseas economic expansion. To illustrate how Wilson fused these elements, Levin quotes from a speech the President gave to a salesmanship congress in 1916:

> with the inspiration of the thought that you are Americans, and are meant to carry liberty and justice and the principles of humanity wherever you go, go out and sell goods that will make the world more comfortable and more happy, and convert them to the principles of America.[21]

Yet on other occasions Wilson made it clear that he saw American prosperity as domestically generated, with exports accounting for less than 4 percent of the nation's commerce. Moreover, he manifested little greater anxiety over America's economic situation than he did over its physical security. On the contrary, in the very speech Levin quotes, he laid stress on the way the war had strengthened America's international payments position. Noting that 'we have more of the surplus gold of the world than we ever had before', he declared that 'we have got to finance the world in some important degree, and those who finance the world must understand it and rule it with their spirits and with their minds'.

As at the time of the Spanish–American War, Wilson evidently had a sense that the growth of America's power had broadened the nation's destiny: 'We must play a great part in the world, whether we choose it or not.'[22] In wishing the United States to embrace wider responsibilities, Wilson was not, of course, alone. Indeed, his efforts to secure a stable European settlement and establish a league of nations won him the support of normally Republican members of the East Coast elite such as the Morgan partners, Thomas Lamont and Henry Davison.[23] Wilson's temperamental predisposition to bold and active leadership was no doubt reinforced by what might be called the presidential perspective. Throughout the twentieth century, there has tended to be more enthusiasm for overseas enterprises and commitments in the White House than in Congress. As well as the differences in their constituencies, this has reflected the fact that in foreign policy the president has greater scope for initiative and unilateral action than in domestic affairs.[24]

Such tensions are all the greater when different parties control the two branches of government, as was the case in 1919. Although Wilson was not prepared to go as far as House advised in giving the new Republican majorities their head in domestic affairs, he was obviously looking to the peace conference and the establishment of a league of nations for the achievements that would crown his presidency – and possibly lay the basis for a run for an unprecedented third term in 1920.[25] For their part, the Republican leaders in Congress, several of whom had developed a bitter hatred for Wilson, had a strong partisan interest in denying him success. As the incoming chairman of the Senate Foreign Relations Committee, Lodge deliberately sought to undercut the President's position in Paris by signaling to the Allies (both privately and publicly) his sympathy with calls for a tough peace and opposition to the incorporation of a league of nations in the treaty.[26] Even before the election, Wilson had been very conscious of the difficulty of securing the necessary two-thirds majority in the Senate for American participation in the League of Nations. This had been why he had argued that the League had to be an integral part of the peace treaty, a matter which he was to be insistent upon in Paris where the forthcoming battle at home was never far from his mind.

To this political stake, Wilson added an intense emotional commitment. He clearly felt the responsibility of having sent so many young Americans to Europe to die. He idealized the motives of these men (who were overwhelmingly draftees), describing them as 'crusaders' and assuming that they had all been inspired by the dream he had articulated of a world both free and peaceful. As he said to Congress on the eve of his departure, 'It is now my duty to play my full part in making good what they offered their life's blood to obtain.'[27]

The course of the conference

The British decided to cooperate with the President's desire that the League of Nations should be the first item on the agenda at the peace conference. This did not represent a wholehearted commitment to the ideal of a new world order, with a concomitant repudiation of the age-old principle that 'to the victor belong the spoils'. On the contrary, most members of the Imperial War Cabinet were looking for concrete national gains, not least those Dominion prime ministers who had their eyes on former German colonies. But Lloyd George and Balfour argued that having the League established would make it easier to resolve potential conflicts with Wilson over such matters as the disposal of colonies, economic issues, and freedom of the seas. In addition, at least two members of the Cabinet, Lord Robert Cecil and the South African J.C. Smuts, were themselves strong believers in the idea of a league of nations, which also enjoyed much public support in Britain, now being marshaled by the League of Nations Union under the presidency of Viscount Grey. Nevertheless, it is striking how a project that had originally been pressed on the American government by Grey, and adopted by Wilson as a means of persuading the British to moderate their war aims, had now become so much identified as an American objective that, as Lloyd George clearly indicated, cooperation in carrying it out was seen as something for which the British could hope to secure some concessions in return. The transparency of Wilson's political stake in the League was primarily responsible for this reversal, but it also reflected the fact, brought out in the British cabinet discussion, that not all Old World statesmen were enthusiastic about the prospect of active American involvement in their affairs.[28]

The proceedings in Paris opened on 12 January 1919, with the first meeting in Paris of the Council of Ten, the heads of government and foreign ministers of the victorious Great Powers (France, Britain, the United States, Italy, and Japan). Within a fortnight, the Council had agreed, at Lloyd George's instigation, that a league of nations 'should be created as an integral part of the general treaty of peace' and a commission had been appointed, under Wilson's chairmanship, to draw up its constitution.[29]

Wilson had not hitherto put forward any detailed plan for the League of Nations. He has been much criticized for this, but it was a deliberate policy which he had held to despite pressure from House. In August 1918 he explained that he did not want to publish a draft 'Covenant' that the two of them had put together because 'it would cause so much criticism in this country, particularly by Senators of the Lodge type, that it would make it difficult to do what we both had in mind at the Peace Conference'. Wilson's political judgment was endorsed by the shrewd Tumulty: 'His enemies here and abroad hope that he will particularize so that they can attack him. People of the world are with him on general principles. They care little for details.'[30]

There was more to this problem than party politics or the need to 'educate' public opinion. In the first place, those who supported the idea of a league of nations did not by any means all have the same conception of what sort of an organization it would be and how it would operate. Any concrete plan would have to address a number of specific issues upon which there were significantly different views, and also frequent ambiguity and confusion. The first was membership – would it be an inclusive organization of the world, or something more like an alliance of like-minded countries? A second was structure, particularly whether all members would have an equal status or if it should be really run by the Great Powers. Then there was the question of what members of the League would commit themselves to. Would it be to renounce completely the use of force against other members – or simply to follow certain procedures (of adjudication, arbitration, or delay) before resorting to war? And if war was outlawed, how would disputes that could not be negotiated be resolved? Would the status quo always be upheld? Or would there be some supranational authority that could impose its judgments? Finally, how would the rules of the League, whatever they were, be enforced? Simply by the moral power of world opinion? By collective economic sanctions? Or by military force? If the last, would there be a League army and navy? Or would individual members be prepared to put their own forces at the disposal of the League? On all these difficult issues, there were complex divisions of opinion that reflected both broader political philosophies and degrees of partisanship in the European war.

Wilson's attitude to the various ideas that were current was not that simply of a neutral arbiter; he had his own firm views. Indeed, his reticence in expressing them publicly may have owed something to the fact that they were very different from those of the League to Enforce Peace, the lobby organization that had done most to develop political and public support for the idea in the United States. In March 1918 Wilson had met two of the League's leaders, Taft and the President of Harvard, A. Lawrence Lowell, in order to dissuade them from promoting a particular plan. At this meeting, Wilson expressed his opposition to proposals for an elaborate constitution, on the model of the American one, and suggested that all that was needed was a mutual guarantee of territorial integrity and a provision for conferences to deal with threats to, or violations of, this guarantee. Although Taft referred to this as a 'minimizing statement', it did not, as time was to show, reflect a lesser ambition for the League so much as a distrust of a legalistic approach. To House, Wilson explained his

> conviction ... that the administrative *constitution* of the League must *grow* and not be made; that we must *begin* with solemn covenants, cov-

ering mutual guarantees of political independence and territorial integrity (if the final territorial agreements of the peace conference are fair and satisfactory and *ought* to be perpetuated), but that the method of carrying those mutual pledges out should be left to develop of itself, case by case. Any attempt to begin by putting executive authority in the hands of any particular group of powers would be to sow a harvest of jealousy and distrust which would spring up at once and choke the whole thing. To take one thing, and only one, but quite sufficient in itself:

The United States Senate would never ratify any treaty which put the force of the United States at the disposal of any such group or body. Why begin at the impossible end when there is a possible end and it is feasible to plant a system which will slowly but surely ripen into fruition?

The explicitly organic metaphor here reminds us of Wilson's admiration for Burke, and indeed of the continuing influence on him of the ways of thinking about society that he had absorbed at Johns Hopkins. He was arguing that a new world order could not be created by a legal contract but, like earlier developments in civilization, would gradually evolve – as he said to Taft and Lowell, 'the common law was built up that way'. But, given his clear recognition of the difficulty of gaining Senate consent for a firm pledge to use America's armed forces in any particular circumstances, his approach to the League could also be seen as an attempt to paper over the gap between what he had long indicated that the League would provide (a guarantee of peace) and what he felt he could make in the way of a specific American commitment.[31]

During the course of 1918 Wilson had been compelled to develop his ideas more fully, particularly in response to a report commissioned by the British government. The Phillimore Report, of which Wilson was sent a copy in July, envisaged an agreement among 'the Allied states' not to go to war with each other before submitting a dispute to arbitration or conciliation. This agreement would be enforced by economic and military sanctions so it was a little strange that Wilson complained that it had 'no teeth'. His objection was more likely rooted in the report's reference to the League as an 'alliance', which associated it with the calls currently being made for the League to be established at once by the nations fighting the Central Powers. This, Wilson explained to Wiseman, would inevitably result in its being 'regarded as a sort of Holy Alliance aimed at Germany' and 'would not be the purpose of the American people'. The President asked House to rewrite the Phillimore constitution in line with his own ideas, and then himself amended House's version in a draft he took to the Colonel's summer home in Magnolia, Massachusetts, in August. House's version had retained many of the provisions of the Phillimore draft but added to it in ways that broadened the scope of the whole project. 'Any war or threat of war' was to be within the remit of the League, an international court was to be established, armaments were to be 'reduced to the lowest point consistent with safety' and arms manufacture by private enterprise was to be ended. International affairs were to be governed by 'the same standards of honor and of ethics' as other realms of human conduct, and both intrigue and espionage were to be 'deemed dishonorable'. Wilson excluded these pious aspirations from his 'Magnolia Covenant' and also cut out the court, but he highlighted the mutual guarantee of political independence and territorial integrity that House had included, while accepting the qualification that territorial modifications could be made 'pursuant to the principle of self-determination' or with the assent of threequarters of the League's members. Wilson followed House in providing that the Covenant's rules would be enforced by economic embargo and blockade, but added an explicit statement that these would be upheld by 'any force that may be necessary to accomplish that object'.[32]

Once in Paris, Wilson gave a further reason for not having committed himself in advance to 'a concrete program' – the need to consult with the European powers and let them participate in shaping the form of the League. A plan published by Smuts particularly impressed him, and he incorporated some parts of it into a revised version of his own Covenant – in particular that territories formerly belonging to the defeated empires should be administered by 'mandatory' states under the authority of the League, and that the League should have an executive council consisting of delegates from the Great Powers as permanent members and a rotating representation from 'middle' and 'minor' states.[33] This last served as a helpful compromise (essentially retained in the composition of the UN Security Council) between those who felt that control should rest with the Great Powers who alone could make the League effective, and those who feared such a condominium and insisted upon the equal rights of small countries. The British government held strongly to the first position, to whose merits House had become persuaded; whereas Lansing, and to a lesser extent Wilson himself, shared the general American suspicion of Great Power imperialism.

Lansing also argued that the positive guarantee included in Wilson's draft was unlikely to be acceptable to Congress and suggested instead that members of the League simply commit themselves not to violate each other's political independence and territorial integrity. Lansing's political judgment was to prove well-founded but Wilson disregarded his suggestion. As we have seen, the mutual guarantee was basic to his conception of the League. The phraseology came from an abortive Pan-American pact but the idea was to establish a new form of security for states to replace that which had led to arms races, diplomatic intrigues and eventually the catastrophe of war. Doing this would require something more far-reaching than the League to Enforce Peace's plan, or what was apparently envisaged by the British government.

On the other hand, Wilson remained very conscious of the political constraints on what he could commit the United States to. In the meetings of the League of Nations Commission, spokesmen for France and Belgium pressed for the authority of the League to be broadened and strengthened with provisions for an international force, or at least military staff, lest the organization be merely 'a screen of false security' for states threatened with attack. Wilson resisted such proposals as firmly as Cecil did, explaining candidly that

> the argument which has been most employed against the League of Nations in America is that the army of the United States would be at the disposal of an international council, that American troops would thus be liable to be ordered to fight at any moment for the most remote of causes, and this prospect alarms our people.

This objection could have been countered in part by restricting the scope of the American security guarantee. Some leading Republicans, notably Senator Knox (who had been Secretary of State under Taft) as well as Lodge, favored a commitment to protect 'the freedom and peace of Europe' against a revival of 'the German menace' – which would of course have been very satisfactory to the French. But such an approach meant participating in, rather than seeking to transcend, the traditional mechanisms of power politics. It would have been undeniably an 'entangling alliance', not what Wilson was to call 'an arrangement which will disentangle all the alliances in the world'. As during the period of neutrality, he sought by such an adaptation of the American tradition to generate a commitment to European security that did not entail taking sides in Europe's quarrels, thereby avoiding alienating any ethnic groups in the United States itself.

All this dictated a commitment that was both universal and rather fuzzy. Seeing the mutual guarantee as the provision which showed that 'we mean business and not only discussion', Wilson sought to make it as strong as possible within the political constraints. Accordingly, he adopted Lansing's self-denying formulation as an addition to, rather than a substitute for, the obligation to protect others against attack. He also accepted Cecil's suggestion that how this commitment should be implemented would be decided by the Council in each case. In its final form, what became Article 10 of the Covenant read:

The Members of the League undertake to respect and preserve as against external aggression the territorial integrity and existing political independence of all Members of the League. In case of any such aggression or in case of any threat or danger of such aggression the Council shall advise upon the means by which this obligation shall be fulfilled.[34]

The provision for future territorial changes in accordance with self-determination had been dropped on the grounds that it would be de-stabilizing, particularly in eastern Europe. Wilson had not protested against the omission; after all, he had always made it clear that 'the peace of the world' was the overriding consideration. Yet the early weeks of the conference also confirmed that Wilson's approach to achieving an ordered world differed from that of conservative Europeans. He firmly resisted pressure, first from the French and then from Winston Churchill, for mili-tary action against the Bolsheviks in Russia and secured agreement for an invitation, which he drafted himself, to all the warring parties in Russia to meet with representatives from the Council of Ten at Prinkipo in the Sea of Marmora (since Clemenceau refused to allow the Bolsheviks on French soil). This initiative was supported by Lloyd George, but the President found himself alone over the issue of the former German colonies. He agreed their return to Germany was out of the question, but insisted that they should become League of Nations' mandates; for them to be annexed by the British dominions and France would 'discredit the conference' by giving credence to charges that it was 'merely to divide up the spoils'. After some ill-tempered exchanges with Hughes, Wilson somewhat reluc-tantly accepted a compromise worked out by Smuts for there to be three types of mandate according to stages of development and geographical location, with places such as Southwest Africa and the southern Pacific islands being 'best administered under the laws of the mandatory states as integral parts thereof'.[35]

Such mandates were little more than fig-leaves for annexation, and the Prinkipo invitation proved abortive. The President's real achievement in the first phase of the conference was securing agreement on the League Covenant. (Smuts was later to write that no one else could have accom-plished it.) Presenting the finished product to a plenary (open) session of the conference on 14 February, Wilson stressed the scope of the League as well as its fundamental importance. He drew attention to the article on labor conditions (that had been included at Lloyd George's initiative) and claimed that, with the mandate system, 'the helpless and undeveloped peoples of the world' would no longer suffer exploitation. Above all, the League was 'a definite guarantee of peace ... a definite guarantee by word against aggression': 'Armed force is in the background in this program, but it *is* in the background, and if the moral force of the world will not suffice, the physical force of the world shall.' However, 'we are depending primarily and chiefly upon one great force, and that is the moral force of the public opinion of the world'. This had been strengthened by the war: 'People that were suspicious of one another can now live as friends and comrades in a single family, and desire to do so.' The League was not so much an institution as 'a vehicle' for the expression and development of such sentiments and the practices that would flow from them: 'A living thing is born, and we must see to it that the clothes we put upon it do not hamper it.'[36]

Later that day, Wilson departed for the United States in order to meet a constitutional obligation to deal with legislation before the old Congress adjourned. As the President boarded the train for Brest, House noted, 'he looked happy, as well indeed he should'. He seems to have believed that he had not only secured the agreement of foreign leaders to his own priority but also thereby outmaneuvered his domestic opponents. He has often been criticized for not adopting a more conciliatory and nonpartisan approach to achieving American adherence to the League of Nations. He had rejected suggestions that he include a senior Republican, such as former Secretary of State Elihu Root or ex-President Taft, on the American Commission to Negotiate Peace, choosing instead Henry White, a former diplomat but not a political heavyweight. The fact that Wilson now landed and made a speech in Boston, the home city of Lodge, has been seen as a further act of provocation. But this had not been his own idea; indeed, he had agreed to the plan somewhat reluctantly at the urging not only of Tumulty but also of House, who was at the same time seeking to open lines to the Republicans in the Senate. Nor was it unreasonable in the aftermath of the election campaign of 1918, in which even Taft had attacked the Fourteen Points, for Wilson to have concluded that having a Republican politician as a peace commisioner would leave him fighting on two fronts at once as he sought to achieve the sort of peace to which he had committed himself. In any case, he clearly trusted no one else to make the delicate political judgments involved in the negotiations, and given the resentment that Lansing came to feel at being excluded from meaningful participation in the proceedings, it would hardly have helped the cause of bipartisanship if someone like Taft had had a similar experience. During the war, Wilson's most irreconcilable opponent, Theodore

Roosevelt, had reestablished himself as the preeminent figure in the Republican party and its likely presidential candidate in 1920. Roosevelt died suddenly in January 1919, but his old friend and lieutenant Henry Cabot Lodge was a no less committed antagonist. During the President's absence in Paris, Lodge had continued to raise doubts about the League idea and to warn that the Senate might reject or strongly amend any treaty it did not approve of. It is true, of course, that Wilson had a particularly low tolerance for criticism as well as a longstanding belief in party government, but he can hardly be held solely responsible for the way that the nation's consideration of the League became so entwined with domestic politics.[37]

Boston, with its Democratic mayor, gave Wilson a great reception. In his speech there, Wilson deliberately eschewed open controversy or any detailed discussion of the League covenant (which he had asked members of Congress not to discuss until he had had the chance to explain it to them). But, knowing that it would be attacked for surrendering America's sovereign rights to an alien 'internationalism', he himself appealed to patriotic pride, stressing the esteem which the nation's war effort had won for it overseas. America was 'regarded as the friend of mankind' and had become 'the hope of the world'. To disappoint this hope and plunge the world into despair and 'hostile camps again' would mean that 'America has failed'.[38] Once back in the White House, Wilson, following a suggestion of House's, held a dinner for members of the foreign affairs committees of both houses of Congress at which he outlined the League and sought to meet objections. Although the atmosphere seems to have been civil enough, his Republican opponents were not won over. In the Senate, two days later, Lodge delivered a lengthy critique of the Covenant, stressing the sweeping nature of Article 10 and what he saw as the restrictions on America's independence of action. Shortly afterwards, he secured the signatures of more than the third of the Senate needed to block ratification for a resolution declaring that the League in its present form would not be acceptable. Wilson responded to this clearly threatening move in two ways. One, which reflected the deeply combative side of his nature, was defiance. In a speech on the eve of his return to Europe, he declared that 'when that treaty comes back gentlemen on this side will find the Covenant not only in it, but so many threads of the treaty tied to the Covenant that you cannot dissect the Covenant from the treaty without destroying the whole vital structure'. Yet he also insisted (as he had earlier to the Democratic National Committee) that 'this is not a party issue' and he walked on to the New York platform arm in arm with Taft, who had been energetically campaigning for the Covenant since the day of its publication. Once back in Paris, Wilson welcomed Taft's offer to suggest 'clarifying amendments' that would undermine the opposition's case. In response, Taft made four suggestions, including an explicit reservation of the Monroe Doctrine which he thought 'alone would probably carry the treaty'.[39]

When he returned to Europe, Wilson's position had undoubtedly been weakened by his political difficulties at home. Lodge's 'round robin' strengthened doubts about whether the undertakings he made would in fact be honored by the United States. It also lowered Wilson's personal prestige, which had been so high after the enthusiastic receptions he had received on his first arrival. The need to secure amendments to the Covenant would give the other leaders the opportunity to demand reciprocal concessions. When Tumulty cabled that reports from Paris that the League was not to be included in the peace treaty were 'doing great damage here', the President must have felt (with some justification) that his antagonists at home and abroad were in collusion. He immediately issued a press release that the prior resolution making the Covenant an integral part of the peace treaty was 'of final force'.[40]

The French-inspired reports had arisen from the moves that had been made during Wilson's absence towards a 'preliminary' peace with Germany. House's participation in this 'speeding up' procedure and his apparent acquiescence in French territorial demands, despite a cabled injunction from Wilson that nothing except military terms should be agreed until he returned, has been seen by some historians as an act of disloyalty. It is true that House's sense (evident in his diary) that his own diplomatic skills and political judgment were superior to the President's seems to have been sharpened by European flattery. But few in the American delegation doubted that he still saw himself as serving Wilson (whose instructions had only reached him in garbled form due to problems with the code), and he may well have been concerned to protect the President from the charge that he was holding up the conference. Nevertheless, Wilson was clearly disconcerted on his return to learn what had been going on and he made little secret of his feeling that House had been overaccommodating. Although to describe this as producing a 'break' between the two men is an exaggeration, it clearly diminished the degree of trust and confidence with which Wilson regarded his friend. House continued to be his chief aide and deputy but the greater distance in their relationship soon became apparent.[41]

As he resumed charge of the negotiations, Wilson found himself facing the strong pressures to which House had yielded. Citing their recent sufferings and need for future security against their more powerful neighbor, the French demanded that Germany lose all its territory west of the Rhine, with the establishment of an independent republic there and the direct cession to France of the coal-rich Saar Valley. Soon after Wilson's return, the Council of Ten was superseded as the prime ministers of France, Britain, and Italy started meeting in Wilson's rooms with only a French interpreter (and later the British cabinet secretary) in regular attendance. Within days, there had been an explosive exchange over the Saar in which Clemenceau accused Wilson of being pro-German and left the meeting. While allowing that the French were entitled to Saar coal as compensation for the Germans' deliberate destruction of their own mines, Wilson firmly resisted the incorporation of the region into France as a betrayal of the pre-armistice agreement, the principle of self-determination, and what he saw as the 'great world movement towards justice'.[42] He succeeded in preventing the transfer of sovereignty but eventually agreed not only to French control of the mines' output but also that the region should be administered by a League of Nations commission for fifteen years, after which its status would be determined by a plebiscite. Moreover, although Wilson (with Lloyd George's support) refused to accept the separation of the Rhineland from Germany, he did concede that it should be permanently demilitarized and that zones and bridgeheads within it should be subject to military occupation for fifteen years. In an effort to persuade Clemenceau to reduce his territorial demands, Wilson had earlier agreed to a suggestion by Lloyd George that Britain and America should offer a treaty of guarantee to come to France's assistance in case she were attacked. Overriding his financial experts, he also accepted that war pensions and separation allowances should be included in the Allies' claims for reparations.

It is upon these concessions, made in the great crisis of the conference in late March and early April, that the criticism of Wilson for failing to stand by his principles has chiefly focused. Keynes wrote that the 'old Presbyterian' had been 'bamboozled' over the reparations issue by 'a masterpiece of the sophist's art' (a reference to a letter from Smuts). At the height of the Cold War, it was suggested that Wilson's readiness to compromise with European conservatives was due to their shared concern to contain the spread of Bolshevism. More recently, some scholars have attached importance to the effects of a viral illness that reduced Wilson to bed for a few days in early April.[43] None of these explanations is very convincing. Most of the concessions had been made before Wilson's illness, from which he seems to have recovered fully as well as promptly. Some – for example, the offer of a security treaty to France – had been made before the communist coup in Hungary that allegedly produced 'panic' in

Paris. In any case, fear of Bolshevism's spreading to central Europe was a reason for treating Germany with moderation, as was pointed out by Wilson as well as by Lloyd George in his Fontainebleau Memorandum – in Hungary, Béla Kun's accession to power had owed much to wounded national pride. And although the President's agreement to the inclusion of pensions in the reparations bill was no doubt eased by his respect for Smuts, he made it clear to his advisers that his attitude to this issue was not determined by logical or legal arguments.[44]

Rather, Wilson's position on this matter, as on others, was the product of the interaction of his own priorities and those of his negotiating partners in the context of the political situation each of them faced. With respect to reparations, the American concern was that there should be a fixed sum that could reasonably be paid over a defined period, so that the Germans would have both the means and the incentive to develop their production and aid the continent's economic recovery. From this point of view, whether or not pensions were included would affect only the distribution of this sum among the beneficiaries; if reparations were limited to the physical damage done to civilian property, Britain would get comparatively little and the Dominions even less. But for that very reason it was a vital issue for Lloyd George, who was at this time under strong domestic pressure not to renege on election promises to pass as much as possible of the cost of the British war effort on to Germany, and who warned that he could not sign a treaty that did not include pensions. With President Poincaré backing Foch's demand for the Rhine frontier, Clemenceau, too, indicated that he 'could not face parliament' without the undertaking that there would be Allied troops in the Rhineland for fifteen years. It was to ease Clemenceau's position that Wilson had acceded to the Anglo-American guarantee proposed by Lloyd George. On the face of it, this was a remarkable concession since such a specific commitment clearly breached the injunction against 'entangling alliances' that Wilson had always insisted that the League of Nations was consistent with; it also seemed to imply a lack of faith in the League. Wilson, who agreed to the proposal on the very day that he returned to Paris, later made the pledge subject to the approval of the League Council and also insisted on a separate US–French treaty rather than a joint one with Britain. When Henry White warned him that the proposal would be unpopular in the United States with both supporters and opponents of the League of Nations, the President responded that 'all that I promised is to try to get it'.[45]

Although Wilson's tenure of office was more secure than that of Lloyd George and Clemenceau, he was at least as subject as they were to domestic political pressures. While in Paris, he was kept in touch with American opinion by Tumulty, who reminded him that the priority remained to establish the League of Nations and advised against alienating the support of other countries for this by taking a stand on reparations, 'which is a paramount question with European nations and only of indirect interest to us'. Wilson not only needed to ensure that the League was an integral part of the treaty but also had to gain the consent of other leaders to the amendments to the Covenant that Taft and others had told him were necessary to win Senate approval. Lloyd George blatantly sought to exploit the President's predicament by saying that his own agreement to an explicit recognition of the Monroe Doctrine would be conditional on a cutback in America's naval building program. Some historians have argued that Wilson could have structured the negotiations more advanta- geously by explicitly stating that the amendments were necessary in order to gain Senate approval since 'the European statesmen dreaded the possi- bility that Europe might be left to cope with her postwar problems – par- ticularly the economic problems – without American help'. But such criticisms are misplaced not only because Wilson did in fact indicate why he was seeking the amendments but also because, as the consequent dis- cussion showed, the more that American reservations and qualifications were articulated, the less value the French in particular were inclined to place on the League.[46]

A further illustration of the way Wilson's bargaining position in Paris was constrained by the need to maintain his standing at home came when, during the impasse over the Saar and Rhineland, he gave orders to the *George Washington* to return to Brest. It is impossible to know if he ever contemplated carrying out this implicit threat to leave the conference but, if so, he would have been dissuaded by Tumulty's report that in America it was regarded 'as an act of impatience and petulance on the President's part'. This strongly negative reaction may have surprised Wilson, as only a few days earlier Tumulty had urged him 'in some dramatic way' to 'take hold of the situation'. But, like other American progressives, Tumulty apparently saw Wilson's confrontation with the leaders of the Old World as analogous to his earlier fight with the bosses in New Jersey, and believed that the same tactic of a bold appeal to public opinion would again carry the day.[47]

Wilson adopted this course on 23 April when he published a statement explaining his opposition to the Italian claims to territory on the Dalmatian coast of the Adriatic, including the port of Fiume. This move has commonly been condemned as a naïve 'blunder' because it provoked a very hostile reaction in Italy, where Americans were officially advised to keep their distance from the demonstrating crowds. Although he had been warned about the excited state of Italian opinion on the subject, the President may have expected a better response after the warmth of his receptions in Italy only a few weeks earlier and in view of his own sense of the reasonableness of his position. As he pointed out in his statement, Italy was to gain her 'natural frontiers', including not only the Alps along the Brenner line in the north but 'the great watershed within which Trieste and Pola lie'. Although Wilson did not mention it, this would involve the incorporation of over 200,000 German-speaking peoples in the Tyrol and a rather larger number of Yugoslavs in Istria, notwithstanding his call in the Fourteen Points for Italy's frontiers to follow 'clearly recognizable lines of nationality'. He had justified these concessions on strategic and economic grounds that he argued did not apply to Fiume and the Dalmatian coast. With the exception of Fiume itself, the Italian claims were based on the 1915 Treaty of London through which the Allies had induced Italy to enter the war and which the British and French governments felt bound by. For this very reason, the issue could be seen as epitomizing the conflict between the old diplomacy and the new, as it was by the scholars of the Inquiry in a strongly worded memorandum. Their observation that, if Italy was granted Fiume and war with Yugoslavia followed, 'the League will be fighting on the wrong side' is likely to have been particularly disturbing to Wilson since American liberals were already troubled by the possibility that the League would become an instrument to uphold an unjust status quo. As the historian Sterling Kernek has argued, in issuing his statement Wilson was probably less concerned with its effect in Italy than with countering the impression in America that he was abandoning his principles. From this point of view, the manifesto was a great success: 'This is your supreme hour and I have never been so proud of you', an exultant Tumulty cabled.[48]

The downside of Wilson's intransigent stand over the Adriatic was the danger that Italy would refuse to participate in the League of Nations – a danger highlighted when, following Wilson's public statement, the Italian leaders left Paris. (They returned twelve days later.) The same dilemma of how to reconcile the demands of the internal and the external realities had by then presented itself in an even more acute form over the issue of Shantung, a province in China where the Japanese claimed the territory and rights that Germany had held before the war. After declaring war on Germany in 1914, Japan had taken these over and had secured title to them through a coerced treaty with China the following year; they were also among the spoils that Japan had been secretly promised by Britain and France in 1917. But at Paris, the Chinese representatives eloquently pleaded for untrammeled sovereignty over 'the home of Confucius', and their position was overwhelmingly supported by American public opinion. Wilson's fellow-commissioners Lansing, White, and General Tasker Bliss expressed in writing their strong opposition to the Japanese claim. On the other hand, the Japanese made it clear that if they received neither Shantung nor the inclusion in the League Covenant of a declaration of racial equality (which was unacceptable to Britain and her dominions), they would not join the League of Nations. 'They are not bluffers and they will go home unless we give them what they should not have', Wilson told Ray Stannard Baker, now acting as his press secretary. With Italy's participation in the League also uncertain, Wilson evidently felt he needed to reach an agreement in this case notwithstanding the strength of American feeling on the subject, of which he told Baker he was well aware. In the circumstances, he did well (with Balfour's assistance) in persuading the Japanese to limit themselves to the economic privileges that the Germans had possessed and to give an assurance that they would remove their troops and restore Shantung to Chinese sovereignty (which they eventually did in 1922). Yet no feature of the settlement was to attract more criticism in America.[49]

In Paris, on the other hand, attention was focused on European issues. With a sense of urgency intensified by unrest and disturbances across the continent, a draft treaty was put together and presented on 7 May to the German delegates who had been summoned to receive it. It was only at this point that the agreements that had been worked out separately were put together; the overall result seemed shockingly harsh not only to the Germans, who still hoped to be involved in real negotiations, but also to several members of the American and British delegations. A troubled Herbert Hoover woke early on the 7th and walked the deserted streets where, he recalled, he soon ran into Smuts and Keynes: 'It flashed into all our minds why each was walking about at that time of the morning.' Smuts wrote to Wilson, pleading with him to 'use your unrivalled power and influence to make the final Treaty a more moderate and reasonable document'. When Wilson replied that he did not think the treaty 'on the whole unjust in the circumstances', Smuts and others who sought a revision of the terms had more success with Lloyd George who was not only anxious that the Germans would not sign the treaty but conscious that much British opinion, including that of the Cabinet, had become increasingly sympathetic to their case. On 2 June Lloyd George bluntly warned his colleagues in the Council of Four that Britain would not be prepared to renew the war and that it was necessary to make changes in order to win German assent. In particular, the British cabinet favored concessions over the German–Polish frontier, the occupation of the Rhineland, reparations, and the immediate admission of Germany to the League of Nations.[50]

Following Lloyd George's *démarche*, Wilson held a meeting of the whole American delegation to consider the matter. However, he insisted that 'if we regard the treaty as just, the argument of expediency ought not to govern', and that the Germans had 'earned' a 'hard' peace. This attitude has been seen by some historians as representing a constant strand in Wilson's approach to the peace – 'a moralistic desire to make Germany an example to mankind of the severe results of international criminality'. Such a view is based on the premise that Wilson's policies expressed a consistent, if complex, vision rather than being adaptations to the demands of a changing situation. Contemporary observers, however, seemed clear that Wilson's attitude at this time was different from what it had been earlier. Even the faithful Grayson noted that the President's position was 'rather a peculiar one inasmuch as the British had now swung squarely over to the attitude which had marked his efforts entirely during the month of March'. Indeed, Wilson himself observed that the British 'ought to have been rational to begin with and then they would not have needed to have funked at the end'.[51]

His irritation at Lloyd George's *bouleversement* did not lead Wilson to oppose any change in the treaty. On the contrary, in accordance with the unanimous advice of his experts, he made another attempt to secure a fixed sum for reparations, warning the Europeans that Germany's credit had to be established and they could not expect the American government to underwrite it (as Keynes had earlier suggested). But when Lloyd George joined Clemenceau in resisting this, the President did not press the point. Although he made little secret of his pro-Polish sentiments (a constant strand in his policy that was reinforced by the Inquiry's expert, R.H. Lord), Wilson also yielded to Lloyd George's insistence that that there should be a plebiscite in Upper Silesia. On the questions of German entry into the League of Nations and the occupation of the Rhineland, he made some ameliorating suggestions but then deferred to Clemenceau's adamant opposition to any changes. Throughout the discussions, indeed, he played a mediating role between the British and French leaders, stressing the need for agreement and making clear his willingness to use force to compel Germany's acceptance of the treaty. 'I am not particularly interested in one solution rather than in another', he told his colleagues. 'But a solution must be reached, and soon.'[52]

This could be seen as the remark of a man at the end of his tether. Wilson had been driving himself hard throughout the conference, forgoing his usual insistence on periods of relaxation and physical exercise.

Following his gastrointestinal illness in early April, he seems to have suffered a small stroke at the end of that month. By the later stages of the conference, he was clearly very tired and showing signs of strain. As the conference ended, it was only the earnest pleas of Henry White that persuaded him not to decline an invitation to a state dinner given in his honor by President Poincaré (for whom Wilson had developed an intense dislike). Yet the most careful and balanced review of the evidence on Wilson's health problems at Paris concludes that they had no discernible impact on his decisions on matters of policy, and there seems no reason to dissent from this view.[53]

Certainly, his attitude on the question of revising the treaty is readily explicable in political terms. Having succeeded in embedding the League firmly in the treaty, Wilson then had to make it as hard as possible for the Senate to reject the latter. The draft presented to the Germans apparently served this purpose very well. 'Publication of peace treaty here great triumph for you', Tumulty cabled. 'Opposition stunned. There will be no serious opposition to it.' German objections to the treaty met with much less sympathy in the United States than in Britain. 'A great many newspapers in this country are worried lest you be carried away by the pleadings of Germany for a "softer peace", Tumulty warned on 22 May. 'I know you will not be led astray.' Wilson cited Tumulty's reports to Ray Stannard Baker when the latter taxed him with the distress the treaty had caused to liberals. Baker concluded that 'the President is evidently now keenly aware of his problem in getting the treaty – with the League – adopted by the American Congress', and that 'it is plain that at every point the President is thinking of American public opinion'. In addition, Wilson was naturally desirous of avoiding both further delay and the possibility of a serious split among the victor powers.[54]

Critics of Wilson's performance in Paris accuse him of playing a lone hand, mismanaging the negotiations, and thereby failing to achieve the objectives he had proclaimed. Although he did in fact make use of the expertise in the American delegation, it is true that the President conducted the principal negotiations himself without really consulting his fellow-commissioners – even, in the later stages, House. As we have become more accustomed to 'summit diplomacy', this may seem less striking, or culpable, to us than it did to contemporaries. Wilson did not play his cards closer to his chest than Franklin Roosevelt was to do. In the framing of the treaty, he did not have everything his own way, but this was inevitable in a negotiating situation, particularly since his bargaining position was in reality much less strong than it had appeared to be. The questions of priority among his aims that had consequently to be decided required political judgments that Wilson could neither delegate nor always openly avow. In the Council of Four, Wilson had not been outwitted or overborne, but neither had he alienated his colleagues – indeed, by the end his relationship with Clemenceau in particular was conspicuously warm. The outcome – the Treaty of Versailles – caused great distress and disillusionment to many, particularly Germans and liberals. But by the test of its acceptability to American opinion – which naturally weighed heavily with Wilson – it was less of a failure. It was certainly preferable to the breakup of the conference in disagreement. Above all, it contained the League of Nations, which Wilson increasingly argued would be able to rectify the treaty's faults 'out of the atmosphere of war'. Throughout, he had been conscious of the forthcoming fight with his domestic opponents to secure Senate consent, and he seems to have been confident that he had positioned himself favorably for this. On the eve of his departure, he told Poincaré that a hard battle lay ahead in Washington but that it would be a one-day battle.[55]

Notes

1 Arthur Walworth, *America's Moment: 1918: American Diplomacy at the End of World War I*, New York, 1977, p. 114n.

2 The next longest period of absence from the United States by a serving president was Franklin Roosevelt's 37-day trip in January–February 1945, encompassing the Yalta conference.

3 Diary of R.B. Fosdick, 14 December 1918; Diary of W.C. Bullitt, 11 December 1918, *PWW*, vol. 53, pp. 384–5, 366–7.

4 Victor S. Mamatey, *The United States and East Central Europe 1914–1918: A Study in Wilsonian Diplomacy and Propaganda*, Princeton, NJ, 1957, pp. 107–8; Klaus Schwabe, *Woodrow Wilson, Revolutionary Germany, and Peacemaking, 1918–1919: Missionary Diplomacy and the Realities of Power*, Chapel Hill, NC, 1985, p. 262.

5 Diary of Dr Grayson, 8 December 1918, memorandum of Isaiah Bowman, 10 December 1918, *PWW*, vol. 53, pp. 336, 356.

6 Diary of Josephus Daniels, October 17, 1918, *PWW*, vol. 51, p. 372.

7 Diary of W.C. Bullitt, 10 December 1918; Diary of Dr Grayson, 8 December 1918, *PWW*, vol. 53, pp. 352, 337. This threat echoed Wilson's statement in his January 1917 Address to the Senate that 'there is only one sort of peace that the peoples of America could join in guaranteeing', *PWW*, vol. 40, p. 535.

8 David M. Kennedy, *Over Here: The First World War and American Society*, New York, 1980, pp. 338, 332; Walworth, *America's Moment*, p. 285; Wilson to House, 21 July 1917, *PWW*, vol. 43, p. 238.

9 For example, Joseph S. Nye Jr, *Bound to Lead: The Changing Nature of American Power*, New York, 1990, pp. 31–3.

10 T.W. Lamont Memorandum of Conversation with the President, 4 October 1918, *PWW*, vol. 51, pp. 222–6; Walworth, *America's Moment*, pp. 138, 72; Inga Floto, *Colonel House in Paris: A Study of American Policy at the Paris Peace Conference of 1919*, Princeton, NJ, 1973, pp. 32–3.

11 Diary of W.C. Bullitt, 10 December 1918, memorandum by Isaiah Bowman, 10 December 1918, *PWW*, vol. 51, pp. 351, 353.

12 W.C. Bullitt to Wilson, 17 May 1919, *PWW*, vol. 59, pp. 232–3; Sigmund Freud and William C. Bullitt, *Thomas Woodrow Wilson: A Psychological Study*, London, 1967, pp. 224–8 and passim.

13 Carter Glass to Wilson, 19 December 1918, 28 February 1919, *PWW*, vol. 53, pp. 441–2, vol. 55, pp. 332–3; Arno J. Mayer, *Politics and Diplomacy of Peacemaking: Containment and Counterrevolution at Versailles, 1918–1919*, New York, 1969, pp. 266–73. For further discussion of this point, see Schwabe, *Wilson, Revolutionary Germany, and Peacemaking*, pp. 166–7 and William R. Keylor, 'Versailles and International Diplomacy' in Manfred F. Boemeke, Gerald D. Feldman, and Elisabeth Glaser (eds), *The Treaty of Versailles: A Reassessment after 75 Years*, Cambridge, 1998, pp. 477–8.

14 W.C. Bullitt to Wilson, 17 May 1919, *PWW*, vol. 59, pp. 232–3.

15 Walworth, *America's Moment*, p. 115; Mayer, *Politics and Diplomacy*, pp. 33, 148–63, 170–87, 194–226.

16 Wilson to House, 30 October 1918, *PWW*, vol. 51, p. 513; Walworth, *America's Moment*, p. 61; Freud and Bullitt, *Thomas Woodrow Wilson*, pp. 180–1.

17 On the attitudes of the American military, see Schwabe, *Wilson, Revolutionary Germany, and Peacemaking*, pp. 224–7.

18 Diary of Dr Grayson, 8 December 1918, address to the League to Enforce Peace, 27 May 1916, Diary of W.C. Bullitt, 10 December 1918, *PWW*, vol. 53, pp. 336–7, 352, vol. 37, p. 116; Schwabe, *Wilson, Revolutionary Germany, and Peacemaking*, p. 28.

19 Imperial War Cabinet memorandum, 30 December 1918; Wilson to House, 31 October 1918, *PWW*, vol. 53, pp. 558–69, vol. 51, p. 533.

20 Protocol of a Plenary Session of the Inter-Allied Conference for the Preliminaries of Peace, 25 January 1919, *PWW*, vol. 54, p. 266.

21 N. Gordon Levin, Jr, *Woodrow Wilson and World Politics: America's Response to War and Revolution*, New York, 1968, pp. vii, 18.

22 Lunchtime address in Cincinnati, 26 October 1916; address to the World's Salesmanship Congress, Detroit, 10 July 1916, *PWW*, vol. 38, p. 528, vol. 37, p. 384.

23 Priscilla Roberts, 'The Anglo-American Theme: American Visions of an Atlantic Alliance, 1914–1933', *Diplomatic History*, 21 (summer 1997): 353–7.

24 Although both the President and the Congress are in a sense elected by the nation as a whole, the political system gives extra weight in the two cases to different elements of the population. The 'winner-takes-all' rule for the votes of most states' delegates in the electoral

college privileges the metropolitan areas because the more populous states are crucial to the outcome of presidential elections and victory in these usually goes to the candidate who carries the big cities. By contrast, the fact that each state has two senators means that thinly populated rural states are overrepresented in the Senate – generally the more important house for foreign affairs.

25 Edith Benham, who as Mrs Wilson's secretary was a member of the Wilson's household in Paris, wrote in her diary that

> I have always felt, though the P. talks of the joy he will have when he is free and how nothing would induce him to run, that subconsciously he has that in his mind. I base this principally on the fact that every candidate mentioned for the Democrats while commending some of their qualities, he always gives conclusive reasons why they shouldn't run, and if they did why they couldn't be elected.

(Edith Benham diary, 12 May 1919)

For House's advice concerning the Republicans, see House diary 1 January 1919, *PWW*, vol. 59, pp. 74–5, vol. 53, pp. 587–8.

26 William C. Widenor, *Henry Cabot Lodge and the Search for an American Foreign Policy*, Berkeley and Los Angeles, CA, 1980, pp. 298–9; Mayer, *Politics and Diplomacy*, p. 19.

27 Speech at a plenary session of the Inter-Allied Conference for the Preliminaries of the Peace [henceforth, the Peace Conference], 25 January 1919; State of the Union Address, 2 December 1918, *PWW*, vol. 54, p. 270, vol. 53, p. 285.

28 Draft Minutes of Imperial War Cabinet, 30 December 1918, *PWW*, vol. 53, pp. 558–69; Thomas Knock, *To End All Wars*, Princeton, NJ, 1992, pp. 199–201.

29 Hankey's notes of a meeting of the Council of Ten, 22 January 1919, *PWW*, vol. 54, p. 206; Knock, *To End All Wars*, p. 209.

30 House to Wilson, 25 June 1918; House diary, 15 August 1918, *PWW*, vol. 48, pp. 424–5, vol. 49, p. 266; Arthur Walworth, *Wilson and His Peacemakers: American Diplomacy at the Paris Peace Conference, 1919*, New York, 1986, p. 106n. For criticism by historians of Wilson's failure during the war publicly to cooperate with others in promoting a specific scheme, see Warren F. Kuehl, *Seeking World Order, The United States and International Organization to 1920*, Nashville, TN, 1969, pp. 254–6, 336, and Knock, *To End All Wars*, pp. 148–54.

31 A memorandum by W.H. Taft [c. 29 March 1918]; Wilson to House, 22 March 1918, *PWW*, vol. 47, pp. 198–203, 105.

32 Reading to Wilson (with enclosure), 3 July 1918; Wiseman to Reading, 16 August 1918; Wilson to House, 8 July 1918; House to Wilson, 14 July 1918, 16 July 1918 (with enclosure); House diary, 15 August 1918, *PWW*, vol. 48, pp. 501–3, vol. 49, pp. 273–5, vol. 48, pp. 549–50, 608–9, 630–37, vol. 49, pp. 265–8. The text of Wilson's 'Magnolia draft' of the Covenant is enclosed with Wilson to House, 7 September 1918, *PWW*, vol. 49, pp. 467–71. On the Phillimore Report and the pressure, especially from the French, for the League to be a continuation of the wartime alliance, see George W. Egerton, *Great Britain and the Creation*

of the League of Nations: Strategy, Politics, and International Organization, 1914–1919, Chapel Hill, NC, 1978, pp. 65–74.

33 Grayson diary, 21 January 1919; Benham diary, 21 January 1919, *PWW*, vol. 54, pp. 177, 197; memorandum, 26 December 1918, a draft of a Covenant of a League of Nations, c. 8 January 1919, *PWW*, vol. 53, pp. 515–19, 655–86.

34 Lansing to Wilson with enclosure, 23 December 1918, *PWW*, vol. 53, pp. 474–6; minutes of the eighth meeting of the League of Nations Commission, 11 February 1919, Cecil diary, 11 February 1919, *PWW*, vol. 55, pp. 72–80; David Hunter Miller, *The Drafting of the Covenant*, New York, 1928, vol 1, pp. 175–81, 168; Cecil diary, 6 February 1919, *PWW*, vol. 54, p. 514; Lloyd E. Ambrosius, 'Wilson, the Republicans, and French Security After World War I', *Journal of American History*, 59 (September 1972): 341–3, *PWW*, vol. 53, p. 481n; address at the Metropolitan Opera House, 4 March 1919, *PWW*, vol. 55, p. 419; Covenant of the League of Nations [28 April 1919], *PWW*, vol. 58, p. 191.

35 Miller, *Drafting the Covenant*, vol. 1, pp. 52–3, 70–71; Wilson to House with enclosure, 7 September 1918, *PWW*, vol. 49, p. 468; minutes of the Council of Ten, 22, 27, 30 January 1919, *PWW*, vol. 54, pp. 204–6, 296, 350–78. For fuller accounts, see Lloyd E. Ambrosius, *Woodrow Wilson and the American Diplomatic Tradition: The Treaty Fight in Perspective*, Cambridge, 1987, pp. 51–79; Knock, *To End All Wars*, pp. 210–13 and Walworth, *Wilson and the Peacemakers*, pp. 64–81, 125–33.

36 Address to the third Plenary Session of the Peace Conference, 14 February 1919, *PWW*, vol. 55, pp. 173–8. Smuts is quoted in Walworth, *Wilson and the Peacemakers*, p. 120n.

37 House diary, 14 February 1919, *PWW*, vol. 55, pp. 193–6; Tumulty to Wilson, 6 January 1919, Wilson to Tumulty, 9 January 1919, *PWW*, vol. 53, pp. 625–6, 698; Widenor, *Henry Cabot Lodge*, pp. 300–15; Walworth, *Wilson and the Peacemakers*, pp. 181–3; Ambrosius, *Wilson and the American Diplomatic Tradition*, pp. 80–87; Knock, *To End All Wars*, pp. 168–9, 176–7, 189–90, 229–30.

38 Wilson to Tumulty, 14 February 1914; address in Boston, 24 February 1919, *PWW*, vol. 55, pp. 184, 238–45. In his speech to the Senate on 28 February Lodge claimed that the country was being asked 'to move away from George Washington to . . . the sinister figure of Trotsky, the champion of internationalism'. Knock, *To End All Wars*, pp. 240–41.

39 *New York Times*, 27 February 1919; House diary, 14 February 1919; Address at the Metropolitan Opera House, 4 March 1919; Remarks to the Democratic National Committee, 28 February 1919; Taft to Wilson, 18 March 1919, *PWW*, vol. 55, pp. 194, 413–21, 313, vol. 56, p. 83; Walworth, *Wilson and the Peacemakers*, p. 186. 'Your dinner . . . was a failure', Wilson told House when they met again. House diary, 14 March 1919, *PWW*, vol. 55, p. 499.

40 Tumulty to Wilson, 13 March 1919; 14 March 1919; R.S. Baker diary, 15 March 1919, *PWW*, vol. 55, pp. 493, 500, 531.

41 Wilson to House, c. 23 February 1919; Grayson diary, 13 March 1919 and note, *PWW*, vol. 55, pp. 229–30, 486–9. Arthur Link writes flatly that House 'betrayed Wilson' at this time: *Woodrow Wilson: Revolution, War, and Peace*, Arlington Heights, IL, 1979, p. 88. The fullest analysis of the decline of the Wilson–House relationship is Floto, *House in Paris* (especially

Chapter 4), but see also Walworth, *Wilson and the Peacemakers*, pp. 145–56, 161–2, 186–91 and August Heckscher, *Woodrow Wilson: A Biography*, New York, 1991, pp. 545–7.

42 Entries for 28 March 1919, *PWW*, vol. 56, pp. 347–54, 360–71.

43 *The Collected Writings of John Maynard Keynes*, vol. 2, *The Economic Consequences of the Peace*, London, 1971, pp. 33–4; Mayer, *Politics and Diplomacy of Peacemaking*, especially pp. 10, 21–3, 29–30, 562–73; Levin, *Woodrow Wilson and World Politics*, p. 171; Edwin A. Weinstein, *Woodrow Wilson: A Medical and Psychological Biography*, Princeton, NJ, 1981, pp. 337–45; Heckscher, *Woodrow Wilson*, pp. 555–62.

44 *PWW*, vol. 56, pp. 557n–8n; Mayer, *Politics and Diplomacy*, p. 563; Lloyd George memorandum, 25 March 1919; Council of Four meeting, 26 March 1919; J.F. Dulles memorandum, 1 April 1919, *PWW*, vol. 56, pp. 259–70, 289–90, 498–9.

45 *PWW*, vol. 56, pp. 6n–7n; Walworth, *Wilson and the Peacemakers*, p. 281; Minutes of the Council of Four, 22 April 1919, *PWW*, vol. 57, pp. 587–8, *PWW*, vol. 56, p. 12n; Wilson memorandum, 12 April 1919; Henry White to Wilson, 16 April 1919; Wilson to Henry White, 17 April 1919, *PWW*, vol. 57, pp. 297, 416–18, 430.

46 Tumulty to Wilson, 9 April 1919, *PWW*, vol. 57, pp. 188–9; House diary, 27 March 1919, *PWW*, vol. 56, p. 335; Cecil Diary, 8–10 April 1919, *PWW*, vol. 57, p. 142; Knock, *To End All Wars*, pp. 248–9; Alexander L. George and Juliette L. George, *Woodrow Wilson and Colonel House: A Personality Study*, New York, 1956, pp. 257–8; minutes of the League of Nations Commission, 26 March, 10 April, 11 April 1919, *PWW*, vol. 56, pp. 301–3, vol. 57, pp. 226–32, 252–57.

47 Tumulty to Grayson, 9 April 1919; 5 April 1919, *PWW*, vol. 57, pp. 177, 37.

48 Wilson statement on the Adriatic question, 23 April 1919, *PWW*, vol. 58, pp. 5–8; Thomas A. Bailey, *Woodrow Wilson and the Lost Peace*, New York, 1944, pp. 261–8; John Morton Blum, *Woodrow Wilson and the Politics of Morality*, Boston, MA, 1956, pp. 176–7; Ambassador T.N. Page to American Mission in Paris, 24 April 1919, *PWW*, vol. 58, pp. 91–3; Ambassador T.N. Page to E.M. House, 17 April 1919; Isaiah Bowman and others to Wilson, 17 April 1919, *PWW*, vol. 57, pp. 434–7, 432–3; Tumulty to Wilson, 24 April 1919, *PWW*, vol. 58, p. 105. For other positive responses to Wilson's statement see George Lansbury to Wilson, 24 April 1919, Bernard Baruch to Wilson, 24 April 1919, Margot Asquith to Wilson, 24 April 1919, *PWW*, vol. 58, pp. 93–5.

Sterling J. Kernek, 'Woodrow Wilson and National Self-determination Along Italy's Frontier', *Proceedings of the American Philosophical Society*, 126 (1982): 242–300, provides a lucid, thorough, and persuasive analysis of the whole issue.

49 Lansing to Wilson, 21 April 1919, *PWW*, vol. 57, pp. 560–61; T.H. Bliss to Wilson, 29 April 1919; R.S. Baker diary, 25 April 1919; minutes of the Council of Four, 29 April 1919; A.J. Balfour to Wilson with enclosure, 29 April 1919; Wilson to A.J. Balfour, 30 April 1919; A.J. Balfour to Wilson with enclosure, 30 April 1919; minutes of the Council of Four, 30 April 1919; R.S. Baker diary, 30 April 1919; Wilson to J.P. Tumulty, 30 April 1919, *PWW*, vol. 58, pp. 232–4, 142–3, 216–26, 228, 245–7, 257–61, 270–71, 272–3.

50 Herbert Hoover, *The Ordeal of Woodrow Wilson*, New York, 1958, p. 234; J.C. Smuts to

Wilson, 14 May 1919; Wilson to J.C. Smuts, 16 May 1919; J.C. Smuts to D. Lloyd George, 22 May 1919, *PWW*, vol. 59, pp. 149–50, 187–8, 413–19; minutes of the Council of Four, 2 June 1919, *PWW*, vol. 60, pp. 22–33. On the background to Lloyd George's *démarche*, see A. Lentin, *Guilt at Versailles: Lloyd George and the Pre-History of Appeasement*, London, 1985, pp. 88–96.

51 Discussion with the American delegation, 3 June 1919; Grayson diary, 3 June 1919, *PWW*, vol. 60, pp. 45–71, 43; Levin, *Woodrow Wilson and World Politics*, pp. 155–61 (quotation on p. 159).

52 Minutes of the Council of Four, 9 June 1919, *PWW*, vol. 60, pp. 316–20; Walworth, *Wilson and the Peacemakers*, pp. 403–6, 413–30.

53 Heckscher, *Woodrow Wilson*, pp. 525, 549, 555; House diary, 23 June 1919; Grayson diary, 24 June 1919; Henry White to Wilson, 24 June 1919; Benham diary, 25 June 1919, *PWW*, vol. 61, pp. 112–15 and note, 119, 132, 180; Walworth, *Wilson and the Peacemakers*, pp. 432–3; Bert E. Park, 'The Impact of Wilson's Neurological Disease during the Paris Peace Conference', *PWW*, vol. 58, pp. 611–30.

54 Tumulty to Wilson, 8 May 1919, *PWW*, vol. 58, p. 561; Tumulty to Wilson, 22 May 1919; R.S. Baker diary, 23 May, 31 May 1919, *PWW*, vol. 59, pp. 419, 447, 645–7.

55 R.S. Baker diary, 3 June 1919, *PWW*, vol. 60, p. 80; Walworth, *Wilson and the Peacemakers*, p. 433.

Chapter 8

Defeat

Wilson's prediction was to prove quite wrong, of course. The fight to secure Senate approval of the treaty he had negotiated in Paris was to last months and to end in failure. Yet his remark to Poincaré expressed two elements in the mentality with which he approached the contest that was to dominate the remainder of his presidency – belligerence and confidence. They set him on a course that most historians have seen as in large part responsible for the eventual outcome. His conduct has generally been attributed to features of his personality, and has provided the main grist for the mill of psychoanalytic interpretations of Wilson.[1] More recently, stress has been laid on the effects of ill-health, before as well as after the disabling stroke he suffered at the beginning of October.[2] However, neither his belligerence nor his confidence was all that remarkable in the circumstances.

It was clear that Wilson was in for a fight. Lodge and his fellow Republican party leaders had been determined to discredit the President's peacemaking from the beginning.[3] It was in no way unusual for American foreign policy to be the subject of party political conflict. Indeed, the first party division had arisen in the 1790s as much out of disagreement about how the United States should respond to the French revolutionary wars as over domestic issues. In the 1840s the major parties had divided over the incorporation of Texas, and in the 1890s over the acquisition first of Hawaii and then of the Philippines. Throughout Wilson's presidency, Republicans had attacked his handling of foreign policy, from the Columbian Treaty through the Mexican imbroglio to the defense of American neutral rights. As we have seen, foreign policy had figured prominently in the 1916 election campaign. It is true that entry into war had produced a form of party truce in the interests of national unity, but this had not shielded the administration from fierce congressional criticism even before it broke down completely with the approach of peace.

For the most part these controversies had worked to Wilson's political advantage. His claim to have preserved both peace and the nation's honor had done much to win him a second term. In his response to the European war he had outmaneuvered his Republican critics by combining a flexible approach with an instinct for the middle ground. By adopting preparedness, committing himself to American participation in a postwar league of nations, and finally by entering the war, he had moved the Democratic party away from its isolationist and pacifist traditions. But he had done so in a way that respected the anti-imperialism and hostility to power politics that had upheld those traditions. Thereby he had not only carried even the Bryanite wing of his own party with him, but had also won the support of many Republicans for his attempt to base a continuous involvement in world affairs upon a reform of the international order on American principles. The instrumentality of this enterprise was a project that had been promoted by the largely Republican League to Enforce Peace before Wilson had adopted it. But he had made the cause his own and would obviously garner the lion's share of the credit for its fulfillment.

However, the Republicans had acquired the means to obstruct Wilson's peacemaking by gaining control of both congressional houses in the 1918 elections. Moreover, under the Constitution, the Senate had to approve treaties by a two-thirds majority. Nor was there a tradition of deference to the executive in this respect. Indeed, John Hay, Secretary of State at the turn of the century, had remarked that a treaty going to the Senate is 'like a bull going into the arena'.[4] Wilson himself had expressed a different view in his book *Constitutional Government*, arguing that the president 'need disclose no step of negotiation until it is complete, and when in any critical matter it is completed the Government is virtually committed. Whatever its disinclination, the Senate may feel itself committed also'. But the unearthing of this passage had only served to strengthen the determination of Republicans in the Senate to reassert congressional prerogatives after the wartime exercise of extraordinary powers by the President.[5]

In these circumstances, House had advised Wilson to seek an understanding with congressional leaders and, as we have seen, had persuaded him to invite them to dinner in the White House in February. Yet when House in his last conversation before the President left Europe (and the last that the two men were ever to have) again 'urged him to meet the Senate in a conciliatory spirit', Wilson chillingly replied: 'House, I have found one can never get anything in this world that is worthwhile without fighting for it.'[6] Wilson may well have been implicitly rebuking his friend for what he saw as House's overaccommodating conduct in Paris as well as expressing his combative temperament. Yet he also had both reason and motive for rejecting the advice. He had gone to considerable trouble to gain the amendments to the Covenant that Taft had indicated would be sufficient to secure Senate approval. By tying the League of Nations so inextricably to the treaty (and by avoiding the charge of having made a 'soft' peace), he evidently believed that he had placed its rejection outside the realm of practical politics. Moreover, the League itself appeared to have wide appeal to the American people. Although the Covenant agreed in Paris differed significantly from its own plan, the League to Enforce Peace (including Taft) had immediately started promoting it. A poll of 1,377 newspaper editors in April had found that 718 unequivocally favored American membership, 478 did so with qualifications and only 181 were firmly opposed. Many of these newspapers were Republican as were several of the 32 (out of the 48) state legislatures that had endorsed the League by the time Wilson returned to America.[7] In contrast to the essentially united Democratic party, the Republicans were thus divided over the League. Tumulty encouraged Wilson in his belief that he could rout his foes and lead the United States into the League of Nations that he had done so much to establish, thereby vindicating his justification of America's war effort and laying the basis for a successful election campaign in 1920.[8]

Seeking to secure approval of the treaty he had negotiated without making any further concessions was not therefore an irrational course for Wilson to follow. It did, however, represent a choice of the more optimistic scenario presented by Tumulty over the warnings of House and Lansing. This choice may well have been influenced by the success Wilson had enjoyed up to this point. As he sailed back to America on the *George Washington* in early July, it was just nine years since he had decided to leave the academic world and plunge into the political arena. In that brief period, he had faced many problems and much criticism, but had emerged triumphant. Winning every election in which he had run, he had acquired total ascendancy in his own party, a dominant position in the nation's affairs and a greater influence abroad than any of his predecessors. There is a natural tendency for leaders who have experienced great success to exaggerate their own power to achieve whatever they desire – one thinks of Franklin D. Roosevelt's 'court-packing' plan in 1937 or British Prime Minister Margaret Thatcher's determination to impose the poll tax after winning her third general election. Such a state of mind induces disdain for opponents, to which Wilson was always prone. He referred to the 'bungalow minds' on Capitol Hill, and when visiting his newborn grandson in March had remarked that 'with his mouth open and his eyes shut, I predict he will make a senator when he grows up'.[9]

While Wilson was still in Paris, Republican leaders were preparing to defeat him. Lodge, majority leader in the new Senate, worked with the party's national chairman Will H. Hays and its elder statesman Elihu Root to find common ground on which all his colleagues could stand. Amidst the complex and unstable shades of individual opinion, there were three main strands. Some, preeminently William Borah and Hiram Johnson, stood firmly on the traditional policy of noninvolvement and were utterly opposed to membership in a league of nations behind which they saw the sinister forces of international capitalism and the British Empire. By contrast, Lodge himself had, of course, desired a closer association with the Allies through the war and the peacemaking. Like Theodore Roosevelt, whose political heir he felt himself to be, he had long opposed American isolationism but from a 'realist' standpoint that despised the utopian hopes and unsustainable commitments that Wilson's scheme seemed to him to embody. Finally, there were some Republican senators who supported the League of Nations, of whom Porter McCumber was the most enthusiastic. Lodge showed his determination to prevent Wilson getting his way by ensuring that there was an anti-League majority on the Foreign Relations Committee. He dismissed the changes Wilson had secured in the Covenant as inadequate, insisting that the Monroe Doctrine was not a 'regional understanding' but a unilateral American policy. In late June a potentially unifying formula was produced in a letter over Root's signature that proposed reservations to 'be made part of the instrument of ratification', excluding Article 10, clarifying the provisions for withdrawal, and asserting US freedom of action regarding 'purely American questions'. The day before the *George Washington* reached New York, Lodge assured Root that all but one or two of the Senate Republicans would approve such reservations.[10]

When Wilson appeared before the Senate to present the treaty, McCumber was the only Republican to join in the applause. Anticipating and despising such hostility while recognizing how much was at stake, Wilson unsurprisingly seems to have been nervous about this speech. He had had difficulty composing it on the return voyage and delivered it less fluently than usual. Clearly addressing himself to a wider audience, he followed Tumulty's advice that he couch the choice in stark terms. After praising the gallantry and idealism of the American 'crusaders' who had turned the tide of battle in 1918 (thereby countering Republican accusations of unpatriotic 'internationalism'), he stressed the need to exorcise 'the demon of war' by creating a 'new order'. Like those twenty years earlier who had sought to persuade Americans to break with tradition by acquiring the Philippines (to whom he made favorable reference), Wilson presented the issue as one of both duty and destiny. 'Dare we reject it and break the heart of the world?' he asked. 'The light streams upon the path ahead, and nowhere else.'[11]

The President had not addressed any of the specific questions upon which opponents of the Covenant had focused, and even some of his supporters criticized him on this score. But one judgment that he and Lodge shared was that the appeal of the League lay in its general conception and promise so it was natural for him to emphasize this rather than the exact terms of its provisions and obligations. He did declare his readiness to discuss any aspect of the treaty with the Foreign Relations Committee, and on the day of his speech held both a press conference and informal discussions with friendly senators. He followed this up over the next three weeks by inviting individual senators for chats in the White House, concentrating initially on those Republicans most favorably disposed to the League. These interviews seem to have been amicable enough, but no senator emerging from one of these well-publicized encounters was willing to admit to having had his mind changed. Meanwhile, the Foreign Relations Committee sought to embarrass the President by summoning to its hearings witnesses with strong objections to the treaty, notably pro-Chinese spokesmen and Irish-Americans who passionately denounced Wilson's disregard of Ireland's claim to independence, and by requesting documents revealing disagreements among the American Commissioners in Paris. Anxious to appear reasonable, the President acceded to these requests to the limited extent he was able to without diplomatic embarrassment, and was only restrained by Tumulty from forwarding a copy of Bliss's objection to the Shantung cession. He also agreed to meet with the whole committee for an open discussion.[12]

This event, which took place in the White House on 19 August, remains the only occasion on which an American president has submitted himself to public questioning by a congressional committee. Wilson began by reading a statement in which he stressed the serious economic effects of delay in ratifying the treaty and reviewed the changes that had been made in the Covenant in response to earlier objections. Although the meaning of its provisions seemed to him 'plain', he had no objections to 'interpretations accompanying the act of ratification' provided that these did 'not form a part of the formal ratification itself' and thus require the assent of other signatories, including Germany. The tone of the subsequent discussion was extremely courteous on both sides, but in substance it mostly consisted of attempts by Republican senators to secure information and admissions that would be damaging to the President and his case. Some of Wilson's responses were disingenuous, including his denial of any knowledge of the secret treaties before he reached Paris. However, he did acknowledge that he was the author of Article 10, which he called 'the very backbone of the whole covenant'. He argued that it created 'a moral, not a legal, obligation' in the sense, not that it was less binding, but that there would always be 'an element of judgment' as to whether it applied in particular cases. The coherence of this distinction came under much pressure in the questioning, revealing again the extreme difficulty of formulating a pledge upon which other nations could rely without constraining the action of Congress in the future – and the virtual impossibility of doing so if, like Borah, one did not trust the US representative on the League Council to reflect the will of Congress.[13]

Not long after this meeting, Wilson made a decision that has been seen as a fatal misjudgment. This was to embark upon an extensive speaking tour to rally public support. The precipitant was evidently the adoption by the Foreign Relations Committee (by a vote of nine to eight) of an amendment to the treaty restoring Shantung to China. Wilson's angry response that, if they wanted war, he would 'give them a belly full' led him to disregard his own pre-presidential judgment that, whereas an 'appeal to the nation' could be resorted to when a president was opposed by the House of Representatives, 'the Senate is not so immediately sensitive to opinion and is apt to grow, if anything, more stiff if pressure of that kind is brought to bear upon it'.[14] During August, those Republican senators most favorable to the League were endeavoring to formulate some 'mild reservations' intended to make possible speedy ratification of the treaty, and Democratic senators, too, were increasingly inclining towards a compromise. This was the time, historians have concluded, when 'the League had its best chance in the Senate'. Rather than continuing his confrontational course, they argue, Wilson should have remained in Washington to aid the efforts to form the necessary bipartisan coalition.[15]

Wilson's failure to do this has been linked to his state of health. In July, he became unwell with what Grayson said was an attack of dysentery. Although he seemed to recover quickly, some now suspect that he had suffered a small stroke which aggravated the decline that had been perceptible for some time in his mental capacity (including memory) and emotional balance. Certainly there was evidence that his temper was growing shorter, and that in face of accumulating stresses and frustrations he was tending to a sort of self-righteous despair. News from Europe of continuing imperialistic deals and Rumanian aggressions led him to exclaim to Lansing that 'when I think of the greed and utter selfishness of it all, I am almost inclined to refuse to permit this country to be a member of the League of Nations when it is composed of such intriguers and robbers. I am disposed to throw up the whole business and get out.'[16]

Yet, Wilson's decision to take his case to the country was neither as impulsive nor as 'irrational' as has been claimed. He had asked Tumulty as early as February to make arrangements for such a tour, and on the ship coming home had actually drawn up a list of titles for speeches. It was, of course, a tactic he had successfully employed in earlier battles with legislatures, both as Governor of New Jersey and as President over preparedness in 1916. In mid-July he told Wiseman that he was 'most eager' to take his case to the country, but would not do so unless he concluded that he could not persuade sufficient Republican senators through his personal meetings with them. By late August, such a conclusion was a reasonable one. It was not only that even the group of Republicans most favorable to the treaty were insistent that reservations should be formally incorporated in the resolution of ratification. It was also that the group was not numerous enough to produce the requisite two-thirds majority and could only hope to attract party colleagues by formulating reservations that would substantially alter – rather than merely clarify – the Covenant. Interestingly, Wilson's judgment that the gulf was unbridgeable mirrored that of his principal opponent. In early August, Lodge assured a correspondent of his confidence that the Republican senators would unite behind reservations that would 'take the United States out of the treaty entirely on all the parts where we wish to refuse obligations'.[17]

Nor was public opinion by any means irrelevant. Lodge's strategy of delay and of giving every opportunity for critics of the treaty representing various interests and ideological perspectives to publicize their objections had been calculated to nourish second thoughts about Wilson's handiwork. By late August senators were perceiving a weakening in public support for the League, and this was having an effect on their attitudes.[18] And even if popular sentiment had no direct effect on the votes of senators (elected for a six-year term), it would be decisive in the larger political battle that was Wilson's ultimate concern. In the last analysis, he could not prevent the Republicans from refusing to approve the treaty except with reservations that reduced the League to what he called 'only a debating society'.[19] But he could hope to ensure that they paid a political price for so doing. Here again, Wilson's perspective was the mirror image of Lodge's. The latter's sympathetic and insightful biographer has written that 'we may reasonably assume that Lodge would have swallowed the League had he seen therein the means of securing a Republican victory'.[20] For his part, Wilson was clearly prepared to see the treaty fail in the Senate if the result redounded to his, and the Democratic party's, political advantage (and hence, he would doubtless have argued, the eventual approval of an unimpaired League by a later Congress). After all, he had launched his political career by securing public vindication after being defeated in a closed political environment dominated by his enemies (the Princeton Board of Trustees).

This perspective also explains Wilson's determination not to dicker over the wording of reservations. Just before setting out on his tour, he gave to the acting leader of the Senate Democrats, Hitchcock of Nebraska, the text of four 'interpretations' to be communicated to the other signatories along with the formal ratification of the treaty. These covered the issues on which most Senate criticism of the League had focused – the right of withdrawal, the exclusion of such matters as immigration and tariff policy, the status of the Monroe Doctrine and Article 10. On the last, Wilson's draft stressed that a Council motion with regard to the use of armed force was 'to be regarded only as advice and leaves each Member State free to exercise its own judgment as to whether it is wise or practicable to act upon that advice or not'. But although Wilson clearly authorized Hitchcock to propose these 'interpretations' at an opportune time, he forbade him from disclosing their authorship. This, Hitchcock recalled, was because he feared that 'his enemies would make use of his yielding to demand more and more because they wanted not only to defeat the league but to discredit and overthrow him'. (One of Wilson's most devoted supporters, Senator Williams of Mississippi, compared the President's critics to the wolf in Aesop's fable whom the lamb could never appease 'because what the wolf really wanted to do was eat the lamb'.) Wilson would also have been particularly anxious to avoid becoming embroiled in a complex semantic controversy before setting out on his tour. Tumulty had advised him months before that the case for the League needed to be presented in simple, clear-cut terms and he would not have wanted to muddy the waters.[21]

In shelving earlier plans for a 'swing around the circle' soon after his return to America, Wilson had taken the advice of Democratic senators that an immediate appeal to the country would create a bad impression. But the postponement had also been welcomed by Edith who told Wiseman in July that she doubted her husband could 'stand the heavy strain of a speaking tour through the country during the very hot weather'. However, the itinerary Tumulty organized when Wilson did decide to go made no allowance for any weakness since it involved traveling ten thousand miles in less than a month and making over 30 major speeches. The President's non-airconditioned train was to criss-cross the vast spaces of the Middle West and West – the area of the country that had given him victory in 1916. Grayson (according to his later account) warned the President about the dangers to his health but was rebuffed when Wilson said it was a duty that he owed to the soldiers he had sent to Europe. There was undoubtedly something heroic about the effort Wilson was about to make, the more so as he was going to address his audiences without benefit of amplification or a text. Before leaving Washington, he did type out eight pages of notes on particular themes, but he continued his preparation *en route*. As his train left Kansas City, where he had just addressed a crowd of 20,000, for Des Moines where he was to make another big speech that evening, he was glimpsed through a railway carriage window at his typewriter, 'pounding the keys strenuously'. But public speaking and campaigning was meat and drink to Wilson, and there is every indication that he was happy to exchange the bitter atmosphere of Washington for auto-parades and lecture platforms in mid-America.[22]

Wilson's speeches as he crossed the country naturally contained much repetition, although there were interesting shifts of emphasis as he progressed. As he had planned in Washington, he began with an emphatic and comprehensive defense of the treaty, presenting it as the fulfillment of all that America had fought for. If the terms imposed on Germany were 'severe', this was not to humiliate her but 'to rectify the wrong that she had done' – she had to pay 'reparation' but 'no indemnity'. Moreover, they were temporary; the permanent feature of the settlement was the liberation of small nations from the oppressive power of militarism and imperialism. The 'land titles of Europe' had been settled, not on the old basis of 'dynastic claims' and 'rival territorial ambitions', but 'on the principles that every land belongs to the people that live on it'. This would in itself foster stability since 'revolutions come because men know that they have rights and that they are disregarded'. But just as domestic land titles had to be upheld by legal authority if they were not to give rise to disputes and even armed conflict, so the new international order had to be guaranteed if it was to remain secure and peaceful. This was the role of the League of Nations, which provided 'the only possible guarantee against war' – not an absolute guarantee but one which Wilson repeatedly described as 'a 98 per cent insurance'.[23]

As Wilson presented it, this insurance would be cheap as well as effective. 'A covenant of arbitration and discussion', he called the League as he emphasized the provision for the submission of disputes to arbitration or inquiry by the Council and the undertaking by member states not to go to war for three months thereafter – a 'cooling-off' period that, he confidently asserted, would have averted war in 1914. The primary sanction for enforcement was not armed force but 'something much more terrible than war – absolute boycott of the nation'. In addition to its devastating moral effect, such a punishment would be crippling economically because 'with the exception of the United States, there is not a country in the world that could live without imports'. It had been the blockade as much as the Allied armies that had 'brought Germany to her knees'. As for Article 10, the League Council could only 'advise' on whether it had been breached and, if so, what should be done, and such advice would require the assent of the American representative (unless the United States was itself a party, in which case 'the scrap is ours anyway'). Nor would the Council expect American troops to intervene in the Balkans or central Europe: 'If you want to put out a fire in Utah, you don't send to Oklahoma for the fire engine.'[24]

While providing such reassurances on the one hand, on the other Wilson stressed the magnitude of the role which the League would enable the United States to play. In a passage probably intended to appease Irish sentiment but which was seized on by his opponents, he declared that under the Covenant 'we can mind other peoples' business' by bringing to the 'bar of mankind any wrong' likely to affect the peace of the world. Seeking to counter Republican charges that he was promoting an un-American 'internationalism', he declared that 'the greatest nationalist is the one who wants his nation to be the greatest nation'. Americans could take pride not only because their soldiers – who 'went only one way' – won the war but because the peace embodied 'the American principle of the choice of the governed'. In evoking the appearance of the doughboys, Wilson recalled 'what I had so often seen on former journeys across the seas: going over in the steerage, bright-eyed men, who had been permeated with the atmosphere of free America; coming back, among the immigrants coming from the old countries – dull-eyed men, tired-looking men, discouraged-looking men'. On 'the noblest errand that troops ever went on', American boys had given their lives not for 'the protection of America' (which had not been 'directly attacked') but for 'the salvation of mankind'. It was this combination of power and idealism that made America the hope of the world; 'if America goes back upon mankind, mankind has no other place to turn'.[25]

Wilson was unapologetic about the exalted nature of this appeal: 'Sometimes people call me an idealist', he told his audience in South Dakota. 'Well, that is the way I know I am an American.' But he went on to say that 'if you want to talk business, I can talk business'. Without the ratification of the peace treaty and the extension of American credits, the war-torn nations of Europe would not provide a market for American exports. Moreover, if America disappointed the hopes that were invested in her, Wilson prophesied that the goodwill with which she was regarded abroad would be replaced by antagonism and that 'by every device possible foreign markets will be closed to you'. Nor would it be only the nation's economic interests that would suffer. 'If we must stand apart and be the hostile rivals of the rest of the world', he warned, 'we must be physically ready for anything to come.' The United States would have to become a great military state in a way that would not only raise taxes and check social reform but also be incompatible with its domestic liberties and open, democratic system of government.[26] (Despite the notable failure of America's interwar experience to vindicate Wilson's grim prophecy, this last argument was revived by FDR and postwar presidents in their efforts to counter isolationism, and has been highlighted by scholars who assume that some sort of concern with 'national security' must have inspired Wilson's policies.)[27]

These dire predictions were part of Wilson's effort to present the choice before the United States as a stark one. The treaty, he kept insisting, could not be renegotiated; 'we must take it or leave it'. As for the League of Nations, 'we must either go in or stay out'. There was no halfway house: 'You have either got to have the old system, of which Germany was the perfect flower, or you have got to have a new system.' 'A great and final choice is upon the people', he declared. 'Either we are going to guarantee civilization or we are going to abandon it.' Or, more picturesquely, 'you either have to be ostriches, with the head in the sand, or eagles'. In taking this line, Wilson was of course closing the door to compromise. If the Senate wanted to add clarifying resolutions to its approval although there was really no ambiguity in the wording of the treaty or the Covenant, there would be 'no harm' to this. But the treaty was a contract and any reservation that changed the meaning of the document, he insisted, would have to be approved by the other signatories, including Germany and 'it would set very ill upon my stomach to take it back to Germany'.[28]

When Wilson received from Washington a draft reservation on Article 10 on which the mild reservationists and Lodge were reportedly agreeing, the President immediately made it clear he saw it as falling into the latter class. He sent a message to Hitchcock saying he would 'regard any such reservation as a practical rejection of the Covenant', and a few days later he developed this argument on the public platform. He now stressed the centrality of Article 10, arguing that 'unless we engage to sustain the weak, we have guaranteed that the strong will prevail, we have guaranteed that any imperialistic enterprise may revive, we have guaranteed that there is no barrier to the ambition of nations that have the power to dominate'. Moreover, the reservation involved requesting 'special privileges' for the United States, so that it would 'get the benefits of the League but share none of its burdens and responsibilities': 'I for my part want to go in and accept what is offered to us – the leadership of the world.'[29]

Indications that the 'mild reservationists' were closer to agreement with Lodge and their fellow Republicans than with Senate Democrats was only one of the pieces of bad news that Wilson received as he progressed through the West. Another was the testimony of William Bullitt to the Senate Foreign Relations Committee. Bullitt, like other former liberal supporters of Wilson (notably Walter Lippmann and the *New Republic*), wanted the Senate to reject the treaty, on the grounds that it was so unjust that the United States should avoid the commitment to uphold it that League membership would involve. More widely damaging than Bullitt's personal articulation of this view was his revelation of a private conversation in which Lansing had condemned several aspects of the treaty and expressed doubts about the League of Nations. The Secretary of State's belated and somewhat evasive letter of explanation was grimly received on the presidential train.[30]

In response to these developments, Wilson began to devote more attention to the objections that had been raised to the treaty. On Shantung, the most criticized provision of the treaty, and the one which Wilson admitted he did not like himself, he stressed both the limited nature of the rights that Japan had been granted and that these had been promised to her by the Allies before the United States entered the war. Above all, he repeatedly argued, rejecting the agreement would do China no good – unless America was prepared to go to war with Britain and France as well as Japan over the issue. With regard to 'other matters with which I have less patience', Wilson insisted that both the Monroe Doctrine and the right of withdrawal were now clearly recognized in the League Covenant, as was the unimpaired sovereignty of member states over domestic issues including immigration and the tariff. To counter the 'bugaboo' that the British Empire would have six votes in the League to America's one, Wilson pointed out that this applied only in the Assembly and not in the all-important Council where no action could be decided upon without the agreement of the United States. Besides, when a vote had been given to American protectorates like Panama and Cuba, 'could it reasonably be denied to the great Dominion of Canada?'[31]

From the beginning of the tour, Wilson had maintained that there was 'no politics in this business', but, following the advice of Tumulty (who was accompanying him), in his later speeches he elaborated the extent to which Republicans had promoted the idea of a league of nations. It is true that the President's reading of earlier statements to this effect by Lodge and Theodore Roosevelt was hardly calculated to appease his enemies, but he also paid tribute to those like Taft who were now backing the Covenant. Above all, Wilson sought to depersonalize the issue, and to counter the hostility aroused by suspicions that he was seeking his own glorification. 'I wish I could claim some originative part in so great an enterprise, but I cannot', he told his audience in San Diego. 'I would be ashamed, my fellow countrymen, if I treated a matter of this sort with a single thought of so small a matter as the national elections of 1920.' But he did not do as some supporters of the League had urged and renounce any intention to run for a third term.[32]

Wilson also followed Tumulty's advice in returning to and developing his central theme – that the treaty and the League represented the fulfillment of the purposes for which America had entered the war. At times, Wilson's attempts to exploit the emotions of the war bordered on the demagogic. Implicitly evoking the mythology of the Civil War, he spoke sentimentally of the family mantelpiece over which hung the musket of the boy who had gone to France. He repeatedly claimed that 'the only organized forces in this country against this treaty are the forces of hyphenated Americans' – 'that hyphen which looked to us like a snake, the hyphen between "German" and "American" has reared its head again'. But it was upon the need to ensure that there should be no repeat performance that he dwelt most effectively. He spelt out the terrible cost of the war, in both money and lives, for all the countries involved, and how it exceeded that for all the wars in the world between 1793 and 1914. Predicting that 'within another generation, there will be another world war' if the League of Nations did not prevent it by concerted action, he warned that the development of weaponry was such that the great guns with which the Germans had bombarded Paris 'were toys as compared with what would be used in the next war'. And the sentimentality did nothing to detract from the eloquence of the passages that were to be replayed on the movie screen in the 1940s as demonstrating his foresight. Should Article 10 be impaired, he said he would feel like asking the Secretary of War to gather the men of the American Expeditionary Force on a field so that he could say to them:

'Boys, I told you before you went across the seas that this is a war against wars, and I did my best to fulfill the promise, but I am obliged to come to you in mortification and shame and say that I have not been able to fulfill the promise. You are betrayed. You fought for something that you did not get.' And the glory of the armies and the navies of the United States is gone like a dream in the night, and there ensues upon it, in the suitable darkness of the night, the nightmare of dread which lay upon the nations before this war came. And there will come some time, in the vengeful Providence of God, another struggle in which not a few hundred

thousand fine men from America will have to die, but as many millions as
are necessary to accomplish the final freedom of the peoples of the
world.[33]

In appealing so heavily to the emotions generated by the war – both the
idealism and the belligerence – Wilson, who had after all been out of the
country for over six months, may well have misjudged the public mood.
The United States was facing many domestic problems at this time, all of
which could be in large part attributed to its involvement in the war. The
vast expenditures had produced inflation, and the consequent pressure on
living standards helped to touch off a wave of strikes. The hyper-patriotic
organizations that had sought during the war to extirpate disloyalty and
pacifism turned their attention after the armistice to the threat of Bolshevism, and the consequent 'red scare' had been given a major impetus
when bombs were sent to the homes of a number of prominent figures
(including Attorney-General Palmer) in May and June. The way the war
had aggravated the internal tensions of American society was further
manifested by race riots, the worst of which in Chicago claimed the lives
of 23 blacks and fifteen whites. Before leaving Washington, Wilson had
felt obliged to address Congress on the high cost of living, and in the
course of his tour he warned of the danger of Bolshevism and condemned
both the race riots and a strike by police in Boston (which had particularly
alarmed middle-class opinion). Earlier he had called in a rather vague way
for 'the genuine democratization of industry', but he now stressed that the
first and most important step with regard to all domestic problems was
the prompt ratification of the treaty. Some observers, including Taft,
believed that Wilson was succeeding in creating 'a sense of impatience
at the delay', but such a feeling could, of course, lead to pressure for a
compromise rather than the unqualified approval that Wilson was
demanding.[34]

Although the audiences Wilson addressed were generally large and
enthusiastic, it is hard to gauge how far his speeches built up public support for his cause. However, it is clear that the effect on the Senate was, if
anything, negative. On 24 September, Hitchcock reported that 'the situation has not materially changed since you left here'.[35] The realization
that, for all his efforts, he was making little headway must have been
frustrating for the President. Messages from Paris that, following
D'Annunzio's coup in Fiume, Lloyd George and Clemenceau were urging
that Italy be granted sovereignty over the city had also done nothing to
improve his temper.[36] Beset by troubles, he drew strength from his religious faith. 'I believe in divine Providence', he told one audience.

If I did not, I would go crazy. If I thought the direction of the disordered affairs of this world depended upon our finite endeavor, I should not know how to reason my way to sanity. But I do not believe there is any body of men, however they concert their power or their influence, that can defeat this great enterprise, which is the enterprise of divine mercy and peace and goodwill.[37]

Wilson was also feeling the physical strain of the tour. Throughout the trip, he had suffered from headaches, which had grown more persistent and recurrent, and from coughing spells. In retrospect, it has seemed likely that these were symptoms of congestive heart failure caused by arteriosclerosis. The high altitudes of the Rocky Mountains did not help, and in Montana on the return journey Grayson noted that the President 'found it impossible to sleep while lying down and would choke up and cough during the night, being unable to breathe'. For all the protective efforts of his entourage, observant reporters noted his exhaustion. On 25 September, despite a splitting headache, he delivered a long address in Pueblo, Colorado, after which he was in such poor shape that Grayson had the train make a stop so that the President could take an hour's walk. Yet that night Wilson was unable to sleep and suffered an even worse 'asthmatic attack' in which 'he could hardly get his breath'. In the morning, having enlisted the aid of Tumulty, Grayson insisted that the rest of the tour be called off. Wilson initially resisted but then conceded, saying to Tumulty, 'I just feel as if I am going to pieces', and giving way to tears. Tumulty told the press that Wilson's exertions had 'brought on a nervous reaction in his digestive organs', and that his doctor had insisted on his immediate return to Washington.[38]

Once back in the White House, Grayson sought to impose on his charge a regime of 'complete rest'. But a few days later, early on 2 October, Wilson collapsed on his bedroom floor, having suffered a severe stroke that paralyzed his left side and badly affected his eyesight. The White House usher, who saw him that afternoon, recalled that the President lay stretched out on the bed 'as if dead ... He was just gone as far as one could judge from appearances'. In fact, the stroke itself was not life-threatening but two weeks later Wilson developed a dangerous infection and high fever as the result of an urinary blockage. For a month he remained confined to his bedroom, seeing only family members, his medical attendants and a few servants, and unable to pay attention to anything for more than a few minutes. However, the public was not informed that the president had suffered a stroke, Grayson's statements referring to 'nervous exhaustion'. Such concealment, inconceivable to a later generation, was at the behest of Mrs Wilson, who was evidently concerned to fend off any suggestion that her husband was so disabled that he should resign. When Lansing raised the possibility of the vice-president taking over, it was scotched by Tumulty and Grayson who, like Edith, were doing what they were sure Wilson would want. Lansing himself began to chair cabinet meetings, but most domestic decisions were made, as they had been for some time, within departments. Such papers as did issue from the White House, including a message vetoing the Volstead Act that enforced Prohibition, were written by Tumulty.[39]

Meanwhile, the Senate was attending to the treaty. In mid-September, while Wilson was on his tour, the Foreign Relations Committee had issued three reports. The majority one, signed by Lodge and his fellow Republicans (with the exception of McCumber) had proposed 45 amendments to the treaty and four reservations. Many of these amendments would have removed the United States from the various European boundary commissions that had been established by the treaty, others would have struck out the Shantung clauses and established voting parity in the League between the United States and the British Empire. In backing these amendments, Lodge indicated how far the development of the controversy had moved him towards an isolationist position. October and early November saw the defeat of all amendments, with 'mild reservationists' defecting from the Republican majority. But the Johnson amendment giving the United States six votes in the Assembly lost only by a narrow margin, and several of the others received the support of more than the third of the Senate necessary to block ratification. Moreover, the Republican senators who opposed amendments made it clear that they saw substantive reservations as essential.[40]

So the question then became what form these reservations should take. After intensive discussions with his party colleagues, Lodge in late October presented a new set of fourteen reservations, including some on the same issues (such as Shantung) as the defeated amendments, together with a preamble declaring that ratification was dependent on the acceptance of these reservations by three of the four principal Allied powers. The general thrust was to assert Congress's prerogatives *vis-à-vis* the Executive as well as America's *vis-à-vis* the League. One reservation stated that

> The United States assumes no obligation to preserve the territorial integrity or political independence of any other country ... under the provisions of Article 10, or to employ the military or naval forces of the United States under any article of the treaty for any purpose, unless in any particular case the Congress, which, under the Constitution, has the sole power to declare war or authorize the employment of the military or naval forces of the United States, shall by act or joint resolution so provide.

This reservation was virtually identical to the one which Wilson had denounced in September. It represented a more thoroughgoing repudiation of any obligation under Article 10 than some of the 'mild reservationists' had originally wanted. They justified their acceptance of the Lodge reservations with the argument that this was the only way to secure ratification of the treaty, given the unwillingness of the Democrats to compromise. The 'interpretations' that Wilson had privately given Hitchcock earlier had not yet been aired, and some historians have suggested that a fit president would at this stage have encouraged his followers to seek some agreement on reservations with pro-League Republicans.[41] Even if this course had been followed, however, the Democrats would not have been able to secure enough Republican votes to muster the necessary two-thirds majority without accepting the sort of strong reservations proposed by Lodge. In any case, this seems an unlikely scenario, not only because of Wilson's own consistent and emphatic rejection of substantive reservations but also because the Democratic leaders in the Senate, Underwood and Hitchcock, themselves saw advantages in standing pat on unqualified ratification. They felt that they could hold all but one or two of their colleagues to this position, but that once they accepted the principle of reservations the party would fragment. They still had enough votes to prevent Lodge passing the treaty with his reservations, and believed that the time for interparty talks would be after they had demonstrated that.[42]

This strategy risked the nonratification of the treaty, especially as there were signs that the public was growing impatient of the long debate. As deadlock loomed, some League supporters urged the Democrats to be more yielding. The League to Enforce Peace, at Taft's urging, called for 'the immediate ratification of the treaty, even with its reservations', but with a change in the preamble to permit the 'silent acquiescence' of the Allies. As the Senate prepared for the final votes, and with some in his own ranks favoring compromise, Hitchcock approached the White House for confirmation that Wilson wanted his supporters to vote against ratification with the Lodge reservations. On an earlier visit Hitchcock had been shocked to behold 'an emaciated old man with a thin white beard', but now he found the President shaved and in fighting mood. Insisting that the Lodge reservations were 'a nullification of the Treaty and utterly impossible', Wilson declared (according to Grayson who was present) that 'if the Republicans are bent on defeating this Treaty, I want the vote of each, Republican and Democrat, recorded, because they will have to answer to the country in the future for their acts'. He let it be known that he would 'pocket' the treaty if it was passed with the Lodge resolution as a part of it. He readily agreed to Hitchcock's suggestion that he write a letter that could be conveyed to the Democratic senators. Wilson omitted from Hitchcock's draft of this letter a reference to 'a possible compromise agreement', but he retained the express hope 'that all true friends of the treaty will refuse to support the Lodge resolution'. Although this letter infuriated the mild reservationists, it may have helped to solidify the Democrats. At any rate, all but a few of them voted against approval of the treaty with the Lodge reservations, and then for the treaty as submitted by the President. But with the 'irreconcilables' voting against both resolutions, neither obtained even a simple majority.[43]

Wilson seems to have been quite content with this outcome. This was because he felt that he had succeeded in placing responsibility for the failure to ratify the treaty on the Republicans, and that they would suffer for this electorally. In his talk with Hitchcock before the vote, he had declared that 'I have no doubts as to what the verdict of the people will be when they know the facts'. In this situation, Wilson reverted to the hankerings he had had as a young man for a political system more like the British, in which the government could dissolve the legislature and appeal to the country. In mid-December he had Tumulty draft a letter proposing that senators who had voted against the unreserved ratification of the treaty resign and stand for reelection on that issue. If the majority of them were to be reelected, Wilson himself would resign the presidency and hand it over to a Republican through the procedure he had thought of following in 1916. The impracticability of this scheme, especially in view of the fact that in many states vacant Senate seats were filled by gubernatorial appointment rather than special elections, evidently caused Wilson to abandon it, but he did express the basic idea publicly in a letter addressed to Democrats attending a Jackson Day banquet in early January. Again drafted by Tumulty, this document proclaimed Wilson's confidence that 'the overwhelming majority of the people of this country desire the ratification of the treaty', citing 'the unmistakable evidences of public opinion given during my visit to seventeen of the States', and called for the 1920 election to be given 'the form of a great and solemn referendum' on 'this vital matter'.[44]

In taking this position, Wilson demonstrated how far he had lost his grip on political realities. Politicians and commentators of various perspectives agreed that public support for the League had waned since the summer. Reservations asserting America's sovereign rights had gained favor, whether on their own merits or as a means of bringing the long controversy to an end and allowing the country to concentrate on domestic problems. (The Senate had voted on the treaty at the time of a national coal strike.) In these circumstances, prolonging the battle was more likely to damage the Democrats electorally than to benefit them. When Wilson, bypassing Tumulty for once, had issued a press statement in mid-December that he had 'no compromise or concession of any kind in mind', many Democratic senators made little attempt to conceal their dismay. In the new year, contacts between Republican mild reservationists and Democrats eventuated in a 'bipartisan conference' attended by both Hitchcock and Lodge. At this stage, apparently with Mrs Wilson's encouragement, Tumulty drafted a letter setting forth in detail and in a conciliatory tone 'interpretations' to which the President would 'have no objection', but Wilson delayed ten days before sending a much-truncated version to Hitchcock. 'The very moment of yielding anything to the Senate seems to drive him into stubborn immovability', wrote Ray Stannard Baker, who visited the White House at this time.[45]

This state of mind was clearly related to the President's illness. It was his isolation, Baker thought, that enabled Wilson to cling to the belief that the receptions he had received in the West reflected the current state of public opinion. More important, probably, were the effects of the stroke on Wilson's psychological equilibrium, aggravating his tendencies towards intransigence, self-righteousness and hostility towards all who did not follow him. As he grew stronger physically (though still largely confined to a wheelchair), he was subject to periods of euphoria in which he belligerently sought to bend the world to his will. February 1920 witnessed several manifestations of such behavior. After Britain and France had agreed to some minor modifications in a proposed settlement for Fiume, the President not only rejected them but, overriding the State Department, threatened to withdraw the treaty from consideration if they were proceeded with. When Viscount Grey, after a short tour as British ambassador (during which his presence had never been acknowledged by the White House), published a letter in the London *Times* defending the actions of the Senate and urging the British government to accept American participation in the League even with reservations, Wilson dictated a press release saying that if Grey had made such a statement while in Washington, 'his government would have been promptly asked to withdraw him'. Shortly afterwards, Wilson forced Lansing's resignation. The two men had not met since the summer and the Secretary of State, still very resentful at having been sidelined in Paris, had for some time been writing in his diary of his desire to leave. For his part, Wilson could reasonably question Lansing's loyalty after the Bullitt affair, but he chose to make an issue of the fact that the Secretary of State had been calling meetings of the cabinet during the President's illness. 'The President delivered himself into my hands and of course I took advantage of his stupidity', the unforgiving Lansing noted.[46] Wilson caused further surprise when he chose Bainbridge Colby, a former Bull Moose progressive without previous experience of foreign affairs, to head the State Department.

These actions, particularly the manner of Lansing's dismissal, raised doubts even among sympathetic commentators about the President's judgment and state of health.[47] Yet it is a measure of the standing he had achieved that he remained a political force to be reckoned with. This was demonstrated when the Senate, reluctant to make a separate peace with Germany, reopened consideration of the treaty. The bipartisan conference had come to nothing after Lodge, responding to pressure from hardline members of his party, had refused to make any significant concessions. But Hitchcock reported to the President that he feared that enough Democratic senators were now disposed to abandon the fight to allow passage of the Lodge reservations 'unless something can be done to regain some of them'. By this time, the great majority of the President's friends and supporters wanted him to allow the treaty to be ratified with the Lodge reservations. Even Tumulty, reporting this sentiment, suggested that Wilson should no longer hold up the conclusion of peace but restate his objections to the reservations after they had been passed. Instead of following this course, Wilson decided to write to Hitchcock before the vote reaffirming the unacceptability of the Lodge reservations. Naturally Tumulty collaborated with the drafting of this letter, but Wilson himself seems to have played the major part in composing what was by far the longest and most polished statement he had issued since his stroke. It concentrated on Article 10, 'the very heart and life of the Covenant itself'. Any reservation which rejected or weakened it 'would mark us as desiring to return to the old world of jealous rivalry and misunderstandings from which our gallant soldiers have rescued us, and would leave us without any vision or new conception of justice and peace'. The choice between the ideal of democracy and that of imperialism, 'which is by no means dead and which is earnestly held in many quarters still'. Indeed, it was 'in control now' in France. 'Practically every so-called reservation', Wilson concluded, was 'in effect a rather sweeping nullification of the terms of the treaty itself. I hear of reservationists and mild reservationists, but I cannot understand the difference between a nullifier and a mild nullifier.' This letter led to a pained protest from the French ambassador and much critical comment in the American press. But even a hostile editor evinced a grudging respect in observing that 'the click of his typewriter is heard round the world'. With its clear implication that even if the treaty with the Lodge reservations were to be approved the President would not complete the ratification process, the letter was enough to enable

Hitchcock to hold about half the Senate Democrats in the last ditch. Allied with the Republican 'irreconcilables', they deprived the treaty with the Lodge reservations of the required two-thirds majority when the final vote was taken on 19 March, and thereby kept the United States out of the League of Nations.[48]

'The Supreme Infanticide', the historian Thomas A. Bailey called Wilson's role in this process: 'With his own sickly hands, Wilson slew his own brain child – or the one to which he had contributed so much.'[49] It is the apparent irrationality of this act that has led to the psychological and medical interpretations of Wilson's conduct. The theory that he was unable to compromise or yield because he unconsciously identified Lodge (like Dean West at Princeton) with his father has lost plausibility as we have learnt more about Wilson's early development.[50] On the other hand, the seriousness of his health problems in the last two years of his presidency has become more apparent with the evidence and analyses now presented in Arthur Link's definitive edition of the *Wilson Papers*. There is no way of knowing how Wilson would have behaved in 1919–20 had he been fully fit, physically and mentally. It is natural to think that it would have been in a more politically adroit way, though he had shown before, notably at Princeton, that he could disregard (and despise) normal prudential considerations in a conflict in which he believed there was a question of principle at stake. And the issue on which he took his stand in the League fight was not only vastly more important but much clearer than those involved in the Princeton controversies.

Wilson envisaged the League of Nations not as a mere forum for diplomatic interchange – the 'debating society' of which he spoke contemptuously – but as the core of a new system of international relations. The skepticism with which this project was regarded in other countries, even by those well disposed to it, had been brought home to him in Paris. The sense of insecurity that underpinned the reliance on armaments and alliances had found expression in the demands, particularly by the French, that the Covenant should contain a formal guarantee and binding obligation. The formulation in Article 10, designed to avoid constitutional objections in the United States, was the absolute minimum that could hope to satisfy such demands. Like other forms of deterrent, the system of collective security that Wilson saw the League of Nations as embodying depended upon credibility. This would be fatally undermined if the United States repudiated any obligation, let alone commitment, to collaborate in responses to acts of aggression. As the historian William Widenor has recognized, Lodge's reservation was incompatible with 'the theory on which collective security was based'. There was thus much more involved in Wilson's commitment to Article 10 than the pride of authorship of which he was often accused. While still in Paris, he had described it as 'the king pin of the whole structure', without which 'the Covenant would mean nothing', and told Lansing that 'if the Senate will not accept that, they will have to reject the whole treaty'. It would be rash to assume that, but for his stroke, he would have abandoned this position when the former alternative became unrealizable.[51] Nor is it easy to see how a more flexible and accommodating stance on his part could have enabled him to secure a compromise on this point that would have seemed credible abroad. As we have seen, even at the most propitious time, before Wilson embarked in his speaking tour, it was clear that the majority necessary to approve the treaty could not be mustered without a substantive reservation to Article 10.[52]

Wilson's defeat thus marked the failure of his attempt to build a bridge between the external and the internal realities. This is what he had been seeking to do ever since it had become evident that the United States had to respond actively to the European war. As Wilson recognized, the problem arose, in the last analysis, from America's having become so powerful that she could not avoid having a great influence on the course of events abroad (as in supplying the Allies with munitions – or refusing to do so). Yet, although the United States had come to possess greater potential leverage in international politics than any other state, the world beyond her borders would necessarily be largely shaped by people living elsewhere. It was a very difficult task to devise a policy for bringing America's influence to bear that both recognized the complexity and intractability of this environment and also commanded broad support in a democratic polity reluctant to meet the costs of strenuous action and deeply persuaded of the superiority and universal validity of its own values. Although Wilson had originally adopted the idea of a league of nations as part of a plan to bring the war to an end before the United States was dragged into it, it had become his solution to this broader problem. By 1916 he was already presenting it as the means through which the United States should seek to promote its interests and values by playing a much more active role in international affairs than it had traditionally done. Associated with the vision of a world without war and in which democracy prevailed, it had become central to his justification for American involvement in the war and the peacemaking.

Wilson's was not the only solution that was on offer to the problem of finding a viable US foreign policy. There were some who believed his scheme was utopian both in its aspiration to end war and in the extent of the commitments it envisaged the United States undertaking, but who nonetheless favored a greater American role in world politics along more limited and more conventional lines. Lodge, like Theodore Roosevelt, had been one of the most prominent representatives of this school of thought, and so some historians, including Arthur Link, have argued that the debate over the treaty was a contest between two versions of internationalism rather than 'a struggle between advocates of complete withdrawal on the one side and proponents of total international commitment on the other'.[53] But this is only part of the picture. The embodiment of the 'realist' approach in 1919 was the bilateral treaty guaranteeing French security, which was never even reported out of the Foreign Relations Committee. Although Lodge blamed this treaty's fate on Wilson's subordination of it to the League, the protests that had greeted the President's agreeing to it in Paris suggest that this unequivocal breach of the traditional injunction against 'entangling alliances' never had a chance of ratification.[54]

In short, the defeat of Wilson's League was due primarily to sentiments, in the country at large as well as in the Senate, that were not conducive to any sort of international commitment or cooperation. The objections to Article 10 focused much less on the geographical scope of the obligations it contained than on the degree of their definiteness. The Senate's determination to preserve unimpaired the freedom of action of a future Congress was clearly incompatible with a reliable commitment to the security of any other country, and the reluctance to accept constraints on the nation's sovereign rights in any respect militated against all forms of international undertaking. In the interwar period this taboo was to extend so far as to include economic cooperation and participation in the World Court. The explanation for this outcome must surely go beyond the peculiar psychology or medical problems of a single individual.

Wilson spent a further year in the White House after the final Senate vote on the treaty, but there is no need to dwell on this sad and relatively uneventful period. Despite his partial recovery, the President remained essentially disabled, still unable to type or to read or concentrate for long. On at least two occasions, he played with the idea of going before Congress in a wheelchair and, in dramatic fashion, resigning. Mrs Wilson opposed such suggestions, probably because she rightly recognized them as the product of passing moods.[55] Indeed, the editorialist who had interpreted Wilson's letter to Hitchcock in March as foreshadowing an intention to run again for the presidency was not far from the mark. When Tumulty urged him to announce that he would not be a candidate for a third term, Wilson told Grayson that, if the Democratic Convention concluded that he was 'the logical one to lead' the party's campaign, 'I would feel obliged to accept the nomination even if I thought it would cost me my life.' His disapproval of other candidacies was manifest. It may seem strange that Wilson should want to continue in an office he knew he could no longer discharge properly, but it was the desire to have his stand on the League vindicated by the people that led him to cleave to this fantasy. In private notes, he sketched out the questions in 'the great referendum' his candidacy would constitute, as well as a possible cabinet for a '3rd administration'. The President's hopes were known to those close to him, and Tumulty and Grayson did all they could to discourage leading Democrats from taking them seriously. But when the first day of the Democratic convention witnessed a great pro-Wilson demonstration, in which Assistant Secretary of the Navy Franklin D. Roosevelt played a prominent part, Colby, who was acting as Wilson's agent, wired that he proposed to place the President's name in nomination. After wiser heads persuaded Colby that this move was doomed to failure, Wilson was clearly disappointed. However, he was gracious when the successful candidate, Governor James M. Cox of Ohio, having chosen Roosevelt as his running mate, called at the White House and declared his full support for the League of Nations.[56]

Yet, if the Democratic convention showed that Wilson still had a devoted following, the election campaign revealed the savage enmity of his opponents and the breadth and depth of his unpopularity. The Republican platform attacked him personally for his alleged despotism and 'disregard of the lives of American boys or of American interests'. Among the public at large, he suffered not only from his administration's failure to deal effectively with the problems of the day but also from his association with the war and the bitter internal conflicts it had generated. Wilson's own utterances and actions reinforced this association, not least his refusal to pardon those convicted for antiwar agitation, particularly Eugene Debs who ran as the Socialist candidate for president from his prison cell. Wilson seems to have felt such a move would be a betrayal of the American soldiers whom he had sent to fight and die in Europe. But his foreign policy, too, proved to be an electoral liability. The Republican National Committee targeted the various ethnic groups whom Wilson had offended, particularly those of German, Irish, and Italian extraction. As the campaign progressed, Cox and Roosevelt found it prudent to qualify their support for the League, and stress that they, too, favored reservations explicitly limiting American obligations. This availed them little, however, as on polling day they were buried in one of the greatest landslides in American electoral history. The Republican candidate, Senator Warren Harding defeated Cox by 404 votes to 127 in the electoral college, and the margin of 26 percentage points in the popular vote was the largest between major party candidates in the twentieth century. The Republicans increased their majority in the Senate from one to 22, winning all the contested seats outside the South. Commentators agreed that the results represented a massive repudiation of Wilson, who had become 'as unpopular as he had once been popular'.[57]

Wilson's political decline had paralleled his physical decline. In his debilitated state, he had developed the habit of watching a film in the middle of each day, and it is perhaps not surprising that he was particularly fond of footage of his time in Europe. Ray Stannard Baker, visiting the White House soon after Harding's election, recalled the poignant contrast between the screen images of the President, 'very erect, very tall, lifting his hat to shouting crowds' and the 'stooped, gray-faced, white-haired old man' who, leaning heavily on his stick, shuffled slowly out of the room when the show was over. On the day that Harding took the oath of office, Wilson was not able to join the outdoor ceremony, driving unobtrusively from the Capitol to the house on S Street in Washington that had been purchased with the help of Cleveland Dodge and other generous friends. Here he continued to struggle against the physical and mental effects of his illness. With enormous labor, he composed a 'document' that he envisaged as a manifesto for the next presidential election, and also composed a very short article that was published in *The Atlantic Monthly* (where, he told the editor, it had been 'his preference and pleasure' to send essays 'in former years'). For a time, he entered into a law partnership with the faithful Colby, but this venture collapsed, in part because of Wilson's strict refusal to touch cases that in any way related to past actions of his administration. The struggles and disappointments were alleviated by some marks of respect and admiration. He had been awarded the Nobel Peace Prize in December 1920. On armistice days, crowds gathered around the house in S Street to cheer the former Commander-in-Chief. But it was his continuing fight for the League that inspired the many who contributed to the fund-raising effort spearheaded by Franklin Roosevelt to establish the Woodrow Wilson Foundation in 1922.[58]

In February 1924 Wilson died at the age of sixty-seven. He had been one of the most successful political leaders in American history, whose only major failure was in a project so ambitious that many have considered it utopian. Yet it was his failure, not his successes, that was to keep his memory alive. In terms of the types of leadership he identified in his own early writings, we may say that his successes were those of a skilled and pragmatic practitioner of the art of politics, but that it is as a prophet that he gained his fame.

Notes

1 Alexander L. George and Juliette L. George, *Woodrow Wilson and Colonel House: A Personality Study*, New York, 1956, pp. 46, 59, 196, 251–2, 270–73, 291, 311; Sigmund Freud and William C. Bullitt, *Thomas Woodrow Wilson: A Psychological Study*, London, 1967, pp. 156, 200, 240–55.

2 August Heckscher, *Woodrow Wilson*, New York, 1991, pp. 585–95, 606–19; *PWW*, vol. 61, pp. viii–ix, vol. 62, pp. vii–viii, 628–38, vol. 63, pp. vii–x, 639–46, vol. 64, pp. vii–ix, 525–8.

3 This emerges even in William C. Widenor's sympathetic study, *Henry Cabot Lodge and the Search for an American Foreign Policy*, Berkeley, CA, 1980. See especially pp. 300–1, 309–10.

4 Quoted in Frank Ninkovich, *The Wilsonian Century: US Foreign Policy since 1900*, Chicago, IL, 1999, p. 45.

5 Widenor, *Henry Cabot Lodge*, pp. 302–3, 280–81; *Constitutional Government in the United States*, 24 March 1908, *PWW*, vol. 18, p. 120.

6 House diary, 29 June 1919, *PWW*, vol. 61, pp. 354–5.

7 Robert E. Osgood, *Ideals and Self-Interest in America's Foreign Relations: The Great Transformation of the Twentieth Century*, Chicago, IL, 1953, pp. 291–2; Thomas J. Knock, *To End All Wars: Woodrow Wilson and the Quest for a New World Order*, Princeton, NJ, 1992, p. 252.

8 Lloyd E. Ambrosius, *Woodrow Wilson and the American Diplomatic Tradition: The Treaty Fight in Perspective*, Cambridge, 1987, pp. 151–2.

9 Thomas A. Bailey, *Woodrow Wilson and the Great Betrayal*, New York, 1945, p. 12; Grayson diary, 4 March 1919, *PWW*, vol. 55, p. 410. The White House usher, 'Ike' Hoover, who was close to Wilson, recalled that on his return to America the President 'was looking to the future with a feeling of satisfaction and confidence'. From a memoir by Irwin Hood Hoover (undated), *PWW*, vol. 63, p. 632.

10 Ambrosius, *Wilson and the American Diplomatic Tradition*, pp. 137–8, 148–51; John Milton Cooper, Jr, *Breaking the Heart of the World: Woodrow Wilson and the Fight for the League of Nations*, Cambridge, 2001, pp. 73–83, 91–108. For Root's letter, see *PWW*, vol. 60, pp. 66n–68n.

11 Tumulty memorandum, c. 4 June 1919; Grayson diary, 1 July 1919; R.S. Baker diary, 1 July 1919; Grayson diary, 2 July 1919; Lamont diary, 5 July 1919; News report, 10 July 1919; address to the Senate, 10 July 1919, *PWW*, vol. 60, pp. 145–7, vol. 61, pp. 360, 363, 369–70, 386–8, 424–36. For the arguments over the Philippines, see Richard Hofstadter, 'Cuba, the Philippines and Manifest Destiny', in *The Paranoid Style in American Politics and Other Essays*, London, 1966, pp. 174–9.

12 H.F. Ashurst diary, 11 July 1919; G.W. Wheeler to W.G. McAdoo, 8 July 1919; Tumulty to Wilson, 4 August 1919, with enclosure, message to the Senate, 8 August 1919, Wilson to H.C. Lodge, 8 August 1919, *PWW*, vol. 61, pp. 445–6, 460, vol. 62, pp. 150, 208–9, 219.

13 A Conversation with Members of the Senate Foreign Relations Committee, 19 August, 1919, *PWW*, vol. 62, pp. 339–411.

14 Lansing Desk Diary, 25 August 1919, *Constitutional Government in the United States*, 24 March, 1908, *PWW*, vol. 62, p. 507, vol. 18, p. 161. (This passage goes on to recommend, in a manner not obviously consistent with the one quoted on p. 220, that a President 'act in the true spirit of the Constitution and establish intimate relations of confidence with the Senate on his own initiative, not carrying his plans to completion and then laying them in final form before the Senate to be accepted or rejected ... in order that there may be veritable counsel and a real accommodation of views instead of a final challenge and contest'.)

15 Herbert F. Margulies, *The Mild Reservationists and the League of Nations Controversy in the Senate*, Columbia, MO, 1989, pp. 47–91 (quotation on p. 66); Bailey, *Wilson and the Great Betrayal*, pp. 90–122; George and George, *Wilson and House*, p. 296.

16 Lansing memorandum, 20 August 1919; Bert E. Park, 'Wilson's Neurological Illness during the Summer of 1919', *PWW*, vol. 62, pp. 428–9, 628–38.

17 *PWW*, vol. 62, pp. 507n–8n; John Milton Cooper, Jr, 'Fool's Errand or Finest Hour?: Woodrow Wilson's Speaking Tour in September 1919', in John Milton Copper, Jr and Charles E. Neu (eds), *The Wilson Era: Essays in Honor of Arthur S. Link*, Arlington Heights, IL, 1991, pp. 199–200; Lamont diary, 5 July 1919; Wiseman to A.J. Balfour, 18 July 1919, *PWW*, vol. 61, pp. 388, 542; Ambrosius, *Wilson and the American Diplomatic Tradition*, pp. 160–61. For a full account of the activities of the 'mild reservationists' in this period (and one that takes a more optimistic view of the potential for a viable compromise), see Margulies, *The Mild Reservationists*, pp. 47–93.

18 Margulies, *The Mild Reservationists*, pp. 67, 83.

19 Press conference, 10 July 1919. In his meeting with the Foreign Relations Committee, Wilson modified this phrase to 'hardly more than an influential debating society'. *PWW*, vol. 61, p. 421, vol. 62, p. 343.

20 Widenor, *Henry Cabot Lodge*, pp. 309–10.

21 Memorandum, 3 September 1919, *PWW*, vol. 62, p. 621; Cooper, *Breaking the Heart*, pp. 152–7; Tumulty Memorandum, c. 4 June 1919, *PWW*, vol. 60, p. 145. On this point, see also Ambrosius, *Wilson and the American Diplomatic Tradition*, pp. 158–9, 259.

22 A.S. Burleson to J.P. Tumulty with enclosure, 25 June 1919, *PWW*, vol. 61, pp. 185–6; Wiseman to A.J. Balfour, 18 July 1919, *PWW*, vol. 61, p. 543; Cooper, 'Fool's Errand or Finest Hour?', pp. 201–5; *PWW*, vol. 62, pp. 507n–8n; Heckscher, *Woodrow Wilson*, pp. 595–8.; Grayson Diary, 6 September 1919, *PWW*, vol. 63, pp. 6, 63–6.

23 Quotations from addresses in Columbus, 4 September, Omaha, 8 September, Bismarck, 10 September, Tacoma, 13 September 1919, *PWW*, vol. 63, pp. 7–18, 97–102, 153–5, 245.

24 Quotations from addresses in St Louis, 5 September, Minneapolis, 9 September, Bismarck, 10 September, Salt Lake City, 23 September 1919, *PWW*, vol. 63, pp. 48–9, 155–6, 38, 41, 453.

25 Quotations from addresses in Indianapolis, 4 September, St Louis, 5 September, Salt Lake City, 23 September, Columbus, 4 September, Sioux Falls, 8 September, Billings,

11 September 1919. For the negative reaction in the Senate to Wilson's remarks in Indianapolis, see R. Forster to Tumulty, 5 September 1919, *PWW*, vol. 63, pp. 27, 33, 450, 14, 107–17, 172, 51–2.

26 Quotations from addresses in Sioux Falls, 8 September and St Louis, 5 September 1919, *PWW*, vol. 63, pp. 113–16, 43–8.

27 See, for example, Ross A. Kennedy, 'Woodrow Wilson, World War I and an American Conception of National Security', *Diplomatic History*, 25 (winter 2001): 4.

28 Quotations from addresses in Omaha, 8 September, Denver, 25 September, Sioux Falls, 8 September, Salt Lake City, 23 September, Shrine Auditorium, Los Angeles, 20 September, Seattle, 13 September, Portland, 15 September 1919, *PWW*, vol. 63, p. 105, 494, 109, 454, 416, 262, 290.

29 From Vance McCormick, 18 September 1919; Wilson to Rudolph Forster, 19 September 1919; address in Salt Lake City, 23 September 1919, *PWW*, vol. 63, pp. 363, 392, 451–6.

30 Lansing to Wilson, 17 September 1919, with notes, *PWW*, vol. 63, pp. 337–40. On the opposition that developed among liberals to the treaty and the League, see Knock, *To End All Wars*, pp. 252–7.

31 Quotations from addresses in San Francisco, 17 September, Reno, 22 September, San Diego, 19 September 1919, *PWW*, vol. 63, pp. 317, 436, 377.

32 Quotations from addresses in St Louis, 5 September, San Diego, 19 September 1919. For Tumulty's advice, see memorandum for the President, 12 September 1919, *PWW*, vol. 63, pp. 49, 374, 222–3. For a strong plea that Wilson announce that he would not, under any circumstances, be a candidate for reelection, see C.W. Eliot to Tumulty, 2 July 1919, *PWW*, vol. 61, p. 373.

33 References to addresses in Sioux Falls, 8 September, Cheyenne, 24 September, St Paul, 9 September, Tacoma, 13 September, Omaha, 8 September, Denver, 25 September, St Louis, 5 September 1919, *PWW*, vol. 63, pp. 116, 469–70, 143–4, 243–4, 102, 495, 42.

34 Address to Congress, 8 August 1919, *PWW*, vol. 62, pp. 209–19; addresses in Helena, 11 September, and in Coeur D'Alene, 12 September 1919, *PWW*, vol. 63, pp. 195–6, 216–17; message to Congress, 20 May 1919, *PWW*, vol. 59, p. 291; Taft, quoted in Cooper, *Breaking the Heart*, p. 163. For the figures on the Chicago race riot, see David M. Kennedy, *Over Here: The First World War and American Society*, New York, 1980, p. 283.

35 Hitchcock to Wilson, 24 September 1919, *PWW*, vol. 63, pp. 482–3. Secretary of War Newton Baker concluded that Wilson's 'work among the people' had had no 'effect one way or the other upon the Senate' (quoted in Ambrosius, *Wilson and the American Diplomatic Tradition*, p. 187). However, the historian Herbert Margulies suggests that Wilson's actions and words helped to drive the 'mild reservationists' towards Lodge (*The Mild Reservationists*, pp. 95–7, 101–2, 108–9).

36 From William Phillips, 18 September, 19 September 1919; Wilson to F.L. Polk, 21 September 1919, to P.A. Jay, 24 September 1919, *PWW*, vol. 63, pp. 364–6, 392–3, 424, 484–5.

37 Address in Berkeley, 18 September 1919, *PWW*, vol. 63, p. 350.

38 Grayson diary, 10, 18, 20, 23, 24, 25, 26 September 1919; A News Report, 25 September 1919. For a modern analysis of Wilson's ailments at this time, see Bert E. Park, 'Woodrow Wilson's Stroke of October 2, 1919', *PWW*, vol. 63, pp. 152, 340, 397, 446, 467, 489, 518–21, 487, 639–42.

39 Grayson diary, 28 September 1919; Irwin Hood Hoover, 'The Facts about President Wilson's Illness' (undated); *Washington Post*, 4 October 1919; Lansing diary, 3 October 1919, *PWW*, vol. 63, pp. 532–3, 634–5, 545, 547–8; Heckscher, *Woodrow Wilson*, pp. 611–16; Cooper, *Breaking the Heart*, pp. 198–212.

40 Ambrosius, *Wilson and the American Diplomatic Tradition*, pp. 173–5, 189–98.

41 Margulies, *The Mild Reservationists*, pp. 60–3, 145–7; Cooper, *Breaking the Heart* pp. 153–6, 200.

42 Margulies, *The Mild Reservationists*, pp. 127–8; Ambrosius, *Wilson and the American Diplomatic Tradition*, p. 198.

43 Ambrosius, *Wilson and the American Diplomatic Tradition*, pp. 201–2, 206–8; Hitchcock to Mrs Wilson, 15 November 1919; Grayson memorandum, 17 November 1919; *New York Times*, 18 November 1919; Hitchcock to Mrs Wilson, with enclosure, 17 November 1919; Ashurst diary, 19 November 1919, *PWW*, vol. 64, pp. 37–8, 43–51, 62–4.

44 Grayson memorandum, 17 November 1919; draft of a public letter c. 17 December 1919; Attorney-General Palmer to Wilson, 22 December 1919; Jackson Day message, 8 January 1920, *PWW*, vol. 64, pp. 43, 199–202, 214–15, 257–9. On the continuity between these ideas and Wilson's earliest ones, see Daniel D. Stid, *The President as Statesman: Woodrow Wilson and the Constitution*, Lawrence, KS, 1998, pp. 163–4. For the procedure by which Wilson had intended to hand over the presidency immediately if defeated in 1916, see above, p. 129.

45 Margulies, *The Mild Reservationists*, pp. 133, 170–71, 179; Bailey, *Wilson and the Great Betrayal*, pp. 201–2; A Statement, 14 December 1919; Lansing memorandum, 16 December 1919; Tumulty to Mrs Wilson, with enclosure, 15 January 1920; Wilson to Hitchcock, 26 January 1920; R.S. Baker diary, 23 January 1920, *PWW*, vol. 64, pp. 187, 192–4, 276–82, 329–30, 320–22.

46 Lansing to H.C. Wallace, 10 February 1920; Tumulty to Mrs Wilson with enclosure, c. 3 February 1920; Press release, 5 February 1920; Lansing memorandum, 13 February 1920, *PWW*, vol. 64, pp. 398–402, 355–7, 363–4, 415.

47 For a survey of press comment, see 'President Wilson "comes back"', *Literary Digest*, 28 February 1920, *PWW*, vol. 65, pp. 5–7.

48 Hitchcock to Wilson, 24 February 1920; Tumulty to Wilson, 27 February 1920; Wilson to Hitchcock, 8 March 1920; F.L. Polk to Wilson, with enclosure, 13 March 1920, *PWW*, vol. 64, pp. 466, 479–80, vol. 65, pp. 67–72, 84–5.

49 Thomas A. Bailey, *Wilson and the Great Betrayal*, pp. 271, 277.

50 See above, Chapter 2, pp. 17–18. The theory is advanced in George and George, *Woodrow Wilson and Colonel House*.

51 Widenor, *Henry Cabot Lodge* p. 339; Wilson to Lansing, 24 May 1919, *PWW*, vol. 59,

pp. 470–71. The French desire that Article 10 should constitute a formal guarantee was strongly expressed at the meeting of the League of Nations Commission on 10 April 1919, *PWW*, vol. 57, pp. 226–32.

    Wilson's response to Bailey's charge would presumably have been that he had not killed a healthy infant but aborted a deformed fetus.

52 In this connection, it is worth noting that although Grey's letter was widely assumed in the United States to represent the view of the British government, this was not the case. In fact, much official opinion in London believed that the Lodge reservations destroyed the value of the League from the British point of view and that, if they were adopted, Britain itself should give notice of withdrawal from the organization. The French government, too, was disillusioned by the Senate's attitude. Ambrosius, *Wilson and the American Diplomatic Tradition*, pp. 235–9, 214–15.

53 Arthur S. Link, *Woodrow Wilson: Revolution, War, and Peace*, Arlington Heights, IL, 1979, p. 108.

54 For the strongly negative reactions, within the American delegation as well as in the United States, to Wilson's agreeing to the French security treaty, see above, p. 207, and the references cited there. Lodge's view that it was doomed by Wilson's subordination of it to the League is reported (and implicitly endorsed) in Ambrosius, *Wilson and the American Diplomatic Tradition*, especially pp. 159–60, 211–14.

55 R.S. Baker diary, 4 February 1920, and editorial note, *PWW*, vol. 64, pp. 362–3.

56 *Washington Post*, 9 March 1920; Tumulty to Mrs Wilson, 23 March 1920; Grayson memorandum, 25 March, 1920; diary of Charles L. Swem (Wilson's stenographer), 17 May 1920; Carter Glass memorandum, 19 June 1920; Colby to Wilson, 18 June, 2 July, 4 July 1920; Wilson to Colby, 19 June 1920; Swem diary, c. 6 July 1920; Grayson diary, 18 July 1920; Swem diary, c. 18 July 1920; news reports, 18 July 1920, *PWW*, vol. 65, pp. 71, 117–19, 123, 291, 435–6, 429, 432, 490, 496, 498–9, 520–25.

57 Republican platform, *PWW*, vol. 65, p. 415n; Heckscher, *Woodrow Wilson*, pp. 643–4; Ambrosius, *Wilson and the American Diplomatic Tradition*, pp. 270–88; Robert H. Ferrell, *Woodrow Wilson and World War I, 1917–1921*, New York, 1985, pp. 224–30.

58 Ray Stannard Baker, *American Chronicle*, New York, 1945, pp. 481–2; Wilson to Ellery Sedgwick, 2 May 1923, *PWW*, vol. 68, p. 354; Heckscher, *Woodrow Wilson*, pp. 641–75.

Conclusion

The image of Wilson created by his fight for the League of Nations was of a visionary and idealist. As such he has been both admired and condemned, and his reputation has waned and waxed as subsequent events have seemed to discredit or vindicate his picture of the future. Thus, when one of his most distinguished critics came to express a more favorable view, he did so in what have long been conventional terms. Wilson 'was ahead of his time', George F. Kennan wrote in 1991, 'and did not live long enough to know what great and commanding relevance many of his ideas would acquire before this century was out'. Through the decades, a minority have retained faith in the vision of a new world order achieved through an international organization. Yet Wilson himself had asserted that 'if you would be a leader of men, you must lead your own generation, not the next', stressing the need 'to fish for the majority', and his career as a politician had generally reflected these prudential maxims. His attitude to issues of policy had been pragmatic, responsive to circumstances rather than expressive of ideological dogmas, and he had demonstrated an instinct for the positions that best represented 'the major thought of the nation'.[1]

What explains this contrast? Were there two Wilsons? Both the medical and the psychological interpretations of his career suggest that there were, and that the balanced judgment that characterized a healthy, unstressed Wilson was lost when he was ill, or, in the other version, when he was engaged in a conflict that aroused the demons of his unconscious. However, even if Wilson's behavior did display such marked variations –which is questionable – such variations would not account for his commitment to a reformed international order. This, as we have seen, was articulated at a time when he was both healthy and politically successful.

That commitment reflected basic characteristics both of Wilson himself and of the country he led. Given the realism with which he played the political game, and the flexibility with which he changed his position on issues, Wilson's career cannot persuasively be interpreted as an attempt to reform human affairs in accordance with some higher, or Christian, ideal. There are nonetheless reasons why he might be regarded as an idealist. In the first place, the objectives he sought to achieve were often bold and ambitious. This applies to his elevated view of the intellectual life that could be expected of Princeton undergraduates as much as to his hope of bringing an end to the First World War through 'a peace without victory', and it certainly applies to the form he gave to the League of Nations idea. He generally aimed high rather than low. This no doubt reflected his self-confidence, his strong drive for achievement and fame, and the high expectations he had held of himself since youth. 'I am not interested in simply administering a club', he told his brother-in-law, when he lost the backing of the Princeton trustees. 'Unless I can develop something I cannot get thoroughly interested.'[2] Secondly, Wilson's persuasive efforts as a leader relied heavily on an appeal to the idealism of other people. This may have been because the form of oratory to which he was most exposed when young was preaching, or a reflection of his, possibly related, admiration for Gladstone. In any case, he seems to have recognized that most audiences liked the implicit (and sometimes explicit) flattery of such appeals, and also that talking in terms of generally abstract values was a way of uniting diverse, and often conflicting, interests.

The ideals that he appealed to were much less often those of Christianity than of America's national ideology. The motifs of Wilson's rhetoric were more consistent than the substance of his policies. Throughout his presidency, and indeed before, he gave classic expression to the view that America had a providential mission 'to show the way to the nations of the world how they shall walk in the paths of liberty'.[3] He invoked this idea in the domestic arena, as justification for the progressive reforms he favored, and as imposing upon the American people a special obligation to behave in a way that maintained a society of ordered freedom. But it was by arguing that America's mission could only be fulfilled through an active foreign policy that Wilson had a profound and lasting impact upon his nation's history.

The core idea, which Wilson first expressed in his speech to the League to Enforce Peace in May 1916, was that the United States should abandon its isolation in order to reform the international system. As we have seen, over time there were variations in the substance of Wilson's program, and in the means by which he sought to achieve it. There were also tensions between the various principles that he proclaimed. He himself was well aware of this, as he showed when he limited the right of national self-determination to cases that would not disturb 'the peace of Europe', and when he distinguished, as Mexico had taught him to do, between self-determination and democracy.[4] Beneath the surface, there was also the difficulty of reconciling the ideal of international cooperation with the habit of unilateral policymaking, a tradition that Wilson generally maintained and, indeed, with the assumption that America's values were those of the future for all humanity.

The complex nature of the package that Wilson put together has made it easier for his successors to claim his mantle, and for commentators to see them as acting in accordance with his legacy. Franklin Roosevelt's 'Four Freedoms', Jimmy Carter's emphasis on human rights, and the first President Bush's invocation of a 'new world order' have all been viewed as 'Wilsonian'. One historian has argued that Ronald Reagan was 'a direct descendant of Wilson' because of his commitment to 'the promotion of democracy' – notwithstanding his administration's disregard for the United Nations and the International Court. The policy of containment, the lodestar for US administrations during the four decades of the Cold War, has been seen by some historians as the apotheosis of Wilsonianism, and by others as its antithesis. The former can cite the ideological and universal character of the commitment in the Truman Doctrine of 1947 'to help free peoples to maintain their free institutions and their national integrity against aggressive movements that seek to impose upon them totalitarian regimes', and the assumption of American leadership. The latter point to the reliance on particular alliances, often with authoritarian regimes, to maintain the balance of power. As Robert W. Tucker has wryly observed, 'Wilsonianism is a many-splendored thing'.[5]

Protean though 'Wilsonianism' is, the constant element is the appeal to values and principles that are seen as universally applicable. It is this which distinguishes it from the other major traditions in American approaches to foreign policy – isolationism and Realism. Isolationism also draws strength from the national ideology, but is at once less confident about America's ability to reshape the outside world in accordance with its own values, and more confident about its capacity to preserve a free society at home regardless of what happens abroad. The Realist approach differs from the Wilsonian in its emphasis on the importance of power as compared to moral and political ideals, and in its readiness to accept the rest of the world as it is, with all its evils and in all its diversity.

Among policmakers who have self-consciously adhered to this Realist perspective, Henry Kissinger is probably the most notable. Like George Kennan, Kissinger was for long very critical of Wilson and of his influence on American attitudes to international affairs. Like Kennan, too, he has recently expressed a much more favorable view, but on interestingly different grounds. In bringing the United States to play a leading role in world politics, Wilson's was 'an astonishing achievement', Kissinger has written. Realizing that the nation 'lacked both the theoretical and the practical basis for the European-style diplomacy of constant adjustment of the nuances of power from a posture of moral neutrality', Wilson 'grasped that America's instinctive isolationism could be overcome only by an appeal to its belief in the exceptional nature of its ideals'.[6] It is hard not to read this as a chastened reappraisal by a man who had experienced the difficulty of retaining political support in the American context for a policy conducted according to the precepts of realpolitik. Wilson may be seen as the prophet of internationalism, but Kissinger's tribute suggests that his real talent was the one he had devoted his life to cultivating – as a leader who could at once interpret and persuade his fellow-countrymen.

Notes

1 George Kennan, 'Comments on the paper entitled "Kennan versus Wilson"', John Milton Cooper, Jr and Charles E. Neu (eds), *The Wilson Era: Essays in Honor of Arthur S. Link*, Arlington Heights, IL, 1991, p. 330; 'Leaders of Men' 17 June 1890, *PWW*, vol. 6, pp. 652, 659; address to the Cleveland Chamber of Commerce, 6 Nov.1907, *PWW*, vol. 17, p. 500.

2 Quoted in John Milton Cooper, Jr, *The Warrior and the Priest: Woodrow Wilson and Theodore Roosevelt*, Cambridge, MA, 1983, p. 103.

3 Campaign address in Jersey City, New Jersey, 25 May 1912, *PWW*, vol. 24, p. 443.

4 See Chapter 6, p. 169.

5 Tony Smith, *America's Mission: The United States and the Worldwide Struggle for Democracy in the Twentieth Century*, Princeton, NJ, 1994, p. 269, 117–18; Frank Ninkovich, *The Wilsonian Century: U.S. Foreign Policy since 1900*, Chicago, IL, 1999, pp. 154–7, 178–83; Robert W. Tucker, 'The Triumph of Wilsonianism?', *World Policy Journal*, 10 (winter 1993/94): 83, 92-4.

6 Henry Kissinger, *Diplomacy*, New York, 1994, pp. 44-5.

Further Reading

In few fields of historical scholarship has a single figure achieved such a generally acknowledged preeminence as has the late Arthur S. Link with respect to the life and career of Woodrow Wilson. *The Papers of Woodrow Wilson* (Princeton, NJ, 1966–94), referred to in the Preface, will remain his major monument; as a very active editor-in-chief he directed the project in every way, and must take the major credit for the edition's quality and thoroughness. The editorial notes embodied in the *Papers* (particularly the earlier volumes) constitute Link's most mature treatments of several aspects of Wilson's thought and behavior, but in their nature these are limited in their focus. Much more comprehensive for the years that they cover are the volumes of his major study, *Wilson*. Unfortunately, because of Link's absorption in the *Papers* over the latter half of his life, this work remained uncompleted. The five volumes that do exist – *The Road to the White House* (Princeton, NJ, 1947), *The New Freedom* (Princeton, NJ, 1956), *The Struggle for Neutrality 1914–1915* (Princeton, NJ, 1960), *Confusions and Crises 1915–1916* (Princeton, NJ, 1964), *Campaigns for Progressivism and Peace 1916–1917* (Princeton, NJ, 1965) – constitute both less and much more than a biography. They are less not only because they stop in 1917 but also because the first 45 years of Wilson's life are dealt with in a brief, introductory chapter of the first volume. They are much more because they provide an authoritative and detailed account of the various issues and events with which Wilson was concerned from his election as president of Princeton University in June 1902 to America's entry into the First World War. Based upon broad and deep research, these volumes contain extensive quotations from primary documents. As the series progresses, Link's attitude towards his subject changes. The first volume contains some harsh criticism of Wilson, but the latter three generally present matters from the President's own standpoint, with implicit sympathy. Link has supplemented this *magnum opus* with several shorter works, the most important of which is *Woodrow Wilson: Revolution, War and Peace* (Arlington Heights, IL, 1979), a compact and lucid review of Wilson's evolving policy towards the First World War and its aftermath that represents Link's most considered interpretation – and assessment – of its character. Also of value is the collection *The Higher Realism of*

Woodrow Wilson and Other Essays (Nashville, TN, 1971), which contains in the title essay Link's defense of Wilson as a Christian statesman.

The fullest, up-to-date biography is August Heckscher's *Woodrow Wilson* (New York, 1991). Based on the *Papers* (with which project Heckscher was associated), this largely supersedes the earlier biography by Ray Stannard Baker, who served as Wilson's press secretary in Paris – *Woodrow Wilson: Life and Letters* (eight volumes, Garden City, NY, 1927–39). However, this old work by a shrewd and insightful journalist who knew Wilson personally retains value, and the early volumes include material (derived from interviews and correspondence) that is not available elsewhere. Much shorter is the biography by Kendrick A. Clements, *Woodrow Wilson: World Statesman* (Boston, MA, 1987), a first-class introduction which devotes considerable attention to Wilson's earlier career and somewhat less to the First World War and its aftermath. The reverse is true of the longer study by Jan Willem Schulte Nordholt, *Woodrow Wilson: A Life for World Peace* (English version, Berkeley and Los Angeles, CA, 1991). Shulte Nordholt, a Dutch historian, sees Wilson as 'temperamentally a poet', who expressed in his oratory the sentimental naïveté of American idealism. This reflects a longstanding European perspective, but John Milton Cooper Jr presents a very different picture in his joint biography of Wilson and his great rival, *The Warrior and the Priest: Woodrow Wilson and Theodore Roosevelt* (Cambridge, MA, 1983). Cooper's original and mildly revisionist interpretation stresses Wilson's pragmatism as well as his intellectual ability and achievements.

Cooper and Heckscher, like Link in his later years, attribute what they see as the variability in the quality of Wilson's performance to the several medical incidents he suffered during his life. The first scholar to argue for the importance of these was Edwin A. Weinstein, a qualified neurologist, in *Woodrow Wilson: A Medical and Psychological Biography* (Princeton, NJ, 1981). As the title suggests, Weinstein's study seeks to explain Wilson's behavior at certain critical points in terms not only of his physical disabilities (which are attributed to progressive arteriosclerosis) but also of his psychological response to these. Weinstein's interpretation of Wilson's medical history has been challenged, most notably by Juliette L. George, Michael F. Marmor and Alexander L. George, 'Issues in Wilson Scholarship: References to Early "Strokes" in *The Papers of Woodrow Wilson*', *Journal of American History*, 70 (March 1984): 845–53. Uncertain as all these posthumous diagnoses must be, Weinstein's interpretation of Wilson's psychology is somewhat better based than that of Alexander L. George and Juliette L. George, *Woodrow Wilson and Colonel House: A Personality Study* (New York, 1956), to say nothing of the crude work by

Sigmund Freud and William C. Bullitt, *Thomas Woodrow Wilson: A Psychological Study* (Boston, MA, 1967).

Such speculative psychohistory has been largely discredited since the *Papers* threw additional light on Wilson's early years. The only study of Wilson's youth and education based on the documentation now available is John M. Mulder, *Woodrow Wilson: Years of Preparation* (Princeton, NJ, 1981). A student of church history, Mulder emphasizes Wilson's religious faith and the influence of the 'covenant theology' he imbibed from his father; while recognizing that Wilson showed little interest in theology, Mulder argues that his heritage shaped his 'way of understanding the world'. Mulder's work originated in a doctoral dissertation directed by Link, as did Niels Aage Thorsen's *The Political Thought of Woodrow Wilson 1875–1910* (Princeton, NJ, 1988), a detailed analysis of Wilson's unpublished as well as published writings on political matters in the years before he entered the arena himself. Arguing that Wilson's scholarly works have too often been interpreted within the inappropriate categories of Beardian historiography or modern political science, Thorsen maintains that they reflect a continuing and evolving engagement with the problems of the American polity and the means by which these might be addressed. Although at times one doubts that Wilson's writings can quite bear the weight of interpretation that Thorsen places upon them, this is a careful and sophisticated study. Less intellectually ambitious is Henry Wilkinson Bragdon's much more comprehensive account, *Woodrow Wilson: The Academic Years* (Cambridge, MA, 1967). Written before the *Papers* appeared, Bragdon's readable book is heavily based on a large number of interviews with people who knew Wilson, supplemented by published memoirs and contemporary newspapers. It thus gives a picture, rather lacking in most later studies, of the context in which Wilson operated, and of how he appeared to his contemporaries. The perspective is very much a Princeton one, and Bragdon presents a vivid description of college life in the late nineteenth century and of the way the university developed. More intimate, and more sympathetic to Wilson, are the only recently published recollections of his brother-in-law and fellow academic, Stockton Axson, *'Brother Woodrow': A Memoir of Woodrow Wilson* (Princeton, NJ, 1993). This charming book contains penetrating insights into Wilson's personality, but should not be relied upon as an account of his views at particular times.

Wilson's political thought is connected to his later practice in Daniel D. Stid, *The President as Statesman: Woodrow Wilson and the Constitution* (Lawrence, KS, 1998). Stid, a political scientist, is interested in the bearing of Wilson's ideas and experience on modern debates about the nature of the presidency, but this well-researched and intelligent work is also a contribution to historiography; in particular, it helps to explain both Wilson's successes and his failures as a legislative and political leader. Less theoretical but also illuminating on Wilson's performance as a president is Kendrick A. Clements, *The Presidency of Woodrow Wilson* (Lawrence, KS, 1992). Based on a very thorough knowledge of the political history of the period, this study achieves originality by describing the activities of the administration in areas where Wilson himself was comparatively little involved, with chapters on the Departments of Agriculture and of Labor. Various aspects of Wilson's life, context and legacy are reviewed by a collection of notable scholars in John Milton Cooper, Jr and Charles E. Neu, (eds), *The Wilson Era: Essays in Honor of Arthur S. Link* (Arlington Heights, IL, 1991).

On Wilson's foreign policy, Arthur S. Link himself has edited a collection of essays, *Woodrow Wilson and a Revolutionary World, 1913–1921* (Chapel Hill, NC, 1982), in which a wide range of topics are discussed from strikingly diverse points of view. The argument that promoting America's exports and overseas investments was a major concern of the administration is most fully developed by Burton I. Kaufman, *Efficiency and Expansion: Foreign Trade Organization in the Wilson Administration, 1913–1921* (Westport, CT, 1974). The general activism of Wilson's policy is highlighted in Frederick S. Calhoun, *Power and Principle: Armed Intervention in Wilsonian Foreign Policy* (Kent, OH, 1986), which examines the seven occasions on which Wilson authorized military action abroad. Although the comparison brings out the consistent firmness with which Wilson maintained civilian control while avoiding interference in operational detail, Calhoun tends to disregard the great differences between the various interventions (not least in their scale). There is an extensive literature on Wilsonian policy in Mexico; the best full account is Mark T. Gilderhus, *Diplomacy and Intervention: US–Mexican Relations under Wilson and Carranza* (Tucson, AZ, 1977).

Naturally enough, it is Wilson's response to the First World War that has attracted the greatest amount of attention. Against Link's sympathetic overview in *Wilson: Revolution, War and Peace* may be set an equally brief one by Lloyd E. Ambrosius, *Wilsonian Statecraft: Theory and Practice of Liberal Internationalism during World War I* (Wilmington, DE, 1991), which is written from a critical, essentially Realist, perspective. Ambrosius is also the author of a much more detailed, and very thoroughly researched, study, *Woodrow Wilson and the American Diplomatic Tradition: The Treaty Fight in Perspective* (Cambridge, 1987). As the subtitle indicates, the main focus of this work is the battle over the League of

Nations in the United States, but Ambrosius traces the story from Wilson's adoption of the ideal while the United States was still neutral through the Paris negotiations and the proceedings in the Senate to the election of 1920; the strength of his analysis is in bringing out the real political interests, on both sides of the Atlantic, that shaped attitudes to the subject. Wilson's fight for the League of Nations is also placed in a broad framework, but from a very different interpretative standpoint, in *To End All Wars: Woodrow Wilson and the Quest for a New World Order* (New York, 1992) by Thomas J. Knock, another of Link's pupils. Knock sees Wilson's liberal internationalism as representative of ideas that were widely current in both the United States and Britain; rather implausibly, he argues that it was only the divisions created by American belligerency, and the administration's own repression of dissent, that prevented Wilson from mustering enough progressive support to realize his ideal. This is certainly not the impression given by John Milton Cooper, Jr in *Breaking the Heart of the World: Woodrow Wilson and the Fight for the League of Nations* (Cambridge, 2001), which exceeds all previous accounts of the domestic battle over the League of Nations in its thoroughness and depth of research. Much less hostile to Wilson than Ambrosius, whose book was previously the most detailed version of the story, Cooper attributes the President's maladroitness and obstinacy to his health problems. A penetrating critique of the whole League idea remains Roland N. Stromberg, 'Uncertainties and Obscurities about the League of Nations', *Journal of the History of Ideas*, 33 (January–March 1972), pp. 139–54. On the second great cause with which Wilson has been widely associated, the best treatment is another article: Michla Pomerance, 'The United States and Self-Determination: Perspectives on the Wilsonian Conception', *The American Journal of International Law*, 70 (1976): 1–27.

The neutrality period, leading as it did to American intervention, has been a historiographical battleground, not least because it has often been thought to hold lessons for later foreign policy. In the interwar years, the running was made by 'revisionists' who traced American belligerency to the non-neutral character of US policy, variously attributed to the pro-Ally bias of Wilson and his advisors, Allied propaganda, the influence of munition-makers and bankers, or the dependence of American prosperity on the war trade. In the 1940s and 1950s, by contrast, it was argued that the real reason for American entry was that the nation's security depended upon the maintenance of British sea power. This thesis was the premise of Edward H. Buehrig's *Woodrow Wilson and the Balance of Power* (Bloomington, IN, 1955), but its historical foundation was undermined by the thorough analysis of administration thinking and wider public attitudes on the issue of security in Robert E. Osgood, *Ideals and Self-Interest in America's Foreign Relations: The Great Transformation of the Twentieth Century* (Chicago, IL, 1953). Further light on public, and particularly congressional, opinion in these years is thrown by John Milton Cooper, Jr, *The Vanity of Power: American Isolationism and the First World War 1914–1917* (Westport, CT, 1969), which focuses on the emergence of 'isolationism' as a distinct political position. Ernest R. May, *The World War and American Isolation 1914–1917* (Cambridge, MA, 1959) was notable for its analysis of the interaction of policymaking in Washington, London, and Berlin, on the basis of documentation from all three countries. This process was taken further by Link in his *Wilson*, the last three volumes of which provide the fullest and best-documented account that exists of the whole complex story. The narrative was brought together in a single large volume in Patrick Devlin, *Too Proud to Fight: Woodrow Wilson's Neutrality* (London and New York, 1974). Devlin, a distinguished British judge, largely relied on Link's researches but contributed on his own account an expert disentangling of the legal issues, a worldly-wise assessment of the personalities involved, and a somewhat more rigorous analysis of Wilson's decision for war; exceptionally well-written in a rather mandarin style, this book is a pleasure to read. More recently, Link's claim that Wilson was guided in his handling of the issues of neutrality by international law has been challenged by John W. Coogan in *The End of Neutrality: The United States, Britain and Maritime Rights 1899–1915* (Ithaca, NY, 1981). Although Coogan succeeds in demonstrating that the administration acquiesced in British violations of previously accepted principles, his neorevisionist suggestion that this paved the way for American belligerency is necessarily undeveloped as he does not carry the story beyond March 1915 or discuss the dispute with Germany over submarine warfare.

A later form of revisionism shaped a much-cited interpretation of Wilson's policy after the United States entered the war: N. Gordon Levin, Jr, *Woodrow Wilson and World Politics: America's Response to War and Revolution* (New York, 1968). Levin's view that Wilson's policy was consistently directed to the establishment of a liberal-capitalist world order against the threats of both traditional imperialism and revolutionary socialism was clearly related to the belief that the 28th president 'laid the foundations' of later American foreign policy. During the Cold War, the US response to the Bolshevik revolution, and particularly the reasons for military intervention in Russia, was the subject of passionate controversy; a review of the different interpretations and a sensible assessment may be found in Eugene P. Trani, 'Woodrow Wilson and the Decision to Intervene in Russia: A Reconsideration', *Journal of Modern History*, 48 (September

1976): 440–61. A less integrated analysis than Levin's, but one that captures more of contemporary perspectives, is David M. Esposito, *The Legacy of Woodrow Wilson: American War Aims in World War I* (Westport, CT, 1996), which, although brief and somewhat disjointed, valuably highlights the significance of Wilson's decision to send a large army to Europe. The ideological as well as diplomatic importance of American intervention from a European perspective is brought out in Arno J. Mayer's *Political Origins of the New Diplomacy, 1917–1918* (New Haven, CT, 1959), a path-breaking attempt to show the connections not only between the actions of different countries but also between policymaking and domestic political developments in each. However, both in this book and in his somewhat less successful one on peacemaking, *Politics and Diplomacy of Peacemaking: Containment and Counterrevolution at Versailles, 1918–1919* (New York, 1967), Mayer's analysis is set within a framework that reflects the Cold War rather more than the preoccupations of Wilson's time. Other studies of the effects of this first projection of American power into European affairs also illuminate the reasons for Wilson's actions, in particular, Victor S. Mamatey, *The United States and East Central Europe 1914–1918: A Study in Wilsonian Diplomacy and Propaganda* (Princeton, NJ, 1957) and Klaus Schwabe, *Woodrow Wilson, Revolutionary Germany, and Peacemaking, 1918–1919: Missionary Diplomacy and the Realities of Power* (English version, Chapel Hill, NC, 1985). A more direct engagement with the processes of American policymaking by a European historian is Inga Floto, *Colonel House in Paris: A Study of American Policy at the Paris Peace Conference 1919* (Princeton, NJ, 1980), which is concerned with broader issues than its title suggests; although focused on House's role, and the question of when and why his relationship with Wilson broke down, it provides a thoughtful analysis of the American conduct of the negotiations. Floto does not, however, offer a comprehensive narrative of the proceedings in Paris; this may be found in the very detailed work by Arthur Walworth, *Wilson and his Peacemakers: American Diplomacy at the Paris Peace Conference, 1919* (New York and London, 1986).

The many ways in which involvement in the war affected American society are authoritatively and perceptively examined in David Kennedy, *Over Here: The First World War and American Society* (New York, 1980). Despite its title, Robert H. Ferrell, *Woodrow Wilson and World War I, 1917–1921* (New York, 1985) is not focused on the President but is a general account of American history in these years. As such, it contains some out-of-the-way information and is particularly good on the experiences of the US army, but it is rather oddly organized and weaker on more conventional subjects.

The concept of 'Wilsonianism', as an enduring approach to American foreign policy and the understanding of international affairs, was largely an invention of its Realist critics. Following such works as Walter Lippmann, *US Foreign Policy: Shield of the Republic* (Boston, MA, 1943) and Hans J. Morgenthau, *In Defense of the National Interest: A Critical Examination of American Foreign Policy* (New York, 1952), Osgood's *Ideals and Self-Interest in America's Foreign Relations* is the most developed application of this perspective to American experience in the first half of the twentieth century. In recent years, Wilson's legacy has often been more favorably assessed, but it has also been interpreted in various ways. Thus, Tony Smith in *America's Mission: The United States and the Worldwide Struggle for Democracy in the Twentieth Century* (Princeton, NJ, 1995) credits Wilson with making the promotion of constitutional democracy throughout the world 'the guiding principle of United States foreign policy'. On the other hand, for Frank Ninkovich in *Modernity and Power: A History of the Domino Theory in the Twentieth Century* (Chicago, IL, 1994) and *The Wilsonian Century: US Foreign Policy since 1900* (Chicago, IL, 1999) Wilson's most influential insight was the interconnectedness of security in the modern age; hence 'the domino theory' that aggression everywhere has to be firmly resisted at the outset is seen as the key feature of his legacy.

Index